Cop Knowledge

Cop Knowledge

Police Power and Cultural Narrative in Twentieth-Century America

Christopher P. Wilson

The University of Chicago Press

Chicago and London

Christopher P. Wilson is professor of English and director of American Studies at Boston College. He is author of *White Collar Fictions: Class and Social Representation in American Literature, 1885–1925* and *The Labor of Words: Literary Professionalism in the Progressive Era.*

This publication was assisted by a grant from the Trustees of Boston College.

The University of Chicago Press, Chicago 60637
The University of Chicago Press, Ltd., London
© 2000 by The University of Chicago
All rights reserved. Published 2000
Printed in the United States of America
09 08 07 06 05 04 03 02 01 00   1 2 3 4 5
ISBN (cloth): 0-226-90132-7
ISBN (paper): 0-226-90133-5

Library of Congress Cataloging-in-Publication Data

Wilson, Christopher P. (Christopher Pierce), 1952–
    Cop knowledge : police power and cultural narrative in twentieth-century America / Christopher P. Wilson.
        p. cm.
    Includes bibliographical references and index.
    ISBN 0-226-90132-7 (cloth : alk. paper) — ISBN 0-226-90133-5 (pbk. : alk. paper)
    1. Police—United States—History. 2. Police in popular culture—United States—History. 3. Police power—United States—History. I. Title.
HV8138.W627 2000
363.2′0973—dc21   99-049209

for Greer and Jesse

Contents

Illustrations

Acknowledgments

For their comments on this project along the way, I would like to thank Paul Doherty, Saverio Giovacchini, Dayton Haskin, Catherine Jurca, Paul Lewis, Robin Lydenberg, David Ray Papke, Judith Wilt, and the anonymous readers at the University of Chicago Press. Lee Bernstein and Jim Smith were intellectual partners more than research assistants, and their thinking guided my own argument from the start. But I would especially like to single out, as well, three people who helped this project in very different ways, yet with equally timely doses of sanity, passion, and intelligence: Alex Chasin, Richard Fox, and Judy Smith. To such friends and scholars I have debts too numerous to list.

With Alex, I also had the good fortune of reading for a year with Paul Breines, Stephen Pfohl, and Juliana Chang. For professional support, counsel, and conversation I would also like to thank Casey Blake, Christine Bold, Ti Bodenheimer, Carl Fulwiler, Gordon Hutner, Lucy Maddox, Teresa Murphy, Elayne Rapping, Joan Shelley Rubin, and Laura Tanner. My home institution, Boston College, was characteristically generous with teaching, research incentive, and faculty fellowship grants, all of which assisted in this project. I am also grateful for the comments of the audiences at Boston University and California Institute of Technology, who listened to this work in some of its earliest incarnations. At the University of Chicago Press, I would like to thank David Aftandilian, Toni Ellis, Russell Harper, Michael Koplow, Randolph Petilos, and Alan Thomas for their generosity and care.

Newspaper microfilms were provided by the Lilly Library at Indiana University; the New York State Library, Albany, New York; the Library at the State University of New York, Stonybrook; the Library at Michigan State University; the Boston Public Library; the Avon Historical Society; Boston University; and the Libraries at Boston College. I must also thank the Stephen Crane and Lincoln Steffens Collections at the Butler Library, Columbia University, which have allowed me to quote from their holdings and use their extensive microfilms. Earlier versions of chapter 1 appeared as "Stephen Crane and the Police," *American Quarterly* 48 (June 1996): 273–315, reprinted here by permission of Johns Hopkins University Press; of chapter 4 as "True and True(r) Crime: Cop Shops and Crime Scenes in the 1980s," *American Literary History* 9 (winter 1997): 718–43, reprinted here by permission of Oxford University Press; and of chapter 5, in "Framing the Shooter: The *Globe* and the Streets," *cultural studies* 11 (1997): 390–417, reprinted here by courtesy of Routledge, a member of the Taylor and Francis Group, Ltd.

Introduction

---•---

Thin Blue Lines:
Police Power and Cultural Storytelling

Everyone who thinks is likely to know that the right of arrest is one of the most dangerous powers which organized society can give to the individual. . . . Theoretically the first result of government is to put control into the hands of honest men and nullify as far as may be the ambitions of criminals. When government places power in the hands of a criminal it of course violates this principle and becomes absurd.
　　　　—Stephen Crane, unpublished fragment (1896)

The essence of the police role in maintaining order is to reinforce the informal control mechanisms of the community itself.
　　　　—James Q. Wilson and George L. Kelling Jr., "Broken
　　　　Windows: The Police and Neighborhood Safety" (1982)

This is a book about police power: those who exercise it, those who would reform it, and those in the popular arts who are drawn to its political dramas, its cultural contradictions, and its fraternal mysteries. More simply, it is a book about a series of literary, journalistic, and mass-cultural encounters with everyday police authority in urban America, as that authority has changed over the course of the twentieth century. These engagements have taken place not only in the cultural imagination, but on the beat, in the squad room, and in the police precinct news bureaus that have come to be known as "cop shops."

As everyday representatives of local municipalities, or as heroes and villains in modern mass media, police forces would seem to have a high cultural visibility. As Stephen Crane's private reflection suggests, they often seem the "first result" of the authority of the state. Certain tools of the police trade—the billy club, the police cruiser, the badge—serve to boldly announce this direct form of representation. Police work is commonly said, meanwhile, to be the most overrepresented profession in prime-time television; likewise, the police disproportionately populate the columns of everyday crime news, the chapters of mystery novels, the action-adventure genres of Hollywood film.[1] Not surprisingly, then, an American child's first idealization of political order, theorists of democratic socialization tell us, is liable to be the mythical beat cop, even ahead of the heroic fireman.[2]

And yet, even though they have this high visibility, municipal police do much of their work, as Wilson and Kelling's maxim argues, in realms that are informal, discretionary, actually out of public view. If Crane's formulation speaks to a familiar liberal construction of police authority, Wilson and Kelling attach themselves to an ethos that is more traditionally communitarian, placing the police's duty of reaffirming order before any obligations stemming from their role as representatives of law. In fact, a persistent theme of my book will be that writers and other observers have been drawn to police authority precisely because of this long-standing cultural tension, and because of the police's "interstitial" social position in modern urban society. Within the cop fraternity itself, police officers commonly cast themselves as sharers of a secret knowledge about urban lower-class criminality, human frailty, and political hypocrisy.[3]

Far from being a well-kept secret, however, over the past three decades policing and the knowledge it holds seemed to be all the more valued in American culture. Ten years ago, for instance, gang-related homicides filled Boston newspapers at the rate of one per month, and the call for more cops on the streets began to reach its now-familiar crescendo. Meanwhile, a series of headline murders spilled over into the genre known as True Crime, which to many observers played to a popular preoccupation with psychological profiling of criminality by FBI-style "mindhunters."[4] In criminological debates, similarly, the prevailing criminal image was often the cold-blooded, under-twenty-one "superpredator," projected into nightmarish, future-imperfect proportions by public alarm—resulting in police vigilance that seems to have led only to world-beating incarceration rates.[5] The sum effect was that academic and public criticism alike were quick to declare a "pathological" public sphere, a national "wound culture," a collapse of American citizenship and community—jeremiads that often seemed to fuel the call for more police.[6] The public image of the police, meanwhile, seemed on the rise: in television melodramas like *NYPD Blue, Homicide,* or *Law and Order;* in live-action shows known as "cop TV"; and finally in the heralding of what has become known as the philosophy of "community policing," claimed to be responsible for reducing urban crime rates in the late 1990s. Along with the misnamed "welfare reform," community policing has now become one of the most tangible victories of neoconservatism, a beachhead for the broader assault on liberal politics and social theory.[7]

Not surprisingly, this climate has led much of contemporary academic study to reexamine both the history of policing and of cultural representations of crime. Like several recent writers entering these fields, however, I did not find my own research falling easily on either police power or upon criminality, but on the symbiosis between these seemingly antithetical forces. As a historian of American literature, news writing and nonfiction, and popular culture, I had already been exposed, in fact, to the ways police power infused and shaped a wide range of cultural representations of disorder. Researching an article on turn-of-the-century journalist John Reed, for example, I ran head on into the pervasive use in the U.S. press of the "police beat" metaphor to describe the doubtful legitimacy of military intervention in the Mexican Revolution. Until I saw a contemporaneous cartoon, I had never fully realized what "speak softly and carry a big stick" originally referred to (that is, to Theodore Roosevelt's prior stint as New York's police commissioner). As I soon discovered, thanks to the work of urban historian Eric H. Monkkonen, the term "police beat" enabled a claim to preemptive but putatively nonpolitical action—a rationale for intervention, alas, still with us. Police power, that is, became a cultural trope, and when exported to the U.S. political debate about Mexico, it acquired extraordinary linguistic power, turning deserts into alleyways, revolutionaries into thugs. But this was hardly the sole metaphorical relocation of police power. While researching turn-of-the-century news writing, I discovered that crime news beats often followed police precinct lines; that in advance of so many other social agencies, the press acquired rooms right inside police station houses; that even famous reporters like Jacob

Riis or Richard Harding Davis spoke of an eerie "double-take" in which they were mistaken by city dwellers for police officers.[8]

Finally, of course, "policing" has acquired a new currency, coming from the new historicism, film and literary criticism, gender studies, and many other quarters. As many readers know, the term "policing"—expanded by the example of cultural theorists like Stuart Hall, Michel Foucault, Jacques Donzelot, and D. A. Miller—has come to be used as a shorthand metaphor for the surveillance work often undertaken by modern social agencies, mass media, and other forms of representation. The predominant blueprint for this broader reformulation has been, of course, Foucault's Panopticon: the disciplinary complex and mechanism of power that "establishes over individuals a visibility through which one differentiates and judges them," leaving "no zone of shade." In this model, forms of representation are often said to have worked in tandem not only with actual municipal policing, but with a much broader machinery of regulation, surveillance, and biopolitics that, it is often argued, came of age in the late eighteenth and nineteenth centuries. This usage has been so widespread, in fact, that many readers in the humanities are liable to think of this broader metaphorical sense of policing before summoning its original one.[9]

The model has infused and reenergized many fields of inquiry. Victorian slum photography and fiction, for instance, have come to exemplify a complex realist imperative, in Mark Seltzer's words, of "making everything visible," a process that "entails a policing of the real." For some time now, in fact, in the documentary fiction film of the 1940s, the invasive eye of the camera, opening up the urban landscape to audience inspection, has been likened to the vigilance of the modern police investigations it often depicted. In recent analyses of crime news, likewise, the policing trope is everywhere made synonymous with the act of reporting itself. By reflecting the enforcement priorities of police; by heroicizing the investigative prowess of the police and the reporter him- or herself; by offering a social-pathology view of crime and by personalizing victims into "all that is pure and admirable"—by these and many other conventions, many an argument goes, crime news legitimates those "narrowed grooves of institutional meaning" that often begin with police departments and intersect with other agencies of cultural knowledge and social control. In one influential study of recent crime reporting, the news media are described as "as much an agency of *policing* as the law-enforcement agencies whose activities and classifications are reported upon."

"Crime reporter," it is sometimes said, is a misnomer; it should be "police reporter."[10]

My various debts to these ongoing theoretical reformulations will be apparent in this book.[11] It will be obvious to many cultural-studies readers, for instance, that my approach is indebted to pioneering work like that of the Birmingham Centre's *Policing the Crisis* (1978), and what it called the "spiral" of "mutual reciprocities and reenforcements" between law and its representation.[12] And yet, I have also come to feel that lost in the shuffle, as it were, between power and representation was what we meant by policing to begin with. Rather, in studies of American literary realism, or documentary film, or crime news, the idea of cultural "policing" developed too independently of the scholarship by historians, sociologists, and criminologists on everyday police power, community politics, and municipal authority in temporally specific settings. This book is partly an attempt to redress this ongoing divide in the academy.

Consistently at the center of my analysis has been a startling paradox of modern American cultural life: the fact that much of our popular understanding of criminality and social *dis*order, particularly street disorder, comes from a knowledge economy that has the police—putatively agents of order—at its center. It is not only that today's police forces feed our "information society" with data on crimes, security risks, and even the most petty forms of social transgression. Rather, it is that the police have always been knowledge workers of a kind. In our neoconservative times, they have often been given a new standing even in formal political debate, taken as seers whose broader cultural understandings of civility American society needs to rediscover and respect. As British criminologist Ian Loader has put it, in our day the power of police

> has become the power of legitimate pronouncement: a power to diagnose, classify, authorize, and represent both individuals and the world, and to have this power of "legitimate naming" not just taken seriously, but taken-for-granted. This does not mean that what the police say about contemporary problems remains contested (that is rarely the case); nor is it to deny that, under "mediatized" political conditions, the police often feel compelled to engage in . . . "promotionalism." It is merely to point out that the police's entitlement and capacity to speak about the world is seldom challenged. They start from a winning position.

What Loader is outlining is a narrative power. It is what one social scientist, writing in the early seventies, described as the police's power to "enter upon a variety of social stages, encounter the actors, determine their roles, and figure out the plot"—often, in fact, determining the "fate" of such "actors." That is, even beyond their more formal roles as sources for crime reporters, consultants for television shows and films, or informants for criminologists or sociologists, the police often offer, as it were, the first drafts of a great deal of our cultural knowledge about social disorder and criminality. And yet, this is a role often overlooked in conventional disciplinary renderings of police culture, political history, or media "images." I realized, in fact, that my own knowledge of the police was, in Loader's terms, already so "mediatized" that it often took up the space where my historical understanding should have been. And I suspect I was not alone.[13]

My necessarily partial and eclectic attempt to come to terms with this deficiency has driven the work of this book. As its title suggests, I mean to explore the role of police power in cultural storytelling, in a broader power to narrate forms of social understanding, particularly about lower-class experience and criminality. More specifically, I have become interested in policing both as a material practice and as a symbolic rhetoric where cultural authority—twentieth-century notions of civility, duty, and public participation—have been reenacted and debated. I have therefore deliberately written an experimental book that, rather than tracing the genealogy of any single popular genre or media form, shuttles across them over time, in quest of these broader issues. My itinerary will doubtless strike some as too diffuse, my methodological eclecticism a sign of theoretical imprecision. But if some of my chapters seem focused primarily on police management, and others on media representation of criminal disorder, and others on these broader issues of political authority, it is simply because I see these as three strands of the same rope. And thus, throughout my historical sequence of chapters, I have been guided by three sets of questions.

First, the historical questions about everyday municipal policing. For instance, what material forms has local, municipal police *power*—understood here to mean, in the broadest sense, all the ways police encounter, manage, and direct the citizenry, not just criminals or the disorderly—taken in the United States over the last century? How has the racial, ethnic, and political character of police forces affected their practice? What have the various phases of police reform done to these everyday practices? How real are these reforms? What is the historical genealogy, in particular, of the recent neocon-servative turn?

Second, a set of questions about cultural engagement and representation. When a writer like Stephen Crane, or Mark Hellinger, or Mike Barnicle, or True Crime writer David Simon enters into police society and culture, and into its everyday management of public order, what kinds of power is such a writer witness to? How does seeing through the lens of police power affect one's vision of the changing industrial and postindustrial city, in particular? At the ground level, how has the emergence of new media forms in which these writers worked—the tabloid newspaper, the fiction film, newer True Crime genres—reshaped their understanding of the police's authority? For instance, how did tabloids of the 1920s actually cover the crime of murder? Similarly, where does what became known (in the 1940s) as the police proce-dural mystery come from, and what are the legacies it bequeaths? Moreover, where and how have police or police reformers entered the territory of cul-tural representation themselves? What happens, for instance, when a police officer becomes an author—that is, when a working cop like Joseph Wam-baugh, or ex-cops like Ann Rule or Robert Daley, enlists the power of pop? And why have journalists and Hollywood producers and True Crime writers been so drawn to the particular cultural experience of the police? As supple-ments to our face-to-face encounters with police in everyday life, how have *our* roles as consumers of media—as mystery readers, moviegoers, newspaper subscribers—shaped our cultural understandings of police authority?

Finally, a set of questions that are perhaps more theoretical, which I ad-dress continuously throughout the book, and more directly in the epilogue. They are, I think, also self-reflexive, moving back from history to how we ourselves conceive of political authority and how we practice cultural inter-pretation about it. How has what anthropologists call the particular ethno-graphic "predicament" of writing about the police—that is, the necessity of working in the terrain the police manage, not uncommonly in their protec-tion, even as you are viewed as a potential threat to an often secretive subcul-ture—shaped traditions of representation, even undermined the business of political exposé itself? To what extent are we still party to this predicament? Similarly, how has academic scrutiny of the police, a relatively recent phe-nomenon, affected political understanding of its authority? Where and when has academic writing about the police created representations that legitimate new forms of police power? Ultimately, what does all of this suggest about how *we* use the term "policing" as a vehicle for our own analysis? That is, what does it really mean, as so much of contemporary theory postulates, to say that a cultural enterprise envies, emulates, or attaches itself to policing power?

I

At its most defensive, there is a profoundly territorial streak in police studies, as in police culture itself. More than once my dreams have been unsettled by the eerie ubiquity of the police tape, with its declaration: CRIME SCENE: KEEP OUT. I have no illusions that my analysis will register within contemporary criminological debates, nor even among many historians of police politics. This is a book for cultural historians and literary critics, for news analysts and news readers, for fans of popular culture and its critics—and if at all possible, for citizen-readers among all of the above. I also hope to bring matters of law *enforcement* to the burgeoning fields examining the relations of law and literature, citizenship and cultural expression.[14] It thus goes without saying that my approach would have been impossible without the extensive scholarly work already available on cultural notions of criminality, on the role of law enforcement in modern media, and on the institutional development of policing in the United States.

One sign of my indebtedness is that the sequence of my chapters follows the familiar contours provided by our institutional political histories of metropolitan policing in the twentieth century. Chapter 1 retraces Theodore Roosevelt's "year of reform" as commissioner of the New York Police Department, not long after the famous Lexow Committee report of 1896. In many ways a benchmark of twentieth-century liberalism, Roosevelt's tenure is generally thought to presage the Progressive era's nonpartisan and professional approach to political reform. In regard to policing, Roosevelt modeled an approach meant primarily to address the corruption of Gilded Age urban political machines. Chapter 2 recounts what historians commonly call the "second wave" of police reform culminating in the mid–twentieth century. In these decades, urban police departments, in part following on Roosevelt's example, sought to further professionalize local law enforcement by emphasizing bureaucratic centralization, modern crime-busting techniques, and scientific procedures in anticipating crime's patterns. In these years the Uniform Crime Reports (UCR) system was begun, establishing the standard method for classifying and measuring crime rates in the twentieth century.* Chapter 3 introduces the paramilitary, rapid-response style of policing made famous in the 1960s by the Los Angeles Police Department; chapter 4, the stalemate produced in subsequent decades as police departments clung to this approach despite the notorious fiscal crises, manpower shortages, and exploding crime rates of that era. Chapter 5 turns to the recent ethos of community policing as it was implemented in the city of Boston in the late 1980s and early 1990s.

The most basic contribution of this book, therefore, is to reintroduce the specific context of police history to the interpretation of literary and mass-cultural genres, where it is long overdue. It is remarkable, for instance, that literary criticism on the police procedural mystery genre lays claim to its authenticity with virtually no recourse to history. Or that our discussions of crime news, let alone popular genres like True Crime, so often neglect a historical view of police power. Even our familiar tracking of police images in television or film—the familiar panoramas, say, from the Keystone Kops to Kojak—suffer from a similar ailment.[15] By the same token, it is striking that supposedly empirical criminological studies like Albert Reiss's *The Police and the Public* (1971) or James Q. Wilson's *Thinking about Crime* (1975)— taken up in my later chapters—have so far eluded scrutiny as cultural story-telling and political rhetoric. Thus, I have attempted in this book to do more than simply import findings from one discipline (e.g., history or criminology) into another (say, literary or cultural criticism). Rather, I have tried whenever possible both to integrate various disciplinary perspectives *and* critique their methods.

I also try to offer a somewhat different story from many of the institutional histories of the police—which were, needless to say, often part of the re-form tradition they depicted. This reformist bent has a long and noble history in police studies. Long before the emergence of formal academic police monographs in pathbreaking dissertations like that of Joseph Gerald Woods (UCLA, 1973), journalistic exposés like Lincoln Steffens's *Shame of the Cities* (1904) and Ernest Hopkins's *Our Lawless Police* (1931) gave us some of our first reformist glimpses of twentieth-century police power and its corruption.

---

*Under this system, the FBI became a national clearinghouse for local police departments, which collected data on *reported* crimes: those either filed by officers on their rounds or reported by citizens (for example, by telephone). These reports are then published annually. The local police officially determine if a crime has taken place, and they decide upon its proper classification.

(Hopkins's book exposed, among other things, the persistence of the "third degree" in modern police interrogations that also was documented by the famous Wickersham Commission of 1931.) Journalist and historian Carey McWilliams, as well, had documented not only the LAPD, but the *private* deputizing that had terrorized migrant workers in California in the 1920s and thereafter. The tradition of engagement continued in the post–World War II era, especially in the aftershocks of inner-city riots, campus protests, and rising crime rates in the 1960s. Historian Robert Fogelson, for instance, did invaluable work debunking the California-based McCone Commission's whitewash of the Watts riots of 1965, well before writing his *Big-City Police* (1977). At the same time, these writers—many of them based in California— told a new story that began to shape academic history writing. They told about how the formerly ward-based policing of eastern and midwestern cites had been transformed into a new western professionalism based in boot camp paramilitarism, aggressive automobile patrol, and intelligence gathering on even the most innocuous of citizen groups. This tradition of largely institutional portraiture, often with the LAPD as its bête noire, has been carried on superbly by writers like Monkkonen, Joe Domanick, John Gregory Dunne, and Mike Davis.[16]

These writings have often had a significant impact in their time. Many a national crime commission in the 1960s, for instance, echoed the new academic theme described above, while showing convincingly that urban disorders had been fueled by past histories of police misconduct—by what one federal panel, following James Baldwin's formulation, deemed "occupying armies" in the inner city.[17] The 1960s also witnessed the emergence of the genre I have dubbed (in chapter 3) "police ethnographies," studies that were products of fieldwork on everyday police routines and citizen interactions. Drawing upon such studies, the new police history justifiably focused upon explaining police complicity in urban disorder, and the apparent breakdown of civility between officers and the public (a theme I also address in chapter 3). If the liberal tradition had previously vaunted professionalism as the cure for corruption and police abuse of power, what now emerged was a critique of this panacea. The police, that is, were subjected to the broader-based analysis of the impersonality of large-scale institutions, and of technocratic liberalism, so central to social criticism of the day. Thus, Fogelson wrote, unlike the original boss system, the police and other municipal agencies "no longer eased social mobility, reinforced political decentralization, fostered cultural pluralism, or otherwise promoted the interests of the lower- and lower-middle-class newcomers." Rather, in a dramatic historical reversal, police forces were described as having turned against these Gilded Age legacies. Instead they had become notoriously resistant to civilian review, bastions of white-ethnic "minorityism"—and, worst of all, those paramilitary armies of occupation. On the cultural front, the *Dragnet* "just the facts ma'am" style of the police procedural genre (on radio and TV) was said to offer up homage to this technocratic authoritarianism. It was an obeisance certainly supplemented, as Richard Gid Powers, Joe Domanick, and Claire Bond Potter have demonstrated so well, by FBI and LAPD sponsorship of the "G-man" style of policing in film, on radio, and on TV.[18]

Of course, I have necessarily simplified this historiographical portrait somewhat. A historian like Samuel Walker, for one, was remarkably self-conscious about where this new critique of professionalism might head. And in recent years, though its fundamental critique is still secure, variations and new forays *have* developed. As chapter 1 shows, much new research has begun not so much to alter our picture of twentieth-century policing as to revise the portrait of nineteenth-century machine politics against which the reform tradition has been foiled. As Monkkonen's work had begun to tell me, professional crime busting, aggressive street sweeping, and paramilitarism have a much longer lineage that we used to recognize. Both within the new social history and recent ethnographic study, there has also been more emphasis on the beat-level, territorial work of police labor: policing, as it were, from the bottom up. And finally, as chapters 4 and 5 discuss, there has recently emerged a largely neoconservative in-house history writing that, like so much social criticism of this stripe, uses the critique of technocratic institutions against itself, and thereby calls for a back-to-basics approach to law and order. As was vividly brought home to me quite recently, this is a story the police often now tell themselves (as Clifford Geertz famously phrases it) about themselves.[19] In fact, I have chosen to follow the course of an entire century, as broad as this approach may be, because of a particular claim in law enforcement today: that the emphasis on civil order, the central plank of back-to-basics policing in the late twentieth century, represents a return to late nineteenth-century beat patrol. But that's getting ahead of the story.

II

So what is different about an interdisciplinary, cultural-critical history of the police, such as I am attempting here? To begin with, despite the salutary interest in the historical development of street-level police labor, police history usually retains its institutional character: focused, that is, on matters like bureaucratic structure, efficiency, accountability, and the like. These are all vital issues. Yet my interest, by contrast, falls on what Loader has recently denominated the police's *symbolic* authority: that is, the neglected parts of police power that involve story-making, the mobilization and differentiation of audiences, the engagement with media, the engineering of consent. By this I certainly mean those elements of police work we customarily deem public or (in softer forms) community relations. But like Loader, I also mean to question the notion that there is a "hard and fast distinction" between supposedly real police labor (e.g., solving crime) and these symbolic or meaning-making functions; indeed, I think the functionality of police symbols (like the badge, or the billy club, or the black-and-white cruiser) points to the opposite conclusion. Thus I intend to suggest how the storytelling capacities I describe above, which play off of and feed back from media formations, become not separate from everyday routines of police work, but actually encoded in them.[20]

This symbolic notion of police labor is crucial to a more flexible sense of the relationship between power and representation. Ironically, where our current police histories and our cultural studies analyses tend to converge is in offering up an essentially instrumental model of the relationship between power and culture. As fruitful as the more all-encompassing uses of "policing" have been in cultural studies, they often have had two related, albeit unintended, drawbacks. First, they have tended to eclipse the original, literal referent of municipal policing. That is, at present the term "policing" threatens to double back, and come to stand for or shape our understanding of the more mundane, but no less vital, role of *literal*, municipal police power in shaping modern urban society. Second, these readings have tended to subsume the quite variable tactics of police power, municipal *and* cultural, under the single, Foucauldian paradigm of surveillance and detection. Questions regarding the differential applications of police power, of how police encounters are shaped by class, race, or ethnicity, of the forms of criminality and citizen addressed or (as I suggest in the title of chapter 4) re-dressed in a particular era—all this tends to be deemphasized. Under the surveillance model of representation, a newspaper from the 1920s seems little different from one in the 1980s, a documentary film no different from a Victorian novel, and so forth. Even our best monographs on the cultural history of American crime, meanwhile, often reconstruct their accounts solely through popular commentary or media representation, effectively segregating police power *from* "culture" itself.

Alternatively, my goal has been to arrive at a view of cultural representations of and by police as products of a complex negotiation within what some critics these days often call a given "field" of social struggle and cultural representation. That is, I have attempted a style of cultural analysis that brings together the material conditions of story-making, the affective and imaginative feel to police power that writers clue us in to, and the institutional forms of media that provide both the tactical positions and the vehicles for cultural representation of police power. In this regard, I have tried to learn from what thinkers like Pierre Bourdieu, Raymond Williams, C. Wright Mills, and others have emphasized as the observational locations within fields of power and representation. Hoping for a more pluralistic and yet synthetic approach than we often find, I have therefore focused on different media locations within the broader field of cultural production in specific eras of modern policing. Following current usage, I have occasionally referred to these various media forms and institutions as "posts" in that field: in other words, offices or positions within a cultural field of professional observation and story-making that is itself situated in the broader field of power relations (for example, within urban politics or class relations). To put it another way, I have tried to juxtapose a revisionist account of modern policing against a cultural history of the various *forms* of representation that have arisen, over time, to greet that power, infuse it, even participate in it.[21]

Each of my chapters, therefore, tries to shuttle between institutional history and the particular media forms that have often, as well, been taken as signature styles of their day. At most these are historical snapshots. Yet one potential benefit of this approach, I think, is that it opens analysis up to what Renato Rosaldo has called the "processual" and emotional dimensions of cultural description. That is, we move past the static playbook norms of culture or discursive iron cages, and closer to the experiential second sense, the emotional gravity, the stakes at play and at work as historical actors traverse complex fields of culture and power.[22] And perhaps closer to the covert identifications that ensue by cultural producers and consumers alike.[23] As Bourdieu in particular has suggested, we need to seek out the professional norms that make cultural players lose themselves in the regulations of a given occupation, often leading them to live "in-difference" to the broader field of power even as their work is shaped by it. And finally, this relational attention to post and field also promises to open *textual* analysis up beyond its intended or singular cultural effect. Rather, as Robert Karl Manoff has suggested, a cultural text can often enact a "polyphony" of meanings by patching together, much like a mosaic, references or citations from other texts. These references then scrimmage and struggle to frame the events they describe. Yet quite often that polyphony is what Manoff calls "merely formal"—that is, it only simulates a democratic colloquy and pluralism in its form. More fundamentally, popular texts often work to orchestrate rival meanings so as to restrict our access to only some of them.[24]

III

This scrimmaging of meanings is fundamental to the political subtext of our history. As I've already suggested, my desire to think about the symbolic dimensions of police power involves broaching how the police have come to dramatize some of the central issues of twentieth-century liberalism. The traditional way in which this story has been told, of course, has it that police corruption has been the cultural foil to modern urban liberalism. Police machines are cast, as everyone knows, as bastions of entrenched cronyism and unaccountability that seem anathema to liberal ideals. Yet what is too often overlooked is that even reform of the police has been accompanied by a more covert emulation of its power. In fact, this emulation informs the cultural notions of order, civility, and freedom that twentieth-century liberal texts claim to foster. One cost of our having neglected this emulation is not only that some of the political antagonisms around policing are miscast—but also that the strategic political significance of police power to the changing lines of liberal democratic theory has been underestimated. Furthermore, ignoring this byplay, often in the name of a reform narrative of technocratic police "impersonality," has caused us to neglect the cultural appeals—to human fellowship, to respectability, to shared proprietorship of neighborhoods—that surround discussions of police power. Or, in turn, why "the community" has so often been invoked, albeit as a nebulous telos, in the last twenty years.

Therefore, I have purposely selected certain themes out of this literature of police history and reform in order to highlight matters central to symbolic representation, political rhetoric, and public consent. In sum, I am interested in police power as a street-level venue for a broader cultural reshaping of political thought about modern democratic society. In particular, this book means to recount how thinking about police power over the last century has been central to what has often been called modern "liberal realism." That is, police reform has been a staging ground where, in historian Dorothy Ross's terms, a certain branch of liberal thought emphasizes "the removal of issues from the political arena of conflict over values and ends to a technical arena in which issues were reduced to the adjustment of means." Not surprisingly, some of the characteristic features of this liberal-realist tradition surface in policing: administrative approaches to the consent of the governed, doubts about the rationality of that selfsame democratic public, pragmatic reshapings of community power and hierarchy that begin to place order as a prerequisite of democracy rather than an effect. Chapter 1 emphasizes the root of this administrative approach to street order; chapter 2, its reformulation in the interwar years, as doubts about public support deepened; chapter 3, its resurgence, under the aegis of police ethnography, within the fragmenting liberal consensus in the 1960s.[25] Chapters 4 and 5, seen this way, demonstrate the process by which these modern liberal-realist premiums, again at the level of the street, in effect turned inside out, and so shaped contemporary neoconservative approaches to law enforcement.

To create the prelude for this final turn, my earlier chapters focus on the police's quest for public support. Or rather, I have tried to trace the changing historical position of the public in two related senses: as an audience for appeals by reformers that legitimizes changing forms of police authority, and as a citizenry that cops must actually encounter on the beat. Clearly, these publics do not always line up, and some citizens are treated more as antagonists to police authority.[26] For example, in my first chapter, I consider how Roosevelt's enforcement of vice laws in New York's Tenderloin district was nevertheless contingent upon an appeal to a public well outside its borders. Simultaneously, I also try to reconstruct an array of newspapers that framed, interpreted, and contested the reforms that Roosevelt implemented; here I try to show one journalist, Stephen Crane, working within that array (as it also worked through him). In my second chapter on policing in midcentury (1920–1960), similarly, I ask how the literary police procedural addressed the competing publics needed by police powers increasingly intent upon a bureaucratic sorting of the "normal" citizen and the uncooperative one.

In these chapters, I broach another theme as well: the development of the fraternal, artisanal, and typically white-ethnic subculture of policing. This theme may be only marginally visible in my first two chapters: in Crane's ambivalence over the typical Irish or German American cop, or in the Irish and Italian American professionals folded into the seemingly technocratic domain of modern procedural mystery. My third chapter, however, develops this theme more extensively, comparing the best-selling novels of Joseph Wambaugh to the liberal-realist redrafting of police authority in the 1960s. It is here that the peculiar weltanschauung of police posts—what I begin to call "police populism"—comes especially to the fore.[27] That is, many of the popular works present police work as the labor of a dedicated, hard-bitten knight of the city, an everyday man-in-shirtsleeves servant of the mostly white working class, solving crimes not through eccentric genius but by shoe leather, hard work, and pragmatic adherence to often-tedious procedure. And as such they exhibit not simple authoritarianism or paramilitary values, but a long-recognized double-edged potential in populist ideology, applications that are progressive and reactionary, liberal and authoritarian all at once. What is insufficiently recognized in much of our scholarship, in fact, is that modern police culture is often a locus of this residual American populism, often embedded in the world of what are commonly called white ethnics, working-class and predominantly Catholic Americans of European extraction. Even with the development of African American electoral pluralities in the 1980s (as I discuss in chapter 4), urban police departments have remained—in part due to family networks as well as entrenched racism—disproportionately male, Catholic, largely Irish, Italian, Polish, and German American, despite modest inroads recently made by women and nonwhite officers.[28] This residual white-ethnic ethos, so bound to urban streets, neighborhoods, and parishes, complicates our understanding of the reciprocities of power that flow through and around cop knowledge. A classic pitfall of critical analysis is to mistake cultural or media entanglement with policing for complicity with a generalized, monolithic (or hegemonic) political authority, rather than with this historically contingent and more particular political subculture.[29]

With this regard for ethnicity comes my interest in the unusual class posting of the police. In particular, we need to recognize that police work takes place in an unusual bureaucratic structure in which beat patrol is still regarded as an ideal apprenticeship even for management. Yet these selfsame "workers" are often called on to police other members of their community and their class.[30] To explore what this contradictory class and ethnic politics might mean in one recent instance, chapter 3 examines how Wambaugh's work contested both the managerial cover story behind the new patrol innovations of the LAPD in the 1960s and the academic ethnographies that also entered the cultural field. I then counterpoint Wambaugh's history with a gang autobiography, Chicano poet and activist Luis Rodriguez's *Always Running* (1993). In concert and yet also by contrast, Wambaugh and Rodriguez illuminate the white-ethnic fatalism—the "blues" of policing recalcitrant disorder—that so often colors our cultural representations of police with a complex populist ethos about jeopardized citizenship and lost communities, elite indifference to those who do their dirty work, and the street-level stalemates that often ensue.

My interest, moreover, is in showing how this ethos so often provides an inertial sense of the rules, a feel for the game, that bleeds over into cultural representations of urban life as well. For instance, I also mean to show how this artisanal ethos was absorbed and emulated by newspapermen like Mark Hellinger, Jimmy Breslin, and David Simon. Thus, in chapter 4, while I examine both the stalemate produced by midcentury police reform and the emergence of the genre of True Crime in the 1980s, I end by focusing on the journalistic emulation of the police's hard-boiled, fatalistic view of the streets. And in my final chapter, there is a homecoming in more than one sense. Here, I am interested in a recent fifth phase: again, in the rise of community policing, as it was framed by and informed by the *Boston Globe*'s depiction of a street murder of two African American boys in 1991. In keeping with my overarching investigation of political authority—and yet, with the police now nearly invisible to representation as such—I try to explore how the *Globe* used street and cop knowledge to construct itself as an authoritative, liberal, civic voice for suburban readers like myself in the 1990s.

IV

As a final sign of the departure of this book from institutional histories, my interest in these symbolic dimensions of police authority is meant to broach, however partially, the constitutive role of academic practice as well. In the epilogue, I mean to reflect briefly on the currency of the policing trope in contemporary cultural studies. Another thrust of my interdisciplinary approach, however, is not to bring academic readings back to municipal police power but to suggest that they have always been there. One quite telling drawback of even our best institutional histories has been that they often remove the university itself from their story. Yet in fact, in the twentieth century the academy has been crucial to police status and power. As my second chapter suggests, for example, the development of police professionalism in the interwar decades might itself be seen as a chapter in the creation of police science and administration as a university division, for example in the careers of Berkeley's August Vollmer or Chicago police chief O. W. Wilson.[31] Conversely, it was the relative absence of alternative university critique, for example, that allowed the Uniform Crime Reports to gain the authoritative ground they did with the American public. In chapter 3, as well, I explore the role of sociology and criminology in shaping discussions of police power and social disorder in the 1960s; chapter 4 takes up the impasse produced in the 1970s and 1980s by these very same academic evaluations of police practices. And in my final chapter, I discuss how the *re*reading of these earlier sociological investigations by police consultants like James Q. Wilson and George W. Kelling Jr. drastically revised the priorities of police patrol. These various academic engagements with police power, because they are fundamentally concerned with how that power narrates itself to the citizenry, are inescapably bound up with symbol and story-making—in many cases, self-consciously so. Indeed, as chapter 5 shows, different kinds of disciplinary understanding have often been at war with each other, and the thrust of much recent neoconservative theory has been to cordon off who has the right to write about crime scenes. Thus, academic stories can be thought of not only as narratives that debunk mass-cultural story-making or police propaganda for their supposed inaccuracy. More to the point, like a silent editor, academic thinking has often been constitutive of the thin blue lines around and within law enforcement authority itself, as twentieth-century America has redrafted police power, licensed it, looked at it—even when society has decided to look the other way.

1

"The Machinery of a Finished Society": Stephen Crane, Theodore Roosevelt, and the Police

In the early fall of 1896, journalist, novelist, and new literary celebrity Stephen Crane, riding high from *The Red Badge of Courage* (1895) and the re-issuing of *Maggie: A Girl of the Streets* (1896), traveled to New York's Tenderloin district to conduct what he called a "study of the life of a New York policeman." The moment seemed auspicious.[1] Two years earlier, the investigations of the famous Lexow Commission had exposed extensive corruption, kickbacks, and political partisanship in the city's police department, making it seem little more than a tool of the notorious Tammany Hall. In reaction, civil service reformers had joined with Republican regulars to elect a fusion candidate, William L. Strong, mayor of New York City. Strong had then named four men—two Democrats, one mainline Republican, and reformer Theodore Roosevelt—to the bipartisan board of the city's police commission. During what Roosevelt would subsequently style his "year of reform," a series of controversies soon erupted: over T. R.'s insistence on strict enforcement of the so-called Raines Law, which had raised excise taxes on liquor and restricted Sunday commerce of saloons, bawdy houses, and public entertainments; over T. R.'s closing down of police lodging houses in February of 1896; and over the new techniques Roosevelt would install in his quest to professionalize the department. Even the district Crane chose for his study tells us something about the centrality of police power to the turmoil of the times. As historian Timothy Gilfoyle reminds us, "the Tenderloin" was itself a police nickname, reputedly coined by the infamous Tammany cop, Captain Alexander "Clubber" Williams, to signify a juicy cut of police duty, full of exposure to temptation and, concomitantly, opportunities to fatten one's pay.

And yet, as far as we know, this was a study Crane never even began to write. In its place, we have only the so-called Dora Clark affair, an episode that has come both to represent the author's strained relations with New York's finest and to explain why his work in Gotham would soon be cut short. On 15 and 16 September of that year, the following events—at least as narrated in R. W. Stallman's 1968 biography of Crane—took place:

> From the Turkish Smoking Parlors [Crane] walked with [two young women] to the Broadway Garden, where another "chorus girl" introduced herself as Dora Clark and joined the group. Unknown to Crane, Dora Clark—also known as Ruby Young—was a streetwalker who had several times been arraigned for soliciting. Crane did not care who they were; it was enough that he had found their types. After he had interviewed them at the Broadway Garden, a resort of ill-repute, he escorted one of the women across the street to catch an uptown cable car, leaving the other and Dora Clark on the corner of Broadway and 31st Street. While they stood there conversing, two men walked swiftly by, as though in a hurry to get home, and neither they nor the two women took notice of each other. However, the women were just then spotted by [police detective Charles Becker], not in uniform, from the vestibule of the Grand Hotel. It was 2 A.M.
>
> Walking back to [the two women] from the cable-car, Crane suddenly realized that they were being arrested [for soliciting the two men who had walked by] . . . and so Dora Clark spent the night in a prison cell, while Crane debated whether he dared afford to damage his reputation by defending a girl of the streets.[2]

Crane in fact did dare, sending a protesting telegram to Roosevelt, a self-professed admirer of the younger man's writing, upon the heels of Clark's arrest. But Crane received no response.[3] Even so, and despite warnings from cops and fellow journalists that Clark was a habitual offender, he went ahead and testified on her behalf on two occasions. Announcing that he must do his "duty as a man" as if "our wives and sisters" were "at the mercy of any ruffian who disgraces the uniform," he first appeared at Clark's criminal trial, which ended in dismissal. Then, as Clark brought charges against Detective Becker at a police board disciplinary hearing, Crane testified on her behalf again. This time, however, the policeman was exonerated, and Crane emerged having been smeared as a habitué of bawdy houses and opium dens. His attention already turning to the growing instability in Cuba that would lead to the Spanish-American War, Crane said he was subsequently hounded out of New York by a notoriously unforgiving police department.[4] Lieutenant Becker, it is often pointed out, went on to become (in 1915) the first New York City policeman given the electric chair, for his implication in the murder of a local gambler.[5]

At first glance, this relatively short-lived scandal might seem to have little significance for the larger contours of the 1890s. Crane's experience is, meanwhile, little more than a footnote in our institutional histories of the police.[6] Nevertheless, this episode provides an intriguing encounter between one of our most elusive yet important cultural interpreters and the politics of policing at the dawn of the twentieth century. Crane's case actually provides this book's first opportunity to explore not only how the emerging reform of police power Roosevelt attempted was played out as political drama in one field of cultural production—that is, in the field of crime news—but also how that field itself became pivotal to the police's own desire to fix, label, and thus narrate forms of social disorder. In this chapter, therefore, I mean to demonstrate that Crane was embroiled in a scandal not merely with the institutional might of the police, but with its powers to frame the symbolic social space of the city streets and their inhabitants. In all, these matters are hardly peripheral to the emerging movement we know as Progressivism, but central to the broader reordination of liberal authority that Crane's street fictions—specifically the sixteen Tenderloin sketches he published in 1896—both consent to and resist.[7]

The way Crane's experience made its way into historical understanding is also telling. As I have detailed elsewhere, interpretations of this episode have been a revealing barometer of the ways historians and cultural critics have, over the years, cast the broader relationship between literature and power at the turn of the century.[8] When Stallman and others prepared their accounts of what they called the Dora Clark affair, for example, they followed the standard Cold War assumptions that conceived of literary power in formalist terms, and thus as something that stood largely outside political events. These scholars naturally produced an author-centered, seamless, and putatively objective narrative with Crane as a heroic "soldier" of realist exposé.[9] With court transcripts unavailable, they reconstructed the event primarily from scrapbooks of news clippings originally compiled for Crane by a subscription service, and subsequently deposited at Columbia University. Ironically, however—by painting Crane as a hero of genteel humanism—these efforts largely followed only one thread of the affair, and had the effect of sealing Crane's history off from changing historiography on Progressivism itself. Moreover, they set Crane up as a straw man for the poststructuralist subversions of the 1970s and 1980s.

In the last decade, that is, Crane's original image as a heroic realist has been not so much subverted as *in*verted, especially as Foucault's influence has been felt. Rather dramatically, Crane's work is now seen as supplementing the very powers of policing he once seemed to resist. The broader reapplication of "policing" described in the introduction has produced this result. That is, like Victorian realism more generally, Crane's work has been affiliated with the spectatorial gaze of modern journalism and the invasive power of late-Victorian reform agencies, and thus made to stand for a middle-class spectatorship that both exoticized the poor and hoped to reform them. For it is Stephen Crane's aesthetic, it turns out, that exemplifies that complex "realist imperative" Mark Seltzer has described: the tactic of making everything visible, a process that "entails a policing of the real." In a reversal characteristic of the new historicism, the agency of the author evaporates while his texts become secret agents of power—specifically, of the panoptical eye of surveillance that, in Foucault's terms, leaves "no zone of shade."[10]

Crane's reversal of fortune is hardly unique to contemporary literary study.[11] Yet it is striking, first of all, how detached interpretations of his work have become from his expressed interest in the symbolic, material, and political powers of the police. Thus key particulars of the historical record (itself so dependent on NYPD constructions) have remained virtually unchanged despite generations of interpretive revision. Many studies continue to take at face value, for instance, the NYPD's claim that Clark had been previously arraigned for solicitation—as if that settled the issue. (Stallman's scare quotes, in other words, still set the tone: the passage above calls her a streetwalker in "chorus girl" clothing.)[12] Similarly, even cutting-edge scholarship continues to refer to Crane's antagonist as Tammany Hall—when, as Joseph Katz pointed out long ago, Crane actually directed his protest at the police department as *Roosevelt* had recently shaped it. Likewise, the casting of the New York media remains surprisingly traditional, in that it remains disconcertingly monolithic. In fact, if the old historicism treated the press (contradictorily) as a sensational yet somehow documentary archive of facts, the new errs in flattening a very partisan field of cultural production into a singular "eye of power." But far from providing a transparent historical lens or singular gaze, New York newspapers embroiled Crane, Dora Clark, and Charles Becker in a maelstrom of political allegories, much as in the famous Helen Jewett murder half a century earlier. Finally, if the old historicism described Roosevelt as "naïve or duped" by his subordinates, dubious of Crane's impractical chivalry, or distracted by the upcoming national elections, now his role is virtually unmentioned. The NYPD itself is still overlooked, eclipsed by a description of policing power that often seems as brittle as the formalism it means to scandalize.[13]

As the fragment quoted in my introduction's epigraph suggests, however, Crane's own account of police power was noticeably more precise than either our traditional or new-historical analysis. Specifically, Crane's interest fell on the particular power of *arrest*. The era's own fascination for the billy club, the police's dominant symbol under Tammany, itself identifies this power: to sweep disorder, corral it, put it under municipal authority. In other words, Crane saw police power as an extension of civil authority—what we might, using his own term, call the "machinery" of governance. But Crane seems to have understood this power of arrest not merely as a prelude to being detained or punished, but as the first step in a seemingly pre-emptive judicial spectacle. The first goal of this chapter, then, is to try to describe the pre-emptive machinery that Roosevelt put into place. By way of contrast with our recent thinking, that is, I mean to show how what I will call the Charles Becker affair can best be understood in the context of these particular social, political, and cultural issues about police power in New York in the mid-1890s.

Recovering this political context also gives Crane's seemingly mugwumpish vocabulary a different slant. To be sure, Crane viewed power as something invested in persons, made manifest in their moral character or their corruption. Yet this was because he believed power (say, contra Foucault) *was* owned or at least politically sponsored. Moreover, as the Clark case made manifest, Crane saw police power as reciprocally bound to responsible citizenship, necessitating a moral response by the individual when abused. Thus, as incisive as the panoptical paradigm has been, it has also eclipsed Crane's specific concerns about the peculiarly discretionary political and moral dimensions of arrest, and the differentiated ways—upon whom and in whose behalf—this power was enacted.

Because it *was* so centered on street-level concerns, in fact, Crane's Tenderloin experience not only provides a fitting entrée into our investigation of professionalization in twentieth-century policing as Roosevelt first modeled it. In addition, Crane's Tenderloin experience illuminates *cultural* facets of this germinal phase we might not otherwise see: the dependence of T. R.'s style of reform upon cultural reshufflings of street surveillance and internal discipline; the seminal role of detectives in vice crusading and yet, less visibly, in internal management as well; the cultural instability of the social terrain that T. R.'s reforms tried, by a complex style of administrative management characteristic of Progressivism, to reordinate.[14] As a reporter who was also a middle-class citizen, Crane brought an important double perspective, at once that of an institutional representative and that of a writer extraordinarily sensitive to the politics of representation, particularly of the poor and the downcast. Alternately mobile to the scene and sometimes stranded in evacuated enemy territory, he struggled both within and against police power as Roosevelt tried to redefine it. Ultimately, Crane's laments uniquely displayed the *stakes* of street-level reordination not only for working-class mobility or freedom, but for the middle-class urban pleasure seeker as well.

Meanwhile, Crane's well-known interests not only in matters of visibility and spectacle, but symbol and speech—the vital question of the political grammar behind who narrates a personal history, as dramatized in *Maggie* and so much of his short fiction—provides a vital complement to our institutional histories about policing and its publics. Indeed, it is perhaps not Foucault's portrait of the Panopticon that best bears comparison to the news coverage of the Charles Becker affair, but of earlier, pre-Enlightenment juridical saturnalia, those public spectacles that were sometimes resisted by the citizenry summoned as audience. In my second section, on the press coverage of the Becker affair, I mean both to recover and to remap this saturnalia that has largely disappeared from academic view.[15] To sum up Crane's predicament I will end with a discussion of one of his more neglected tales, "An Eloquence of Grief," which represents the mechanics of a police court as a mixture of piety, agony, and blindness. The police court was not only where Dora Clark was herself tried. It was also the very place where a representative from

William Randolph Hearst first urged Crane to begin his Tenderloin expeditions.[16]

In contrast to the earlier efforts of Stallman and others, my strategy is partly to see Crane's scrapbooks not only as an array of representations surrounding his Tenderloin sketches, but as representational tactics, or powers, reemerging *within* those pieces. Crane's writings are neither documents of liberal exposé or scandalously complicit police "bookings" as our new historicism has it. Rather, they are hybridized texts with variable voices of chivalric sentiment and scathing self-condemnation—mosaics of realistic penetration and blank spaces, administrative fact and profound social symbol, vocalization and bereft silence. Whatever residual traces of power are left in his scrapbooks are not, then, a matter of their documentary authority. Rather, it is that they provided, at the time, the very tissues of Crane's eloquence, or lack of it, in representing Dora Clark's grief at the machinery represented by her arrest.

I

One of the classic, or at least more familiar, accounts of police power and corruption during the 1890s comes from *The Autobiography of Lincoln Steffens* (1931), a memoir that crystallized many of the observations from Steffens's earlier *Shame of the Cities* (1904). Steffens had been hired by the *New York Post* in 1892, apprenticing first as a financial reporter on Wall Street before being assigned to police headquarters on Mulberry Street to cover the reform crusade of Rev. Dr. Charles H. Parkhurst. Eventually, Steffens would become an advisor to Roosevelt himself, urging upon the commissioner the rehiring of Max Schmittberger, the Tenderloin cop who had been the chief witness for the Lexow Commission. Steffens's memoir offers one of the more biting portraits of the Tammany machine and, specifically, its style of "invisible" government.

This particular characterization, so axiomatic to liberal muckraking, is encapsulated best in a scene where Steffens is discussing a recent police raid with Jacob Riis, the well-known crime reporter and photographer and the author of *How the Other Half Lives* (1890). Riis is shocked by Steffens's assertion that the motive for this raid was not moral zealousness, but the "failure of some one to come through with the regular bit of blackmail overdue" the police themselves. Steffens then elaborates on this invisible system and its cover story:

And so with prostitution, so with beggars, so with thieves, and I gradually learned, first from the reporters, then from police officers I came to know well, then from the crooks themselves who learned to trust me, and all the while from [Chief Inspector Thomas] Byrnes. When he discovered that, while and because I did not write criminal news, he could interest and trust me with it, he used to call me in and tell me detective stories of which he was the hero. He was bragging, and he was inventing, too. This I knew because I found out where he hid the detective story-books he was reading, and borrowing them when he was not looking, I read and recognized in them the source of some of his best narratives. Thus I discovered that instead of detectives' posing for and inspiring the writers of detective fiction, it was the authors who inspired the detectives.[17]

In histories of modern liberalism, lessons like this are usually interpreted as characteristic of the Progressive reform style. In its tone and ironic disposition, the passage is hard-boiled, urbane in the reportorial manner so typical of the day: it pits realistic, empirical fact gathering against political deception, romantic narrative, and public naiveté. Steffens thus aligns himself with Roosevelt's cause, both of them serving as emissaries for an enlightened "public"—at the time a term synonymous with "good men"—intent upon police professionalization and overthrow of a system of entrenched power and corruption. Writers like Steffens, that is, viewed the Tammany police as the fundamental instrument in the "boodling" of city services and franchises, a "nervous system" connecting vice to private interests.[18]

This was essentially the emphasis, in turn, bequeathed to academic police history. Decades hence, historians would begin by emphasizing the strategic, institutional position of police within machine politics. Though periodically buffeted between state and municipal authorities, police power was described as ultimately residing in the local ward boss, who in turn distributed it to precinct captains who were, as Steffens claimed, more than deferential to the well-to-do. Police forces were themselves characterized as predominantly local, decentralized, civilian (nonmilitary), and unprofessional in nature. Before formal academies began in the early 1900s, it was pointed out, police officers had been political appointments, with slots often being awarded to the highest bidder; officers worked regularly at polling places, and rarely in an impartial way; internal discipline was a scandalous affair. And as Steffens surmised, when it came to vice crime, brothels and gambling houses were confined to certain areas, regulated so long as they were not unduly disruptive, and shielded by elaborate protection schemes.[19]

Against this backdrop of tight political control and lack of public accountability, Roosevelt's tenure would become, not surprisingly, an oasis of reform in many a history of the police. Roosevelt installed new entrance exams, putatively setting higher educational standards; he put policemen in charge of eliminating election fraud, a notorious abuse under Tammany's reign; he claimed to base his department appointments and promotions upon merit rather than party patronage. He successfully argued for adoption of the double-breasted British army box coat and U.S. army leggings, and the institution of frequent (and surprise) inspections of patrolmen; he also awarded merit certificates and medals.[20] Meanwhile, regular pistol practice was added to supplement the use of the police billy club, which had become the reformers' symbol for the abuses of power by Tammany. Streamlining the management of internal department matters, he also instituted procedures for prompt disciplinary action against police brutality. T. R. even implemented a bicycle squad for swifter apprehension of street criminals, a reform that looked forward to future police reliance on the automobile. Contrary to the Foucauldian paradigm, Roosevelt's campaign to abolish the police lodging house also indicated his goal of moving police duties *away* from the broader community service functions he thought of as sentimental and ill-advised. To his public, Roosevelt stressed military discipline as a means of closing loopholes of corruption, instituting better morale, and assuring equal enforcement.[21] Most important for the Charles Becker affair, he pressured police forces toward equal enforcement of the Raines Law.[22] Not only did law enforcement under Roosevelt seem more vigorous; to some eyes it was nobly even-handed, even egalitarian. T. R. even went on record saying that Irish Americans still made the best police officers.[23] Many historians still call Roosevelt's example the stimulus for first wave of twentieth-century police reform.

Meanwhile, however, more recent scholarship has begun to challenge the muckraking portrait of the Tammany system T. R. claimed to replace. It now seems clear that earlier histories of reform tended to underplay the mid-nineteenth-century expansion and professionalization of northern urban police forces that had established this machinery to begin with.[24] Chief Inspector Byrnes, in fact, had published a folio photo gallery of local criminals organized by type and modus operandi, a practice hardly suggestive of unprofessional policing, much less the invisible government that the muckrakers liked to castigate.[25] The heroic portraits of Roosevelt's drive toward professionalization also tended to downplay earlier innovations in police technology like the rogues' gallery (in New York in 1857, and again a particular favorite of Byrnes); the call or signal box, instituted in the early 1880s; and the patrol wagon, undoubtedly a factor in mushrooming misdemeanor arrests in these years.[26] Indeed, the paramilitary emphasis some of our older histories tended to emphasize—as a distinctive approach of Progressive police reformers like T. R.—actually had earlier roots, particularly in the south. Nor was street vigilance entirely new above the Mason-Dixon line. Even before their formal institutionalization, northern police forces—sometimes backed by affluent, nativist, and often anti-Catholic forces even in the 1830s and 1840s—had gravitated to wider use of the billy club, of the "drunk and disorderly" charge and, in the postbellum years, of stricter vagrancy laws. As recent scholarship demonstrates, the late nineteenth-century evolution of the police court itself was a manifestation of new state powers that had enhanced the legal status of police testimony and made criminal prosecution an administrative rather than a civil matter.[27] When joined to the emerging use of state militias, Gilded Age policing in the north hardly looks as decentralized, lax, or unprofessional as it once did. As Sidney Harring has shrewdly observed, even its characteristic corruption may have been itself a by-product *of* the particularly systemic form professionalization had already taken in the Gilded Age.[28]

Meanwhile, while still acknowledging the local, machine-based, and often corrupt nature of Gilded Age police forces, historians have now begun to emphasize the role of beat officers in providing municipal services for their communities and—albeit paradoxically—in periodically disciplining those communities, often with brutal force. We now know, for example, that the vast majority of arrests in the Gilded Age itself were for misdemeanor crimes, notably public drunkenness, vagrancy, and the like.[29] On the one hand, this was a reflection of the idea of a beat cop as (in Alexander Von Hoffman's words) a "versatile official of the neighborhood where he patrolled," having his work routine largely dictated by the citizens who lived along his beat. Contrary to the popular image of heroic detective work, a beat cop would be very lucky ever to find or return stolen property or catch a burglar by ratiocination. Rather, his main job was the protection of private property, investigating local crimes only after the fact, perhaps thwarting sporadic vandalism and resolving petty disputes. He would also provide blank permit forms or licenses for construction and other businesses, report on broken sidewalks or poor trash collection, even answer fire alarms.[30] And when called upon, he would also maintain street order through the use of force—as Steffens and Crane both saw, through often brutal application of the billy club.

These functions themselves indicate why the vast majority of criminal cases in the Gilded Age and beyond—again, reversing the older tradition of private prosecution in aldermanic courts—were brought to court by police charges, a systemic reform that made Dora Clark's case hardly atypical of her day.[31] This catchall function of the police court again not only illuminates Crane's concern over pre-emptive arrest, but clarifies the particular way in which disputants who have often seemed peripheral to Clark's trial as biographers like Stallman described it—squabbling neighbors, a janitor, cabmen, and others—were actually part and parcel of the adjudicative process. In all, this new scholarship on Gilded Age policing suggests that Roosevelt's liberal reforms were in some ways more continuous with Tammany Hall than he would have liked to admit. The considerable attractiveness of the kind of *mobile* power that police represented was something Roosevelt was not, in fact, going to forsake. Indeed, even the passage I have quoted from Steffens's *Autobiography* seems strangely enamored of the systemic knowledge of a figure like Byrnes, his ability to control not only police power but its cultural representations.

Many of Roosevelt's own reforms simply extended *and* refined the machinery of street justice in places like the Tenderloin. But there were important differences as well. For one thing, despite Roosevelt's nonpartisan patina, his reforms often had highly partisan effects. For another, they reintroduced moral outrage into police regulation of vice, fundamentally altering whose interests were being protected by police vigilance. Moreover, T. R.'s reforms relied upon highly problematic use of surveillance and disguise, techniques with ramifications for police officers and urban citizens as well. Finally, as Crane's protest highlights, Roosevelt's administrative approach to police power was driven largely by telling presumptions about habitual criminality. All of these themes would be central to the Becker affair.

T. R.'s paramilitary emphasis, to begin with, actually compromised his egalitarian aura of reform. For one thing, it gave Roosevelt's well-known ethnocentrism more than a minor role in restructuring the department. It should surprise no one that combating what was often called the comic-paper image of the Tammany cop—a label again suggesting the importance of cultural framing and symbol-making by the press—meant combating its traditional ethnic constituencies. Thus T. R.'s claim that ninety-four of a hundred policeman appointed during his year of reform were "native born" implied a subtle distinction resulting from the new entrance exams, which Roosevelt explicitly compared to naturalization tests. Not surprisingly, then, newspapermen like Abraham Gruber, editor of the German American New York *Staats-Zeitung*, objected to exams that included, for instance, questions on American history.[32] Irish Americans actually remained a strong presence on the force; early on, Steffens's *Post* reported Roosevelt's lament that they were the only ones not scared away by these exams.[33] Meanwhile, the value T. R. placed on prior military experience, collaborating with this implied generational cutoff of naturalization, obviously penalized more recent immigrants. Indeed, when Roosevelt praised what he continued to refer to as the Irish "race," he said it was for the "soldierly virtues" it had demonstrated in the Civil War. Irish American appointments proved a useful symbol of nonpartisanship. Yet as recent studies of the liberalization of postcolonial police forces suggest, Roosevelt may even have preferred some Irish patrolmen on the force merely because he thought it politically prudent. So much for egalitarianism.[34]

Collaterally, under the cover of nonpartisan vice enforcement, the reformed NYPD now directly challenged the fabric of Democratic political culture. As his speeches and essays on police management make clear, Roosevelt himself fully understood the central role of saloons (and Tammany's police itself) to this seedbed. In essence, he agreed with Jacob Riis's assessment that the saloon was a "boy's club" for the worst type of political education: "The saloon is the natural club and meeting place for the ward heelers and leaders, and the bar-room politician is one of the most common and best recognized factors, in local political government." By contrast, T. R. himself appointed officers from temperance societies.[35] As far as internal discipline went, a streamlined command structure provided the internal policing Roosevelt needed to overcome entrenched Democratic opposition *within* the force. To further this end, Roosevelt argued for centralized, hierarchical command led by a single commissioner. As Steffens himself put it in an unpublished essay from this decade, the ideal requisite for success was one honest man from whom all power flowed. Using the metaphor of military discipline, Steffens wrote that the best course to solidify that command "would be to deprive the police of all discretion in the enforcement of the laws." Although Democratic opposition thwarted the particular goal of a single commissioner, internal surveillance on the force became routine, and not only in T. R.'s much-publicized midnight inspections. Standardized police pistols and ammunition, for instance, could be registered and thus monitored. As Hearst's *Journal* noted all too blandly, standardized equipment also facilitated swifter exchanges during riot control.[36] In turn, detective bureaus, perhaps Roosevelt's main point of pride, became central to this paramilitary command structure.

Whereas some literary analysts cast the institution of plainclothes detectivism as a sign of Foucauldian surveillance, in fact the manipulation of uniforms and their absence (that is, a return to civilian guise) was more complex.[37] The new uniforms, for example, allowed citizens *and* police superiors to identify a patrolman on the job, and thus monitor his performance. The coat served to keep a patrolman on duty, a citizen his inspector (a reciprocity, again, Crane felt he must enforce). However, when it came to the arrest of vice offenders, Roosevelt preferred to rely upon *plainclothes* detectives. T. R. announced that "there are certain kinds of crime which can be reached only by the use of detective methods—gamblers, keepers of disorderly houses, and law-breaking liquor dealers can hardly ever be touched otherwise. It would be almost useless to try to enforce the law against any of them if we were confined to employing uniformed police." Once again, however, Steffens uncovered a less obvious function detectives served. Decades before becoming enamored of Bolshevism, and before partly distancing himself from T. R. in the sardonic hindsight of his *Autobiography*, Steffens argued that the key to police reform was to promote one's own appointments as spies. "In other words treat the detectives as a confidential guard, and use them, half for the detection of criminals off the force, half for the capture of criminals on the force."[38] "The detective force of a police department," Steffens argued, "is the key to the system . . . The man who controls it, controls the situation." As the *Times* revealed, the detective bureau of the NYPD was in fact called the secret service branch.[39] For his part, Roosevelt compared detectives to military spies, and defended their use even in labor actions. He buttressed his case by referring to the suppression of the Molly Maguires.[40]

Charles Becker—a Republican-leaning second-generation German American from Sullivan County, New York, who had been on the force less than three years—was himself a police detective. Though appointed under Tammany, his rate of promotion under T. R. was significant.[41] And of course, when he arrested Dora Clark he was in plainclothes. Taken as a whole, his actions in arresting Clark were quite characteristic of the differential order

Roosevelt now attempted to install. Whereas a Gilded Age beat patrolman, for example, would have normally treated a well-known local drunk more leniently than an inebriated stranger, T. R. reversed these priorities. In a longer view, in fact, we can see that Becker was trained in the proactive ethos soon institutionalized in twentieth-century police culture. As many sociological studies would later show, modern patrol officers would be *trained* to be suspicious, to weed out anything on the street that seems threatening to citizens or to themselves. (See especially chapter 3.) Becker's actions were thus not those of a criminal cop or Tammany hack, but of an apparently educated and ambitious man.[42] Caught in the paradoxes of beat authority I have described, they were also quite typical of what Jerome Skolnick would later call the professional officer's characteristically "administrative" and "crafts" approach to law enforcement. In this emerging framework, as long as an officer can retrospectively identify, to his superiors, suspicious behavior that led to the collar, he is doing his job. Even a "bad arrest"—that is, one not leading to conviction—will be deemed legitimate by his peers. As Skolnick writes:

> In contrast to the criminal law presumption that a man is innocent until proven guilty, the policeman tends to maintain an administrative presumption of regularity, in effect, a presumption of guilt. When he makes an arrest and decides to book a subject, the officer feels that the suspect has committed the crime as charged. He believes that as a specialist in crime, he has the *ability to distinguish between guilt and innocence.*

These days, this rationale negotiates the potential illegitimacy of entrapment, not an issue in Clark's arrest. Yet everything about T. R.'s system emphasized pre-emptive action against habitual criminals. It was significant, for example, that the NYPD now adopted the Bertillon system of criminal anthropometry, which added a formula of bodily measurements to repeated offenders' files.[43] Criminality was thus *in* habitual persons and classes. As Roosevelt himself noted proudly: "We did not possess a particle of that maudlin sympathy for the criminal, disorderly, and lawless classes which is such a particularly unhealthy sign of social development."[44]

Meanwhile, these class attitudes intersected with the gendered character of vice reform. Becker's obvious disdain for Clark, reported in several interviews, was hardly atypical of police-prostitute relations then or now. Though many modern officers believe that it is often more efficient to affect sympathy for the prostitute's sense of herself as a "working girl," degrading banter has a longer in-house history. Clark's class status was clearly discounted by this reflex. Crane's "Adventures" provides but one glimpse of how the entire Tenderloin station house relegated Clark to her preassigned role as common prostitute. Clark's prior arraignments had already positioned her, in police culture, for a scripted role whether she suited the part or not. It also seems likely that Becker treated Clark as a noncomplying player of a new game that would not accord her the status of entertainer or working girl. And she fought back.[45]

In the aftermath of the arrest, Roosevelt may well have been distracted or indifferent. But it seems more likely that, in leaving Crane unprotected, T. R. saw himself as closing ranks behind a foot soldier—that is, Becker. Yes, Crane's focus upon Becker's individual moral fiber was limited—yet it also captures another paradox of police power. Contrary to Steffens's more naive outline of the flow of power, pre-emptive action at the point of conflict actually *enhanced* discretionary power on the street by men in Roosevelt's secret service. "Equal enforcement" simply provided the cover story.[46] Becker himself could hardly have been confused on this score. We often forget, for instance, that he let the *second* "chorus girl" accompanying Dora Clark go. (And the johns.) In fact, another policeman named Rosenberg, himself an antagonist of Clark, had been embroiled in an absurd case of aggressive misidentification just three weeks earlier.[47]

Roosevelt's crusade, explicitly coordinated with private reform groups, also meant changes in the *dynamics* of police regulation of prostitution. We customarily assume his campaign was to expose hidden vice. Yet in many respects his effort could make "vice" only more elusive.[48] For instance, the incumbent New York comptroller now complained, with no small irony, that since protection money from brothels had dried up, he needed new appropriations to reimburse police officers for the expenses now incurred in legally securing evidence against prostitutes. (Crane, as we shall see, jokes about detectives as profligate spenders.) Limited funds might also have meant that Becker had to resort more often to the threat of arrest to enforce his rule on the street.[49]

Meanwhile, the Raines Law also had ironic effects by its blurring of boundaries previously distinguishing various forms of commercial sex, theater, and hotel management. As several historians have shown, the cause of equal enforcement only drove saloons into calling themselves hotels to evade the letter of the law. We might thus reverse the effect of Stallman's scare quotes, and take them literally as a reflection of how disorderly urban space had become. Becker's testimony, for instance, positions him in a "hotel" lobby before he goes out to Clark on the street; she and Crane's other companion are "chorus girls," and have come from "entertainment halls." We don't know how Becker was dressed (except, again, that he was in plainclothes); one report nevertheless tells us that Clark had, earlier, mistaken a policeman for a man seeking an assignation. In other words, Becker was intent upon reducing the visibility of prostitution and preserving T. R.'s sense of cultural ordination. However, the ground of urban space was slipping beneath them.

Indeed, this contest over the meaning of urban space not only casts a different light on Clark's claims, but on the implicit testimony of the marginal street women, boardinghouse residents, and workingmen whose appearance at these trials has, until now, seemed so comic, tawdry, or incidental. (As Gilfoyle reminds us, the Tenderloin was also the site of many small industries.)[50] News reports, for example, mention a janitor, one James O'Connor, and a second woman, "Big Chicago May," both possibly police collaborators, who testified that Crane frequented the company of thieves and prostitutes. Reports also mention a woman named Effie Ward, who, in several accounts, assaulted O'Connor after he testified. Finally, mentioned in the news but minimized in every historian's account are the ironworks foreman, driver, and cabmen who also testified that they saw Becker brutalize Clark on Sixth Avenue several weeks *after* her first arrest. In criticism on Crane centering on his biography, these all seem bit players. What we have overlooked is that when the police slandered Crane, they also slandered the residents of the boardinghouse he inhabited and the neighborhood that surrounded it.[51] Indeed, the above-mentioned chorus from the margins, trivialized even in the nominally Democratic press, opens up yet another class dimension to vice patrols: the way—as was frequently true in Progressive thought—the public would be overtly invoked only to be covertly delimited, even displaced, by administrative control. Thus, though Becker's plainclothes dress might seem a form of disguise, used for what we commonly call undercover surveillance, it actually expresses this ambiguity of public representation. As Skolnick points out, in the so-called victimless crimes Roosevelt stressed, the cop actually stands in as a surrogate complainant for a third party not present to the crime (and in some cases nonexistent). Thus even the reform-minded newspapers pointed to the ambiguity of having a man dressed like a pleasure-seeking civilian making vice arrests. Thus the "disguise," such as it was, actually made momentarily visible the groups whose tacit political will probably made such arrests possible. And, in turn, they provided a symbolic expression of the citizen Crane felt was an impostor, and who had to be re-dressed by the author's protest.[52]

Oblivious to such ambiguities, the Tenderloin campaign was nonetheless waged with utter confidence. Some in the press chimed in. Just two months before the Becker affair, in an article entitled "[The] Tenderloin as It Was," the *New York Times* carried the department's banner in announcing that "THE SINFUL DISTRICT HAS BECOME MEEK." The article draws upon the report of Captain Chapman to Chief Conlin; these are the officers who, the *New York World* would charge, would orchestrate the testimony against Crane's character. The article is virtually a précis of Roosevelt's ethos. Underlining that Captain Chapman had "a fine war record, and that he had shown that he has not forgotten his training as a fighter by his aggressive policy in the suppression of crime,"[53] the *Times* presented the glory days of vice as if they were already a thing of the past. "Since Capt. Chapman has been in command," the *Times* pronounced, "he has pursued a vigorous and aggressive policy against the vicious characters who have always infested the precinct." Now, the *Times* added, "[i]t is . . . possible to walk on Sixth Avenue at all hours of the evening without being accosted by disorderly characters." Sixth Avenue, as Katz has discovered, was the site of Stephen Crane's first protest of a solicitation arrest—one month after this victory proclamation, and a month *before* the Charles Becker affair. Crane in fact once began a sketch about Sixth Avenue, but he did not complete it.[54]

As the final endorsement of T. R.'s crusade, the *Times* ran a page-one story arguing that newspapers should desist from illustrations of police detectives, since such sketches jeopardized their undercover work.[55] Thus the political absurdity was not only that Dora Clark had been arrested on sight. Additionally, some voices within the press, the social institution supposedly harboring the cult of exposure, argued that the policeman arresting her should be allowed to remain invisible. Indeed, in many news reports there is virtually no record of the man identified, originally, as a codefendant in Clark's complaint: a detective named Conway. Perhaps he was unmentioned so as not to blow his cover.[56]

II

For late nineteenth-century police trials and the NYPD's internal disciplinary hearings, such as the two involving Crane, Clark, and Becker, news reports are virtually the only extant record. And so far, I have been following customary historical practice, treating news reports as a factual archive. The truth is that news accounts variously disagreed, in ways that may well be factually irreconcilable, over what Dora Clark said in court and what her background was; whether the presiding magistrate in her trial, one Judge Cornell, knew Crane, and why; whether Clark pressed her complaint against Becker over Crane's reservations, or the reverse; whether Police Commissioner Grant protected Crane's reputation or left it exposed; and more. Add to this the fact that, as the federal elections approached in this critical autumn, news writers, editorialists, and cartoonists rarely overlooked an opportunity to polemically link street crime to even the most remote items of national debate. In one Republican cartoon, a silver mine operator was cast as a street mugger; in one Democratic news report, an arrested tramp claimed his name was Willie Bryan.[57]

The 1890s, of course, are notorious for volatility in the journalism trade; partisan transcriptions of court proceedings are to be expected. Yet the problem goes beyond factual discrepancies or simple political distortions. Rather, it is that this decade marks the moment when the familiar classifications in the historiography of journalism—party labels, chronological distinctions, and differentiations by audience—start to come unglued. With the rise of Hearst's *Journal* and Joseph Pulitzer's *World*, the purchase of the *Times* by Adolph Ochs in 1896, or the reversal by Charles A. Dana's *Sun* of nearly thirty years of partisanship in endorsing William McKinley, party affiliations and audiences shifted ground; news conventions within crime reporting, meanwhile, were also in a considerable state of flux, as the recent migration of Steffens's own *Post* into the post of crime news suggests. And as I have shown elsewhere, those most committed to the "new" journalism of Hearst and Pulitzer, and by partisan ties antagonistic to Roosevelt, were ironically the papers most dependent upon the police for their staple of crime news. The sheets that habitually defended Roosevelt, on the other hand, were those most likely to regard crime reporting as a sordid affair.[58] Roosevelt himself added to the scrambling of local press allegiances by his controversial foreign policy positions and by the "big stick" aggressiveness of his vigilance about vice.[59] Even without the recurrent political turmoil over the NYPD, the figure of the *individual* cop on the beat did not, himself, easily conform to prevailing political sympathies. Then as now, the police officer was a fluid representational icon, appearing sporadically in the news as a working-class hero, as a symbol of community order, or as a stock villain in tales of urban corruption.

All this being said, it *is* possible to provisionally describe a local triangle of mainstream English-language newspaper styles in these years. Each corner of this triangle contained several New York papers and represented one location where partisanship, class accents, and conventions of crime reporting formed a common social rhetoric. Necessarily, this triad of newspaper styles was also a fluid configuration, marked by fragile alliances and often crisscrossed by unacknowledged mutual imitation.[60] At one corner stood the largely Republican anti-Tammany cohort of newspapers: the *Press, Tribune,* and *Times,* the last being locally Democratic and nationally Republican. Like Steffens's *Post,* this cohort habitually adopted a somewhat antiseptic tone toward crime news. They used court reports as nonlocal or comic column filler, or as occasional news oddities of amusing arrests or unusual court orations. This material was considered "beneath the fold" matter, far less important than political news. Primarily, these papers interpreted their role as providing public notice. The editorial page of the *Times* even ran notices for unfilled positions in the NYPD, assuring applicants that the process under Roosevelt was now "perfectly fair and open."[61] At a second corner stood the more traditionally Democratic sheets—some affiliated with Tammany, like the *Sun,* and others, like the *Brooklyn Daily Eagle,* more mugwumpish—which had always been more at home with crime reporting. At the third corner stood what journalism historians, reflecting the elite denigration of the day, still often call the new "yellow" papers, Hearst's *Journal* and Pulitzer's *World.* These two sheets, in fact, competed vigorously with each other and marked, as we shall see, some distance from their reputed working-class orientation.

The cultural narrative varied accordingly within and across this field. Within the first cohort, the Becker affair seems a minor episode indeed. The three anti-Tammany dailies each devoted at most four to six column inches to the Clark and Becker trials. Only the *Press,* which had habitually backed Roosevelt and thereby earned the NYPD's own advertising account, moderately dramatized the affair. Having already experimented with melodramatic reports of brutal crimes and police heroics, often accompanied by set scene Victorian woodcuts, the paper ran the Becker hearing under the headline

"Red Badge Man on a Police Rack." But beneath this medieval banner head-line, putatively inside information both minimized the affair and confirmed the case of authorities: that Clark was "well known" by the Tenderloin police, and that Crane's present address was a known opium haunt.[62] The under-cutting by the *Times* was more subtle. In reporting on the charge against Clark, mistakenly minimized as "loitering" by this paper, the *Times* simply converted all courtroom testimony into the indirect third person, ending with the judge's assurance to Clark that he would guard against any further police harassment. Of Becker's hearing, the *Times* reported only that Crane was "subjected to a very severe cross-examination," and added that Grant upheld Crane in his refusals to answer damaging, but again unspecified, questions. On the whole, in the *Times, Tribune,* and *Press* reports, the dominant impres-sion is of an orderly proceeding, a watchful judicial system responding honor-ably to rather minor charges. Yet something more complex than mere parti-sanship, or "surveillance" by the "media," was in play. Rather, within this anti-Tammany reform cohort, upper-class reticence, collaborating with self-styled nonpartisanship and identification with governance, worked to mute Crane's charges and reinforce the apparent civility of police and judicial pro-ceedings.[63]

Indeed, these class idioms of civility crossed party lines. They were quite visible within the second cohort—for example, on the pages of Dana's *Sun.* In earlier days, the *Sun* had taken notorious glee in the flops and foibles of day-to-day police management; even in 1896, *Sun* columns were still littered with comedies of drunken patrolmen, mistaken arrests, and absurd court ora-tions. From its example Pulitzer's *World* would learn a great deal.[64] Like the locally Democratic *Times,* the *Sun* did occasionally take a moderate tone to-ward vice crusading. It cautioned, for example, that enforcement of the Raines Law needed to be more practical in its legal approach to probable cause. But now the *Sun*'s attitude toward Dora Clark and her sisters on the street epitomized its recent drift from working-class to elite audiences. The *Sun*'s legal quibbles did little to disguise, in 1896, its newfound enthusiasm for rig-orous law enforcement; indeed, even its traditional satire of ineptitude could now be claimed as having endorsed such vigilance. The *Sun*'s long-standing defense of experience as the main criterion for public duty—often held up against the rubes, novices, and gentleman amateurs of civil service reform—also made Dana's organ now a tacit ally of cops regardless of their political leanings.[65] Therefore, the paper congratulated Roosevelt's NYPD in October not only for increased arrests, but for increased prosecutions of street women, a trend it called "salutary and pleasing." Similarly, its Brooklyn neighbor, the Democratic *Eagle*, praised Roosevelt's judgment about the need to lock up habitual criminals and gang associates to preempt subsequent disorder— a policy, again, crucial to the Clark case.[66]

The *Sun* and the *Eagle* thus saw Dora Clark's arrest as a routine affair. Where they differed from the anti-Tammany cohort was in their modest protest of the vilification of "knight-errant" Crane. The *Sun*'s 17 September report gave voice to Clark's complaint of harassment, yet cast her voice in a bourgeois, chiseled diction that again only enhanced the court's aura of civility while confirming her status:

> "All I have to say is that the charge is false," was the girl's answer. "The charge is founded, not upon fact, but upon the desire of this policeman to assist a couple of brother officers in gratifying a spite they have against me."

> "But you do not deny that you frequent the Tenderloin, do you?" asked the Magistrate.
> "There would be no use in making such a denial," was the answer.

Into this polite melodrama, the "'red badge of courage' flaming on his breast," Crane is cast as the champion of Clark's cause, asserting that "[i]t would be well if others would follow my example." Crane is a righteous gentleman, indeed a man Judge Cornell himself knows and believes. Yet this time, the judge does not promise to safeguard Clark, but instead warns her "against placing [her]self in a position that will justify [her] arrest again."[67] In short, the *Sun* managed to one-up its anti-Tammany opponents by salvaging Crane's chivalry while still casting Dora as a woman of questionable character. The *Sun* did so as well, without questioning the police in making the initial arrest. Less than four days after the Clark trial, when Charles Becker shot and killed an escaping burglar (as it turns out, a young boy), the *Sun* reported said that he had "the reputation of being an efficient policeman." No partisan bickering here.[68]

This cross-partisan support of police authority, however, left the field open for the so-called yellow journals, which punctured all pretense of civility. For example, whereas the *Sun* and *Eagle* had supported an appeals court decision to overturn the extortion conviction of William McLaughlin, an inspector of police implicated in the Lexow scandals, the *World* crowed that "M'Laughlin Is Lucky," and couched the court's finding in a rogues' gallery report of police officials still unpunished. In much of its coverage of police affairs, the *World* inherited the *Sun*'s traditional satire to create a believe-it-or-not, Keystone Kops–style pageant. Sunday *World* editions, under the heading of "One Day's Life in Greater New York," included short articles about bears locked in police cells; wildly improbable court reunions; and, perhaps most humorously, the saga of policeman John Hughes, who said that he never drank to excess until he joined the force.[69] All of this could be done, of course, while now supporting Dora Clark. Thus, though in its editorials the *World* decried Clark's arrest, in its news coverage it used Crane's status as a writer to create a "racy" story of bohemian adventurism. Leading with "With Himself as Hero" and "Crane Had a Gay Night," the *World* cast Crane as "A NOVELIST IN SEARCH OF TYPES, [who] FOUND HIS HEROINE AND SAVED HER [and] PICKED UP A PLOT IN THE STREETS." Not surprisingly, it is in the *World* that we see that "EFFIE WARD PULLED THE JANITOR'S HAIR AND PLANTED HER FIST IN HIS FACE" at the end of the Becker hearing. And if the *Sun* had quoted Clark as saying, ever so civilly, that "I am almost sure to be arrested the very next time I appear in the precinct, no matter if I am simply walking along," the *World* depicted Clark as a more colloquial heroine: "I will be arrested again on sight the moment I show my face in the precinct." On top of that, the *World* said that Judge Cornell sympathized with Crane not because of shared reform intentions (as the *Sun* claimed), nor because of Crane's literary reputation (as the *Eagle* had). Rather, it was because the author had been sitting up on the bench for a week, studying "types among the prisoners."[70]

One reason for the *World*'s levity, of course, was that Crane worked for its chief circulation competitor, Hearst's *Journal*, which likewise came to Clark's defense. Yet yellow sensationalism did not necessarily generate a common ground regarding police authority. On the contrary, the *Journal* ran by far the most romantic representations of crime busting of any of the papers considered here: contests between reform and Tammany detectives; breathtaking accounts of arrests; and, of course, thrilling exposés of corruption.[71] The *Journal*, then, cast Crane within this heroic idiom, and made him a contestant for justice amid a gallery of passionate combatants that included Clark herself. The *Journal*'s elaborate woodcuts, often used to present "authentic" simulacra of news artifacts (checks from Mark Hanna, a diplomat's cane, the actual

1.1
Detective Charles Becker
(from the *New York Journal,*
19 Sept. 1896).

hand of Laura Jean Libbey), accentuated this gallery effect by re-creating the narrative for its audience. Illustrations showed Crane and Clark's evening gambol, their arrest, and their courtroom appearance; in fact, the middle panel inaccurately presented Becker in uniform (figures 1.1 and 1.2). Moreover, the *Journal's* set scenes unwittingly served to anticipate the dimension of the drama so threatening to its author: they made Crane look like Clark's suitor (or john). Crane's role as heroic realist nevertheless rose to save the day.[72]

The *Journal* cast Crane as hero by turning the *World's* lampooning on its head. As within the *Sun* cohort, within the *Journal* Crane is a valiant knight. Yet it is his skill as a literary realist, not only his gentility, that is put at the service of justice. In the opening of the *Journal's* first report, Crane is portrayed as an intense writer who, even in the hubbub of the courtroom, concentrates upon "the tide of human Misery" passing before him. Clark is led in weeping, under the cruel gaze of officers and onlookers; she is shamed by the charge. Meanwhile, *Journal* sketches (compare figures 1.2 and 1.3) seemed to repudiate the popular iconography of the predatory chorus girl, and cast Clark in prim, nearly matronly garb, and Crane as the man of letters in a studio portrait (figure 1.4). In the news text, the courtroom crowd develops a deep sympathy for Clark's plight. The report asserts that her fears of harass-

1.2
"The Arrest of the Girl"
(from the *New York Journal*,
20 Sept. 1896).

ment are well founded and invites admiration of her defiance. She speaks eloquently of her own plight:

> The Magistrate was annoyed, for he had often listened to baseless charges against policemen.
>
> "It's the truth," she cried, "but what is a girl's word against a policeman's? And so he's right, Judge, when he says I've been arrested."
>
> "Haven't you anything definite to say?" asked the Magistrate, sharply.
>
> "I have the truth to say," she replied, defiantly. "I was in Broadway Garden last night with a woman and two men. I know it was late and I suppose I ought to have been in my own room alone—but I wonder if men can understand how deadly lonesome that is? I was out where there were people and lights and music."

If in this report the *un*sympathetic "reform Police Magistrate" does *not* recognize Crane, Dora Clark is a quite recognizable literary type: the sentimental working girl of dime novel and story papers whose fall, such as it is, stems from impoverishment, loneliness, and urban temptations. Crane's complementary role is that of the male chivalric protector.[73] Indeed, to signify this ready-made role, the *Journal* reported the assurance of Clark's lawyer that

1.3

Dora Clark (from the *New York Journal*, 20 Sept. 1896).

two charity organizations had taken an interest in her case. In short, in the *Journal* Clark became one of the "unfortunate," where class relationships were subsumed under the sign of the patriarchal protection of womanhood.[74] Thus, even if the *World* and *Journal* came to Clark's defense, they did so only by first positioning her, as the *Journal* illustrations show, in a respectable zone above the Tenderloin itself. When Crane states in court that Clark was, by virtue of her gender, under his "protection," the *Journal* observes: the other "women [in the courtroom] were puzzled. Being of the Tenderloin, it was utterly impossible for them to understand the motive Mr. Crane expressed."[75]

Our traditional scholarship errs in several ways, of course, by having elevated this last narrative as an objective, author-centered, even sentimental history. On the other hand, neither can the image of a monolithic, Panoptical media gaze with "no zone of shade" capture the competing array of press allegories around this affair. Indeed, one might say that it is precisely *by* al-

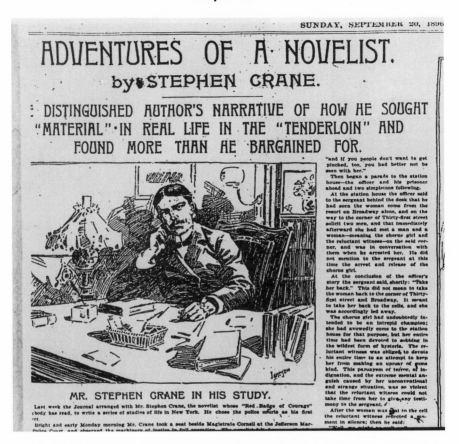

1.4

"Mr. Stephen Crane in His Study" (from the *New York Journal*, 20 Sept. 1896).

lotting various spotlights and shading—that is, by intricate local decisions about what was beneath view or simply out of it—that the New York press competed over and complied with the process of Progressive social reordination. In retrospect, it was the virtual silencing of the affair by *both* the anti-Tammany cohort and the older Democratic papers that seemed most collaborative with the police; these papers and their readers might be said to represent Skolnick's absent third party, citizens who would just as soon avoid direct involvement but want the police work done nevertheless. Yet even the yellow papers drew Clark *out* of the Tenderloin in order to save her. And although we may never know whether a real Dora Clark's voice was silenced by the press's own, we should recognize her resistance despite the odds. We might also notice that the reports of her recurrent grief and shame seem, rather dramatically, to contradict the presumption by the police, the press, and even Crane biographers of her habitual status as a prostitute. Indeed, it was this particular contradiction that seemed to leave its mark on Stephen Crane's eye.

III

By the mid-1960s, the chivalric frame Hearst's *Journal* placed around the Dora Clark affair dominated academic criticism, reinforcing the reading of Crane's work as liberal exposé. A familiar collaboration of traditional archival practice and biographical scholarship had taken place: Crane's interpreters took it as their task to *reconcile* conflicting news accounts into putatively objective historical narratives that focused on the risk the affair posed to the heroic "realist" and his reputation. Yet only by selecting a few of these representations could critics have produced the author-centered history in the first place.[76] Even when this image waned in the 1970s and 1980s, descriptions of Crane's writing retained this association with urban exposure. For example, even as he argued that Crane wrote from "a perspective disengaged from that of the typical middle-class viewer," Alan Trachtenberg nevertheless adroitly placed Crane's work as subtly modifying the tradition of "unveilings" of urban mysteries exemplified by Eugene Sue, George Foster, and Jacob Riis himself. Yet if Crane exposes anything in his sketches of 1896, it is that his Tenderloin was already a reformed, policed space. His musings on systematic police reform, therefore, go out as ironic asides, or meditations on the ethos embedded within an individual patrolman. Taken collectively, his writings offer a kind of postscript upon the vice campaign's mop-up stages, sketches where he could turn the victory chants of the *Times* and police captains into loss and lament.[77] Where the Becker affair had shaped his vision, it was in a growing dispiritedness and even ambivalence about police power.

To be sure, Crane's sketches retained the basic parameters of the journalistic genre long devoted to unveiling the city's mysteries. Taken collectively, Crane's Tenderloin pieces offer a panorama that seems to survey the district from street level to rooftop, entering into zones of urban friction and examining their social mechanics. The moral geography of Crane's sketches typically reduced the city to its microcosmic spaces, to encounters on street corners, in cable cars, bars, restaurants. Often essentially tour guide estimates of these haunts, his articles speak in the language of social generalization, the estimation of "how hot" or "how not" a given locale was. Crane's sketches also convey that conventional ambiguity about their speaker, who seems not only knowledgeable about vice but experienced in it. The *Journal* seemed fully ready to capitalize on these traditional generic expectations. When it ran Crane's "The Tenderloin as It Really Is" in the wake of the Clark trial, accompanying drawings depicted three descending social layers, with a woman's visage in the center of each panel (see figure 1.5). At the top, a maiden gazes longingly out at metropolitan high life; in the middle panel, knowingly at the working-class world of rough amusement; and at the bottom, drunkenly out of jail bars at depravity. To an extent, these descending circles evoked the risky pleasures of a border district, and portrayed at least one issue at work in Crane and Clark's encounter: at what level it could be classified by type (famous author/showgirl; struggling writer/working girl; bohemian opium smoker/prostitute). These alternative possibilities, once again, signified the relative instability of ordination that the police sweeps tried to fix.[78]

Nevertheless, the conventional framing of the *Journal* is misleading. In fact, Crane now seems almost dispirited by how little there is to unveil. For example, in his first article after the Clark trial, "In the Tenderloin: A Duel," Crane begins by characterizing the district as so overwritten about that every common man claims to be an expert. Citizens base their claim, Crane notes ironically, on the "truth which the world's clergy and police forces have collected" (384), a clear reference to campaigns like those of Reverend Charles Parkhurst and Captain Chapman. However, Crane himself characterizes the region as a "corpse" (388) over which requiems are said, and where windy anecdotes are told of the "open days" when vice and drink had flourished. Though he partly retracts his epitaph, Crane admits that the "croakers have clinched" one "mighty fact": that the days of "freedom and fraternity" have given way to a more hollow, garish display.[79]

Other Tenderloin pieces similarly deflate expectations of thrilling picturesqueness by citing the lamentable effects police reforms have had on familiar urban scenes. On "New York's Bicycle Speedway," for instance, Crane writes that a "new game" has arisen between "the Bicycle Cop and the Scorcher" replacing the old of "Fat Policeman on Foot Trying to Stop a Spurt . . . they changed all that," Crane writes. "The un-police-like bicycle police are wonderfully clever and the vivid excitement of other days is gone. Even the scorcher seems to feel depressed" (372). In "Opium's Varied

1.5

"The Tenderloin as It Really Is" (from the *New York Journal*, 25 Oct. 1896).

Dreams," the Tenderloin is a once-splendid space in which vice has "retired to private flats" upon the "appearance of reform" and the police (365). Up in "The Roof Gardens and Gardeners of New York," Crane discovers one restaurant famous for receiving "injunctions" that has shifted to "entertainment" in the aftermath of the Raines Law (380–81). Here Crane refers obliquely to the politics of the new game of vice enforcement: prodigal spending by "Central Office detectives" and reporters (378), while the "civil service commission" (379) absurdly monitors the waiters. In a swipe at the paramilitarism of police, Crane muses that "[s]ome day there may be a wholesale massacre of roof-garden waiters" (379), for such establishments are now "what might be called a county of unoccupied land" (381). No so Minetta Lane, which several newspapers puffed as one of "Gotham's Most Notorious Thoroughfares" when Crane explored it. Yet Crane himself reports that it has been reformed over the last two years (401); now saloons are "restaurants" (403), and the police are ever-present "under the reign of Police Captain Chapman." "Any citizen can walk through there at any time in perfect safety," Crane writes in mockery of *Times*-like approval, "unless, perhaps, he should happen to get too frivolous" (405). What Crane set between the lines of his columns was a war not "in" the streets, but one declared upon them—and virtually over.[80]

Therefore, it is again telling that Crane's tentative postulation of police power centers on the power of arrest. That is, he seemed especially concerned with the threat to the mobility and passage of individuals, and with that, the power of an arrest to inaugurate a legal proceeding without a judicial finding—a power that, as he soon knew, proceeded by its own logic and had drastic consequences. In this way—even as he reproduced the late-Victorian mugwump rhetoric of "honest men"—his formulation reflected the way turn-of-the-century policing still revolved around the management of street order, and proceeded upon the long history of essentially administrative notions of managing the poor. Nevertheless, even as Crane's writings lament the subduing of pleasure, his depictions of the police themselves cannot easily be categorized as conveying simple distrust of police power. On the contrary, Roosevelt's paramilitarization of the NYPD sporadically created a spectacle for Crane's own enrapture. Crane was fascinated with the fortitude, presence, and courage that the cop often embodied in presiding over small dramas of everyday social ordination. Crane's patrolmen appear not, that is, as Victorian villains or buffoons, nor in the mid-twentieth-century garb of the crime buster. Rather, they double both as everyday workmen who arrive at an outbreak of disorder, stanch the flow, cart the disorderly offstage in a grim and archetypal ritual—and as peremptory judges whose decision seems pre-ordained. In "The Fire," for example, it is the movement of the towerlike (344) policeman's fingers that calls the fire department's to battle with the flames of Nature. In "When A Man Falls, A Crowd Gathers," a patrolman deters a crowd with a "sweep" of "two huge buckskin gloves" (348). Like his counterpart the fireman, the patrolman is also cast by Crane (as by Roose-velt) as intrinsically a veteran figure, "evidently in an eternal state of injured surprise at [the civilian crowd's] persistent desire to get a view of things" (344). As Crane puts it in his late novel *Active Service* (1899), the police are part of "the machinery of a finished society that prevents its parts from clashing."[81]

Here again one discovers the limits of fixing Crane's position with a simple partisan label. Even though he resisted the explicit brutality of police, and Becker's personal ruffianism, Crane also spoke on behalf of good police man-agement and seemed drawn to the cop's military consciousness, which sepa-rated him from the gaping public.[82] Both of these latter ideas placed Crane uneasily in the camp of a cross-partisan reform alliance that figured crime enforcement (and, more broadly, achieving political consensus) as largely an administrative matter of efficiency and expertise. The ambivalence of Crane's position is perhaps best represented in "When A Man Falls," when a cop arrives to disperse the gathering crowd:

> [H]e came swiftly, his helmet towering above the multitude of black derbys [*sic*] and shading that confident, self-reliant police face. He charged the crowd as if he were a squadron of Irish lancers. The people fairly withered before this onslaught . . . He was evidently a man whose life was half-pestered out of him by the inhabitants of the city who were sufficiently unreasonable and stupid as to insist on being in the streets. His was the rage of a placid cow, who wishes to lead a life of tranquility, but who is eternally besieged by flies that hover in clouds. (347)

If, again, Crane reads the patrolmen as an intermediary figure, he is also an object of real ambivalence. Seen one way, he is a paramilitary being confident of his superior, practical crafts approach to law enforcement. He keeps those pleasure-seeking spectators at bay "before his threats, his admonitions, his sarcastic questions" as well as the sweep of those gloves. Part of his tool kit, therefore, is a battery of explicit force and brutality, but part is also the machinery of language: sarcasm, warnings, the rhetorical coups that both identify the game at hand and monitor against rule breaking. Like Roosevelt, Crane implicitly deploys a number of racist notions about Irish character that, the passage implies, suit this man for an advance-guard role: animalistic placidity and obedience as well as soldierly fortitude. But here the alliance with reform ended, for in Crane's sketch the cop is also a figure of rage and unreasonability. Pestered by encounters that are both episodic and dispiritedly routine, he is a man deprived of life and thus angry to see it relished by those taking pleasure in the streets.

Crane's ambivalence, as well as a less-than-heroic *self*-evaluation, also made its way into perhaps the richest panel in his Tenderloin panorama, "An Eloquence of Grief." As archival research has shown, this tale was written in September 1896. It returns, in a sense, to the scene of the crime: that is, to the police court, where the authority of patrolmen like the one before whose onslaught "the people fairly withered" was often legally sanctioned. Here Crane sums up not only the machinery of justice in the 1890s but the mixture of piety, routine, and cynicism that oiled its administration. The sketch depicts a brief hearing involving a servant girl charged with petty theft, and it opens ominously, shot through with the dispirited aura of his other excursions:

> The windows were high and saintly, of the shape that is found in churches. From time to time a policeman at the door spoke sharply to some incoming person. "Take your hat off!" He displayed in his voice the horror of a priest when the sanctity of a chapel is defied or forgotten. The court-room was crowded with people who sloped back comfortably in their chairs, regarding with undeviating glances the procession and its attendant and guardian policeman that moved slowly inside the spear-topped railing. (382)

Crane's imagery, a devious mixture of the Christian and the barbaric, positions the uniformed cop as both priest and usher, enforcing civility to a comfortable audience assembled as if for theater. As the case opens, however, the arresting officer for the case actually at hand is in "plain clothes," a sign Crane twists, now, to a demonstration of how "uniform" proceedings are turned from the street into oh-so-civilized proceedings. Rather quickly, Crane turns the setting into a bleak Last Judgment, a mural of bodies brought before an unnamed magistrate, some well-dressed plaintiffs made to depart "one way" while Crane's protagonist, called only "the girl," is turned another, "towards a door with an austere arch leading to a stone-paved passage" (383). The metaphor of Final Judgment is especially macabre in its irony, given that what we are witnessing is only a preliminary hearing. To Crane's eyes, however, this was precisely the dark absurdity that a street arrest like Dora Clark's had represented.

The "procession of misdeeds" of the police court led one genteel observer, William Dean Howells, to wish that criminal trials could be "kept private as hangings," a nineteenth-century desire Foucault would certainly recognize.[83] But layered within the imagery of Crane's depiction is a dark rendering of administered justice as a force superseding all democratic resistance by the creation of spectacle. The passive crowd is there for the show but not able to locate the seat of power:

> All persons connected with a case went close to the magistrate's desk before a word was spoken in the matter, and then their voices were toned to the ordinary talking strength. The crowd in the court-room could not hear a sentence; they could merely see shifting figures, men that gestured quietly, women that sometimes raised an eager eloquent arm. They could not always see the judge, although they were able to estimate his location by the tall stands surmounted by white globes that were at either hand of him. (382)

It is true that in this proceeding, as in the modern forms of power Foucault describes, authority is recessed from view, so as to thwart incitement to counterviolence. In this sense it operates much like Roosevelt's police department, doing the work of the even more invisible "respectable" citizens who supported it. Yet as the blending of medieval and modern iconography in the passage above also suggests, the time frames to which Crane's imagery allude make the proceeding's Foucauldian shape apt in yet another way. Now in a second sense—in addition to the press's saturnalia—it is as if we are witness to the spectacles of punishment that Foucault's *Discipline and Punish* places in history *before* the arrival of the Panopticon: that "theatre of hell" where "the cries of the condemned man . . . already signify his irremediable destiny . . . Hence the insatiable curiosity that drove the spectators to the scaffold . . . there one could decipher crime and innocence, the past and the future, the here below and the eternal" (46).

On the other hand, it seems unresolved how decipherable *this* proceeding really is. In a technical sense, Crane's point of view within the courtroom might seem, as critics have often described the surveillance power of realism, invisible to the action and immune to it. But this stance is only temporary. As if the *World* was right about Crane's true position, his narrative view shifts from the audience to the judge's bench itself. From this closer vantage point, the distanced, ironic voice gives way to something different from detachment, indeed to melodrama that might have been pasted in from the *Journal*'s portrait of Dora Clark:

> In a corner of this space, devoted to those who had business before the judge, an officer in plain clothes stood with a girl that wept constantly. None seemed to notice the girl, and there was no reason why she should be noticed, if the curious in the body of the court-room were not interested in the devastation which tears bring upon some complexions. Her tears seemed to burn like acid, and they left fierce pink marks on her face. (382)

Here, Crane juxtaposes a close-up of the acidity of suffering against the cold stone backdrop of the court. One cannot overstate how suffused Crane's prose is, in this moment, with the array of news representations surrounding the Becker affair. Like his own scrapbooks, the two main vehicles of Crane's "Eloquence" display an ambivalent counterpoint between a *Times*-like indirect quotation of testimony, the civil authority through which the judge decides *against* the defendant, and a more heated prose of yellow melodrama that is drawn to her agony. Like the Dora Clark in Hearst's *Journal*, this girl "believes that she was lost" (383). And then, at his climax, Crane's counterpoint positions the eloquent cry of this girl against the consciousness of an unnamed, witnessing "man":

> People pity those who need none, and the guilty sob alone; but innocent or guilty, this girl's scream described such a profound depth of woe— it was so graphic of grief, that it slit with a dagger's sweep the curtain of common-place, and disclosed the gloom-shrouded spectre that sat in the young girl's heart so plainly, in so universal a tone of the mind, that a man heard expressed some far-off midnight terror of his own thought. (383)[84]

The momentary linkage between the "girl" in agony and her now-terrorized male interpreter is striking. It is possible to read this as a chivalric plea, or as an exposé of the scene: the curtain of the commonplace is rent. Yet the

passage above is pointedly not an appeal based upon the unnamed girl's putative innocence. Rather it depicts the violence beneath the proceedings and
one's own immobility in the face of it. The "girl" resists both her preliminary
and final convictions; the interpreter, however, seems frozen. Crane's title
thus potentially doubles as bitterly self-condemning: there is no eloquent
male knight present at all.

Meanwhile, the machinery rolls on. And as if transposing the male observer's dispirited terror to the reader, *our* eyes have been dissuaded from realistic
objectivity, confidence in secure social ordination, faith in administered justice. In Crane's denouement, another case comes on. This time, it is a hearing
for a routine drunk (or is he, we now ask?) who protests that he is not a
habitual offender. Nevertheless, this plea only causes, in the last lines, "[a]
court officer [to lift] his hand to hide a smile" (384). Here again, with the
"cry" of the girl silenced and Crane's male witness immobilized, the system
produces only forgetfulness and further violence. Whatever "eloquence" remains survives in the smile of the "officer," a pre-emptive vanity to which he
is clearly not entitled.

IV

Given the systematic character of Roosevelt's campaign, it does seem likely,
as our received account has it, that Crane soon felt under siege following the
Becker hearing and was forced to leave New York for Cuba and the Spanish-
American War. In this respect, that Crane's sketch of Sixth Avenue remained
unfinished is telling. "An Eloquence of Grief" performs an interesting turn
on Crane's interest in police power as centering on the power of arrest; in
the end, the observer is, as it were, "arrested" in the presence of an essentially
peremptory power. As the *Times* recognized, the machinery intent upon reforming the Tenderloin focused not only upon reforming the men who policed it, but the men who reported on it. Yet on all three fronts the campaign
proved incomplete. Even my provisional shorthand label of the "Charles
Becker affair" ultimately proves inadequate. Despite the temptation to scapegoat Becker or personalize his action, the fact is that whatever enhanced
power he experienced was itself a product of work discipline from above;
soon, Tammany would be in charge again. Roosevelt's vice campaign also
had its own limits. As Richardson reports, arrests for prostitution rose precipitously in the year leading up to Clark's trial: there were 403 convictions

from May 1895 to May 1896, compared to only 172 the previous year.[85] Yet whether this reflected vigilance or proliferation of the trade is not easily sorted out. But in either case, as the *World* liked to muse, if Crane had stayed longer to pick up his plot, he might have seen that the Raines Law, in Gilfoyle's estimate, "produced results entirely contrary to its supporters' intentions."[86]

These ironies in themselves point to how brittle the Panoptical paradigm is in deciphering urban power. Roosevelt's own police machinery was definitively shaped by ethnicity, exercised within prevailing norms of patriarchal authority, orchestrated in a class context, and shaped by political contingency. The risk, I think, is that the Panopticon can turn many of these contingencies into a gothic abstraction, Foucault's "machinery that no one owns"; it can easily silence a voice like Dora Clark's and her own agency in pressing her case; and perhaps just as importantly, it overlooks the vocal resistance like that of the audience in the raucous Becker hearing. Our sense of "public" involvement, and its important differentiations, is thus flattened, much as the news field itself is. Indeed, journalistic reports work intertextually with other forms of media representation and public understanding, providing reference points and backdrops that citizens inevitably reassemble for their own ends.[87]

Meanwhile, it is curious how our new historicism has only obscured, or rendered marginal, the vexed class position of Becker himself. Becker would certainly go on to develop a reputation for overzealousness within the department, lining his pockets from gambling halls. To a degree, he *was* emblematic of the system of police corruption that Tammany seemed to perfect (and, as I have tried to show, liberals like Roosevelt covertly tried to master). Yet it is also telling that our only full-length study of the Rosenthal murder argues that Becker was a political scapegoat, and possibly framed. Freelancing on the system that had educated him, Becker seems to have developed a Rooseveltian taste for celebrity: as the heroic cop making his name not just with the local ward, but with the public and at central headquarters.[88]

In contrast, Roosevelt's machinery left a less sensational but more profound legacy. Seen from the ranks, Roosevelt's campaign, first of all, introduced those administrative elements of reform liberalism in which, again in historian Dorothy Ross's terms, emphasized modern civic life as "a technical arena in which issues were reduced to the adjustment of means."[89] Yet seen from the street, the effects were much broader: here, in a relatively remote corner of American literary history, we see vividly Crane's recognition that the power of arrest worked as a form of humiliation, a stripping of prior identity—in terms the Chicano poet Luis Rodriguez will exploit, the stitching of a criminal "jacket." In these ways, Crane's writing is a testament to what, following Ian Loader, I have suggested is the symbolic power of the police over "legitimate pronouncement." As sources for crime reporters, as administrators in their own police court, and most of all by the power of arrest, Roosevelt's NYPD used its "taken-for-granted" position, even in such partisan times, wielding material force by simply narrating events. To begin with, they held the power to make Dora Clark's status (as prostitute) a given. As Crane's own self-reflexive moments in "An Eloquence of Grief" suggest, this power could be tantamount to freezing Crane's own expression. No wonder, then, that so much of our histories—literary, political, cultural—have accepted this social given.[90]

Crane, of course, was not wholly silenced. At his best, in fact, Crane tried to leverage the *Journal's* partial opposition of the police's naming power into his own voice, saturating his fictions with the doubt that the police hoped to erase through their administrative action. As well, Crane can be said to have marshaled a battery of literary iconography—medieval, Christian, the smiles and evasions of social satire, as people slope back in their chairs as the "girl" is silenced—in order to challenge this administrative silencing, portray the drastic contradiction that pre-emptive arrest was, in Clark's case, tantamount to final Judgment. Indeed, to the extent that a story like "An Eloquence of Grief" served as exposé, it forecast how much of modern police power would be invested in symbol, pre-emptive action, spectacle, and the demonstration of power.

And yet, our estimate of Crane's powers of resistance should not exceed his own. If Crane's traditionally chivalric image obscures his fascination with authority, and the Panoptic revision overestimates it, both overlook how exemplary he was of an emerging middle-class ambivalence about the kind of power turn-of-the-century policing represented. Crane's awe for police veterans, his concern for effective crowd management, and his anxiety over the danger inherent in the police's submerged envy and antipathy for urban frivolity—this uneasy mixture makes Crane's posture quite suggestive of how many in the urban middle classes would view police power in these years and after. These conflicted attitudes entangled Crane in a loop of bad faith that made him both exemplify, in the public eye, genteel class paternalism and yet become its opponent when it was more aggressively and systematically implemented.

In these lights, the Spanish-American War could provide little escape. "Police actions," in time, would not only be cross-referenced rhetorically from domestic to international fronts, but in a real sense superimposed as a guide to action, as intervention could be legitimated with or without a civil (read: "national") complainant. When Roosevelt declared, in the cloak of nonpartisanship at home, that "[o]ur duty is to preserve order, to protect life and property, to arrest criminals, and to secure honest elections," he might have been providing a blueprint not just for the NYPD but for future Latin American policy. (We might also remember that the Spanish-American War was precipitated in part by the illegal search and seizure of an American woman by Spanish forces, an action Hearst's *Journal* virtually invented.)[91] Even the plot of *Active Service*, which depicts a chivalric rescue mission of a newspaperman undermined by a confident showgirl and uncooperative military men, belies one character's assessment that a foreign landscape could be " 'a long way from the Bowery' " (151). Perhaps it was only as far as the Tenderloin, a land Crane felt had already been occupied.

2

". . . And the Human Cop":
Professionalism and the Procedural at Midcentury

In the opening frames of the 1948 black-and-white film classic *The Naked City*, viewers are treated to an overhead view of the Manhattan skyline, the heavy drone of an airplane or dirigible in the background. Then, the voice-over: "Ladies and gentlemen, the motion picture you're about to see is called *The Naked City*. My name is Mark Hellinger. As you can see, we're flying over an island, a city, a particular city." In an evenly paced yet snappy Brooklyn accent, the narrator informs us that the film is about to tell a story of that city. The film was not, he assures us, photographed in the studio but on the hot streets of the city itself. We will therefore see, he tells us, "buildings in their naked stone," and "the people" without their "makeup." The story begins at one in the morning on a hot summer night, with the city's machines shut down, people asleep on fire escapes. Then, rather dramatically, we peer through window blinds into an apartment, where a faceless woman is being chloroformed—being murdered.[1]

All too quickly, this woman's death becomes fodder for mass consumption. Before long, newspapers in the film are calling the crime, erroneously, the "bathtub murder." In words recalling Dora Clark's plight, we are told that "yesterday [the victim was] . . . just another name in the phone book," today, she's "the marmalade on ten thousand pieces of toast."[2] Ultimately, however, the film will not linger in these headlines, nor take us on anything like one of Stephen Crane's Tenderloin expeditions. Rather, we are initiated into what is known as the "police procedural," a genre centering on the collaborative labor of a force of dedicated white-collar police officers. Specifically, we follow detective Dan Muldoon and his protégé Jimmy Halloran as they patiently solve the murder of this woman, a young model named Jean Dexter, by a circuitous course leading to a ring of con men and jewel thieves. Along the way, in scenes soon to become typical of this genre, the audience glances over the shoulder of the police sketch artist, watches the medical examiner snap on his gloves, sees the radio dispatch operator send out ambulances and police cars, follows the homicide squad tailing suspects. To give the film its authentic feel, producer Hellinger had also hired the famous police and news photographer Weegee (Arthur Fellig), appropriating the film's title from Weegee's book of 1945. With street scenes shot from behind a one-way mirror in a van, the film (like Weegee's work) also invades city shops, subways, apartments, bedrooms, while we listen to the vocalized interior monologues of city dwellers.[3] In many ways, therefore, *The Naked City* seems to draw upon a familiar element in cultural storytelling about criminal detection. We are not passive viewers of the investigation, but secret accomplices. The film's screenwriter himself, Malvin Wald, claimed that the very ethos of his "fiction documentary" was to simulate detection: "strictly analogous with the method of logical deduction," it was a process of "seeking out and following up clues."[4]

And yet, in its focus on the lab, on teamwork, and on mundane police routines, the film also offers a more modern, state-centered parable, as if documenting the progress of police history since the heyday of Poe's Dupin or even Thomas Byrnes. Muldoon, we discover, is a former beat cop. We see him rising in the morning, boiling an egg in an urban flat, singing an Irish workingman's ditty. But as Robert Fogelson suggests, the younger generation of police officers, represented by Muldoon's junior partner Halloran, seem comparatively "deethnicized" and middle class.[5] As if anticipating the upward mobility of Irish Americans after World War II, Halloran is a middle-class professional, fresh from the battlefields of Europe, who commutes from a modern streetcar-suburban row house to the downtown headquarters.[6] Police labor is also specialized, hierarchical, and centralized in a way Theodore Roosevelt could only have dreamed of. The lead detective Muldoon interviews the socialite victims and their elite sting man, often at police headquarters, while his foot soldier Halloran seeks out the brutish enforcer of the jewelry operation, a former circus wrestler named Garza, by relying on shoe leather, the pay phone, and tips from citizens. We also learn about the merits of centralized, coordinated teamwork. When the rookie Halloran naively overextends himself from central headquarters and delves too deeply into the city, he is mugged and nearly killed in Garza's own flat. The day is saved, however, by the more experienced Muldoon, who marshals his troops via radio dispatch and arrives by automobile.

The genre would thus seem to herald the progress of scientific technique, particularly as it was shaped during what historians like Fogelson call the "second wave" of police reform culminating in the mid-1950s. Indeed, the creators of what was alternatively called "the police method" genre, which would soon come to dominate film, mystery writing, and television at midcentury, often made themselves available for police propaganda purposes. Wald himself, after apprenticing in documentary training films during World War II, had spent a month with the NYPD in a police academy refresher course, an arrangement worked out by none other than New York's mayor at the time, William O'Dwyer.[7] The procedural's technocratic, just-the-facts aura seems to turn the police into the professionalized organization men that FBI, LAPD, and NYPD literature at the time trumpeted. As Samuel Walker, Richard Gid Powers, and Claire Bond Potter have shown, the FBI had deliberately managed public views of law enforcement in the 1930s by directing the New Deal's rhetoric of "national emergency" toward public mobilization against organized crime. In addition to supporting the notorious Hollywood codes, the Bureau also sponsored films in which lone wolf gangsters were defeated, typically, by scientific Bureau men. At the municipal level, meanwhile, the new professional was often foiled to the beat cop. The LAPD, for instance, would rule out the word "cop" from the opening monologue of Jack Webb's *Dragnet* as too reminiscent of the older *c*onstable *on p*atrol.[8] As NYPD commissioner Lewis J. Valentine put it in 1946, a real detective was not the Irish beat officer of yore, nor the maverick loner of hard-boiled detective stories. Rather he was a modern office worker with his eyes "on his problem."[9] Police work was a matter of crime labs, telephone dispatch systems, and police teamwork, Webb wrote in his documentary account *The Badge*, "the work of many hands and many minds."[10]

In the more prosaic and less propagandistic haunts of the literary procedural, meanwhile, a set of standard conventions took hold. The trademark of the procedural mystery would be that moment when the everyday policeman steps forth to belittle the illusory mass-cultural image of Holmesian ratiocination, and expound upon the tedious necessity of humdrum police procedures and human contacts.[11] Emblematically, procedurals would come to mimic a technical yet also fatalistic detachment generated, in particular, by repeated exposure to grisly crime scenes: the autopsy would typically be their prologue and generic keynote—in the medical examiner offshoot, even their central MO. (Wald, not at all coincidentally, referred to Muldoon's squad as the "police of the blood" watching over and eventually purifying the "social body.")[12] Readers, in turn, are reputed to be enthralled by such procedural authenticity: by the way, as William Stott puts it, documentary power "imposes" its conclusions upon readers. As novelist James Ellroy describes the claim, the procedural seems to deliver "the real goods from the gate."[13] Just as the police professionally severed themselves from machine politics, the argument goes, so too the literary procedural puts the city at a distance, positing it as an object of detached, impersonal investigative skill, a naked body subject to its heroes' professional diagnosis.

This conventional way of reading the procedural is quite compelling; once again, realism is the organizing rationale. On the other hand, what I will also argue in this chapter is that our historical understanding and even our genre descriptions suffer a bit from this seductive homology, a problem that often happens when "the documentary" (like the term "realism" generally) is invoked so broadly. The term "the procedural" is itself a bit monochromatic, making the form into a simple, formulaic reflection of history. We are left to wonder why writers like Hellinger or Wald became so enamored of an actually quite *un*romantic form of police power—a recipe that, Wald's remembrances aside, relies less on following clues than on creating a procedural net into which the criminals inevitably, under pressure, fall. More importantly, the conventional reading of the procedural has the effect of implicitly endorsing a Whiggish narrative of police history itself, making midcentury police reform seem a mere elaboration of Roosevelt's Progressive ideals in the name of ever-greater police impersonality. Rendered so pure, police history itself is thus rarely reexamined.

If only to trouble the implicit idealism of current approaches, in my first section I want to critique what I will call this "narrative of police professionalization." The emergent ethos of midcentury crime busting can best be understood not as an inevitable by-product of the impersonal processes of historical modernization, but as part of a broader reforming of political consent to police power. This consent was sought not only through the symbolic power of crime-busting professionalism, but through a more subtle blend of routinized procedures and modern public relations. To begin with, therefore, I will try to distinguish a newer midcentury style of public cooperation from the aggressively moralistic and political styles of enlistment used previously by a Teddy Roosevelt or even a J. Edgar Hoover, and suggest *how* it blended with the proceduralizing of power. Although Hoover's stylization of a war on crime of course persists even today, municipal police reformers in the interwar years, in fact, took a slightly different tack. Rather than merely heroicize policing, or emphasize *only* its technical rationality, they actually sought to stress *both* professional status and the *similarity* of police work to their constituents' labor. Contrary to our customary ways of thinking about an evolving police impersonality, I will argue, instead, that this was a mobilization that proposed to give the cop a human face. A key part of the story, that is, is how police hoped to *represent* that public—that is, both "stand for" public authority and "stand in" for citizens themselves. As it were, they hoped to make the simulation between policing and citizenship reversible.

In my second section, returning to the field of cultural production, I will demonstrate how this reversible simulation capitalized on a commerce between the press and the police peculiar to these same decades. Not surprisingly, interpretations of *The Naked City*, like those of the procedural generally, has tended to emphasize the investigative, documentary, and God-like eye of the camera lens. Enacting the tactics of detection and exposure the police themselves undertake, the film seems to perform the kind of Foucauldian surveillance Victorian realism had earlier modeled, and which so much of our criticism now emphasizes.[14] Alternatively, I mean to place the procedural genre in the context both of changes in police power and in the field of cultural representation. Thus, while (as in chapter 1) I will track two former journalists, Hellinger and Weegee, as they migrate across a terrain managed by cop culture, this part of my essay will fall more directly on the film's tabloid antecedents, particularly press coverage of the crime on which *The Naked City* was based. In this part, I want to demonstrate the development of the style I will call "popular proceduralism," and suggest how the populist styles of tabloid journalism in the 1920s proved fundamental to the central political idiom of *The Naked City* and its cultural narrative about public order. To show how these political idioms and anxieties became constitutive of the genre more broadly, I will supplement my reading of the film with a look at Ed McBain's *The Con Man* (1957). Like *The Naked City*, this work is commonly thought of as prototypical of the midcentury's procedural style.

My focus on the police procedural's roots in the knowledge economy between American police reform and modern journalism is hardly comprehensive. From other vantage points, for example, a film like *The Naked City* reflects that classic Hollywood hybridization that was retrospectively labeled "film noir." A collaborative project, this film brought together (among others) a son of Russian Jewish immigrants (director Jules Dassin), eventual victims of anticommunist hysteria (Dassin and coscreenwriter Albert Maltz, one of the Hollywood Ten), and migrants from the journalistic world of the Manhattan smart set (Hellinger, Wald, and Weegee).[15] This last lineage is the thread I emphasize, if only because it is the one the film seems most intent upon repressing. In order to dismantle the procedural genre's documentary claim, I mean to recover the traces of police human relations and tabloidism *in* it, and show how they help us rethink the class and cultural narrative we find there—in particular, its popular narrative about civility, middle-class normalcy, and the pros and cons of social order. In my third and fourth sections, therefore, I mean to trouble these texts' representations, respectively, of police labor and the seemingly placid urban public it serves. It turns out that, like Crane's Tenderloin sketches, the police procedural often does expose an underworld as well as a surface world of fragile middle-class consensus. But in these two particular procedurals—as if turning the more familiar lesson of film noir upside down—that underworld seems intimately dependent upon the respectable citizens the police, contradictorily, so hoped to enlist and simulate. Ultimately we need to read the procedural not merely as a mystery subgenre, but for the way it drafts a new police-citizen relationship. In that drafting we may find, as it were, an unstable micropolitics of authority in the modern industrial city.

I

The story of the second wave of police reform culminating in the interwar years is the standard narrative one can find in liberal historiography, much of it written in the aftermath of the 1960s. Broadly speaking, in these accounts police have been taken to be typical of a twentieth-century organizational trend outlined by historians such as Samuel Hays and Robert Wiebe. Between

1920 and the early 1950s, the story goes, urban police reformers like Raymond Fosdick, August Vollmer, Bruce Smith, O. W. Wilson, and William Parker sought to professionalize law enforcement, particularly by enhancing its civil-service and crime-busting orientation. The emphasis fell on rank-and-file training, bureaucratic efficiency, and political autonomy from urban machines. While the literary procedural would conventionally belittle book learning in favor of police experience, in many ways this was merely a cover story for the evolution, even academicization, of what became known as police science.[16]

As Walker has written, the Depression provided the main impetus to reform. Capitalizing on vehicles like the Wickersham report of 1931, which exposed the persistence of corruption and the infamous third degree, pivotal organizations like the International City Management Association focused police departments on cost-cutting efficiency, cooperation with the FBI, and learning scientific techniques for crime measurement and prevention. Police reformers also followed Roosevelt's earlier example, upgrading entrance requirements for recruits, and now instituting character checks and even psychological profiles; expanding T. R.'s notions of specialization in crime control, they assigned civilians to nonenforcement tasks like office work or jail management, thereby freeing up officers for crime busting. The Depression itself allowed for great selectivity in hiring: by 1940, half of the entering academy class in New York had bachelor's degrees. The evolution of Berkeley (and briefly LA) police chief Vollmer was exemplary: at one time a famous advocate of a social-service orientation for beat officers, in the 1920s Vollmer reversed himself, becoming an advocate of automobile patrol, crime labs, even firearms expertise. But as if following Roosevelt's lead, the keyword really became police "administration." Vollmer was, for example, the first American police chief to implement a formal modus operandi classification system for departmental criminal records. Reformers also subjected police management itself to modern manpower measurements, making police efficiency a matter of rapid response, via the radio dispatch, to calls from civilians. The reforms of Chicago chief O. W. Wilson, Vollmer's protégé, altered standard shifts from eight-hour watches to patrols distributed according to the need demonstrated by prior crime patterns. Policing thus became a matter of professional crime-busting techniques and proper *procedure*, a bureaucratic code word for anticipating future criminal actions by following an actuarial logic based on past cases.[17]

Meanwhile, reflecting a widespread cultural belief about crime in the 1920s, police advocates buttressed their case by arguing that criminals had themselves professionalized. Crooks were conceived as mobile, even migratory; organized in specific hierarchical command structures; and violent. Of course, even in the mid-1930s, law enforcement agencies still circulated folkloric criminal nicknames like "Bluebeard" as old as Chief Thomas Byrnes's Gilded Age folio. But a newer, more polished image of criminality also emerged, too mobile and cosmopolitan to be defeated by older methods.[18] Crime's putative organization, that is, was repeatedly used to justify greater integration of traditionally decentralized policing agencies.[19] In an era when holdup men no longer bothered to cover their faces, Vollmer said, a photo gallery like Byrnes's seemed antiquated at best. Yet what is even more surprising is the veneer—as it were, the face itself—that criminality putatively had adopted. It was not that T. R.'s image of the disorderly criminal classes was abandoned. But in public pronouncements, advocates now focused more often on what they termed the "intelligentsia" of the criminal craft, cast as "well educated, gentlemanly appearing, and fond of good music, good literature, and good living." The criminal ostensibly spoke several languages and could enter any social group without arousing suspicion. He frequented and lived in the very best hotels and high-class apartments. Such a criminal was, therefore, "quite unlike the 'plug-ugly' of the past," Vollmer said. The quintessential criminal, in other words, was the Con Man, a social parasite who was mirror and mock antithesis of everything the middle-class citizen stood for; conversely, it was the status-seeking middle-class professional who had much to fear from crime.[20] Such was the covert class appeal in the broader rhetoric of professionalization.

Many historians, of course, have been quick to point out the shortfalls in the new professional reforms. Civil-service professionalism is now widely seen more as a cover story. Not only was it able to quash rank-and-file unionization in this era (as so vividly seen in the Boston police strike of 1919), but it also provided a counteroffensive against demands for civilian review. And even as cop salaries stayed ahead of those in the manufacturing sector, most historians have emphasized that professional status remained elusive. Even by 1947, Fogelson has pointed out, cops still ranked below bookkeepers in some studies of occupational prestige.[21]

Meanwhile, the recurrent claim that the police simply abandoned their traditional functions was little more than a myth. Professionalizers like O.

W. Wilson, for instance, actually claimed that police functions had *broadened* to encompass countering "delinquency-inducing influences in the community" and providing "suitable treatment for the maladjusted" as part of the crime-busting program. Even the Wickersham report had affirmed the importance of addressing juvenile crime and argued that police training had relied too much on mechanics and too little on the "fundamentals of human psychology." Wilson likewise continued to speak of patrolmen as social workers, primarily as symbols of decentralized municipal service; the cop was best understood, as a Wilson or a Bruce Smith would say repeatedly, as a policy maker in miniature. In turn, as field studies of police in the 1960s (discussed in the next chapter) would also clearly show—*Dragnet*'s opening to the contrary—departments had hardly abandoned their traditional functions as managers of street order; nor had boss system corruption been so neatly excised as, say, the LAPD would claim.[22] Historians like Joseph Gerald Woods or Joe Domanick, for example, make the case that Vollmer's tutelage in Los Angeles laid the groundwork for the dragnets invented by James Davis in the 1920s, the notorious "bum brigades" of the Depression, and the LAPD's notorious history of intelligence operations, spying, and illegal activity. Commissioner Valentine, his polite interview manner aside, was also famous for his "muss 'em up" order (directed at street toughs) in New York in 1934. Thus, the radio dispatch and the automobile are better seen not merely as patrol tools, but as technocratic symbols of a long-standing faith in demonstrations of authority on the street. To an astute critic like Mike Davis writing in the 1990s, they were harbingers of a dispersed, mechanized policing style that, eventually through helicopters and satellite links, expresses its technological domination of the world below.[23]

Thus our police histories cannot be accused of the benign historical profile the procedural genre, much less hagiography like *Dragnet*, offers up. And yet, it is telling that even our most incisive institutional histories seem, at times, to be bereft of standards other than the professionalism so often found at the root of the police problem. Their focus on status, meanwhile, sometimes unwittingly reinforces the police's own repeated claim that it lacked the public respect it deserved. Thus, it is perhaps the brittle, abstract, and even ahistorical notion of professionalization itself that bears reconsideration. In particular, professionalization narratives often confuse authority with "being looked up to": that is, with achieving *status*, rather than *consent*. Seen this second way, reform might look less like professional status seeking and more like a rewriting of police labor into an administrative and middle-class iconography that presumed resistance from delinquents, from the rank-and-file cop, and even, it seems, from the broader public as well. The trope of professionalization, that is, especially misconstrues how these police advocates approached the entire issue of managing the "public." Even the term itself now referred not to T. R.'s absent moral elite nor to citizens actually encountered on patrol, but to distinct audiences for effective public relations.

When police reformers spoke so insistently in these years about public relations, they of course used the term in the sense in which it had been used by Hoover's FBI. As LAPD division commander G. Douglas Gourley put it, the real problem was that citizens didn't have any feeling of "alliance"—or, as Parker loved to philosophize, the "police function" wasn't "considered by the members of the electorate to be a vital element of their life together." At least since World War I, indeed in Progressive reform well before that, PR had been seen as a device of moral mobilization.[24] However, in the professional handbooks, management advice, and public treatises from police reformers in later years—Vollmer's *The Police and Modern Society* (1936), Wilson's *Police Administration* (1950), and the consensus textbook from this period, Smith's *Police Systems in the United States* (1949)—one also finds a rather different refrain, not uncharacteristic of the new democratic realism of the post-Progressive years. It was now not that public attitudes toward policing were merely indifferent, but that they were "sentimental," "irrational," even "maladjusted." As Vollmer put it, the heaviest handicap to effective policing was "the overwhelmingly indifferent, negative attitude of the public, punctuated by spasms of short-lived, ineffectual indignation, that in no small degree nullify the effectiveness of police."[25] As Gourley complained:

> Among these are the widely held beliefs that policemen are uneducated and of low mentality; that they are selected for physical strength and courage alone; that they are of doubtful honesty and integrity; that they are engaged in a continuous offensive against society; that they are often rude and domineering; that they get angry easily, and assume a "smart-alecky" attitude even more easily; that they resort to the illegal "third degree"; and that the only way to be safe from this tyranny is to have either wealth or "pull."[26]

It certainly didn't help that, in the mid-teens, Charles Becker's execution drew public attention once again to police corruption. Indeed, anticipating

the miscasting of Stephen Crane scholarship, Raymond Fosdick would explicitly refer to the Becker case as indicative of the nagging persistence of the
old system.[27] But three decades later little seemed to have changed. "In city
after city," Bruce Smith could complain, "and in state after state . . . the
general public does not want law enforcement in the strict sense of the term
. . . The instrumentalities of the law have been deliberately weakened . . .
and even law observance by the law-observing has suffered a severe decline."[28]

As extreme as this complaint may seem, it contained a rather precise sense
of history. It was not only, in the aftermath of Prohibition, that gangsters
had been elevated to the status of cultural icons, or that the cultural field
"depict[ed] the policeman as a fool, a knave, or a hero, and not as a man
working for a living." Rather, the inner lesson reformers had learned, particularly from Prohibition, was not that criminality was beyond containing, but
that the public had not really wanted it to be. Former Progressive reformer
Fosdick, for instance, explicitly connected the conclusion of his *European Police Systems* (1915)—that European police were less corrupt than American
because they were "not called upon to enforce standards of conduct which
do not meet with general public approval"—to the teachings on morality and
liberty of his mentor Woodrow Wilson, indeed to Wilson's own doubts on
Prohibition.[29] Vollmer, similarly, pointed to a "vicious circle":

> [L]egislators pass laws prohibiting activities for which a demand per-
> sists; illegal means for meeting the demand are devised and support of
> the people makes them profitable; political influence, with its inevitable
> accompaniment of corruption and inefficiency, prevents enforcement
> of the law and engenders disrespect both for law and for the agents of
> law enforcement; reformers are aroused; and more laws are passed in
> the vain hope of effecting a remedy and the circle starts again. The
> police, in the center of the maelstrom, are the helpless tools—and vic-
> tims—alternately of politician and reformer, and the indifferent, un-
> comprehending taxpayer foots an enormous and perfectly needless
> bill.[30]

Not uncommonly we treat the idea that reform only leads to the perfection
of corruption as the sardonic hindsight of beleaguered radicals. The idea appears prominently, for instance, in the writing of Lincoln Steffens. But as
Christopher Lasch pointed out long ago, this skepticism about the public
had actually become axiomatic to mainstream liberalism in the 1920s. Walter

Lippmann, once a protégé of Steffens, was arguing precisely the same thing at this time.[31] Like these journalists, Vollmer himself understood the power of the press in creating spasmodic crime waves, followed by bouts of temporary reform so demoralizing to police—indeed, the kind of saturnalia chapter 1 describes. Little wonder, then, that the Uniform Crime Reports, initiated in the late 1920s by Vollmer, Smith, Hoover, and others, were explicitly designed to circumvent not only the suspicious bookkeeping of local precincts, but what Fosdick called the "hysterical headlines" of the press. So it was no longer a matter of corralling individual press members like Stephen Crane. The more important point is that the UCR were not, as they are so often cast, simply empirical registers against which "images" of crime or policing can be debunked. Rather they are themselves a by-product of both management science and public relations.[32]

Naturally, the FBI and the LAPD often made their infamous, red-baiting appeals to a mythic, transhistorical need for collective security, ushering in the kind of paramilitary elitism with which the LAPD would enlist (and then alienate) war veterans like the young Joseph Wambaugh. The rhetoric of war and collective security never dies.[33] But historical focus on this storm trooper mythos has tended to obscure the less visible application of the new science of human relations to police labor. Police reformers (and novelists after them) disparaged bookishness in part to elevate the benefits of human interaction—public relations in a double sense. On the one hand, as Department Inspector Asenhurst in Dallas described this effort in 1956, "The public must be shown by positive action that a police officer is a worker." But the corollary idea was to reform the police image *and* public sense of alliance at once by making the cop have a more human face, and then deploying that human face for more effective, discretionary power on the beat. The police must, as Police Commissioner Valentine put it in 1944, "above all else, be human. While they should know how to salute snappily, they must be intelligent citizens, ready to protect, direct, and advise the rest of the community." Removing the crime-busting cop from traffic duty, for instance, was not only a more efficient and professional use of manpower. It also diverted the cop from one of the most likely friction points with the public. Reassignment of police duties to civilian personnel, in a similar reciprocity, established public outreach, both in terms of public relations *and* its incorporation of civilian staffs.[34]

In turn, Wilson, for instance, advised departments to sponsor civic events, conduct public speaking tours, issue an annual report to the community, establish junior police patrols. He even told officers to brush up on their telephone "etiquette": as the "Square Deal Code" of his Wichita department put it, the style was to "never to scold or reprimand, but to inform and request." Wilson advocated starting his tours of public inspection with leading luncheon clubs and then church, industrial, and professional groups. He also recommended taking "influential men of the community" for rides in police cars, preferably with "some type of emergency run . . . When suitable tactics are employed, the citizen will be favorably impressed with the speed and thoroughness with which the point of attack is covered."[35]

Of course, this strategy of simulation was, as it were, the cultural mirror image of how the actual counts of prior crime had legitimated that attack in the first place. In this sense, police work did indeed become procedural: that is, not in the way it worked by the book, but in the way it aimed at a statistical offender. Many of these reforms inscribed the idea that criminality was a recurrent state of affairs, appearing in predictable locations and, quite often, from a predictable class of perpetrators, a self-fulfilling and often racist redundancy that the LAPD made infamous. Moreover, the aforementioned emphasis on the problem of delinquency was not only in reference to an age cohort; rather, it anticipated one by-product of the increasingly actuarial logic of policing, the discovery of the so-called "18+" offender, reputedly the demographic category most responsible for the *volume* of crime. Policing now also inscribed a self-fulfilling redundancy: those in the system provided the logic not only for ingesting others (anticipating crimes criminals have yet to commit), but for differential treatment on the beat. For example, this logic might legitimate rougher treatment in high-crime areas.[36] One might reasonably ask whether this system was replacing the boss system or merely redesigning it, blending professional expertise and actuarialism with the long-standing fatalism of cop culture.

Paralleling what is, our hesitations about jargon aside, legitimately called a reification of criminality was a differentiation of the public being served. When Wilson spoke of giving inspection tours to "[i]mportant groups," or Parker of cultivating "business and professional groups of the city," what was happening was an internal differentiation of *publics*. In the 1950s, likewise, when the LAPD began to conduct its own public opinion polls, it typically ranked attitudes toward the police by occupation. The reorganization of public alliance with the police, however, did not break down purely along class lines. Unskilled laborers, for instance, turned out to be the most favorably inclined toward police, followed most closely by skilled laborers. Among professional and corporate groups, meanwhile, executives rated police highest, and entertainers lowest.[37] This array could have manifold interpretations: in an open-shop world like LA, however, where "Hollywood" actually signified a political alliance and a cultural power, the moral was quite clear. (In a Joseph Wambaugh novel, this terrain would be a hostile beat to actually police.)

Such differentiations were, meanwhile, hardly incidental to the structuring of professionalism as such. Rather, they reflected the way the most technical of innovations by police actually encoded ideas about managing a citizenry whose sense of alliance was often in doubt. As was pointed out in a volume of the *Annals of the American Academy of Political and Social Science* edited by Smith in 1954, the zealousness about various forms of forensic identification, for example, reflected a preference over the notorious unreliability of eyewitness testimony. Or take, for instance, the expanded use of the paneled police van, the technological device that would so fascinate Weegee. Of course, the van was a sign of centralization, used for the hustling of offenders to downtown offices for lineups that, in New York City, Commissioner Valentine began to require in mid-1940s.[38] But the van was now also clearly an instrument of crowd and press control, as Weegee's photographs attest. In a quite literal way, the van signified the police's reclaiming of the streets as its own, as grist for the downtown mill and not for voyeurism and public consumption.

Perhaps I can best crystallize this reformulation of the profession of policing, and its rethinking of the public, by closing with a series of lectures given by Boston Municipal Court Judge Elijah Adlow to the graduating class of the Boston Police Department's academy in the mid-1940s. As much as Adlow took the pragmatic jurist's approach to keeping the court system unclogged, he granted considerable legal authority to the police to make that possible. Even if it risked a return to vice protection rackets, Adlow emphasized to his academy class how important it was for beat cops to exercise greater discretion, cultivate public respect, so as to overcome the indifferent, even fashionable hostility to the police. His reasons were clear: "The policeman is really the public's public relations man," Adlow claimed, "and he's doing a mighty good job at it." "What makes the policeman peculiarly different in our civilian set-up," the judge argued, "is that he alone can speak for the public with authority." In other words, the police officer actually *becomes* the public's representative, agent of its own desire for order. However, Adlow goes on to argue—and here is the turn of the screw—*actual* members of the public should not interfere with the policeman's sworn duty. The professional cop thus doubles both as the antithesis of the leisure-class man, and as the *real* public itself empowered with the badge.[39]

And so, when one reform advocate spoke of "Mak[ing] People Like You," the pun was a telling index of what professionalization really meant. Non-delinquent citizens would ally themselves with the ordinary professional workingman; in turn, the cop, becoming more like these (not-always-so-) average Joes, would cultivate civilian sources. Human relations thus bled quite easily back into intelligence gathering; it also meant, in Los Angeles and else-where, human relations that actually reinforced persisting racial divides. The cooperating citizen, meanwhile, simulated the cop. Citing an informant who was a bellhop, one advocate wrote: "This man does not live by criminal activity himself. He works, but he sees things."[40]

Ultimately, the Uniform Crime Reports can be seen as perhaps the arche-typal symbol of this secret meaning of police proceduralism as it attached itself to public relations. In one way, the UCR were professional records of crime. Yet seen as a cultural text, they were more accurately statistical render-ings generated by the willingness of *some* citizens themselves to report to police departments or, in other cases, submit to police interrogations. That is, to ally themselves. More importantly, this trademark reform shows how policing now concretized, inscribed, and centralized its own institutional memory: the often fatalistic knowledge of what crooks *had* done and thus what they were likely to do again. Thus it was fitting that the basis of *The Naked City* was not a murder from the 1940s; rather it was an unsolved murder from the 1920s. And, as it turns out, a tabloid murder, the aftermath of which may have been witnessed by Mark Hellinger and his good friend Walter Winchell while riding, one night, in a police car.[41]

II

So where does the police procedural come from? Popular culture theorists date its modern emergence from the mid-1940s, when the police officer, long a stock character in Victorian fiction, moved to the center of the mystery genre. For one thing, we now know the genre's emergence allowed paperback publishers to restake a claim to male audiences early in the 1950s after mys-tery novels had declined as a percentage of softcover books sold, in part due to official censorship of more sensationalistic genres. As I have noted, the normalcy of the procedural is taken as a sign of a supposed postwar cultural consensus. The procedural's paramilitary and documentary aura, for example, is often attributed to the prior example set by FBI series and propaganda, while its premium on domesticity and middle-class normalcy is attributed to the broader structure of feeling provided by World War II. (We see Jimmy Halloran, for instance, chastised by his wife for not disciplining his son, while sitcom Muzak plays in the background.) More locally, the procedural's technical accuracy and its emphasis on the prosaic boredom of collaborative labor are seen as a repudiation of the romantic individualism and implausibility of hard-boiled detective fiction. *The Naked City* can be said to be reworking a plot typical of the earlier gangster films David E. Ruth has described so well.[42] To many critics, then, the procedural is *the* romance not only of police authority, but of the broader postwar age.[43]

Yet, as I have suggested in my first section, these arguments often reproduce a familiar and rather static picture of the interwar years, and proceed upon an unexamined sense of police history. Indeed, *The Naked City*'s plot is actually based upon the Dot King (Dorothy Keenan) murder of 1923. In this crime, a young model, drawn into dalliances with a Boston con man and a wealthy, married businessman from Philadelphia, had been mysteriously killed in her New York apartment. As in the film, she had died by suffocation due to chloroform. Early reports indicated that jewelry worth as much as twenty thousand dollars, ostensibly a gift from that mysterious, initially unnamed Philadelphia suitor, had also been stolen from the scene. The NYPD and district attorney's office pursued several leads in a real-life mystery that saturated not only the new tabloids just emerging in the 1920s—the *New York Mirror*, the *Daily News*, and others—but also the front pages of the *New York Times*. For nearly two weeks in late March, the case attracted national attention, involving various reports of a telltale comb left at the scene, love letters and the threat of blackmail, rumors of political dealing, and protection of the suitor the papers named as "Marshall," who turned out to be the married John Kearsley Mitchell, the son-in-law of one E. T. Stotesbury. (Fortuitously, to some editors' eyes, an associate of J. P. Morgan.) The crime was so sensational that a half hundred newspapermen and photographers followed the movements of Mitchell and his wife by the end of the investigation. A decade later, the case would still provoke press commentary and political charges over its handling.[44]

At first glance, the Keenan case seems subject to the same kinds of allegorizations and saturnalia that had surrounded Dora Clark's trials in the 1890s. Certainly, as murder seemed, to many eyes, to rise phenomenally in the post–World War I years; as organized crime seemed to link the glamorous world of celebrities to that of criminality; as a widespread cultural debate emerged on the causes of criminality—as all this happened, yellow journalism seemed to experience a resurgence. Following up on conventions from the turn of the century, the *New York Daily News* even cited a policeman and fireman each month for heroism. And yet, thanks to the work of scholars like Michael Schudson and John Brazil, we now recognize that the news field was undergoing subtle changes as well: a complex pattern of consolidation, polarization, and tabloidization. In 1920, New York had eleven dailies; a decade later it had only seven, but two of them were now the new picture tabloids, the *Daily News* and the *New York Mirror*. The *Daily News* became the nation's largest paper, and Mark Hellinger its highest-paid columnist, in the same decade that established powers like Pulitzer and Hearst had actually been overthrown.[45] Meanwhile, with a steady fare of murder, startling photos of crime scenes, and courtroom drama, the tabloids of the twenties ran, scholars now estimate, many *times* more crime stories than in the 1890s. The kind of carnival atmosphere more typical of the Sunday *New York World* of Pulitzer's day had become a daily affair. Alongside Keenan's murder, a paper like the *News*, which staked its claim as "New York's Picture Newspaper," ran the funnies, movie contests, society confessions, or, for instance, its weekly hundred-dollar contest for the best tongue twister.

At first glance, of course, all of this seemed to merely bleed over into the alliterative and sensational idiom *The Naked City* would parody. When it turned out Dot King had frequented the theaters of Broadway and its high life, the floodgates were thrown wide open. The *News*'s reporter Julia Harpman cast King as the "Broadway Butterfly" or the "dashing Dot," a wordplay upon the telegraph, "who combined in her slender beauty the gay cloak model of a thousand loves and the doleful daughter of Melancholia." Keenan/King emerged as a woman who had invited her own fate by "liv[ing] on the bubbles of life." She quickly gravitated, that is, from "model" to a bright-lights girl who used the "mysterious" Mitchell as her rich "Angel." Her epitaph, the *News* lead announced the next day (18 March), might well have read "Here Lies Broadway." This was certainly reminiscent of Dora Clark and the Tenderloin.

At a deeper level, however, the tabloid precedents to the film reveal important differences from the 1890s: clues, as it were, about its scene of the crime, the recasting of New York itself. We also get a glimpse of the New York publics that newspapers in the twenties meant to represent. A more staid paper like the *Times*, for example, now seemed to have secured the high ground for which the mugwump cohort of the 1890s once competed. If one looks at *Times* ads running immediately adjacent to coverage of the Dot King murder, one sees that they addressed high-profile leisure products, product engineering, enclosed cars—and, that quintessential sign of the modern successful man, bran flakes. For these readers, a rich man's flirtation with Dot King might well have been read as a cautionary tale about what not to do with one's disposable income.

By contrast, the *Daily News* is famous for having wooed advertisers in the early 1920s by sending a young woman to the East Side "to find out what people [there] bought, why they bought it, and how much they could spend for it." This young woman, Sylvia Dankin, had actually convinced her editors to resee the ghetto as a rich market of potential immigrant buyers; the *News*'s slogan, as a result, became "Tell it to Sweeney." As Pete Hamill has recently recalled, the *News*'s managers thought of the newspaper as something like citizenship papers for many immigrant audiences, who they thought actually learned the city's byways, and English itself, through the mastering of trademarks.[46] Thus, while hardly excluding luxury items, the *News* ads adjacent to Dot King's tale promoted gas and motor oil, foreign music like Hungarian Rhapsodies and Irish melodies, and music halls. Interestingly, the *News* also advertised everyday grocery items, which as today might have reflected the paper's site of sale. What's in evidence is a more pluralistic, mixed audience of recent immigrants, young mothers, urban singles, on balance more female: precisely those who walk the streets of "the naked city." For these readers, a different angle of identification may have ensued. (Jean Dexter herself, we discover, is Polish American.)[47]

What was that difference? For one, this popular plebiscite was engaged by a style that involved potential readers in the scene the crime vivified: not just in its details of ratiocination, but the larger social stage it engaged. The paradox, long true of mass journalism, was that the tabloid press had (in comparison, again, with the *Times*) more police access, less regard for privacy, and more sources in the Broadway life (including gossip) with which to contextualize crime and thereby both mimic police sleuthing and allegorize it.[48] That is, at precisely the historical moment the police not only began to manage their crime-busting image, but sort the publics for their reliability, the King murder exemplified the way the slow release of investigative details had now become a valuable tool for managing interest, in all quarters, in the deductive labor of police investigation.[49]

The *News*'s stories, of course, were peppered with facts that named each player with his current address, or dutifully cited the medical examiner and "Inspector Coughlin of the Detective Bureau." Stories provided lead-ins and italicized passages—not unlike the soap summaries of TV guides today—to update readers on the progress of the investigation. Indeed, the particular convergence of police power and cultural narrative meant that popular proceduralism of this kind actually cut across the news field. The *Times* itself, for instance, also tracked right through the grainiest details of the case, reporting the initial investigative clues at the crime scene, the work of the autopsy, and the rounding up of suspects; clues were sifted, like whether it was "possible for a person to descend" a back stairway "without being seen by the elevator operator." Even the careful attributions of "objectivity" often said to be in embryo at the *Times* could just as easily blur into the gossip and hearsay on which the *News* depended. (For example, "it was said that several detectives were assigned to find . . . [witnesses] who, it was believed, could supply information about a man who was said to have been seen.")[50] This was the kind of vigilance in which Hellinger and Wald were actually schooled: tabloid proceduralism that mimicked the police's own.[51]

This schooling in scandal seems especially important when one examines the inner political rhetoric that proceduralism at the *News* conveyed. As if feeding back from its ads aimed at trademarking its own populist, immigrant audience, the *News* worked in a visual key. That is, tabloid coverage was genuinely illustrative, both serial and picture oriented: it used its photographic emphasis to explicitly resuscitate Dot King's body, to drape it with luxury, and then juxtapose it with Mitchell's image, or his wife's, or that of a petty con man. The effect was to create a gallery of thieves and upper-class hypocrites, not unlike a Broadway marquee itself (see figure 2.1).

That the police seemed content to shield Mitchell's identity at first seemed sufficient evidence, to tabloid story makers, of political collusion. Indeed, the entire political rhetoric of the tabloid was intended to build this kind of bridge between class levels. As Brazil points out, quite a few murder trials in this period involved not the high-profile celebrities, but more mundane average citizens,[52] as if the tabloids were anxious to situate their readers in the

2.1

"Model's Death Showers Fiery Light on Broadway Jackals"
(from the *New York Daily News*, 18 March 1923).

melodrama of sensational crime. As if hybridizing its broader rhetoric of puzzle solving, celebrity photography, and confession, the *News*, for example, offered up this portrait of Dot King's past:

> Dorothy King was enamored of the sparkle of wine. She knew not when to say "no" and when the fumes of alcohol stole away her senses she had a predilection for kicking the glass out of taxicab doors.
>
> She was not averse to "smoking hop" and often she was found at the "layout" of a man friend in his apartment on West Fifty-fourth Street.

One thinks here of Stuart Hall's comments on what he calls the "demotic populism" of tabloids, which Hall calls a "complex species of linguistic ventriloquism" aimed at mobilizing readers. Using this kind of echo of the hard-boiled argot of the day, the *News* re-created a moral drama via a strategy of populist affiliation with temptations its own readers could imagine.[53]

Acknowledging this political idiom also helps explain why Mark Hellinger came to establish the *News*'s trademark style. Hellinger had actually just arrived at the *News* in 1923, and would soon stake out a columnist post right on the borderland captured above: the world of celebrity gossip, human inter-

est, and the allure of criminality. (We also know that, like Crane, Hellinger had covered night court and sensational trials himself.) In several ways, of course, Hellinger's art was an old one, albeit seasoned with tabloid interests: in the love nest, in the double-cross, and most of all in racketeers themselves. Not unlike his best friend Winchell, or Damon Runyon, Hellinger paraded the fact that "over a period of years, I have—in the pursuit of my trade— fraternized with the underworld more than any other class of society." Indeed, like police reformers themselves, Hellinger depicted the underworld as principally a world of rackets, or confidence games. By doing so, however, he also bolstered his own image as a middle-class urbanite fully versed in the con. Typically, his books enumerated favorite cons of the urban world, thus presenting himself as the antithesis of the citizen-sucker who could be caught.[54]

But the ethos Hellinger brought to his columns, and then to his films, was not merely cosmopolitan savoir faire. Rather, as his literary guide to this realm, he drew upon example of the so-called Caliph of Broadway, the writer O. Henry, whom the *New York World* had celebrated twenty years earlier as a chivalric protector of the "little people" inhabiting the city's byways. That is, like O. Henry's, Hellinger's art, in stories collected later in *Moon over Broadway* (1931) and *The Ten Million* (1934), was one of exposé only in the sense that it revealed the private stories of people making real or potential headlines, celebrities transformed into commoners or the reverse. In Hellinger's fictional world the well known and the half known merge with the millions of little people inhabiting the city. Commoners could thus, in effect, be lifted into one of his columns, as if by an act of patronage. In ways that looked forward to working-class populists like Jimmy Breslin or Mike Royko, the city in Hellinger's work became a series of galleries that implicitly positioned the reader within the news, again as if receiving sponsored tabloid re-creations of their own lives. The O. Henry inheritance, in fact, allowed Hellinger to present his work not as documentary at all—but rather as what O. Henry had called "semifiction." That is, rather than working in strictly realist mode, Hellinger presented stories with fictionalized names, "as if" tales that nevertheless teased the reader with their potential authenticity. The effect was not unlike the tabloids' famous chromosomographs, photos that allowed readers to place their heads on the bodies of celebrities.[55]

As *The Naked City* would also show, Hellinger presented the city as a place of millions of individual destinies, stories of individual loneliness, private

dreams and often ironic and dreary fates. Take this depiction of a coat-check girl in *Moon over Broadway*, which one might compare to the *News*'s casting of Dot King:

> Sadie worked in a joint. As the star hostess in one of those minor dance halls that dot the livelier sections of Manhattan, she was the queen of a dive that catered to all comers—young, old, white, or yellow . . .
>
> You can take my word for the fact that Sadie was a mighty tough baby. As they say in the underworld, she would fight at the drop of a gat. She shook a mean hip as she waited for customers . . .
>
> . . . Sadie's history was just a blot on life's copy book. She hadn't reached any goal, unless it was the long-distance chewing-gum championship, and she wasn't going anywhere. More, she didn't care particularly. As long as she had a place to sleep and a slug of gin to wash down the hash, she was fairly contented.[56]

Again, the hard-boiled rhetoric of this portrait works to strike populist affiliation *with* its subject and yet partly disclaim her mundane history by making her a momentary star. In the end, however, she is restored to the status of a citizen who plays the game in a border zone between the underworld and more respectable citizens. This modification on exposé—and what in many ways is an emulation of the police's reliance on tipsters—was what allowed Hellinger to wrap his columns up in aphoristic but sly O. Henryesque snapper endings: gangsters who really have human hearts, or this hard-boiled coat-check girl who nevertheless takes the time to sew a button on your coat.[57] All personalities were reversible, able to simulate marginality and normalcy at once.

When it came to *The Naked City*, Hellinger's choice of Weegee as his photographic consultant was also homage to this older journalistic ethos. Even more than Hellinger himself, in fact, Weegee used police power as a lens through which to view both criminality and the spectator-public. If Hellinger and Winchell rode in police cars and hobnobbed with gangsters, Weegee had set up shop at Manhattan police headquarters in the 1930s, renting a room right behind it; he had his room wired to pick up signals from the police radio dispatcher, before becoming the only freelancer to acquire his own radio in 1945.[58] Selling his photographs of murders, fires, and other forms of urban carnival especially to papers like Hellinger's *News* and the *Mirror*, Weegee spoke of police headquarters—in an elaboration on

Steffens's earlier strategy—as "my headquarters," his "private island," his "club," a place where he could fraternize with "dicks" and gangsters. He later boasted of having taken "a leaf out of the racketeers' book" and made Manhattan Homicide his "exclusive" territory. In quite deliberate ways, however, Weegee put his camera into police service: filling in at line-ups, publishing photos of lost children and acknowledged gangsters, even helping to break a few cases. Out on the street, his photos had the quite intentional effect of turning even spectators into a crime scene for police use.[59] Weegee's obsessions were in fact often those sites that police professionalizers themselves seized upon as places where delinquent citizens could be sorted out: the police van, the line-up, even the crime scene of a homicide itself, with bodies draped on the pavement. Indeed, this final set of pictures often seems little different from autopsy shots themselves. They were, however, merely the negative image of Weegee's own personal fantasy, of what he called "Psychic Photography": that is, photos that might actually be taken *before* a crime or news scene would take place. Weegee's trademark fantasy, that is, was of a supplementary proceduralism—or, perhaps less charitably, of being a kind of junior police cadet.

Of course, not all of Weegee's pictures are of crime scenes, any more than Hellinger focused exclusively on the gangster. Along with his panorama of gaping fans, Weegee also photographed dwarfs, victims of muggings, fire victims driven into the street in their bathrobes or their underwear. Seen from the end of the twentieth century, these more Barnumesque shots might seem to be little different from the exploitative voyeurism of today's tabloid fare. But it is important to see that this very split in Weegee's gallery merely serves, once again, to segregate the police from the gaping public—a line, in return, we can see is demarcated even in individual photos themselves—but occasionally placing the camera eye in alliance with the police line of vision. This is perhaps nowhere more evident than in the famous photos that, laid across the spine of his book to provoke us with their juxtaposition, and the caption *"The crying landlord . . . because his property was damaged . . . and the human cop"* (figure 2.2). As in these photos, Weegee's tabloid portraits of distress and human comedy often place heroic firemen or police on the margin as actors *and* as spectators, here expressing populist rage at the landlord who sees his tenants as mere property. Here the cop is positioned not only as "middle"-class—between owner and tenant—but as a split persona: having to cultivate dispassion in the face of the outrageous sorrow of the landlord,

The crying landlord . . . because his property was damaged   . . . and the human cop.

2.2

"The crying landlord . . . and the human cop" (from Weegee, *Naked City*
[New York: Essential Books], pp. 68–69).

and direct, human witnessing at the prone (female) victim. Not surprisingly,
then, a few of Weegee's interpreters saw his work not as invasive at all, but
as populist, even as occasionally working in an O. Henry vein itself.[60] Hellinger seems to have viewed Weegee's photographs this way: in the way they
provided, that is, individual stories of longing, pleasure, capture, and courage
in a naked city where tragedy could render all bodies ultimately equal: police
stories in and of themselves, to which cops and journalists were bound together as the most knowing readers.

III

The tutelage of Wald, Hellinger, and Weegee in both police labor and tab-
loidism decisively shaped the invasive, fatalistic, and semifictional feel of *The
Naked City*—as it were, creolizing the popular tabloid proceduralism and
Weegee-esque carnival I have described above. Through its populist gallery

of private longings, the film presents the city not only as a crime scene for technical analysis, but as a collection of commoners' narratives—as the famous lines went, the "EIGHT MILLION STORIES IN THE NAKED CITY." But I mean to stress that these elements provide far more than stylistic window dressing; they also include ideological work that affects the genre's symbolic rendering of police power and the democratic populace as well. To begin with, tabloid protocols invade the class and cultural rhetoric of the police procedural, especially its representation of police labor, my focus in this section. I want to demonstrate, therefore, how these populist legacies unsettle the realist authority of the genre, its presentation of middle-class normalcy, and any utopian reading of scientific police procedure that seems, at first glance, the genre's emphasis.

To bring our view to matters of genre criticism, it will also help to widen our lens now to include Ed McBain's *The Con Man* (1956), the fourth novel of the famous 87th Precinct series widely regarded as the genre's midcentury benchmark. Much like *The Naked City*, McBain's novel follows the work of a squad of homicide detectives, led by war veteran Steve Carella, a coat-and-tie guy and the devoted husband of a deaf mute named Teddy. And like Hellinger's text, McBain's emphasizes the tedious, office-bound, paper-bound quality to police routine. The narrative voice is once again that of a privileged deflation of romantic expectations:

> The work was not exactly unpleasant, but it was far from exciting. The average misconception of the city detective, of course, is one of a tough, big man wearing a shoulder holster facing a desperate criminal and shooting it out in the streets . . . The only desperation he knew was of a quiet sort that drives many city detectives into the nearest loony bin where they silently pick at the coverlets. [The detective], at the moment, was involved in routine—and routine is the most routine thing in the world. (37–38)

Cast in resolutely professional yet somber terms, homicide work is shown as a matter of cultivating dispassion, like the coroner who begins working on the heart of the young female victim (19). Likewise, when Teddy sees her husband fight a man in a restaurant, McBain observes that she "had just had a visit to her husband's office and seen him at work," and that he is a "technician" (87, 88). The reader, in turn, is made to walk through the tedium of

```
RESIDENT KNOWN CRIMINAL
Name  Frederick Deutsch    Command  2
Alias  Fritzie, Dutch, The Dutchman
Address 67 South 4th Street  Precinct  87th
Floor  1st   Apartment No.  1C   House  ———

CHANGE OF ADDRESS
    Moved to Hotel Carter, Culver and
    South 11th
Criminal Specialty  Confidence man
Names of Associates  ———   Prison (In or Out)  Out

D.D. 64b  Note—If criminal moves, forward card to Resident Precinct.
                                                    (Over)
```

2.3

Resident Known Criminal Card
(from Ed McBain, *The Con Man*
[1957; reprint, New York:
Signet Books, 1974], p. 63).

police procedure, even to stall over the seemingly incomprehensible file that may nevertheless contain a decisive detail. Through these devices, procedurals expose how contingent police work actually was upon the kind of integration and federalization of record keeping that reformers like Bruce Smith called for (like the Teletype sent to Baltimore in *The Naked City*). Professional procedural work depended entirely on citizen cooperation, indeed the entire net of commercial record keeping and files of the society's own mainstream life. In *The Naked City*, the detectives trace a prescription, sales receipts, newspaper files, shopkeepers' records. Meanwhile, *The Con Man*, like most of McBain's books, even offers actual print simulacra of fingerprint files, autopsy reports, and—perhaps most illustrative of police actuarialism—what are called "Resident Known Criminal" cards (figure 2.3).[61] These documents both re-create police proceduralism and yet also restrain alternative speculations by the reader; he or she is kept on the case of a serial killer of women who answer personal ads. In the finale of this novel, Carella is even forced to heroically save Teddy herself from the clutches of this criminal.[62] With these documents in front of us, it is not hard to see why the procedural makes the realist claim upon many readers that it does.

In addition, Carella's careful craft is counterpointed, simultaneously, to the unfocused lives of reckless citizens, hopeless romantics, mere amateurs— and especially criminals themselves. Although of course the presentation of criminality in procedurals would vary over the decades, in this signature novel McBain's counterpoint to the pro, as in police reform accounts, was the con, the racketeer. In *The Con Man* it is the figure of Donaldson, a man who seems to distill the rejection of middle-class professional norms. And the image here is again directly parallel to Vollmer's archetypal criminal:

> You can remain a gentleman, pursue a life of romantic criminal adventure, see the world, meet a lot of nice people and drink a lot of cool drinks, and still make a lot of money—all by fooling people.
>
> You can, in short, become a con man. (8)

Both texts present criminality, that is, as a kind of social fraudulence, a pretty-boy, leisure-class racketeering that makes a mockery of real work. Like *The Naked City*'s front man Niles, who claims army experience when he has had none, the con reflex is antisocial mostly in its inability to suppress its ego and appetites. Niles courts two beautiful women simultaneously, while he bilks their friends for jewelry; McBain's Donaldson complains, " 'The trouble with my business is that you can't enjoy yourself . . . Plain girls are good. They buy whatever you sell . . . Being good looking, it's a pain sometimes, isn't it? Men get to hate you, distrust you. Me, I mean. They don't like a man who's too good looking.' " He tattoos his victims with a Valentine heart because he feels that "[l]ike a great painter, he must sign his work" (130).[63] Meanwhile, it is not merely the fashionable upper class, or the criminal, who come under derisive scrutiny for unruly appetites. In a dual action quite typical of tabloid representation, lower-echelon criminality also takes on the foiling role to middle-class norms, indeed an almost Weegeeish carnivalizing of readers' own tastes. After following Halloran as he descends through the underworld of gymnasiums, and then climbing up an unfinished skyscraper, we ultimately see the harmonica-playing Garza performing calisthenics (a wrestler's bridge)[64] in a bathing suit in his flat. In Garza, we see a criminality that is arrogant and cagey at the core, contemptuous enough of social authority not be fooled by Halloran's lame attempt at a con while trying to arrest him. Like a wrestler, Garza threatens to overturn, upend Halloran's normalcy: " 'Try and find me,' " he sneers as he ties Halloran up. " 'This is a great, big, beautiful city.' "[65]

As I have suggested in the introduction, this all-encompassing class wisdom, seeing into every cell of the city, is predicated on police power, on the fatalistic knowingness that Muldoon certainly models in this film. Ever-human, Muldoon doubles as the little guy and the cop. But on the other hand, it would be misleading to say that the film's eye and voice are wholly congruent with this mystique. On the contrary. Though Hellinger's voice does present itself as an accomplice to the detective's labor, it also supersedes the working cop in its worldly wisdom—again, not merely its urban savoir faire, but its tendency to divert each story into what we might call cracker-barrel cosmopolitanism, such as we see in Hellinger's columns or Weegee's captions.[66] Even McBain's voice reflects a residue of this tabloid disposition, a smartness that is all-knowing, sentimental but also jaded, invasive yet at times contemptuous or hectoring of his own characters. As with Hellinger, this voice functions in complicated ways, both to ventriloquize police reasoning and yet—and here is the important distinction—also depart from its reformist nostrums by mocking the design in which police laborers are forced to work.

Both McBain's and Hellinger's voices take special pleasure, that is, in not only acknowledging the tedium necessary for investigation but taunting their police detectives with it. Hellinger in particular uses folkloric wisdom like "button button" or children's rhymes ("out went the doctor, out went the nurse . . .") to parallel yet mock the elimination of murder suspects. Indeed, in these lights, like Weegee's fantasy and Hellinger's columns, *The Naked City* is not so much documentary as psychic crime semifiction, with the average workaday cop trying to discover what we as smarter viewers, or particularly the narrator, already know. As if reflecting its dual posting, the police "procedural" might be something of a misnomer, since the cultural form really tries to have it both ways with the police and tabloid knowledge. If the news version of the crime is mocked as tabloid sentimentalism, half-knowledge, belatedness—mocked as the police would—in the voice of the film's storytelling wisdom the tabloid version is actually redeemed. The redeemed tabloid voice becomes anticipatory, again not unlike an O. Henry tale in that its knowledge reveals inevitable, secret, often circular ironies and outcomes. In the film, every social fact is turned into its antithesis: a model into a set-up girl, a college man into a fraud, a well-to-do doctor into a lovelorn, suicidal "sap." This is in many ways the antithesis of the documentary's resolute presentism. As Neal Gabler has suggested in regard to Hellinger's comrade Winchell, the essence of slang or gossip is to make the reader feel knowing, ahead of the curve.[67]

The populist affiliation with a cop's knowledge is thus a tricky business. Here the procedural actually serves, in one register, to speak back against managerialism, in a tabloid ventriloquism of the hard-boiled resistance of police labor to the boss's plan.[68] That is, the narrator's hectoring is not directed, precisely, *against* the working cop. Rather, the power of procedurals often lies in the way they depict men working *in* the managerial utopia of an O. W. Wilson, but experiencing it both as labor they publicly claim but sometimes privately disclaim. As McBain repeatedly shows, actual crime cases always seem to toy with actuarial expectations, or with the idea that the forensic clue will lead you to the criminal. The entire opening of *The Con Man* is built upon a comic by-play about a corpse that doesn't fit the profile for missing persons or a summer homicide. Soon, we are witness to a line-up at police headquarters—one of the main centralizing reforms, to which the NYPD renewed its commitment in 1945[69]—but it doesn't work, and the con man Donaldson goes free again. In fact, it is *not* really the case, in *The Naked City*, that the newer, more professional generation breaks the case. Rather it is the patient, fatalistic, still quite Irish Muldoon who draws his pleasure from exposing those who aspire to upward mobility, those who try to avoid labor and its necessary drudgery. In *The Con Man*, it is the police ally the tattoo shop owner, again an ethnic small businessman named Charlie Chen, who really helps capture the criminal. Indeed, in striking contrast to what David Ruth describes as the tendency of earlier gangland depictions,[70] ethnicity is a marker of the city's defender, not its alien threat. This double-sided populism thus also invades the depictions of the public sphere, and the utopian claim of citizens' alliance with police power. A city of a million lonely souls promised to be as much a gallery of victims as it would an allied army. It is to this final tension that I would now like to turn.

IV

As I have argued, police procedurals often exhibit the ordinary longings of little people in order to establish a populist link with the humanity of the cop. Following Hellinger's preamble, the earliest shots of *The Naked City* seem to demonstrate that respectability is rooted not in mere appearances, but in a commitment to routine behavior, hard work, nuclear families, and the rest. In *The Naked City*, we actually see the film's characters before we know that they will central to the main plot line: we could be looking, that is, at the public (and documentary shots of them). Niles and Ruth Morrison, for instance, are seen enjoying New York nightlife long before we know that he has begun to victimize her. In a devious parallel, we also see Muldoon and Halloran getting ready for work, just like any men in the mass, before we know they are cops. Then we segue to Jean Dexter's maid, who is about to have, we are told by Hellinger's voice, something other than her ordinary day. *The Con Man*, likewise, obsessively establishes the social boundaries of normalcy: loyal husband, dedicated office staff, cooperative citizens, all serving as a bulwark against the corrosive temptations of urban life. The simulation, again, is reversible, as if faith in these totems is its own justification.

But there are limits here. Whereas the police seem masculine masters of their trade in *The Naked City*, the public is by contrast almost exclusively naive, unschooled in cons, and feminized—again, tabloidesque.[71] Moreover, the form's periodic distrust of this feminized citizenry seems to spill over into the faith in normalcy it means to proclaim. Indeed, in many instances the differences between the professional cop and the con man are made to seem negligible. A persisting paradox of these police procedurals was often that, even as they tended to sanitize and normalize police labor by emphasizing its scientific, technical, and professionalized character, they also isolated systematic flaws in its utopian vision of police power: flaws not only in the true nature of precinct labor, as I've suggested, but flaws in the citizenry it proposed to protect. Returning to the opening scenes of *The Naked City*, we reflect that, untutored and unmobilized as we are at first viewing, we ourselves cannot easily separate the pros from the cons. McBain similarly plays with such reversals, constantly reminding us of the thin boundaries between vice and crime. We discover, for instance, that Teddy has been reading the personal ads all day (51–52), just as the floater victim had been. McBain adroitly performs a segue similar to that of Hellinger's film, when he cross-cuts cinematically from Teddy to Donaldson's next victim, disguising our misrecognition by using the abstract phrase "the girl" (53) before we realize he's referring to Carella's wife. She in fact nearly becomes a victim. Even as police labor became the basis of internal fraternal affiliation, some in the public were necessarily outsiders.

Even the police's procedural knowledge of criminality is double-edged. In one subplot in *The Con Man*, for instance, one of Carella's rookie colleagues forges a letter to his fiancée's college so they can plan a vacation together. We forgive the minor crime because, putatively, we are witnessing true love in action. Indeed, that love is documented: McBain prints a graphic of another Valentine they create. Yet of course what our trained eye now sees is that this image is eerily similar to the tattoo that Donaldson leaves on his victims.

In another subplot, readers are led to mistake an undercover cop for a potential victim, when he is actually trapping a con. That is to say, readers are
conned by the cop's (and McBain's) actuarial knowledge of how cons work.
Finally, at the close of the novel we even see Teddy *voluntarily* tattoo herself
as a testament to *her* love for Steve Carella. The question lurking here is why
the normal or pro side of social affirmation would fall so readily for the con
side, if, in fact, the boundary was as secure as the genre's professional idiom
seems to want to make it. (We are back to Vollmer's lament about the vicious
circle.) In the imaginary terrain of the procedural, the mutual simulation of
citizen and cop has its underside. As much as the public's own gullibility
legitimates the need for police authority, it also threatens to disable police
work.

In *The Naked City*, this underside is established by the early scenes with
Jean Dexter's maid. Too horrified by the crime scene to think clearly, she is
viciously patronized by Muldoon, who even plucks her hair to use it for a
forensic comparison. Or take this by-play between two women outside a dress
shop window. The women are ventriloquized, and, as if we're hearing radio
comedy from inside these characters' heads, we witness a kind of tongue twist-
ing of their desires, expressing the film's own populist ambivalence:

FIRST GIRL: Imagine me in that [dress].
SECOND GIRL: I can't imagine.
FIRST GIRL: . . . in the Waldorf Astoria, with Frankie singin' . . .
SECOND GIRL: I can't imagine.
FIRST GIRL: Oh, you. You're so unco-op-era-tive. I could slam you.[72]

If we have found ourselves looking for Jean Dexter's body, here it is: the
hidden node of appetite and dream work that Jean (like Dot King) quite literally, in her profession, "models."[73] In fact, the cultural work of police procedure is often to take us on a tour of leisure-class phonies, celebrity wanna-bes,
and salon parasites: Dexter's friend Ruth Morrison, unaware of her fiancé's
criminality; then her mother, an aimless social butterfly; then (importantly)
Dr. Stoneman, the doctor who has actually given in to the disease of this
city's "blood," loneliness and hopeless passion. The film's famous final chase
scene, soon so much a trademark of police melodrama, thus can be taken as
working out a certain fantasy of control: as if chasing its antagonist through
the streets of the city, the work of these procedurals is to sift through and

initiate, separating out the allied public and the nonaligned. But out on the street, once again, the public is overwhelmingly feminine, virtually helpless, like the cliché baby carriage that crosses in our path. In this film, the cops encounter a female fashion store owner, who hires models; a hesitant receptionist-nurse; a woman in a grocery store; then, children on the street. Finally, in Garza's escape, the most telling icon of all, we pass a blind man and his dog. The public does not see, of course, because it has been too busy gawking, looking at crime scenes like Jean Dexter's apartment building, looking at mannequins in shop windows, dreaming of Frank Sinatra—another clear Weegee touch—or reading the tabloids themselves.[74] In *The Con Man*, victims are similarly infantile, or feminine, lonely: a Negro child, conned by a man playing a priest; a lonely man on a business trip, conned by his own greed; and, most centrally, those lovelorn girls who look for their desire in the classifieds (53).

The procedural's trademark dunning of the feminine style of murder mystery takes on more complex functions than is often recognized. When, in *The Naked City*, a woman dressed like Miss Marple comes into the office with mystical solutions to the crime, having just read the tabloids, she appears of course as the pilloried, feminized amateur, the symbol of domestic parlor ratiocination. Even the one citizen other than Carella's wife who *does* come forth to help in *The Con Man*—that tattoo parlor owner Charlie Chen—is dismissed on the phone as "Charlie *Chan*" by a detective with, quite obviously, bad phone etiquette. But what is especially striking here is that the turf of the office covertly challenges or rivals domestic normalcy itself. Even the Donna Reed–like domestic counterpointing of Halloran's home to the high life of the criminals, normative as the suburb seems, is a bit counterfeit. He proves actually unwilling to submit to his wife's authority at home, demonstrating that his core family is more the office bureaucracy and the paternal Muldoon; Jimmy clearly prefers the spontaneous generativity of white-manly work so typical of romance forms. Women are either victims or bad citizens in the way of real work.[75] Indeed, both of the citizens in the film proposing to solve the crime (Miss Marple and the grocery boy) are certifiably insane.[76]

Yet the linked plot involving Charlie Chen and Teddy in *The Con Man* is where this tension about public mobilization (of the domestic, the civilian) becomes more complex. For Teddy is more than the requisite sex kitten of this masculine genre—the totally solicitous, even intuitive mate for the romantic hero Carella. She is also clearly a surrogate for the public, a reader amateur, another version of the anti-pro. Her mobilization to help solve the crime probes the central contradiction of the procedural's populism. On the one hand, Teddy is explicitly linked to, and gradually set up to serve as, the con man's ultimate victim. After witnessing Carella at his office—a lesson that tells her that it is always open, that he is never off duty—she eventually participates in the investigation, first accompanying her husband into the tattoo shop. But like Charlie Chen/Charlie Chan—and thus like Halloran too, who now can be seen as doubling uneasily for the citizen public—Teddy gets in too deep, confuses the game of clue gathering with the brutal business of police work. Like a naive girl working from the script of "Hansel and Gretel," she drops clues in the form of strips of paper asking citizens to call her husband at work. And when she solicits a cabby to assist her in a dangerous tailing operation, his response speaks outward, to the cultural field: "Women writers!" he says, in obvious exasperation.

If we understand that Teddy's status as public surrogate also functions as reader surrogate, then we can better see the hybridized nature of what seem like training or tutelary functions of procedural narratives. For if the reader is meant to vicariously relive the mundane, white-collar labor of police investigation, he or she is *never*, in this alternative reading, to mistake the simulation for the real thing. Even those documentary simulacra in *The Con Man*, then, do not necessarily function in the way commonly supposed; after all, the tabloids were famous for them. Nor do they work only to train the eye so that the citizen can better recognize criminality, or resist future cons. Rather, the effect of these documents is partly in their *il*legibility, the manner in which they provoke awe in the reader for the practiced skill of a more disciplined reader—that is, the cop himself. Though partly drafted, a reader might also be licensed, as it were, to skim over the documentation, admire the actuarial, but to leave the actual to the professional. This same tension is played out, again in mirroring contemptuousness, by the con man himself, the final tutor whose course you don't really want to take, much less fail. As one cop says of another con man in the novel, "'He said he wanted to teach the girl a lesson'" (159). Teddy's new and eventual willingness to tattoo herself, marking her naked body with her own badge of alliance with the pro man, her husband, might be said to register her acknowledgment of subordinating herself to Carella's real skill, to admire at a distance. His, we feel, is now the real art. In a similar vein, Jimmy Halloran in *The Naked City* often seems not merely the pro's protégé, but more the comic-book sidekick, on junior police patrol, unable to con the con man, and upended by Garza's naked social body.[77]

Niles and Garza are of course organized crime—in the term so evocative of the day, a racket. But McBain and Hellinger's fondness for this term itself—supposedly the antitype, the con, to the resolute pro and his procedural knowledge—actually exposes the particular slipperiness of the professional claim to humanity. In colloquial usage, the term "racket," of course, came to apply to *anyone*'s form of employment. Both McBain and Hellinger in fact blur this boundary, tapping into the idea (evident even in O. Henry) that urban capitalism produced artificial personalities that in the end fostered only isolation, loneliness, and despair. McBain's tale goes to great lengths, in fact, to list all of his culture's mainstream cons: advertising, love, politics, and even book publishing itself. Then he writes: "[M]aybe it's stretching a point to say that every human being has his own confidence game, that every human being has a tiny touch of larceny in his soul but be careful, friend; the television is on, and that man is pointing at *you!*" (25). Hellinger chimed in with an observation in *Moon over Broadway*. "It is interesting to note," he wrote, "that the most successful rackets are invariably worked upon victims who have a touch of larceny in their own systems. A man who is not looking for something for nothing . . . has little to fear from the racket guy."[78] Thus, the real threat of a con man was that he was a kind of recruiter of social disorder or delinquency, a man who drew out the lonely person, or the con, in each of us. He draws out the antisocial and the potentially delinquent, identifying and differentiating the public*s* that could or couldn't be counted upon—in short, who could be "co-op-era-tive" and who couldn't. It was perhaps only too fitting that while *The Naked City* was shot behind that one-way mirror, Hellinger also made sure to hire a juggler down the street, to distract unsolicited passersby from too much involvement in his plot.

V

There are, of course, important legacies of popular proceduralism, and its collaborative, tabloid-generated populism: lines of descent, for example, from Hellinger and Winchell to Jimmy Breslin or Mike Barnicle. Even Weegee has his legacies, and not just in the tabloids.[79] What is striking about the procedural, I have tried to suggest, is not its aesthetic uniformity but its pliability, its ability to cut across and suffuse various posts within the field of cultural production. *The Naked City* is an excellent illustration, in fact, of this cultural mobility. Based on a tabloid murder story, it became a fiction documentary that would later become a popular TV show. One thinks, as well, not only of the crossover from radio to television by shows like *Dragnet*, but by comic-strip series like *Dick Tracy*—which, incidentally, ran in the *Daily News*—and which used adventure formats and technical wizardry to facilitate juvenile identification and hero worship (elements, as we've seen, at work in *The Naked City*). As critic Larry Landrum has argued, the peculiar hybridity of the procedural also made it eminently suitable for television. With ensemble productions so suitable to new pressures for multiethnic casts, serialized formats, and yet case-centered episodes, the procedural became especially well suited to television's notorious balancing act of moral stereotyping and disruptive violence. The form embodied, that is, an idea of policing as a "response to a series of disruptive crises," a crucial legacy.[80] (McBain, in fact, frequently grouses about the plagiarism of *Hill Street Blues*.) Even the "real TV" of the 1990s inherits the pseudodocumentary "crime stoppers" aura developed forty years ago. In turn, the procedural's romance of crime busting becomes a field of force across which Wambaugh moves and then rebels; the nostalgia to which television melodrama often clings; the whipping boy of neoconservative reformulations of public involvement and community policing in our own time. McBain's Donaldson is, as well, clearly a prototype for the normal-seeming serial killers who haunt True Crime.

My goal here, however, is not only to come up with a story of influence. Rather, I've tried to show how the cultural posts of police reform and tabloidism found common *political* ground in the literary procedural, establishing a benchmark not only for literary culture but for how the police would cast its own symbolic power. The procedural expressed a common desire, in the news and in the police, to strike populist affiliation with a lonely and dependent public; each also wanted to supersede that public with its own urban savvy. Both, meanwhile, constructed criminality as a threat to a fragile consensus about hard work and middle-class normalcy, yet both also glamorized the racket as the con in all of us. Rather than merely an instrumental tool of Hoover or the NYPD, these shared passions nevertheless did supplement procedural faith in actuarial, preemptive knowledge and proactive policing. But the faith took many other turns as well. Once built into modern work routines, these passions would commingle, for example, with what national commissions on crime, in the 1960s, would rename as the "rotten apple" fatalism of increasingly paramilitary police forces. In this way, the procedural would ultimately reinforce not the faith of midcentury, but police fatalism about a public stirred to cycles of outrage and then indifference, but ultimately outside its own secret, sometimes dark, unchanging fraternity of knowing.[81]

The procedural genre is not, then, simply a testament to a classless of "deethnicized" professionalism, our standard critical categories notwithstanding. Nor is the boss system really displaced in the genre's inner mythology. Indeed, the ethnic heroism and labor consciousness of the form speak of older police traditions—as it were, older precincts in both culture and in power. These texts covertly pillory naive faith in professionalism even as they seem to vaunt it. One should not overlook the fact, for instance, that the feminine name "Teddy" was also a famous name in New York police lore, the name of an Anglo commissioner who—as my previous chapter suggests—placed a naive faith in professionalism and the ability of the police to stand in for the public. Drawing upon this repressed institutional memory, the political rhetoric of the procedural thus offers more than a simple hymn to social affirmation and professional expertise. On the contrary, it drafts many different cultural icons into its mosaic of faith. Its police heroes contain traces of the professional, the dutiful servant—yet also the urban savant, the white ethnic, the amateur and the pro, the laboring guy who puts in his week: Joe Friday.

By emphasizing these laboring dimensions, I do not mean to discount the procedural's propagandistic potential for police managers. In many ways what I have called "popular proceduralism" did go hand in plastic glove with the forensic passions of the new downtown headquarters. Weegee's fantasies, for one, might be said to reflect back these passions; even O. W. Wilson's reforms, that is, wanted to greet a crime before it happens. But in many respects the cultural field had a slightly larger role to play. We might end by remembering, for instance, that the Dot King case itself was never actually solved. If the cultural work of these procedurals is populistic, their work is often not merely to enlarge upon the class accents of police labor, but in some fundamental way to try to unalienate that labor, to use the cultural field to settle an account with the public—in this instance, on a case that, privately, the NYPD felt it had solved but could not prove.[82] " 'The Department never calls a case unsolved,' " Muldoon says in *The Naked City*. " 'Great,' " Halloran replies. " 'Twenty years from now I'll put my kid on it.' " *The Naked City* ends, in fact, by giving ritual thanks, in its credits, to "the Mayor and the Police Commissioner" of New York for their assistance. We should not overlook, however, the fact that the NYPD was on the brink of yet another of its recurrent scandals, or that Mayor O'Dwyer was, in point of fact, in bed with racketeers. Commissioner Valentine, however, had moved on to work in radio and the movies.[83]

3

Blue Knights and Brown Jackets:
Beat, Badge, and "Civility" in the 1960s

Sheriff's helicopters were a nightly annoyance. It could have been Vietnam, only we were the enemy. They hovered above the slopes and ravines, covering the ground with circles of lights. Deputies drove by often, pushing dudes against walls, detaining them and dispersing crowds of two or more. The homeboys shot out the few lampposts to keep the place in darkness. We hid in bushes, in basements and abandoned buildings. We were pushed underground. Codes, rules and honor became meaningless.
—Luis Rodriguez, *Always Running* (1993)

Within the seemingly placid black-and-white world of police proceduralism, offering up a workaday world of national consensus, a certain midcentury fantasy of police power and criminal predictability was enacted. Police science had yoked itself to the language of human relations, and imagined that routinized, bureaucratic work was the best way to anticipate public disorder. Under the progressive-sounding banner of efficiency and actuarialism, the procedural approach aspired to make policing into a predictive, rather than merely reactive enterprise.

And yet, as years of historically informed scholarship have also made clear, in the 1960s crime itself seemed to elude prediction. Not only was the public image of American affluence matched by rapidly escalating crime rates, but street disorder seemed to blur easily in and out of political protest. The police suddenly found themselves not heroes of an American consensus, but accused as provocateurs: on the streets of Birmingham and Detroit and Los Angeles, at the riots at the Chicago Democratic convention, and of course among the disruptions on college campuses during the Vietnam War itself. Indeed, the conservative backlash that ensued from the 1960s remains to this day part of law enforcement's long memory, where political protest and civil rights activism are often conflated with the countercultural permissiveness that supposedly undermined authority at home as on the front lines in Vietnam. To this day, police politics continue to be read against the legacies of that war: a police union lawyer in Boston proudly recalls defending Lieutenant William Calley; community policing advocates invoke the lessons of Richard Nixon's Vietnamization program; Hispanic and African American street gangs are compared to the Vietcong. No visitor to the National Police Memorial (dedicated in 1991) in Washington, D.C., can escape the fact that he or she is looking at a sculptural retort to the Vietnam memorial across the Mall. And nowhere is this aggrieved sense of historical mission more persistent than in the superheated worldview of the Los Angeles Police Department.[1]

As historians have long recognized, in the aftermath of the second wave of police reform in the 1960s, the LAPD moved to the center of national attention as a model of a newly professional, aggressively paramilitary style.[2] Now, the world into which police rookies were initiated was not that of *The Naked City*'s mundane, office-centered proceduralism, but what has been termed "western"-style preventive patrol. Whereas crime busting in the years between the wars had, as chapter 2 shows, emulated the FBI's bureaucratic proceduralism, the LAPD evoked the national security apparatus, in its fetishizing of intelligence gathering, massive shows of force, and technological domination.[3] William Parker, chief of the LAPD from 1950 to 1965, repeatedly pilloried the idea that a cop was a social worker, much less the crime-busting civil servant we see heroicized in *The Con Man*. Rather the cop was a soldier of what was called "proactive" law-and-order maintenance. Being proactive meant going beyond mere actuarialism and trying to prevent crime by reducing its likely opportunities by scientifically managed patrol patterns and coordinated action. Rather than recognizing historical neighborhood borders, police precincts were now reorganized for the most efficient automobile response-to-call patterns; patrol beats were normally rotated among officers, sometimes on a daily basis; after rigorous, paramilitary training in

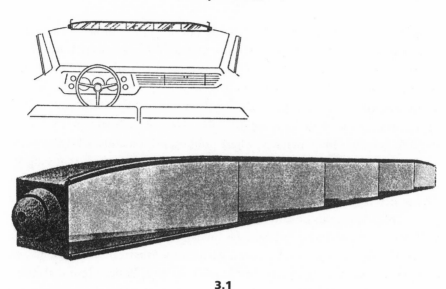

3.1

Multiphasic mirror (from George T. Payton, *Patrol Procedure* [Los Angeles: Legal Book Corp., 1967], p. 139). Reprinted with permission.

the vaunted LAPD academy, rookies spent a probationary term in different precincts not of their choosing. Patrolmen were even taught how to work with split-screen, "multiphasic" mirrors to better scan the street over their shoulder (see figure 3.1).[4]

And, of course, as our institutional scholarship has made clear, this scanning emerged from a fatal mixture of anti-Communist zealotry, self-appointed territorialism, and racism. The growing coinage of "civilian" in place of "citizen," for instance, reflected how paramilitary norms implicitly overlapped with a self-conscious strategy of political exclusion of the changing ethnic constituencies of Los Angeles.[5] To this day, street patrol continues to be exercised in highly differential ways by neighborhood, race, and class, as a matter of policy and training, not happenstance or overzealousness. As Steve Herbert and Mike Davis have shown, many street-level officers conceive of themselves as agents of moral order, as if still scripted by Parker's paranoid speeches about public dependence and anarchy.[6] And nowhere was this new-style professionalism made more explicit in the world of mass culture than in the work of Joseph Wambaugh, the former LAPD burglary sergeant turned pop cop extraordinaire.

In the aftermath of the 1960s, particularly with his first two best-selling

novels, *The New Centurions* (1970) and *The Blue Knight* (1972), then as creator
of his own ensemble television serial *Police Story*, and even finally as the producer of *The Onion Field* and other films, Wambaugh became the cultural
figure perhaps most responsible for creating the modern mass-cultural image
of the paramilitary patrol cop. He did so by detaching police iconography
from the power of the police procedural and enfolding it within the new
realist aesthetic of the nonfiction novel, televisual and cinematic vérité, and
the ensemble production. Meanwhile, Wambaugh's work also positioned a
generational story within a broader political, cultural, and even mythological
chronicle of public malaise and the decline of modern civilization.

The New Centurions, for instance, proceeds in sections marked by successive summers starting in 1960, as we follow three rookie cops as they move
through police academy training, probationary apprenticeship under veteran
officers, and then the rigors of automobile patrol—all marked by encounters
with a violent, recalcitrant, and uncooperative citizenry. Five years later
Wambaugh's officers meet again, now veterans themselves, at a mock "re-
union": the Watts riot at which Wambaugh was himself present, and which
is presented as anarchy let loose upon the world.[7] Meanwhile, the novel adapts
to its metaphorical design the historical clichés that customarily structured
the political jeremiads of Chief Parker, who, in an event the novel itself would
allegorize, died of a heart attack in 1966. With characters espousing sexist,
racist, and homophobic opinions on many a page, heroes pitted against impossible odds, men returning home to collapse into the arms of conveniently
willing women, Wambaugh's writings seem, in this potential reading, merely
a downshifting of Parker's phantasmic paramilitarism to the cultural and domestic front—to Vietnam, as it was said, on the streets.[8]

To read Wambaugh only in this way is tempting. Certainly to do so would
be to reinforce that superb strand of revisionist historiography—pioneered by
writers like Jerome Hopkins, Carey McWilliams, Joseph Woods, and Robert
Fogelson, followed up by Davis, Herbert, Joe Domanick, and John Gregory
Dunne—on which I have relied so much myself. In police studies per se, the
LAPD has come to stand for the midcentury emphasis on professionalization
and bureaucratic impersonality gone sour. But in a broader sense, our cultural
criticism continues to draw upon that strand of social criticism that viewed
Vietnam as the watershed (and Waterloo) of technocratic liberalism. The
contemporary cultural-studies fascination with the LAPD, that is, often
merely transposes the themes of "authoritarian" personalities or "occupying

armies" that were originally crafted in the 1960s by national crime commission reports. Much like the work of historian Samuel Walker in the late 1970s, this ongoing critical tradition has played a valuable role in unearthing the relationship between Parker's paramilitarism, the "rotten-apple" moralism espoused by generations of police leaders, and the order-maintenance tactics of our own day.[9]

On the other hand, as Walker also suggested, this narrative of LAPD impersonality can easily perpetuate a misconception about the police power actually emergent in the 1960s and the cultural forms that arose to legitimate or contest it. Even in institutional terms, this narrative has tended to overdraw the differences between western and eastern police machines, leading to the neoconservative nostalgia for the watchman ethos that I will discuss in chapter 5.[10] Primarily, however, much like the narrative of professionalization used to recount midcentury reforms, the paramilitary motif of LAPD portraiture can obscure a crucial way that power was actually reframed by public and academic debate in the 1960s themselves—as it turns out, not in military terms at all. To begin with, then, we need to recapture a less obvious but actually more enduring thread of the debate in those days. And that was the idea, emerging from academic scrutiny at the time, that the proper lens for understanding law enforcement in a democratic society was not only in measuring the police's political sympathies, or assessing its forensic crime-busting techniques, or even analyzing its own work culture—but *in examining the interstices of individual interactions between police officers and civilians.* That is, everyday police encounters with the public, negotiations described as the very microcosm of civil life itself, were where police power was said to be enacted.

To a degree, this idea of casting police authority in terms of the citizen encounter accommodated itself to long-term police desire to see itself as a form of mobile political authority—in O. W. Wilson's vein, to view the cop as a roving magistrate. The police preference for "civilian" over "citizen" thus not only spoke to paramilitary norms, but to an attempt to redescribe the way police power was seen—as an essentially civil enterprise that relied on public cooperation. Additionally, however, this new cultural frame around police power was the by-product of the migration of academic sociology, in the 1960s, into debates about the police, in particular via an emergent form (or genre) we might call "police ethnography." In other words, when sociologists and criminologists took it upon themselves to write about the work life of police officers, they did not represent it as a spatially bounded culture unto itself. Rather, cops were presented in an episodic narrative of patrol encounters with citizens and offenders. In the first section of this chapter, I want to explore how this formulation about police-civilian interaction was rehearsed in two seminal studies, Albert Reiss's *The Police and the Public* (1971) and Jerome Skolnick's *Justice without Trial* (1967).[11] Then, I want to take up a few ways in which this foundational issue of public civility, and thus the representation of LAPD power itself, made its way into popular culture and memory through Wambaugh's work.

The relation is not a simple one. The LAPD emphasis on paramilitary discipline, intelligence gathering, and slick public relations often did breed propaganda and rigid script control of mass media, and Wambaugh most often saw himself as a loyal son.[12] Each episode of *Police Story* opened with the trademark squawk of the LAPD dispatcher; Wambaugh even once received a department commendation for his many labors.[13] Yet when we turn to examining that work, in fact, we actually find that it suggests how the revisionist historical narrative can tend to produce a static, instrumental, and managerial reading of the relation of mass culture to police power—which, ironically, doubles back upon how we read the LAPD itself: that is, within its own fantasy of centralized command and control. In point of fact, Wambaugh's cultural posting in the field of imaginary production was shaped by many factors beside its LAPD assignment: by his ethnicity and class background; by the feel for the game he derived from the labor of policing, not its upper management; and by his own migration from policing into the business of mass-cultural representation, and the contradictions that move created.

The son of an Irish Catholic East Pittsburgh police chief and steelworker, a father who never joined the LAPD, Wambaugh brought a bawdy, nearly Joycean, grunt-level working-class disposition to his fiction. In many ways, Wambaugh's might be termed an "antiprocedural" idiom, accentuating the white-ethnic, blue-collar undertone that was always present in that genre. In a play on the garb and class status of his heroes, Wambaugh's cops were (and had) blue k/nights, and thus emerged in tension with the bureaucratic paramilitary imperatives of Parker's mission. Police labor is cast as an artisanal practice, a secret—but also a dirty one. "I'm a G-Man," one cop in *The New Centurions* says; "G for Garbage" (180). In my second section, therefore, I mean to recover the imprint of this white-ethnic and even artisanal disposition, and to demonstrate the contradictions that occurred when Chief Parker's self-avowed "minorityism"—the bizarre, but hardly technocratic claim that the LAPD itself was a kind of ethnic "minority"—found its way into Wambaugh's dream work.[14] In the end, we find Wambaugh challenging popular understandings of police power on several fronts: mocking mass-cultural fantasies while attempting to seize power over them; carrying on the department's own lament about public incivility while lampooning the elite paramilitary code that only worsened it.[15]

All that being said, we nevertheless must also avoid falling into the sterile argument that Wambaugh's idiom simply subverted LAPD-speak from below. If Wambaugh readapted the police populism described in chapter 2, he also hardened it into a grunt-level mystique both better and worse than what guided it from above. Moreover, as I hope to show, Wambaugh's claims to his own "minorityism" had severe contradictions. Thus, if only to give us some glimmerings of the street encounters that academic ethnography theorized and Wambaugh mythologized, I will close by turning to Chicano poet Luis Rodriguez, specifically his memoir *Always Running: La Vida Loca: Gang Days in L.A.* (1993). Rodriguez's memoir not only offers a look back at gang conflict with the police in the exact same era Wambaugh chronicled; just as substantially, it counters Wambaugh's Yeatsian gyres of Chaos with the passional, epic sweep of Diego Rivera, refashioning the seeming nightmare of Watts to remind us of its original political dreams. Each writer, as we will see, cloaks his history in paramilitary terms, so resonant in the backdrop of Vietnam. But it is not only that Rodriguez challenges the official ideological complex of LAPD "minorityism" and citizen dependence with pride in his past Chicano activism. It is that Rodriguez also helps us recover the subtexts obscured by the dominant formulation about "civility" in the 1960s when it came actually to policing the streets—codes of fraternal obligation, class, and ethnic difference that certainly undermined any police claim to "impersonality." As the site of an important contest over civil authority and public accountability—a struggle that still haunts popular memory—the streets were very *much* about "personhood" and political identity. Indeed, a struggle that began, in large part, with the LAPD's mistaken belief that, behind its western badge, *it* was really the only public left in town.

I

One should not be surprised that many contemporary accounts of law enforcement in the 1960s begin to read police power in explicitly political and partisan terms. That decade, it is often said, constitutes the historical moment when a presumed liberal consensus, especially about the value of administrative expertise in managing public consent, foundered on the oppositional shores of civil rights, antiwar activity, and Vietnam itself. Yet what is often less appreciated is how, at the same moment, a particular turn in criminological study and discourse, some of it avowedly liberal, actually supplemented and legitimated a consensual view of law enforcement that both relayed a police view and fed back into it. The renewal of understanding police power in civil, not paramilitary, terms also had the long-term effect of buttressing the neoconservative turn, in which public order became not an effect of democracy but a prerequisite.[16]

Of course, the principal legacy of Progressive reform, which was to measure that power in terms of its efficiency, hardly disappeared from view. On the contrary, measurements like the UCR or rapid-response rates only opened the door to increased academic scrutiny.[17] As both criminology and sociology increased their emphasis on participant observation, city-based ethnographies and research projects, often linked to federal commissions on crime or disorder, began to flourish in these years. And like more in-house portraits of police personality (like former New York police lieutenant Arthur Niederhoffer's *Behind the Shield* [1967]), polls of public esteem, and economic profiles, these studies often began to tell a dismal story. In contrast even to midcentury standards, police salaries in southern and northeastern cities now fell behind skilled labor, and the vast majority of officers still had no college education.[18] Police work had begun to seem more hazardous while its public prestige only seemed to plummet. When pollsters questioned police themselves, officers listed lack of public respect as their main complaint, followed most closely by the liberal Supreme Court decisions that, many officers felt, only made their work more dangerous and more difficult.[19] This grim picture received official sanction, for instance, in a 1969 staff report from the National Commission on the Causes and Prevention of Violence. Like many analyses, this report concluded that the police were "overworked, undertrained, underpaid, and undereducated," and fully alienated from their own citizenry. They had turned to greater militancy and political activism, their work now fueled by a reactionary rotten-apple philosophy that saw criminality as the product of individual moral choice alone.[20] The Watts riot itself had been ignited by a confrontation between a highway patrol officer and a crowd, a crisis that Chief Parker, quite typically, tried to pass off as the result of poor procedure on the officer's part. And also quite typically, he insulted the black community with racist remarks predicting an ominous Negro take-over of Los Angeles.[21]

This defensive, reactionary, and paramilitary image was only reinforced by portraiture emanating from those branches of social science now tending to depict political conflict as rooted in rival personality types. In 1968, for instance, political scientist Seymour Martin Lipset, in "Why Cops Hate Liberals—and Vice Versa" (his contribution to the special supplement of the *Atlantic Monthly* on the police), sketched a frightening portrait of police as typical of the "authoritarian personality" disposed to right-wing fanaticism. Lipset enumerated police affiliations that went beyond mere PBA activism: sponsorship of the John Birch Society (author of the "Support Your Local Police" slogan), or even Ku Klux Klan affiliation. In all, Lipset found police exemplifying a monastic outlook that oversimplified political conflict into moral categories, and readily fell victim to conspiratorial thinking. Mean-while, Lipset added, cops found themselves the antagonist ("pigs") of a rival cultural formation emerging in the universities. To Lipset, student antipathy to the police was symptomatic of an emergent elite class's countercultural disrespect for authority. Not unimportantly for the future shape of neocon-servative thinking, the police provided a vital supporting role in a broader allegory about the supposed deterioration of political authority.

The tenor of Lipset's portrait was typical of a polarized time.[22] And yet, underneath these polemics, and beneath the surely legitimate application of the military metaphor of occupying armies, was a less obvious but longer-lasting theme to public debate, not unlike the contribution to our political vocabulary of the Nixonian silent majority metaphor. In tandem with the paramilitary motif, a more subtle theme had emerged that Lipset's case now assumed: a political framing that directed debate about police power away from the midcentury emphasis on crime busting to closer scrutiny of the social role that civil society had supposedly *already* asked the police to play. In subsequent years, it would seem altogether natural to view the interaction between the individual cop and the citizen as a microcosm of political author-ity itself. And indeed, a microcosmic dramatization of a largely dependent and hypocritical public.

The initial ramifications of this reframing, however, were many. First, it tended, quite reasonably, to shift public focus from the more sensational epi-sodes of urban disorder. Instead it proposed to view riots, for instance, in the context of the more mundane, long-term, historical profile of everyday police work.[23] This produced terribly important work on police brutality and justifiable citizen mistrust.[24] Far less reasonably, however, this reframing often confined debate with an inside view of civil society. Indeed, it tended to suggest that the very thing many activists sought *from* the system at the time—civilian oversight—was *already* built into the order-maintaining practices of the cop himself. Collaterally, then, the new framing also included the public in any estimate of the policeman's poor performance. That is, if personality studies often had the effect of isolating the frontline patrolman as the problem, thus allowing him (sometimes her) to be scapegoated in stories of a continuously aggrieved managerialism, now the public itself also came under scrutiny as a silent and negligent partner in the failures of civil policing.[25] We thus find a style of analysis that did remarkably flexible yet devious cultural work: an analysis that both lamented the class status and political loyalties of the (white working-class) cop and yet also offered a critique of the citizens who did not respect him. At its worst, this new framework co-opted the citizen's own desire for order while undermining any genuine assertion of civil rights; quite often it also let the police's own claim to professionalism go unchallenged.

How this reframing worked is perhaps best seen in Albert Reiss's *The Police and the Public*, an ethnographic study based upon observations of police-citizen interactions while Reiss and his assistants accompanied cops on mobile and foot patrol in high-crime white and black areas of Boston, Chicago, and Washington, D.C., in the early 1960s. Essentially, Reiss and his fellow observers classified the demeanors of cop and citizen (e.g., "agitated" or "hostile" or "authoritarian") in these encounters, and logged them in for aggregate statistical analysis. From the start, then, Reiss's study concerned itself with the ostensibly integral role citizens themselves played in the reactive system established by the radio dispatch and automobile patrol. The first main conclusion of his study, in fact, was that "[c]itizens exercise considerable control over the policing of everyday life through their discretionary decisions to call or not to call the police" (69–70). Reiss discovered, for instance, that 87 percent of patrol mobilizations were actually initiated by citizens (11); that 30 percent actually led to no police-citizen interactions whatsoever (13); that 70 percent of citizen-initiated encounters took place in private, not public spaces, in part because people often left a public scene after the police had been called (14–15).

However mundane they may seem in hindsight, these are probably still the most influential conclusions of their kind in law enforcement circles. Yet Reiss's work was also marked by its own time. For instance, one is immediately struck by how the language of Talcott Parsons's functional sociology often gives Reiss's recounting of police labor a kind of eerie theatricality, blending the paramilitary with the performative. "Modern patrolmen," Reiss writes, "must move continually from 'stage' to 'stage' in response to commands from general dispatchers . . . The scenery, the plot, and the actors may change dramatically in the course of a tour of duty" (4). Or here, for example, is the boilerplate version of Reiss's account of a cop arriving at a crime scene:

> We see, then, that it is incumbent upon a police officer to enter upon a variety of social stages, encounter the actors, determine their roles, and figure out the plot. Often, before they can act, the police must uncover the "plot" and identify the roles and behavior of the actors . . . The fate of the actors and the situation in such cases may reside with the police. (45)

Seen one way, Reiss's phraseology might initially appear intent upon exploring police discretion, even the cop's ability to narrate a crime story—something we'll see other studies figuring out. But in fact we discover that Reiss's account sets its "stage" this way because Parsons's influence tilts his analysis in the direction of measuring the police's professionalism in terms of preassigned social theater: role playing that reflects, decidedly, the status quo.

This consensual effect can be seen in the way Reiss described the police's social role to begin with. By locating his research in the more traditionally reactive dispatch systems in eastern cities, Reiss clearly hoped to restore the sense of policing as a form of municipal duty rather than modern professionalism. He moved in sequence through the various stages of police labor in order to demonstrate its differences from most real white-collar professions. So, for instance, Reiss argued with no small irony, the location of the cop's "office" was the street; his work routine was arbitrary and unpredictable; most importantly, his clientele didn't always request the actual execution of his services. Yet perhaps the most enduring effect of Reiss's municipal service paradigm was that it also returned the object of police power to a more consensual liberal category of "the public," a term that now referred vaguely to a presumed social norm of civility.[26] This connected directly to the discovery about policing private spaces. Reiss emphasized, for instance, that eight out of ten calls for police assistance involved what the police themselves deemed noncriminal matters (70, 73). In Reiss's account, that is, citizens often confused what was morally offensive with what was illegal, just as they confused civil matters (e.g., a landlord-tenant dispute) with acts that were actually criminal. In other words, as Samuel Walker has pointed out, despite the Parker-esque refrain that a cop was not a social worker, the new technologies brought with them just the thing the cop's professionalism was supposed to ward off: his encroaching imbrication with those social services he claimed, officially, he had outsourced to other agencies.[27]

And yet, in Reiss's consensual view, it was here that a gap was opened up between police and citizen expectations, with startling effects. On the scene, Reiss said, cops typically encountered two kinds of clients: those who called the police and those who were ultimately to be policed themselves in some way. And, not too surprisingly, those arrested often expressed considerable hostility. One half of those arrested were deemed insulting, explosive, argumentative by academic observation (54). "Generally, police officers regard citizen resistance as routine, and our percentages agree" (55). Officers wanted deference to their authority, and civilians wanted to be treated with personal involvement and attention (181)—here, in Reiss's view, was the source of friction, again in the roles everyone played. Particularly in arrests for disorderly conduct, disturbing the peace, and so forth, citizens viewed police authority as illegitimate: they complained because other perpetrators got away, or because they viewed the conflict at hand as a personal matter. "Police dealings with lower socio-economic groups," Reiss added, were where one seemed to find the most friction (17).

It would seem, again, that this observation would open up the issue of police misconduct. But since (under that observation) Reiss's cops exhibited very little abuse, Reiss's emphasis fell on *citizen* misunderstanding of the process. Indeed, Reiss noted blandly, "the most common complaint officers in our studies voice about citizens is their failure to show respect for authority" (47). Although Reiss observed that over 75 percent of white police officers made prejudiced statements about Negroes, he claimed that "in actual encounters they did not treat Negroes uncivilly more often than they did whites"—that they were, in fact, more likely to exhibit force against members of their *own* race. "[I]n the final analysis," his book declares rather incredibly, "race is not an issue in the unnecessary use of force by the police" (147). "I submit," he wrote in his conclusion, "that in a civil society no one should be trained or paid to accept incivility; to accept invectives that begin with 'mother' or animal names . . . failure to sanction incivility towards the police on the grounds that the police should expect, and therefore accept it, is to lay the ground for even less civility of citizens toward the police and for the police to respond in kind when opportunity presents itself" (184–85).

In retrospect, of course, one can see that Reiss's book is very much shaped by its time—and that it encounters the limits of what is now called "ethnographic realism." It is not only likely that the presence of Reiss's own observers doubtless muted police misconduct. There is also very little re-creation of the actual gathering process, of interactions *between recorder and subject*; rather, such observations are recessed, resurfacing only when broader statistical results are presented. One can also feel the particular framing power of the Uniform Crime Reports' response-to-call approach to measuring crime. Crimes occur, in Reiss's framework, not when citizens issue the call but when the police legitimate it. The positionality of analysis in the squad car ends up being *quite* determining, since Reiss assumes crime is happening, and being dealt with, only when the police decide to play their role on the scene. (Crime is, despite Reiss's own literary trope, really authored by cops who make the plot anew).

Not too surprisingly, therefore, Reiss's observations blur easily into his informants' story, as if echoing the police's own lament.[28] What is especially striking, in particular, was how Reiss's model reinforced the police's own lament about a hypocritical, dependent citizenry, in need of the police to solve its most private matters, yet often leaving the scene before the police arrive. What was really being reinscribed here, of course, was the police's long-standing representation of the public, discussed in my previous chapters. Even minor asides supplemented this familiar picture. In some cases Reiss even blamed citizens for failing to file police reports, supposedly thwarting insurance claims; thus in his view they had the power to subvert the system by their decisions to call the police or not (68). When so-called victimization surveys found more crime than in the UCR, citizens again were faulted for not reporting in.[29]

The determining role of the squad car is especially apparent in the study's treatment of racism as a matter of individual, microcosmic interaction. Even leaving aside the pressure of academic observation, this treatment could easily overlook racism built into institutional practices. In its vaunted Academy, for instance, LAPD officers were trained to read the street for nonnormative and potentially threatening behaviors. Take, for example, George Payton's textbook *Patrol Procedure* (1967), part of the Peace Officers Standards and Training (POST) used in southern California in these years. Included in the POST manual's list of suspicious persons in the 1960s, however, were "[d]rivers that don't fit the car they are driving" and "[p]ersons wearing dark glasses at night." Of course, the author advises, mocking the hipness of the day, "There are certain groups that wear them at night because it is 'cool' and all the 'cats' wear them. A person from this group bears close watching anyhow, since they are often anti-social and antipolice."[30] Here street behavior is deemed criminal merely because of its presumed antipathy to police presence—a policy foreboding conflict if there ever was one—a training that serves only to mark proactively the very groups it expects trouble from. And that Chief Parker had himself marked in public speeches.

Therefore, Reiss drew conclusions that went beyond mere consensus seeking, or midcentury laments about citizens' failures to ally themselves with police out of their supposed love of vice. Moreover, in Reiss's framework, criminality is so rooted in incivility that the obverse becomes true: assertion of civil protest is seen as a form of street disorder. In Reiss's final plea quoted above, the counterculture is clearly the veiled antagonist: the university is lumped in with the ghetto as a site of such incivility—and Lipset, not surprisingly, is cited (185). Likewise, when Reiss admits that nonwhites account for a higher percentage of arrests, and for higher friction in the encounter itself, he allows that "the emergence of organizations or groups that generate citizen complaints" (155) is probably "the most important factor of all" in the statistical weighting. Reiss leaves unclear whether it is in *reporting* or in *creating* such incidents that the weighting occurs. Of course, he has to leave that distinction unclear, since to explain that gap would be to dismantle his central governing assumptions.

There are many other limits to Reiss's account, but I will not belabor them further. The central point is that very little in his study showed significant containing power of citizens over the discretion officers asserted on patrol. On the contrary, seen institutionally, his reactive model did more than discount the proactive model actually emergent at the time—it literally took it off the page.[31] Indeed, by showing how cops weeded out merely civil or moral complaints by retrospective narration, Reiss showed quite the opposite of what he intended—that is, a kind of ruling authority over what constituted civil rights themselves. This is why it is important to compare Reiss's account with that of Jerome Skolnick's *Justice without Trial,* which put police discretion at the *center* of its analysis.

Also an ethnographic study, this time of the Oakland Police Department, Skolnick's book is anything but consensual in its approach. Nor does it accept the idea that public respect for police professionalism was the panacea for social ills. Rather, the problem was not that professionalism had failed in its public accreditation—Reiss's case—but that it had been too narrowly defined, Skolnick argued, as merely a matter of managerial efficiency and technical expertise, a tradition he explicitly connected with LAPD Chief Parker and O. W. Wilson. Indeed, Skolnick pointed to a contradiction in the emerging slogan of "law and order" itself, for which liberals like Reiss seemed to have such sympathy. Contrary to contemporary usage, Skolnick claimed, the twinned terms "law" and "order" were not always synonymous in daily police practice. In America, rather, the police operated more as interpreters of criminality, often at the street level. They were the primary agents, in other words, of a society working largely to adjudicate "justice without trial" (13–14).

This challenge to the dominant framing of the day was not merely a by-product of Skolnick's politics, nor of his choice to center his study, again contra Reiss, in a decidedly proactive western department. Nor was it solely a matter of returning analysis of police culture and personality to the discussion about interaction with citizens. In many respects, in fact, Skolnick's account of the policeman's "working personality" (43) actually worked to refine the more sensational accounts like Lipset's (235). Most police did subscribe, Skolnick conceded, to a "Goldwater kind of conservatism" (60), and negative attitudes toward Negroes were a norm (81). But Skolnick did not find policemen intrinsically "moralistic" (57) as such. Instead, he found their personality shaped by persistent, ingrained *suspicion* (48), engendered by the institutionalized training the POST manual made so vivid.

Drawing a subtle distinction, Skolnick said the cop's training in suspicion meant that he was a man engaged in enforcing a set of bureaucratic rules against a citizenry from which he felt alienated (62). That is, cops were shaped both by their own weltanschauung as craftsmen and by modern bureaucratic norms imposed by a production schedule from above. Like other artisans, cops were proud of their skills but frustrated by the production demands, the the clientele, and especially the systemic flouting of their own decision making, as for example in the courts. Moreover, it was their perception of danger, rather than their adherence to authority as such, that contributed to conduct that was not predictable or reasonable at all, but often arbitrary (90). As a result, the cop develops "resources within his own world to combat social rejection" (51), particularly a high degree of occupational solidarity (52).

This solidarity played directly, albeit in contradictory ways, into the cop's view of his own labor. Contrary to the customary liberal view of the police role as occupying armies—a paramilitary trope that played off the familiar idea of "two nations"—Skolnick argued that the cop was alienated not just from everyday citizens, but from the ruling forces he often served. In philosophical terms, Skolnick said that police work was rooted in a "nontotalitarian ideology of the relation between work and authority" (235). More simply put, Skolnick's cop was not a mere instrument of law or of his managers, as Reiss (and too much of our history) would have us presume. Rather, as I mention in chapter 1, when an officer makes an arrest, Skolnick observed, he feels that "as a specialist in crime, he has the *ability to distinguish between guilt and innocence*" (197) on the spot. To be sure, in some cases, what Skolnick calls this "probabilistic" thinking—the cop's working presumption of guilt—did play directly into bureaucratic hands. As a worker, a police officer often sought out the means to carry out the "production demands" put upon him (243). But more characteristically he made order seem continuous with law by the *way* he did his work. That is, faced with the kind of interpretive dissonance Reiss describes on the scene, or administrative indifference from his superiors, a policeman will usually shape his account of events "in the interest of justifying a contention of legality, irrespective of the actual circumstances" (214). In fact—and here was the clincher—beat officers often identified this latitude with the power and prerogatives of their craft. Thus it was not merely bureaucratic laxity, much less citizen resistance, that often made street encounters so volatile. Rather, it was that "the more police tend to regard themselves as 'workers' or 'craftsmen,' the more they demand a *lack* of constraint upon initiative" (235, emphasis mine), making their own standards arbitrary. In direct contrast to Reiss's study, Skolnick thus closed his book not with a plea for civility, but for closing the gap between police practice and the rule of law (239, 245).

In at least one important respect, then, Skolnick brought to the surface something that the political debate would soon efface: the artisanal status of the cop. In so doing, he ventured the stunning observation that the prevailing managerial ideology of policing, which O. W. Wilson and Chief Parker indeed exemplified, actually *promised to weaken the accountability* of policing (237) by failing to bridge the gap between law and order. And Skolnick was certainly right to insist that this managerial conception was shared not only by police officials, but by civic groups and leaders—the "power structure" (241–42)—of cities themselves. Skolnick's warning about proactive managerialism was an important one, and to be sure the rival histories of *The New Centurions* and *Always Running* can both be illuminated by understanding his central paradox: of the cop's essentially artisanal notion of autonomy and freedom, forced into excesses by the managerial authority he deems denies him his true rights to police. And into excess that, in turn, denies rights to others. (Vietnam, indeed.)

And yet perhaps it should also not surprise us that Reiss's framework actually ruled the day. It was not merely that Reiss's more conventional liberal categories of "the public" and civility tended to overshadow Skolnick's more radical, and more incisive, concerns about the effects of the cop's contradictory class position. Reiss's dominance was also partly a product of the synergy between academic ethnography and the drives of police managers themselves—and indeed, even the liberal trope of occupying armies itself. However much Skolnick tried to investigate the cop's own sense of his labor, ultimately Reiss's focus on the microcosmic stage ended up by casting the individual cop, in line with paramilitary language of the day, as a soldier besieged by a hostile populace. Necessarily, as popular histories of their day, the works of Wambaugh and Rodriguez readapt much of this sociological imagery about paramilitary drives, fraternal longings, Vietnam subtexts. Yet because they are partly written from the street, they also offer a partial retort to the dominant LAPD-speak, in which calls to civility were actually put to quite uncivil uses.

III

As I have said, Joseph Wambaugh's work can often seem little more than a reactionary mythological chronicle of the modern LAPD—a form of cultural expression dispatched, as it were, by central command. In *The New Centurions*, William Parker's sayings are voiced by a knowing veteran named Kilvinsky, who meditates on how centurions so trained would greet the forces of anarchy (86). There seems, as well, a vicious machismo, rooted in Hemingwayesque reticence (215). Thus what the public calls police brutality is described simply as what citizens would do under the same stressful conditions (161). Homosexuality is classified as one of many forms of sexual pathology (218); indeed, LAPD lore says "fruits," above all kinds of perpetrators, must be handcuffed.[32] So notoriously, homosocial fraternalism literally has it both ways. If Chief Parker is called a man to "love" by Kilvinsky (63), another cop's criminology professor who defends search-and-seizure laws is discovered, by cop intuition, to have been gay (195).[33]

On the other hand, we might take our cue from the plaintive tenor and static of the dispatcher's voice as it actually blared during those opening moments of *Police Story* episodes, suggesting as it does both the urgency and yet also the illegibility of command—as well as the dangers of carrying orders out. Wambaugh's work, it turns out, expressed something different from a simple ideological echo of the managerial ideology emanating from what, in the fatalistic humor of patrol, became known as the "Glass House" (the Parker Center) in the 1960s. As I've already suggested, read against Reiss and Skolnick, Wambaugh's prose narratives might better be understood not as fictionalizations, but as hybridized productions, partly themselves street-level (antiacademic) ethnographies, encounters with citizens of the 1960s recast into the cultural authority of the novel and the most popular mass medium, television. Beginning here, we can better see how the emergent discourse of civility both played into and reinforced Parkerism, and yet exposed the gaps between (in Michael Herr's terms) the Mission and the motion. It is not simply a matter, then, of Wambaugh's cultural migration serving to support or subvert the new dynamics of police power. Much in Wambaugh's emergent beat mythology worked to honor Parker's authority, even attempting to offer it as a cultural retort to liberal pluralism itself; it also helped ground, in cultural terms, the new geographies of authority (beat, community) on which neoconservatives would later build. But at the same time as it commingled with the G-man ethos, its fatalism also allowed the cause, in key moments, to be turned into sad farce.

Seen as literary ethnography, *The New Centurions* seems at first to serve the chief well. On the one hand, the book appears to reaffirm the findings of the McCone Commission, which had attempted to explain (away) the Watts riot of 1965. Wambaugh's cops encounter the main elements—

criminals, "riff-raff" (e.g., the uneducated or unemployed), juveniles, recent southern migrants (who always say "PO-lice"), and politicized Negroes— which Chief Parker and the McCone Commission said (so misleadingly) were the key players in the Watts riots. As it were, Wambaugh worked to legitimate those findings by a kind of *retro*spective cultural account of *pro*active policing, serving up his fiction as fieldwork that the Commission, as its critics pointed out, never undertook itself.[34] Moreover, in a metaleptic move Parker made famous and, as I've shown, even academic ethnographers like Reiss fell victim to, civil rights agitation is made *responsible* for the decay of white authority, and thus further criminality. As one cop puts it, blacks have been promised "nigger heaven." The crime-busting lens is apparent: just as LA is itself cast as an industrial magnet for immigrants, the riot is seen as a thousand felonies happening at once (313). At the close of the novel, the cops themselves muse how long it will take for someone to come up with a "just cause" explanation for the riot (353).[35]

Wambaugh's first book then, as it were, becomes a narrative of class in at least two senses. First, the fraternalism of the "Academy" (a rival university) transfers to that of Parker's thin blue line. As if confirming this translation, Wambaugh's writing depicts cultural locations with the names "University" and "Hollywood" not only as literal beats, but as posts of rival representations of police labor that are to be beaten, debunked by the centurions' class (labor) experience. Indeed, the physical location of Hollywood is a key to the political understructure of this novel's assault on the liberalism and permissiveness of the 1960s. Hollywood is presented allegorically as the land of "the Lotus Eaters," whom the force (implicitly, the Warlocks) must literally police—and presumably gather data (intelligence) upon for one's novel.[36] Cop knowledge is in fact proactively positioned against Hollywood versions of the street: rookies, from the moment they enter the Academy, are told to abandon their faith in winging an assailant (11–12), in paraffin traces (119), in being able to subdue resisting citizens single-handedly (11). Indeed, Hollywood—which will become, in one rookie subplot, one beat that itself is saturated with phonies—serves only to create a hostile audience for cop work, as juries quesytion police judgment by using these very same phony standards on the real.

And at first, therefore, the rookies' and veterans' daily encounters with citizens seem quite congruent with the chief's macropolitical crusade. Wambaugh is especially adroit at re-creating this mission—as, for instance, in this portrait of a cop scanning the street:

> I saw a Negro woman get off a bus and walk down a residential block from Central Avenue and I turned on that street for no reason . . . Then I saw a black guy on the porch of a whitewashed frame house. He was watching the woman and almost got up from where he was sitting until he saw the black-and-white. Then he pretended to be looking at the sky and sat back, a little too cool, and I passed by and made a casual turn at the next block and then stomped down hard and gave her hell until I got to the first street north . . . It was an old scam around here for purse snatchers to find a house where no one was home and sit on the stoop of the house near a bus stop, like they lived at the pad . . . Most black women around here don't carry purses. They carry their money in their bras . . . [citizens] don't get suspicious of a guy when he approaches you from the porch of a house in your own neighborhood. (*Blue Knight*, 179–80)

One could hardly imagine a more bookish application of POST manual advice, indeed extrapolated beyond the mere conflation of antipolice responses with criminality. Citizens are virtually lifted off their porches, as the cop's knowledge claims to be more in tune with black consciousness than that of the public themselves. It is important for much of what I've been calling police populism that Wambaugh reasserts, in passages like these, a cop claim to *ownership* of the streets—a strategy so resonant with the new framing of police power around civility.[37]

Yet in some ways the ideological reading above is a little too pat. It is more accurate to say that Wambaugh's books look back to Parker as a *lost* leader by wrapping him in transhistorical wisdom. If the cop world is a secret fraternity, it is one marked by this sense of loss, a full flowering of the alienation *The Naked City* tried to salve. Quite soon, it is the very insistence upon street-level teaching that opens up a subtle gap with the Glass House's *own* Academic vision.

Wambaugh offers his alternative explanation by positioning the explicitly Parkeresque vision of Western declension against a more covert, interior narrative about class in its second, sociological sense. Wambaugh's main protagonist, Marine veteran Serge Duran, is a blond Mexican American Catholic who learns the Anglo fraternity from the inside. Augustus ("Gus") Plebesly—his very name combining Roman rule with plebe status—is a provincial freshman in from Azusa, straight out of junior college and work as a bank teller. Roy Fehler, whose last name (probably pronounced "Feeler") identifies him as the liberal foil to the narrative's tutelage, is a self-styled empathetic intellectual with an interest in criminology and abnormal psychology. The book thus casts these three rookies typologically; the street is a gauntlet that tests religious belief, or physical endurance, or liberal empathy. Over time, however, it is the cop fraternity that becomes the true guild, a secret world not unlike that evoked by Tom Wolfe's "right stuff."

But what happens is that a subtle gap is opened up between one's professional academic training and one's older-style guild apprenticeship. There are the little tricks of the trade veterans teach: keeping your baton next to you in the car, "lancelike" (35), or learning street number patterns on patrol (37). There is the manly pride in the sensory apparatus, which improves with exposure to danger and vice. Real life is defined, of course, as sordidness: as one cop puts it, one wishes one could "bottle the smell" of an apartment and take it to court as proof of an "unfit home" (274). In Wambaugh's quite Catholic fiction, as well, constant exposure to human sinfulness serves to further bond the male cops across generational and ultimately ethnic lines, and thus partly *against* management and the streets alike. Policing is itself credited with creating a pluralistic fraternity far superior to the neighborhoods one polices. As was typical on Wambaugh's television series *Police Story*, crooks of color are often collared by cop partners of color, and immigrant—often Irish American—parents are sympathized with as their children wander into crime.[38]

Even more suggestively, *The New Centurions* demonstrates, in particular, how the task of policing incivility was an impossible one from inception. Exposing the very thing Reiss identified and Parker denied, Wambaugh's cops are indeed called in to handle what they call "beefs"—again, civil disorders in which residents claim to want criminal adjudication. If social workers and judges worry about criminals' rights, " 'we're the only ones who see the victims' " (51), one veteran testifies, portraying (as Skolnick tells us) a knowing assurance that a cop can recognize guilt when he sees it (160, 161, 357). The typical cop's estimate of the public, it follows explicitly, just doesn't measure up to his estimate of the cop fraternity itself (77).[39] And in these dispersed, ethnic publics we see not a simple affair with vice rackets, but a love of sheer disorder. In one telling example, procedure dictates that police officers should doff their hats on the scene, to better address the citizen in a domestic dispute; this is the proper military code. A veteran, however, teaches Roy to wear his hat to keep both hands free in case of unpredictable violence (97). Thus Wambaugh records the blue fate of having to police a community that, privately, he no longer thought *was* one.

Parker's own tragic sensibility tried, of course, to encompass this fate: the thinness of the blue line, for instance, was itself a covert claim to *true* minority status. But almost from the start, the narrative design of *The New Centurions* undercuts the progress and orderliness of the LAPD lessons that it claims to be confirming. Rather than an easy translation from academy to street, cop knowledge actually involves an often-violent unlearning that strips not only preconceptions, but the very markers of the Academy itself—and, with it, middle-class status: certainly liberal attitudes, but also faith in the law or one's professional training (e.g., in those criminology courses). Department procedure is itself exposed as a fiction; in a reflex Skolnick recognizes, the brotherhood of fraternal wisdom teaches resistance to both bureaucratic routine and the law itself.[40]

Again, that cops *do* actually manage beefs (96) itself subverts the Glass House mentality, with its myopic insistence that cops were not social workers. While Chief Parker is off pontificating about that "Thin Blue Line," therefore, carrying out his work becomes, in Wambaugh's narrative, "the Blue Enema." In this particularly bawdy scene, the blue-collar cops become an ambiguous battering wedge, ramming into the portals of a gay bar called The Cave. It is not merely that gays supposedly threaten civilization, or even that they embody a street illegibility. Rather, as Wambaugh reports it, gays threaten because, once their straight cover is blown, they can become dangerous—that is, they turn into a mirror image of you. (As an echo of the chaos of Watts itself, History is itself unmanned: hence, as well, another layer to the joke about being a "G-man").[41] It is thus telling that Kilvinsky not only vocalizes the chief, but (through the conversion of a heart attack to suicide) evinces the futility of the chief's program at the street level.[42]

Veteran fraternalism thus has this double-sidedness as well. Initially, the rookies disdain the outdated veterans under whom they apprentice: an experienced cop named Milton, a worn-out drinker named Whitey who keeps his bottle in his call box, even Kilvinsky himself. Yet as the rookies are stripped of their status differentiations from the old-timers, they ironically take on the veterans' bad secrets of divorce and self-doubt, stress and alcoholism—learning from Whitey, for instance, *how* to hide your bottle in that call box. One is, over time, handcuffed to the veterans' ills. At the end of Wambaugh's first novel, just as this class has earned its stripes (353)—a marker of imprisonment as much as of paramilitary pride—Roy is killed right as he feels he had begun to know. Even his "know, know, know," however, is misheard as saying "no" to death (358).

If anything, this ambiguity of veteran status becomes even more pronounced in Wambaugh's second novel. *The Blue Knight*, in fact, is entirely an interior monologue by beat cop Bumper Morgan, still patrolling on his last five days before voluntary retirement after twenty years, gathering up his pension so he doesn't have to become a desk man downtown (279). To a degree, again, Bumper *is* a company man. He backs the department's version of the Century City riots explicitly (87–88), and takes pride in Parker's western ethos. LA would be a frustrating place, he tells us, "if it weren't for the fact that the West in general is not controlled by the political clubhouse owing to the fact that our towns are so sprawling and young . . . it's still the best system going" (191). On the other hand, as the following meditation on his badge reveals, Bumper also defines himself partly in opposition to the auto-culture of the Glass House (55):

> Most of the ridges had been rounded off long ago, and twenty years of rubbing gave it unbelievable brilliance. Turning the face of the shield to the white sun, I watched the gold and silver take the light. I pinned the badge to my shirt and looked at my reflection in the blue plastic that Rollo has over his front windows. The plastic was rippled and bubbled and my distorted reflection made me a freak. I looked at myself straight on, but still my stomach hung low and made me look like a blue kangaroo, and my ass was two nightsticks wide . . . It was ugly, but what made me keep looking was the shield. The four-inch oval on my chest glittered and twinkled so that after a second or two I couldn't even see the blue man behind it. (10)

At one level, Wambaugh's second book covertly uses its nostalgia to stake a claim to the beat that has been lost. But like the passage itself, the shield, in turn, both embodies and disembodies Bumper's claim to that authority. On the beat a symbol of his authority and experience, the badge is nevertheless something that hides his blue state. If *The New Centurions* is a historical meditation on the terrors of an aggressively modern, western, forward-looking, proactive warding off of chaos, *The Blue Knight* illustrates its complementary nostalgia, a longing for an essential policing that the community relies upon but cannot respect. In this state, LAPD paternalism is exposed as farcical and pathetic.

In a curious interplay of surface and depth behind that badge, Bumper is a flatfoot whose feet literally have fallen beneath him, relegated to a patrol car whose ethos he barely abides (13). Bumper resists even answering calls on his car radio (70); he wears the eight-pointed hat instead of the new, Air Force–style cap (3); he keeps his leather thong for his baton at his hip, even after the department wanted it (in a public relations move as old as the Progressive era) removed from view. In another interesting byplay on academic knowledge, it is the downtown office that is now called an "ivory tower" (67); Bumper and his friend, Sergeant Serge Cruz, mock the very language of the " 'new breed of professionals' " coming from downtown (72). Over the course of the novel, we acquire more detail about the blue man, Bumper: a man whose parents died young, who was raised by his brother; a divorced World War II veteran who lost his only son, Billy (his namesake), when the child was only five.

The thread Wambaugh pulls out of LAPD ideology, in other words, is a decidedly blue-collar one. Wambaugh's quest for the secret knowledge of the police fraternity has led him to mythologize an essence of frontline policing, again a kind of class-inflected transhistorical knowledge embodied, so ambiguously, in the Bumper Morgans of the world. Returning to the beat leads Wambaugh to policing's medieval truth, where a cop carries not merely a badge but his "shield" (10), calls his car seat his "saddle" (21), and calls women "wenches" (16). His chief antagonist is a bar called The Pink Dragon (14)— a hybrid antagonist with traces of liberal permissiveness, political radicalism, and a newly exotic (eastern) landscape. For the first several chapters, Bumper Morgan is literally adored by community members whose ethnic foods and daughters come to him as a kind of tribute. It is his girlfriend who dubs him the Blue Knight, one who " 'joust[s] and live[s] off the land' " (103). He gathers knowledge not merely from his snitches but from residents themselves (42), and engages in preventative jousting merely to assert his authority on the beat.[43] Working across this familiar community treats Los Angeles as if it were a small town, where a little bumping, not really harassment, works to preempt larger threats to order.

And yet this is also a place where his blue coat turns into a "sackcloth" (26) in the heat. To Wambaugh's way of seeing, cop knowledge becomes a matter of *instinctual* learning, even a form of faith, and yet a dubious one. The knowledge learned on the street is not, strictly speaking, empirical. Quite importantly, in Wambaugh's work it was always to some degree intractable and unpredictable, hardly reducible to something like the POST manual's nostrums. One early plot line in *The New Centurions*, for instance, follows Fehler, who must, according to even black veterans, unlearn his liberal tolerance about blacks. Nevertheless, it is his ultimately *learned* racism that causes him to relax, and be shot by, as it happens, a *white* assailant (250). The teachings of this labor turn out to be anything but securely reactionary at all— but again, something better and worse than Academy learning. Likewise it is not, as so much popular culture criticism states, that violence is eradicated in Wambaugh's fictive beat; both novels end, in fact, with the brutal street murder of a fellow cop. The unpredictability of violence unsettles the cop psychologically, making learning from it fully improbable, the very antithesis of going by the book.

Meanwhile, the fact that the essence of cop knowledge is derived from the citizens' vassalage to the cop on his beat actually turns out only to deepen his sense of their dependency. As in Reiss's consensual frame, Bumper is appropriated by community members as a symbol of order that they long for. Yet beneath the surface of this faith, one can see that if this knight is a kind of border guard of civility, his world is also borderless, and the beat itself is prone to decay. Burlesque houses, for instance, turn into skin-flick houses (25). Even more fundamentally, Bumper's beat is exoticized and rendered unfamiliar as well, not only in the familiar essentializing of Hispanic and Negro difference—as I will suggest in my final section, a kind of border patrolling of whiteness—but in the populating of the beat with radically *non-*western types. Negroes become less street legible as they become Muslims; Arabs appear or, most tellingly, Gypsies, whom Bumper casts as the very antithesis of civilization (185–86). In a very real sense, Bumper finds himself the knight in a last, and again lost, crusade for civility; the beat is itself labeled by his Hispanic friends, as another parody of chivalric knighthood, Bumper's *puta* (whore). In a scene that provides an important harbinger of the close of this novel, a mother pauses on the street to tell her little boy to watch out for the cop, like a bogeyman and enforcer of right and wrong (20). Significantly, however, Bumper worries that this role will merely breed fear and hatred in the future. ("She gave me a sweet smile," Bumper says of the mother, "very smug because she thought I was impressed with her good citizenship" [20].)

At many levels, then, the downshifting of LAPD managerialism to a street-level populism now picks up the ethnographic framing that covertly equated not only citizen dependency, but citizen protest, with potential criminality. As if in search of a rationale that justifies increased police assertiveness in the face of this dependency, moreover, what Wambaugh comes up with is the idea that the community is Bumper Morgan's, too—an idea with a long history in police ideology, but now more forcefully expressed. The rationale emerges when Bumper recalls an older beat cop who enforced his will by beating up a lowlife named Angie rather than booking him downtown. This was a crook who, not coincidentally, was "from the same dirty town in Pennsylvania" (60) as the cop himself. The older cop explains the "unofficial" beating this way:

> ". . . I convicted [those bookies] and saw them get pitiful fines time after time and I *never* saw a bookmaker go to state prison even though it's a felony. Let somebody else work bookmaking I finally decided, and I came back to uniform. But Angie's different. I know him. All my life I knew him, and I live right up Serrano there, in the apartments. That's *my* neighborhood. I use that cleaners where the old man [Angie's victim] works . . . The books'll be scared now for a little while after what I done. They'll respect us for a little while." (63)

Bumper Morgan shows that the turn to History has only reinforced the present quest to set "the books" straight. And of course, like "Hollywood," or "University," or with that cop tutor of man's inhumanity named "Milton," this isn't just books in the Glass House, but in the house of culture: both the books of social accounting and literary books. The pattern of partial recuperation is reinforced here by the entire trajectory of *The Blue Knight*'s plot, in which Bumper Morgan lets go of his plans for early retirement, cuts off his relationship with his new fiancée, and gets in his "saddle seat" again, facing westward to do battle at the end of his book (316).

The dark face of this recommitment is partly shown in the way loyalty to one's original, even prehistoric oath allows for the legitimation of harsher, more violent authority. There is in Bumper Morgan actually *more* violence than in Wambaugh's new centurions—a reflection of the increasingly defensive directions Wambaugh's populism seemed to move when remembering the 1960s. In one particularly telling moment, Bumper fantasizes about sticking his baton "three inches in [the] esophagus" of a "scuz" protester, then imagines the citizen crying police brutality (77). Here, putting the beat in the patrolman's words works to legitimate LAPD wisdom at the street level—and, in a curious but crucial turn, also lets the workaday cop off the hook, since he's only doing (supposedly) what secret lovers of order would want him to. Like the young centurion Roy Fehler, who begins to "know" only in death, Bumper's secret knowledge is too deep for real verbalization: it can only *be* in what he does (bumping). It is thus contrasted with those who talk back, or who protest.

This double-sided binding of nostalgia with a new claim to force—an ideological crucible, I think, of neoconservatism—is evident in the episode designed to reveal, even more directly, the already-absent community into which Bumper has grown: a Vietnam protest. Here, we hear for the first time the popular derogatory term "pig" (80); rather intriguingly, Bumper rejects the social worker image of the cop as public relations management of this epithet. (And protests, Bumper tells us [83], only take him away from the beat.) Bumper, however, gets up on his own soapbox, and speaks from his posting as "'only a neighborhood cop'" (80). He pleads that we often praise cops for delivering babies, or being a good scout leader, but never because they simply do their job—in Bumper's formulation of the crime-busting ethos, making "'thirty good felony pinches a month for ten years'" and sending "'a couple hundred guys to San Quentin'" (85). But what is actually revealing about this episode is Bumper's inability to read this particular crowd: he thinks he identifies all of the "pros" (subversives) and the hangers-on, and he's completely wrong in every case. At the end of his speech, he discovers that the subversives will tape, edit, and distort his police story for consumption in the mass media.[44] His skin is saved by a colleague from the intelligence division. Bumper inquires:

> "I had a feeling something wasn't right," I said, getting sick because I was afraid to hear what I figured he was going to say. "Did they set me up?"
>
> "Did they set you up? No, they didn't have to. You set yourself up! Christ, Bumper, you should know better than to make speeches to groups like that. What the hell made you do it?"
>
> Stan had about fifteen years on the job and was a sergeant, but he

was only about forty and except for his gray sideburns he looked lots younger. Still, I felt like a dumb little kid sitting there now. I felt like he was lots older and a damn sight wiser and took the assbite without looking at him.

"How'd you know I was speechmaking, Stan?"

"One of them is one of us," said Stan. (91)

That this sergeant of "about fifteen years" could easily be Wambaugh himself points to the two sides from which history is written here. If there is heroic appreciation for the beat cop, and anger at the new noncommunity, there is also a telling supplement on Wambaugh's part. For more than anything else, there is surreptitious admiration for the *new* LAPD here—reversed parentage, even—for the efficiency and necessity of counterintelligence in a hostile world. In short, the rhetorical nostalgia for the essence of beat patrol is conjoined with a fatalistic acknowledgment, sub rosa, that the world now has to be policed in a different way.[45]

This tacit acknowledgment dominates the close of *The Blue Knight* as well. All through the novel, Bumper is haunted by the memory of his lost son, also named Billy. Near the end, encouraged by his fiancée, Bumper courts the idea of adoption and counsels a young street kid to whom he takes a shine. But in the end, Bumper recoils from this role, while the young kid also turns against him, saying that "[y]ou're just a cop." (309) The novel ends by returning to Bumper's self-doubt as we now re-view the overweight cop climbing back into his car. Or rather, Bumper's view of himself:

> Then he fastened his shield to his chest and urged the machine westward . . .
>
> I laughed out loud at him [his own reflection] because he was good for no more than this. He was disgusting and pathetic and he couldn't help himself. He needed no one. He sickened me. He only needed glory. (316)

Of course, Wambaugh hopes to redress the contemptuous rookie he once was, as well as the Hollywood-swayed public who can view the cop no more critically than he can view himself. Yet a shield, of course, is both a thing in which one finds one's reflection and something behind which to hide: in many ways Bumper is hemmed in by the fictional double he must himself construct, the culturally acceptable image he cannot, over time, abide. Astride his machine, he becomes a little like a bumper on the auto-culture of the LAPD itself. In the course of Bumper Morgan's street trek, Bumper returns to his beat by taking up, as it were, the Billy (club) to which he was born.

Of course, this was the reverse of the direction that Wambaugh himself had migrated. Indeed, as one final twist on the problem of LAPD allegiance, Wambaugh's own migration into the mass media seemed, at times, to undermine his standing as the loyal son. As yet another realist, of course, Wambaugh claimed to master the field of mass culture by denying his membership in it, a pose that allowed him to act as if the real force (LAPD) was still with him.[46] However, having his street stories out in public often put Wambaugh in a double bind. Being loyal to working-class patrol forces, and depicting their plight, also meant exposing their secret world, and their public story making—and again in some ways departing from the official line. To write up this secret knowledge, and send it out to the very public cops so distrusted, was even to broach betrayal, because the secrets so publicized might only enhance the vulnerability of cops to the incivility of the job and the streets.[47] To tell the secret was potentially to betray one's class, not only the teachers of the Academy. The problem is addressed explicitly when Bumper Morgan admits that he no longer uses the wall search because citizens have learned from the media how to evade it (241). Perhaps even more tellingly, Bumper both admires the military hero T. E. Lawrence and wonders whether he should have revealed his secrets to the natives (108).[48]

IV

Given the above, it is remarkable that some of the most probing meditations on LAPD culture in Wambaugh's novels come from Chicano characters. The centurions apprentice mainly at the feet of white ethnics—veterans named Galloway, Kilvinsky, and rather tellingly Whitey; street Negroes, conversely, are represented as the direct threat to civilized order. Mexican Americans, however, occupy an adjacent, more complicated space, as both racial others intent upon asserting their rights and yet also a Catholic, seemingly fraternal people, respectful of authority.[49] In other words, Chicanos seem symbolically at the crux of Wambaugh's representation of the debate over the future direction of civility, criminality, and rights. For these reasons and others, it is therefore helpful to counterpoint Wambaugh's fictive history with that of

Luis Rodriguez. On the one hand, Rodriguez's memoir debunks the portrait of public dependence proffered by law-and-order advocates, their allies in sociology, and Wambaugh's own chronicles. On the other, Rodriguez's memoir does more than simply subvert this dominant frame, or even of the populist history Wambaugh imposed, in the name of Chicano activism or, to be sure, gang rights. Such a subversion might, after all, simply reaffirm the lyrical marginality of gang life in the 1960s and beyond. Instead, what Rodriguez does, in part, is expose the curious mirroring and mutual dependency between cop culture and its gang nemesis during that decade—a grim forecast of days to come.

In *The New Centurions*, Chicanos are seen as new migrants. They are presented as drawn to the centripetal "steel and concrete" power that is LA (257). The once predominantly Jewish division named Boyle Heights is thus overrun, now deemed a barrio named Hollenbeck or just East LA (38–39), the division in which Wambaugh himself worked. Eminent domain, we are told, breaks up Chicano gangs better than the police can (257). Yet even our understanding of these transformations is filtered through the character of officer Sergio ("Serge") Duran—as I've mentioned, a hidden ethnic and Marine veteran, a former altar boy from the barrios of Chino. Such changes in LA, then, are seen with a mixture of disdain and regret. Initially, Duran "looks paddy" enough to disguise his ethnicity on the force. "He told himself," Wambaugh writes, "he was not ashamed of being Mexican, it was simply less complicated to be an Anglo. And an Anglo he had been for the past five years" (41).

Of course, the tension between looking "paddy" and passing for Anglo captures a deep contradiction in LAPD-style "minorityism" that Wambaugh cannot overcome. This split identity, momentarily contained by racial self-identification with the Anglo Glass House, eventually reopens in much the same way the class divisions I described earlier do. First refusing to offer intelligence on barrio residents and gang members by repressing his knowledge of Spanish, drawn into the cop fraternity when he nearly kills a Hispanic gang juvenile (116), Duran is nevertheless eventually drawn back to the mystical faith and peace he rediscovers in Chicano culture. But if his nostalgia for this essential order initially binds him to whites, soon it only redoubles his antipathy to the Anglo downtown. A Mexican American citizen who mistakes Serge for an Anglo tells him, in a conversation about Negro disrespect for law:

"I used to feel very proud to be accepted like an Anglo because I know of the bad treatment of Mexicans not too long ago. But as I watched you [Anglos] grow weak and fearful that you wouldn't have the love of the world, then I thought: look, Armando—*Mira, hombre, los gabachos* are nothing to envy. You wouldn't be one of them if you could. If a man tried to burn your house or hold a knife at your belly you kill him and no matter his color. If he broke your laws you would prove to him that it's painful to do such a thing . . .

". . . Forgive me, señor, but I wouldn't be a gringo. And if your people continue to grow weak and corrupt I'll leave your comforts and return to Mexico because I don't wish to see your great nation fall." (325)

Once again, the pluralism of Wambaugh's police fraternity thus turns out to be a contradictory dimension of the larger mission.

"Minorityism" does more than inoculate the force against the charge of institutional racism. Rather, it is precisely Serge's persisting isolation, his own version of minorityism, from both his potential communities—Lotus Eaters and East LA—that causes him to cast his lot, though not his full heart, in with Whitey's. In structural terms he is quite like the white ethnics before him (like Charles Becker or Dan Muldoon); one thinks here, as well, of the colonial position of the Irish in the British Empire. Nevertheless, within the entire framework of civility, Duran's passing fails to obscure the vexed question of his national self-identification. As if pondering this play upon ethnic priorities and his own class location, the problem appears, for instance, in his interrogation of a Chicano gang member named Primo, who seems not to know which nation gets his first priority. To expose his provincialism, the cops ask him, "Ever see the ocean?" (120–21).

It is a question like that one that makes Wambaugh's vision seem so incommensurate, at first, with that of Luis Rodriguez's eloquent nationalist Chicano memoir[50]—where, in one of the most dramatic scenes, it is the cops who *prevent* Chicano youths from enjoying an "American" beach. In this scene, Rodriguez's gang mistakes a "van of white dudes" in the distance for the "surfers" and "paddies" with whom they customarily battle; the paddies turn out to be cops who provoke their arrestees into retaliatory violence (65). The scene is quite emblematic of how the police conflate racial, national, and criminal identification. Indeed, as the epigraph to my chapter explicitly claims, gang existence is seen as a Vietnam underground actually created by these occupying colonial forces (121). In a logical reversal so reminiscent of the antiwar movement, Rodriguez even takes the western label "outlaw" and turns it into a subversion of domino theory, into being outed by the law itself. Referring to criminality as a "jacket" imposed from without, he writes: "Why not be an outlaw? Why not make it our own?" (84) Thus over time, it is this street education that causes young Luis to move into Chicano activism, and thus to repudiate the "running" (as in drug running) that conflates his identity not only with criminality but with cowardice (running away). As the helicopters hover over what is seen as a generations-old war (53); as police are said to engage in drug sales and drive-bys (72, 205); as the barrio is cordoned off (204)—we are witness to the imposition of police rule that seems, in contrast to Wambaugh's novels, to bear anything *but* civility.

The dominant consensual framework is shattered in many ways, in fact. Against Wambaugh's somber and apocalyptic historical chronicles, imposing a realism both political and aesthetic, Rodriguez uses a surrealist narrative technique not unlike the Mexican and Mexican American murals he praises (201). He turns his remembrances into dreamlike, fragmentary, and poetic images in which the body becomes a "thing" of bone and skin that desires fluidity and life, but is embroiled only in the blood, the running of always being the prey (36). "Mama and blood and Watts" collapse into broad-stroke, fluid metaphors that recur like poetic refrains (24); Luis himself is a "ball" that initially just takes up space and accepts its direction from others (34).

And if Wambaugh does see Los Angeles as an industrial magnet—created, we might note, by the defense and aerospace complex that flowed to the Vietnam War itself—and gang turf as only the site of juvenile crime and incivility, Rodriguez instead sees Chicano gang wars as the heirs to at least three belated yet ongoing political expropriations.[51] The first, of course, is the history of northern Mexico: being an outlaw is played off against the memory of Pancho Villa, while police nicknames like Cowboy (145) or words like "sheriff" or "deputies" speak volumes. The second displacement is that of residential development, which works by restrictive covenants to leave barrio turf actually unincorporated by adjacent townships (17). Civil policing is thus transformed into a kind of border guard activity. And then, finally, Rodriguez's memoir ends by invoking a new era of Pacific Rim development, a global capitalism that again dwarfs the "Hills" on the globe (236, 242). Ultimately, then, while Wambaugh used Watts as a historical code word for anarchy—those thousand felonies at once—Rodriguez sees both the "Watts Rebellion" and subsequent protests as landmarks in a developing multiethnic political consciousness (162). Indeed, contrary to Serge's white identification, black identity is the canvas for the dreams of Rodriguez's youth. Black music and politics flow together, as one of Luis's earliest gangs is called—in a name expressing both the technique of mimicry and its object—Thee Imperson-ations (84), while African American civil rights activism is a model as well.

In keeping with this rewriting of the civil frame, Rodriguez's historical mural, meanwhile, specifically targets a debate about police authority he knows is still ongoing in the early 1990s.[52] In particular, he exposes the limits of the debate that made the "stage" of the police's story making—here, I am citing Reiss's metaphor for the street encounter—look as if it is an egalitarian and uncontested theater. By contrast, Rodriguez's invocation of gangs as rival *nations* works to establish how even the most fundamental political ground of U.S. nationality was itself contested. In a telling moment, when faced with the offer of tighter policing oversight, more police on the streets—the nos-trums of our own day, but forecast by Wambaugh's covert claim to ownership of the community himself—Rodriguez and his Chicano cohorts reject the model of dependence that they realize police presence often foments. The reasoning for this rejection is espoused by Chente, Luis's mentor:

> "We should organize a meeting in which the various groups [in the barrio] could agree to a truce," [one member proposes.]
>
> "I don't know if we should condone their existence by doing this," a woman from the Zapopan Community Center countered. "We need more police protection—we need to stand up to these hoodlums and put them behind bars."
>
> "That sounds like cops talking," Chente said. "These aren't criminals without faces. They are our children! What you propose only pits the community against itself—and the police would like nothing better than that." (193–94)

Here, talking like cops is exposed as a political ventriloquism antithetical to true Chicano identity.

Nevertheless, it would be a mistake to think that Rodriguez stakes this claim *only* on the ground of a rival nationality. Rather, in the gang's refusal of such truces, Rodriguez's memoir shows how a choice between political dependence, in U.S. terms, or a life or futile, cyclical, retaliatory violence and further repression is really no choice at all. As Rodriguez makes clear, *la vida loca* also cannot be read as a lyrical political resistance alone. To be sure, gang membership is a means of acquiring authority over turf, a way to repudiate both police dependence and the feeling of "locura" (206)—that one is simply taking up space and having no bearing on one's time, like that ball (125). But Rodriguez also translates *la vida loca* as "the insane nation" (251). And in fact, moments like the one above mark an important turnabout in the young Rodriguez's thinking, voicing a desire that he says is fundamentally American at its core (185). Ultimately, the older Rodriguez wants to legitimate the political resonances of gang nations without becoming guilty of romancing what he sees as a fundamentally suicidal violence (9). In fact, this is where the curious mirroring and collateral dependency between cop culture and its gang nemesis emerges. For if anything, *Always Running* is *also* a story, like Wambaugh's, of initiation into a culture of *veteranos*, of soldiers. When the last line of his book reads "Stop Running," it is a plea not only to repudiate that jacket of criminality—jacket, of course, being a slang word for a criminal record—but also to challenge the machismo that only inculcates self-destruction in the young, in an underground that is no nation. Indeed, in a telling counterpoint to Bumper's paternalist fantasy about the lost Billy, this is advice that Rodriguez is offering to his *own* son.

My claim is not that Rodriguez's memoir transcends the dominant framework in the 1960s about civility—quite the contrary, it shows our continuing indebtedness to it. Instead, what emerges in Rodriguez's adult voice is a complex recuperation and repudiation of the uncivil nation of gang life. Perhaps the best poetic distillation of this complex position comes in Rodriguez's revisionary meditation on a pool hall, where a gang leader named Puppet—who, we discover, "didn't care about anybody" (115)—seems to dominate the scene:

> The cue ball rolled across the tattered green felt and struck an odd-numbered striped ball like a firecracker, the violence sending it twirling into the corner pocket. Smoke curled through the luminance of fluorescent light hanging by wires over the billiard table. Puppet gazed momentarily at the remaining balls which lay scattered on the playing field . . .

Puppet's forearms were a canvas of extremely elaborate, interwoven, and delicately-pinned tattoos that danced on skin with *cholo* images, skulls, serpents and women's faces. On his neck was a stylized rendering of the words *Las Lomas* [the gang's name, referring to "The Hills" themselves]. At 20 years old, he was a *veterano* and just out of YTS [Youth Training School, a juvenile corrections facility] . . .

. . . The game belonged to Puppet. (114–15)

In the dream logic that has earlier associated Luis's identity with a ball, the older Rodriguez now expands the analogy to take up a more sophisticated story about turf and its mastery. In this elaborate play upon a field so like the killing fields of Vietnam, with the idea of violent cornering and elimination of rivals—colored like gang colors are—Puppet likewise becomes a canvas in which the nightmarish consequences of veteran status are etched on his own brown body. In the glow of remembrance, Puppet might seem a figure of manly dominance. And yet of course one also notices that, in Rodriguez's retrospective counter-History, it is a white cue ball that drives the violence, whether its origin is in the downtown or that van of white dudes we saw on the beach. And in real terms, of course, neither the paddies nor a Puppet own the game.

V

It's not uncommon in our institutional police histories to think of the LAPD's presence in popular culture as a manifestation of its continuing institutional sponsorship: *Adam-12*, *Hunter*, *T. J. Hooker*—the list is indeed endless. But Wambaugh's influence, working in what I've suggested is a more artisanal, populist, and conflicted vein, is not to be discounted. *Police Story*, for instance, not only had its own spin-offs, imitators, and crime-buster shows staffed by the actors the original show had featured. Wambaugh also established a vision whose influence, sociologist Todd Gitlin tells us, worked its way into the 1980s' *Hill Street Blues* and has remained a benchmark even today.[53] Indeed, Wambaugh's early fiction and television work help explain how Vietnam-style police paramilitarism could be combined, in mass-cultural representations, with a seductive precinct pluralism, a fraternal mystique rooted not in Hawkeye and Chingachgook but in the unique "minorityism" of post-Parker cop culture. In popular fiction, meanwhile, Wambaugh demonstrates how that covert pluralism provides a hubristic counterclaim to the way that, as David Glover and Cora Kaplan have put it, so many contemporary mystery novels continue to rewrite sixties and seventies radicalism as "the thinly disguised criminality of the children of the idle white rich or lumpen black poor." And while we often attribute the jump-cut graininess of cop TV to the technology of the handheld video-cam, in fact it was Wambaugh's *Police Story*, capitalizing on the nonfiction feel of his beat-level chronicles, that brought vérité to illegible dispatch calls, rough-and-tumble car rides, recalcitrant citizens. Looking back, we might see that Wambaugh bequeathed to police melodrama stylistic gestures soon to emerge in True Crime. In the TV series he sponsored, if the streets of LA often look more like Beirut, the criminals that walk them look more like implacable Gothic villains.[54]

Perhaps the most important legacy, however, is that Wambaugh and Rodriguez can be seen, together, to rebut the seductive narrative of police impersonality that now dominates both official and neoconservative remembrances of the LAPD's rise to power. They both demonstrate the codes of class, ethnicity, and race that suffused the Vietnamization of the streets, and how those codes, and the contest they represent, persist despite the cleansing of popular memory the more official LAPD line attempts. But in the ways that these two writers are often mutually incommensurate, they also bring back from history disheartening memories of a spiraling standoff that might well have made the Glass House vision even more potent in its day. Parker's own reading of Watts had its own legacy to bequeath: a renewed commitment to paramilitarism and brutality and intelligence gathering, even more self-appointed minorityism.[55] Blue and brown jackets, blood and memory and Watts, only flowed—as my next two chapters will show—into subsequent decades. The bad western that was Vietnam at home hardly died; indeed it lived on in the populist imaginings of police and gang storytelling, and in the streets themselves.

4

---•---

Hardcovering "True" Crime:
Cop Shops and Crime Scenes in the 1980s

What's black and white and read all over? The answer is true crime.
—*Publisher's Weekly*, 1 June 1990

The hardcover dust jacket for David Simon's *Homicide: A Year on the Killing Streets* (1991) is set in stark production values—indeed the color scheme—that came to be identified with the genre known as True Crime in the 1980s. The book depicts a squad of Baltimore homicide detectives through the course of a calendar year. And yet, as if trying to evoke the criminal violence this squad will face, the book used the trademark red-black-white cover publishers consciously deployed as an audience cue for recognizing the genre: its title is cast in blood red against a black background, in a typeface sharp-edged to the point of Gothic effect.[1] And on the back cover, we find a black-and-white glossy of a man standing in an office door, under a sign that reads HOMICIDE UNIT. The man appears in the workaday yet forceful posture of the police detective: jacketless, sleeves rolled up on a wrinkled button-down shirt, top button undone and tie knot pulled down, a wristwatch standing out prominently on well-shaped, masculine arms. The image is resolute and direct, authoritative in a way befitting its office.

Four decades earlier, this picture (figure 4.1) could easily have been a still photo from *The Naked City*.[2] True Crime descendants of Dan Muldoon and

4.1
Cover photo from David Simon's
Homicide: A Year on the Killing Streets
(Boston: Houghton-Mifflin, 1991).

Jimmy Halloran, the squad of Baltimore homicide detectives depicted in Simon's nonfiction narrative are urban heroes, men burdened with impossible loads of imponderable cases in a largely indifferent metropolis. The photo itself seems to speak of a populist heroism; as in the police procedurals of midcentury, it seems to present not only an everyday cop, but a fictional double of the responsible citizen as well. Police labor thus seems unalienated, returned to civic normalcy, as if stepping away from the excesses of western, LAPD-style paramilitarism: instead, this eastern man is garbed in the attire of white-collar, workaday, hands-on labor. We have a man who seems to embody responsible citizenship, a cop who evinces public duty by standing resolutely at his post. Or so it would seem. For of course, the photo is actually not of a police detective, but of the book's author, the journalist David Simon himself.

Wittingly or not, the photo thus recapitulates a "double-take" that, as my introduction recounts, has haunted the urban crime reporter for over a century. But in the late 1980s, in the superheated climate of True Crime, the implied claim of a secret fraternity (indeed, near equivalence) between journalism and cop knowledge took on a new meaning. As if synthesizing the rhetoric of hard news with the allure of the bodice slasher, True Crime narratives are often said to be "ripped" from headlines, and audiences to "feed" off a fare unabashedly recycled from crime news itself. However secondhand or parasitic the form, the trade category has nevertheless become extraordinarily popular. After what publishers generally describe as a mid-decade take-off point, True Crime garnered some thirty trade imprints by 1990 alone, and consequently earned its own shelf space in the mass-market bookstore. In these years, writers like Joe McGinness, Ann Rule, Jack Olsen, Edna Buchanan, and countless others had risen to the top of bestseller lists, characteristically by penning tales of brutal (often domestic) violence, serial murder, and the disruption of otherwise normal communities—a formula some see as a downscale, pop documentary adaptation of Truman Capote's *In Cold Blood* (1965). Spinning off television exposure, moving faster in the paperback market, and selling as both a front- and backlist phenomenon, True Crime was the signature category of the new blockbuster book climate, itself super-heated by media mogul acquisitions in print and electronic media.

One could easily forget that Simon had originally been a humble *Baltimore Sun* crime reporter who had spent a year as an official police intern to research his book (the *Publisher's Weekly* joke, after all, used to refer to newspapers). A sign of a new crossover climate, however, was that *Homicide* won prizes in mystery categories normally reserved for fiction, and then, of course, became the basis for director Barry Levinson's Emmy Award–winning NBC series.[3] Given this track record, it was not surprising that Simon's book was quickly followed by two similar accounts, also by prizewinning reporters, that blurred the line between cop and pop: *Crime Scene: On the Streets with a Rookie Police Reporter* (1992), by *New York Newsday*'s Mitch Gelman, and *The Cop Shop: True Crime on the Streets of Chicago* (1993), by Robert Blau of the *Chicago Tribune*. Again, the cue for these books was a grisly firsthand encounter not so much with crime, but with crime scenes. For its jacket, Blau's book presented readers with a photo of a police shakedown of gang-bangers against a wall scrawled upon with graffiti. If Simon's colors were suitably neogothic, Blau's were police blue and gray. Gelman's *Crime Scene*, meanwhile, used a Weegee-like overhead photo of a chalk outline on a city sidewalk, with a lone cop facing bystanders; the photo was then bisected by yellow police line tape (see figures 4.2 and 4.3). Indeed, in mass-market books, the police tape seemed to be everywhere: in testimonials by police officers like E. W. Counts's *Cop Talk: True Detective Stories from the N.Y.P.D.* (1994) or Chicago professor

4.2
Cover photo from Robert Blau's
*The Cop Shop: True Crime on the
Streets of Chicago* (Reading, Ma.:
Addison-Wesley Pub. Co., 1993).

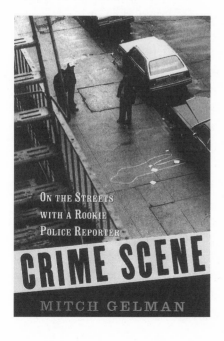

4.3
Cover photo from Mitch Gelman,
*Crime Scene: On the Streets with a
Rookie Police Reporter* (New York:
Times Books, 1992).

Connie Fletcher's *What Cops Know* (1991); in exposés of police corruption, like *New York Daily News* reporter Mike McAlary's *Good Cop/Bad Cop* (1994); in books that presented themselves as case files of brutal homicides, like Ann Rule's Crime Files series; in other reporter narratives like Edna Buchanan's *The Corpse Had a Familiar Face* (1987). On prime-time TV or the syndicated live-action cop TV shows, meanwhile, police officers were now viewed over the shoulder in their squad cars, scrutinized at the point of making arrests, or reimagined as locked in battle (or in interrogation rooms) with seemingly irremediable and often "low-life" foes.

To date, of course, books categorized as True Crime have been attacked for their voyeurism and sensationalism. Criminologists have been quick to point out, for instance, that True Crime offers a terribly unrepresentative look at American violence. It is clearly a murder-based genre; it overempha-sizes female victims, older victims, and—intriguingly—white offenders and white victims.[4] Cultural studies discussions of True Crime, meanwhile, have focused almost exclusively on the staple serial killer narratives that often dom-inate sales. The popularity of this subvariant, and thus of True Crime as a whole, has been attributed largely to public hysteria about crime rates in the 1980s, to the propaganda efforts of local and federal forces (notably the new visibility of FBI profiling of serial killers)—and, perhaps most of all, to the enduring power of gothic literary conventions. True Crime, it is often said, plays to readers' seemingly insatiable appetites for villains of motiveless ma-lignity, normal-seeming monsters who make readers grateful for their ordi-nary lives: in sum, a killers-next-door thrill based in sex, violence, and voyeur-ism. At the same time, of course, hyperbolicizing crime is often taken to be synonymous with supporting a generalized law enforcement ethos. As Robin Anderson has suggested, cop TV itself seems little more than an updated version of the propagandistic crime-busting shows of yesteryear, simply recal-ibrated to the Reagan-Bush war on drugs. The case history format common to these shows and novels, moreover, is often said to give readers the comforting illusion of police expertise.[5]

These critical commentaries all represent valuable work. To be sure, a book like *Homicide*—set in Edgar Allan Poe's adopted hometown, depicting a possible serial crime itself, and organized by case and chronology—resonated deeply with many of the conventions critics have described.[6] And yet, our criticism has been far better at demonstrating the gothic or crime-buster precedents of these books and their eerie postmodern redundancies than at articulating their relationship to contemporary urban crime and its actual policing.[7] In fact, beneath all the hype, all the attention devoted to serial criminology and pop profiling, and all the critical absorption with the Ted Bundys and the Jeffrey Dahmers, was an even more mundane yet quite startling paradox about the emergence of True Crime in the post-Vietnam decades. And that was that at almost the precise moment when police labor seemed to acquire this startling new visibility in American mass culture, metropolitan law enforcement in the United States reached what was arguably, since Prohibition, its nadir in terms of effectiveness and public esteem. Ironically, our often exclusive focus on voyeuristic, propagandistic, and case-study elements of True Crime—all commonly lumped into a generalized category of "policing" discourse—has tended, I think, to obscure our understanding of what policing actually came to mean in the years that saw both urban deindustrialization and the draining of news markets as well. That is, the very conditions of urban life not only made True Crime possible, but shaped the political fables it often told to American audiences.

It is in this more prosaic light that the books by Simon, Blau, and Gelman, in particular, offer a unique opportunity to readjust our view. Focused in a nearly naturalistic way upon the politics and practice of metropolitan policing during the decades when LAPD-style paramilitarism ran head on into budget cuts, bureaucratic intransigence, and white flight from the inner city, each book speaks of a growing urban malaise about policing and the men left to the task. Second, each is to a greater or lesser degree a journalist's memoir, an account of an apprenticeship in crime reporting that begins and ends at the seat of police power in its day. More to the point, these books provide an inside account of what tabloidization really meant in the decades long after Mark Hellinger put the *News* to bed. And finally, each book offers itself, again with greater or lesser degrees of explicitness, as a form of political confessional, rehearsing what we might call a 1980s clash of posts and dispositions: the encounter of young liberal reporters, in the twilight years of Reagan-Bush America, with the supposed pathology of our inner cities. In other words, as memoirs of both the harvesting of headlines and the killing in the streets, they help us understand the cultural fields that generated True Crime in the first place. Indeed, by putting street crime in a self-consciously political register, these books implicitly offered to "out-true" mainline True Crime itself.[8]

This final dimension is also what will allow us to move slightly away from the model of reading that our criticism on the serial killer often presumes.

Instead, I will suggest we might well read True Crime books as "entertainments" not only in the sense that they generate compulsive viewing—as modeled by the fan of serial killer narrative—or how they offer spin control for modern law enforcement agencies. Rather, we need to regard them as narratives that draw upon a much broader set of cultural and political values, "as if" political fantasies by citizens beyond the private consumerism that the voyeurism model often rehearses. All along, my argument will be, in fact, that *Homicide* and the books by Gelman and Blau might best be described *not* as exposés—though this is the tradition they invoke—but essentially as literary hybrids: pop-culture ethnographies of modern police departments combining conventions from professional autobiography, political confessional, and crime news itself. In this way, they help us understand the *relations* among seemingly disparate cultural trends.[9] My first two sections will thus take up the contemporary, post-Vietnam history of news writing and policing that shaped these writers' apprenticeship; the third, their own account of the political dimensions of their initiation. My fourth part will then turn more directly to their portrait of police culture and consciousness.

A covert entertainment of these reporter stories, I am suggesting, may not be solely in their attention to crime. And that is because, even as they convey their grisly fare, these books also present themselves as liberal-realist initiation narratives, political stories of baptism into an urban, street-smart wisdom mediated by the fraternal work culture (and inertia) of police power in the 1980s. Ultimately, then, I want to explore how the cultural poetics of this True Crime variant resonated within the larger field of power in urban politics—specifically, to show how, reengaging a populist root already present in police culture, this genre covertly fashioned a rapprochement between liberal realism and an emergent neoconservative ethos. In this reading, True Crime becomes a kind of crucible and vehicle for what Stuart Hall, Lawrence Grossberg, and others have denominated the authoritarian populism or popular conservatism emergent in the 1980s. In my final section, therefore, I want to reconstruct the complex of ideas about class, ethnicity, and race that these books entertain. Specifically, I will argue that they entertain an imaginative engagement by these liberals with the sense of powerlessness among urban Catholic, working-class white ethnics, the figures for whom cops might be said only to stand as surrogates.

Indeed, the true prototypes for this allegory about a mutually alienated citizenry and police are not so much Capote and other new journalists of decades past, but the multigenre field of urban police populism I have described in earlier chapters. That is, even in their most dismal of assessments of police ineffectiveness—indeed, almost now taken as a badge of martyrdom—they often return to representing policing as the labor of a dedicated, hard-bitten knight of the city. Moreover, wittingly or not, these books document why urban journalism as a cultural field became so captivated with this populist posture—the "double take" both covered over and betrayed by their True Crime, pop-cop packaging (such as Simon's photo). In the decades they strove to portray, however, this emulation (or, as in the midcentury procedural, a simulation) could only be an increasingly defensive posture. We might therefore expand my *Publisher's Weekly* epigraph into a joke with a broader range of reference. That is, if we recognize that the joke alludes not just to blood on the page, but to the standard slang for a police car, and even more inadvertently to one field of contemporary race relations—then, in these larger senses, True Crime really *can* seem "black and white" all over.

I

In their typically extravagant blurbs from the likes of Pat Conroy, Studs Terkel, William Kennedy, and Nicholas Pileggi, Simon, Blau, and Gelman's books were originally hyped as gritty, realist portraits of a new American underside. They garnered authenticity, in part, because they were written in (as Blau's title signaled) the so-called cop shops, those news bureaus housed in police precincts that have, for over a century, typically provided the base camp for crime reporting. As if evoking this dateline tradition, the print of Gelman's book even reverted to the look of the old-fashioned typewriter, while Blau's led each chapter with a news clip or headline. And indeed, each book presented a dismal urban prospect: rust-belt cities faced with fiscal stagnation, bred of corporate, white, and middle-class flight; police forces experiencing shortages of manpower and of public respect; inner-city neighborhoods devastated by poverty, drug use, and record-setting homicide rates. The publicity for each book, meanwhile, resurrected a long-standing stylistic convention of the hard-boiled news memoir: paralleling the rookie reporter's initiation into the streets, and his supposed loss of innocence, with the fall and shame of American cities.[10] And yet, what was also striking about these books was that they were *not* simply exposés of machine politics or police corruption, in the vein of Peter Maas's *Serpico* (1973) or Robert Daley's

Prince of the City (1978), much less Lincoln Steffens's famous benchmark for the form, *Shame of the Cities* (1904). On the contrary, these 1980s reporters seemed curiously attracted to the heroic if weakening spectacle of literal police work, to police power in its most fundamental, routine form—at precisely the moment that power seemed to stall and wither. We need to better understand, then, how these cop shop books—intrinsically, as it were, border narratives between the news and law enforcement—registered changes in the power relations in *both* fields.

Because so many True Crime authors are former reporters, the genre is often seen as a mere spin-off from the tabloidization of crime news in our time. But to rephrase a point media critic Jon Katz has made about cop TV, it was more accurate to say that True Crime entered into a terrain where crime news itself now often feared to tread. In the 1970s and 1980s, to begin with, the news field was deeply unsettled both within its own professional norms and in its relation to traditional audiences. Urban deindustrialization, that is, impacted not only the fiscal well-being of cities, nor even simply the staffing and funding of police departments, but the structure of news markets as well.[11] Just as American municipalities now faced white flight, eroding tax bases, and the unsettling of white-ethnic political machines, urban newspapers had similarly found themselves in competition for ever-dwindling audiences at the precise moment crime rates began to escalate. To take but one example: in Philadelphia, Anthony Smith reports, total local circulation had already dropped from 1,643,000 in 1960 to 1,223,000 by 1975.[12] Though readers abandoning newspapers were counted among the young—from those eighteen to thirty-four—the effect was also particularly pronounced among working-class readers, upon whom (as I've shown in chapter 2) the tabloids in particular had built their base. As one contradiction not a few observers noted, the sensational harvesting of crime might have actually given one's audience more reason to depart the city. Changes in the institutional character of tabloids, however, went deeper than this irony.[13]

As is often the case in large-scale business, deindustrialization had profoundly "delocalizing" effects on news production, opening up, as it does, local establishments to external control. Dwindling news markets had been accompanied by a flurry of chain building, consolidation, and absentee ownership, much of it fueled by opportunities created by new information technologies. In the 1970s and after, corporate conglomerates and media moguls had tried, in the main, to diversify their holdings in the news business and, through that diversification, provide a cushion against future economic down-turns. The result was that larger companies both expanded their hold upon a range of markets, and readership constituencies, by buying papers in several cities at once, while at the same time extending these papers' reach into more affluent suburban areas. Thus, what could look like a resurgence of local com-petition and tabloid news in the city was partly generated by forces outside the city limits. Here the migration of the previously suburban *Long Island Newsday* into New York City in 1985, hoping to strike a niche between the tabloid *Post* and the *Daily News* (and compete with the more upscale *New York Times*), was telling. (*Newsday* was where Mitch Gelman would apprentice.) Despite being greeted as a brash newcomer in Manhattan, *Newsday* was actu-ally owned by the Times Mirror company of Los Angeles, which had engaged in buying up newspapers for years. (In southern California, it had done so in order to stifle competition with its own *Los Angeles Times*.)

It is virtually impossible to synopsize the musical chairs of ownership in the news field in these years, but even at the older tabloids absentee ownership became the rule, not the exception. The *Post* had been owned by Rupert Murdoch until the early 1980s, when it was taken over by a real estate devel-oper; Mark Hellinger's former employer, the *Daily News*, was now owned by the Chicago-based Tribune Company. David Simon's *Baltimore Sun*, its esteemed Menckenian tradition notwithstanding, was in fact also owned by Times Mirror at this time. Times Mirror had already bragged it would make the *Sun* the most modern computerized paper of the day, and made explicit its plans to extend the paper's reach into suburban markets. We are a long way from the local and largely partisan field of Stephen Crane's 1890s—indeed, a long way even from those days, as Pete Hamill has pointed out, when the tabloids of the 1920s serviced their largely immigrant constituencies with their own populist style.[14]

As Hamill also notes, on the scene and in the cop shop, absentee or con-glomerate ownership paradoxically meant intensive managerial oversight and an emphasis on cost-cutting technological innovation.[15] Gelman, for instance, mentions in passing how even following up assignments was now predicated on getting budget approval via computer terminal, either for individual stories or what were now called "pak" tales, stories bunched around a single crime.[16] Thus while *Newsday* made its splash in New York, for example, by hiring away seasoned reporters from older tabloids—Jimmy Breslin, Hamill, and others—truer to pattern, it also hired on a new, college-educated breed (like

Gelman) more at home in this high-tech environment and more in synch with the upscale audiences advertisers actually coveted. To some, this meant absentee owners were matched with news gatherers wholly unfamiliar with the tabloid's clientele. A covert generational war ensued, setting the stage for the kind of memoir rookies like Gelman and Blau would write. Yet *New York Times* columnist Bob Herbert was hardly alone when he turned up his nose at the invasion of his own trade by the upscale, yuppie staffers at papers like *Newsday* who "know next to nothing about the real lives of the people they purport to cover."[17]

This seemingly internecine, professional squabble therefore spoke to the audiences—particularly the class and geographical location of those audiences—journalists purported to be serving. It is a bit misleading, as a result, to describe tabloidization in the 1980s as a return to the style the 1920s made famous, since the link between tabloids and their constituencies was being reformed. Conservative hand-wringing, and even the phrase "tabloid TV," can be quite misleading on this score. This polemical headline, as it were, has tended to disguise the fact that many of the newspaper chains sponsoring local tabloids had actually begun, simultaneously, to turn away from hardcore crime news in other markets. Simultaneously, that is, they began aiming at what their advertisers clearly wanted: more highly educated, suburban, younger, and upscale readers—after all, like *Newsday*'s original Long Island clientele.

Computer typesetting—not the older typeface within Gelman's book at all—also made possible the creation of zoned editions keyed to different municipal districts ("boutique" marketing). The same computerization that allowed news gathering itself to be more closely managed from above, in other words, also allowed papers like, say, the *Los Angeles Times* itself to try to extend their local dominance by producing multiple regional editions, a strategy soon evident *within* city limits.[18] A book like Blau's *Cop Shop* therefore shows a city in which the old tradition of reporters racing to meet multiple deadlines had been replaced by a single, 9:30 P.M. cutoff for an edition that would then be modified in *production*. (Blau's *Chicago Tribune* had nine such zoned editions as early as 1980.) And according to Anthony Smith, these zones were explicitly "designed not to cut across blue-collar and upper-middle-class neighborhoods," because publishers wanted each edition to create a feeling of "hometownness" among its otherwise segmented readers.[19] Computer typesetting even allowed some papers to remove crime news from certain zoned editions.

(As it were, crime news redlining. Another key development had been to challenge grassroots community newspapers, a phenomenon I touch briefly upon in chapter 5.)[20]

Here and there, a few commentators at the time seemed aware that *Newsday*'s arrival in New York City could mean several different things. At first, there were the complaints about the resurgence of the tabloid wars; recurrently, legitimate complaints about the invasion of absentee-owner, bottom-line journalism. Over time, when some saw that the flirtation with tabloid news (in publications with more upscale aspirations) actually could not last, nostalgia for the tabloids' original urban aura set in. But for now, the important point is that crime news stories in the 1980s, and hence True Crime itself, were not simple manifestations of a return to supposedly traditional sensationalism. Rather, again as Katz's model suggests, it is more accurate to say that the same quest for high profit margins that would fuel the blockbuster book climate, and help to create True Crime, simultaneously found its way into the news trade. Yet because tabloidization would be relatively short lived, and the urban segmentation of news so pronounced, newspaper chains eventually had the effect of creating a series of cultural vacuums that True Crime itself would try to fill.[21] Books like Simon's, Blau's, and Gelman's are thus not merely crime stories. Rather, as I will suggest in subsequent sections, they are also partly stories of an evacuation, retrospective accounts of how upscale tabloidization actually disguised a more desperate segmentation within and between urban and suburban, white- and blue-collar audiences. Thus, it is not surprising that these books rehearse that segmentation autobiographically: that is, within their personal accounts of news gathering as a profession.

II

Meanwhile, another crucial dimension of True Crime's genesis was taking place on the cop side of the cop shop. For as I have said, in the aftermath of the standoff in the streets in the 1960s, the post-Vietnam decades were a period in which metropolitan police departments, particularly in these larger rust-belt cities, found themselves faced with fiscal crises, resurgent scandals and public ridicule, and of course escalating crime rates that, quite simply put, made it seem as if the police were out of answers.[22]

Reform itself had seemingly ground to a standstill. To be sure, there had been modest gains made, from the mid-1960s to the mid-1980s, in the educational level of police officers, in hiring women and some minorities, in decentralization (e.g., establishing local district substations), and in favoring community mobilization over reactive policing. Several cities, such as New York, Houston, and Detroit, also took important steps against the use of deadly force by the police. A few departments, mainly in western cities, were moderately successful in incorporating civilians into police bureaucracies, thereby also addressing citizen mistrust.

The more pervasive pattern, however, was that police departments had generally stopped growing and, in many respects, stopped changing. Especially in the Northeast, where per capita spending on crime control was nearly double what it was in other regions in 1980, police found themselves bogged down by the notorious fiscal crises of the late 1970s and a virtual collapse of public support. New York neither hired nor trained any new police officers from July 1975 to November 1979, and then scrambled in the 1980s to overcome an age, experience, and management gap that only led to further problems on the force. This stagnation only worsened the general isolation of departments from their rapidly changing cities by reinforcing the historic mismatching of white-ethnic departments with their constituencies. In Chicago, Blau notes, residency requirements had only forced many cops into white-ethnic enclaves, beyond the inner city albeit legally inside municipal limits.[23] At the start of the 1970s, the percentage of police who were nonwhite was one-third of that in the general population in Gelman's New York; one-fifth in Boston; one-sixth in Simon's Baltimore. By the mid-1990s, the profile was only moderately better, as affirmative action on police forces struggled to keep pace with the new electoral power of nonwhites. Even Chicago, which made some headway in the early 1970s, by the mid-1990s still had a police department that was two-thirds white in a city whose population was only 38 percent white.[24]

We need to remember, as well, that police corruption, yet another sign of stagnation, grabbed the headlines in these years well before violent crime did. Until murder rates ballooned in the late 1980s, ideas about how to improve police effectiveness took a backseat to various now-well-known corruption scandals rivaling even those of the Gilded Age: in Chicago starting in 1972, in Philadelphia in 1973, in New York—well, most infamously in the early seventies, and then about every other year through the 1980s.[25] These dismal stories of kickbacks, brutality, and discrimination are all by now quite familiar tales. But in fact, the telling feature of these scandals was not only how extensive or implicitly sanctioned corruption was, as New York's Knapp Commission so notoriously declared. Nor was it merely that new technological devices—for instance, the stun gun—had only escalated the potential for new styles of police brutality. Rather, what was telling was how immune corruption now seemed to the familiar panaceas of professionalization offered up in the midcentury's "second wave."

The experience in New York, particularly under self-styled reformers like its police commissioner Benjamin Ward, was exemplary. Initially, for example, following the Knapp Commission report of chronic "grazing" by precinct officers, police reformers in New York had tried to reduce the chances of payoffs to beat cops by turning away from street sweeps and low-level drug arrests. But over time this had only seemed to sanction an ever-expanding drug trade. No surprise, then, that street sweeps would return.[26] In the face of such reversals, the familiar tools of professional reform took on the look of a management shuffle one step behind the crime: for instance, transferring supervisory personnel, or insisting upon drug testing or lie detector tests— all ventured by commissioners like Ward. These strategies withered not only because of bureaucratic inertia, but because, in many cases, the crime-busting pros had actually been the leading criminals in the department. The Knapp Commission's own conclusions reflected this dismal fact. In Frank Serpico's NYPD, just as in the Chicago scandals of the mid-1970s, elite plainclothesmen were the key links to payoffs, and some of the most corrupt cops were also the most skilled crime busters in the department. In Chicago, it was not the rookie who might be better professionalized, but the career vice cop squads that been the seedbed of extortion; in *Prince of the City* Robert Leuci's case, it was NYPD's Special Investigative Squad that *itself* came under investigation, turning into a case that produced over fifty indictments in a squad of approximately seventy officers.[27] Spreading personnel to new precincts could mean only dispersing corruption to new venues.

In such contexts it is not surprising that, in the estimate of many police analysts—Robert Fogelson, Samuel Walker, Jerome Skolnick, and others— reform of police management and patrol had nearly come to a standstill in the late 1970s and early 1980s. Though the tendency was to blame dwindling urban resources, many factors had contributed to stagnation: the precipitous rise in the cost of policing, in part due to police benevolent association gains, which only led to labor conflict when the fiscal crises struck; the intransigence of police bureaucracies in responding to outside recommendations, including riot commission reports, in the late 1960s and onward; and, of course, the riots themselves, which only seemed to increase police defensiveness and further legitimate paramilitarization of police command (Daryl Gates's new resolve after Watts being the notorious example). Traditional appeals for civilian oversight also seemed futile. Many so-called civilian review boards were actually staffed by police employees or mayoral appointees; by the mid-1970s the general consensus was that, seriously underfunded and ignored, most of these boards had proved to be mere window dressing. They became a lost cause of groups like the ACLU and NAACP, organizations themselves under conservative attack. Joseph Wambaugh, for one, tells us much about how frontline cops viewed the entire notion of Glass House review to begin with, much less civilian oversight.

Of course, as I've already suggested in chapter 3, this history of post-Vietnam stagnation would be turned to neoconservative conclusions and must be approached guardedly. As Walker, Jack Greene, Skolnick, and others have pointed out, reform experimentation was still sporadically under way. Partial solutions from a return to foot patrol, to so-called problem-solving policing that designed tactics in response to community complaints, and to so-called team policing all received attention from the late 1970s to mid-1980s. (In this final strategy, endorsed by a presidential commission in 1967, integrated teams of police subdivisions, like vice and homicide, were delegated to concentrate on single zones of the city and encouraged to coordinate their crime-busting tactics.) Likewise, the much-hyped and various cause of community policing (discussed in chapter 5) *was* on the horizon by the mid-1980s, though mainly in smaller cities.

But in many an observer's estimation, these experiments were very slow to germinate, largely due to resistance by middle-level managers, by unions concerned about unequal workloads, and, again, by a bureaucratic intransigence that one study compared to trying to bend granite. At first, the notion that police officers should return to a less paramilitary, more generalist approach—which many saw merely as a return to foot patrol, or even to one-man patrol cars—hardly received a warm welcome from the ranks, let alone from unions or upper management. Many cops were still likely to see foot patrol as a downgrading of their work, and forms of community outreach as not real police work at all. Contrary to the experimental spirit that analysts like Skolnick now found in places like Detroit, Santa Ana, or Houston, many other departments seemed instead to cling to conventional response-to-call policing. Even Wambaugh's mythologizing of the beat, after all, reflected this very same intransigence: Bumper Morgan thinks being a cop is putting people in jail. In all, these patterns suggested a subtle synergy between computer-assisted news gathering of crime and police retrenchment.[28]

Of course, the chalk outlines and killing streets that would litter True Crime in subsequent years cannot be laid solely at the feet of police intransigence or futility; too many other factors (the crack cocaine economy, deindustrialization itself, structural unemployment, and more) were at play.[29] Nevertheless, the stagnation within police culture did breed a more subtle and destructive reciprocity between the streets—that is, these same causes of crime—and everyday police tactics than has commonly been recognized. That is, it was not only in how crime occurred, but in how it was responded to.

As Stephen Mastrofski has suggested, the insurgent neoconservative interest in proactive defense of street order, when combined with technological changes in police management itself, had itself subtly altered the dynamics of street policing. The supposed turn against crime busting, which neoconservatives would say marks the post-Vietnam era, in fact isn't quite what was happening. Rather, many departments seemed to move less *against* response-to-call strategies and more toward *refining* them, in particular by computer-assisted stacking and prioritization of citizen calls. In the same way, Mastrofski argues, the facilitation of onboard computer checks, for example, in those black and whites, tended to enhance not simple order maintenance, but the crime-busting proactive policing that the LAPD made infamous—particularly in so-called "pretext" busts that then turn up prior violations and lead to arrest. (The computer, as it were, sweeps the street for you.) And meanwhile, with increasing public pressure, from the 1980s onward, to criminalize and increase the severity of punishment for activities such as drunk driving, spousal abuse, drug abuse, and prostitution, the crucial point was that the boundary between order maintenance and crime busting was actually blurring—or rather each was absorbing the other. What was left was a hollow shell of the administrative approach to crime that I have described in earlier chapters. If anything, if UCR reports were deemphasized, it was only to discount their usefulness as a way to measure the success of what began to be called "fear control" programs. But how the effectiveness of these programs *was* to be measured was not clear.[30]

Another quite fatalistic twist on crime-busting efficiency measurements was especially telling in this regard: the so-called clearance rate.* Many police departments in our time, of course, have become fully cognizant that effective crime busting can actually lead to the appearance of higher crime *rates*, which can then be used against them by a cost-conscious public and publicity-conscious mayors. Many departments have fallen back, therefore, on the in-house emphasis on clearance rates—which, as we'll see, Simon emphasizes—notably for homicide detectives. And yet, even leaving aside how low some of these rates became in the 1980s, the clearance rate was a rather ambiguous index of the relationship of police consciousness to their work.[31] At one level a sign of public pressure for greater efficiency and productivity, at another it reflected a reactionary, artisanal, and (in Skolnick's older terms) administrative insistence upon control over one's labor—in many instances, degenerating into a unilateral *police* decision on when a case was closed. The irony was that crime busting thus retained its in-house glamour, even found itself reinforced by the seemingly antithetical insistence on order maintenance. And internally, of course, the clearance rate remains the sole measure of your work: busting a crime.

As if all of this wasn't bad enough, the opening up of police departments to academic scrutiny, such as I describe in chapter 3, had in some ways backfired. That is, there had developed a certain destructive byplay between the new social-science scrutiny of the police on the one hand and traditional bureaucratic and artisanal intransigence in cop culture on the other. And its fatalism. The immediate result was that considerable doubt had been cast on the effectiveness of almost any standard patrol practice in combating crime.

Police themselves continued to point to the need for increased manpower, better automobile coverage, saturation patrolling, and improved rapid response times. But as Jerome Skolnick rather breezily summarized it in 1986, all these time-honored police strategies seemed to have little or no effect on public satisfaction *or* on crime rates, much less on the violent crimes that now terrified Americans most. As Greene ironically surmised at the time, the main refrain emerging from academic scrutiny, from the left and the right, was

---

*A clearance rate is the percentage of crimes that a police department feels it has closed (in most cases, solved). Department divisions often assign cases to detective teams that then have their efficiency monitored, though some cases (for instance, drug-related homicides) are notoriously difficult to clear. From the police vantage point, a cleared case, of course, need not result in a conviction in court, though certainly closed cases can be reopened (e.g., by political pressure, confession, or new evidence).

that *"nothing worked."* A typical example was the Rand Corporation report on criminal investigation practices from the mid-1970s. This report found, for instance, that only about three percent of arrests for what are called index crimes—"serious crime against unwilling victims"—appeared to result from special investigative efforts. Contrary to the romance of the police procedural or television melodrama, studies like the Rand report showed, the vast majority of crimes were solved by incidental factors like immediate apprehension or witness identification; that investigators spent more time in postarrest processing than in apprehending a suspect; that matches of latent prints with known offender files were rarely even attempted because they were so notoriously ineffective. Such findings, as Skolnick put it, were virtually "devastating" to how policing had been conceived since midcentury, and policing seemed "bankrupt" in more ways than one.[32] Clearly what had also happened was that the discrediting of public civility, in books like Reiss's *The Police and the Public*, had now become a pretext for the hand-in-glove grasp between public relations and sterile order maintenance. As Greene has argued, academic scrutiny had both put more emphasis on measurements of productivity (like those clearance rates) and at the same time turned many a department toward new tactics in managing public perception, largely through controlling disorderly behavior. But there is also a sense in which social-science measurement, falling back upon these appeals to community perception and fear reduction instead of crime rates that refused to budge, had already granted too much ground to the discourse of public relations.[33] One will feel this standoff between command spin control and cop labor in my True Crime narratives: Simon's Baltimore, for instance, would have one of these showcase programs aimed at public perception of crime. His cops, however, disdain any mention of it. They're too focused on "true" crime.[34]

This was only one of the ways in which the genre by that name carried forth the more traditional conventions of the cop shop; in the world True Crime makes manifest, all is still 911. But it was not merely that True Crime duplicated some of the bad habits of the news trade, and the policing, that had fostered it. More precisely, the genre reflected the disjunctures generated by the reshuffling of cultural posts and police power: upwardly mobile, college-educated professionals mimicking the men in stagnant police bureaucracies; tabloid news gathering riding its computer circuits, but perhaps short-circuiting its traditional audience; young True Crime writers on the trail of murder scenes while some of the police, quite wittingly, were actually scanning the streets in quite another way. And as I will show, even the fiscal crisis of the 1970s circles back into the political entertainment of these books in unsettling ways. Inevitably, True Crime inherited some of the contradictions of its writers' own fluid cultural location—and indeed, some of the chaos of the streets themselves, byways many among the police felt they could no longer save.

III

At least since the mid–nineteenth century, when newspapers first posted themselves at police station houses, reporters' memoirs have traditionally been initiation narratives. At one level they are tutorial memoirs, professional stories that serve potentially to inspire aspiring reporters as well as educate the general middle-class reader. Even before Steffens's *Autobiography*—and later, in memoirs by Russell Baker, Harrison Salisbury, Pete Hamill, and many others—these books have told the story of a neophyte's initiation into the group mentality of the cop shop, usually described as a baptism into a cynical, hard-boiled, and often hard-drinking world. Typically, the lessons of formal education are supplanted by the tutelage of the street, disillusioning encounters with incrementally more grisly crime scenes. Along the way, the reporter's progress is often registered by his acquisition of the hard-boiled gallows humor of the cop shop; as Stephen Crane's contemporary Vance Thompson put it in the 1890s, the police reporter's daily lesson is the "fall of man." In time, however, his fall proves to be fortunate, as he succeeds an older generation too hardened by routine to serve any longer as the public's witness; the profession of journalism is thus renewed. These generic conventions underwrite the *habitus* within a professional field like journalism, the persisting "second sense" or "feel for the game" that becomes the cop shop's cultural residue.[35]

Gelman's *Crime Scene* and Blau's *Cop Shop* conform most closely to this pattern. Recounting a twenty-six-year-old's first year in tabloid reporting as the fulfillment of a boyhood dream,[36] Gelman's book tells the story of a rookie breaking into the ranks of tabloid journalism at *Newsday* in 1988. The book casts its rookie persona as potentially an inheritor to Steffens, Hamill, and Breslin, rising through "shoe leather" in a world where the crime beat still "drove the daily paper," an American witness who becomes gradually so inured to record-breaking violence that he decides to move on.[37] Told by an editor to eliminate all conjunctions from his writing for a probationary year, the rookie earns the hard-boiled nickname of Bulldog along the way.[38] *The Cop Shop* likewise covers a three-year apprenticeship in crime reporting (starting in 1988), focusing especially on the Chicago Police Department's attempts to cope with drug- and gang-related crime. Like Gelman's book, Blau's was marketed as a True Crime underground voyage, up close and personal with police incompetence and his own growing indifference. Though Blau describes his beat as less driven by the police blotter and New York–style tabloidism, he too claims to have resurrected what he calls "staircase reporting" from the inertia of old-timers who no longer even visited a crime scene.[39] A by-product of a sabbatical from crime reporting for the *Baltimore Sun*, Simon's *Homicide* follows a third-person story of a year-in-the-work life (again, 1988) of a shift of that city's homicide detectives. Simon is sure to offer a few asides that let us know that daily newspapers are actually out of touch with what his book documents;[40] the obvious claim is that the reporter need not tell his own story, since the proof of his education is in the literary pudding.

Claiming to go beyond these routine reflexes, and hence behind the news, thus itself becomes part of the generic pattern. If neither *Crime Scene* nor *The Cop Shop* offers itself as an exposé, they do take on the scandals of their own profession. Gelman, for example, shows how the aforementioned managerial monitoring of story selection curtailed his occasional efforts to follow stories with a more progressive angle. His editorial superiors are ever-present in the narrative, ensuring a high-pressure harvesting of police reports, graphic picture copy, and headline-grabbing quotes. Blau offers a slightly different but equally dispiriting picture of his own news climate. "Nearly everyone was tiring of cheap crime," Blau writes, "crime that happened daily, in the places it always did,"[41] a phenomenon Simon implicitly attributes to the Baltimore press as well. In the stratified and zoned news market of these years, it seems that young reporters could be faced with (at least) two equally unappetizing alternatives: the deadening, relentless harvesting of crime, oddity, and perversion, or—worse yet?—simple ignoring of urban violence, on the grounds that it had become so routine it was no longer news.

Meanwhile, these books demonstrate how the aura of inexplicability that crime often acquires is actually reinforced by the hit-and-run habits of news conventions themselves. As a great deal of media analysis has shown, these practices dictate that the news usually does little to seek out the causes of a crime, much less stay through to its verdict in court.[42] Blau and Gelman also come to recognize that the status of the victim often dictates the *amount* of coverage given a violent crime. Beyond always being on the lookout for the tabloid hook of oddity—say, as Gelman observes, a man killed by a bayonet[43]—they recognize that news stories with "legs"[44] or "wings"[45] are stories with white, white-female, upper-class, or "innocent" (often meaning young) victims. By contrast, stories of minority gang members with long police records have started to seem less newsworthy. ("[B]lack and Hispanic teenagers were dying by the score," Blau writes, [and] "there didn't seem to be any way to keep their memories alive. Too many had fallen from grace to make big news").[46]

Again, some of this may well be a reflection of police fatalism and shifting priorities. In Blau's account, police withhold gang-bangers' names for fear they will see themselves as celebrities. In Simon's book—as so often in a Joseph Wambaugh novel—juries' understanding of legal requirements are distorted by expectations set by television courtroom dramas. In all three books the police seem especially wary of the spotlight of media attention, yet aware that their own resource management is partly dictated by anticipation of the very same thing. That is, what in Blau's police department is called a "heater" case,[47] and in Simon's a "red ball,"[48] generates manpower assignments not because of its intrinsic difficulty, but because of the potential headlines it will generate. As Blau's cops put it, "The media decide what's important and what's not—not us."[49] Simon similarly tells the story of a fourteen-year-old shot down "without any apparent motive as he walked home from his job at a fast-food restaurant."[50] Newswriters, like the Baltimore cops themselves, immediately recognize that the case is a red ball because of its *story* potential as a social allegory. Not unlike in Crane or Hellinger's day, "true" crime is a static player, a threat to normative citizenship.

True to convention, this dispiriting portrait of the news trade is accompanied by a foiling to the old-timers of the profession, too inside the game to see what ails them. The physical setting of the cop shop sets the tone. Blau, for instance, depicts his cop shop as a decrepit building, saddled with an out-of-date communication system, and most of all, populated by men of the old school.[51] His predecessor had been called "the Commish" by the detectives themselves, and would be given a funeral the police normally reserved for a fallen comrade.[52] Blau portrays himself, by contrast, as a "short Jewish guy from New York" who only knows cops from TV.[53] Established journalists are also portrayed as the bearers of the double-edged cynicism that rookies both aspire to, as a mark of initiation, and fear as a sign of professional malaise. Blau, for instance, is advised by an old-timer to " '[m]ake 'em laugh, make 'em cry' . . . [to] showcase the facts that awakened readers' greatest fears."[54] Gelman similarly associates old-timers with deadlines, bookies, and booze. These are men who are not college educated; Gelman finds himself called "Joe College" by old-timers, and feels ostracized for his "California" looks.[55] Gelman too introduces an old-timer who, like Blau's Commish, actually looks like a cop.[56]

Initially, Blau and Gelman seem ready to use this narrative foiling as the opening gambit in an eventual story of professional upward mobility. Even as more mature, retrospective narrators, they seem inescapably the young professionals whom old-timers like Bob Herbert resented. They feel guilty about their personal priorities[57] yet often track how much ink their stories generate.[58] Initially, Gelman's memoir seems little different from the traditional heroic narrative of reportorial ingenuity, about beating deadlines and outmaneuvering competitors. He even reprints his first laudatory internal review at *Newsday*.[59] In Gelman's case, even compassion can be sublimated into ambition. Learning from one story that "empathy is more important than intimidation or subterfuge," he goes on to explain why: "If a reporter could win a person's trust, the person would give up almost anything you asked for, often a lot more than you ever expected."[60] Beaten to a crime scene because he traveled by subway, Gelman goes out and buys a car;[61] summoned from a love tryst by his beeper, he swears off love—temporarily.[62] To their credit, Blau and Gelman try to follow stories more suited to their own liberal self-image: an attack on an interracial couple, or on women of color who are rape victims. Yet they find their disenchantment deepened by editorial and public apathy.[63]

Thus, a pattern of disillusionment sets in, a burnout created by the high pressure of the now-computerized cop shop. The original goal of a career in crime reporting is *itself* exposed as a sickness, a harvest in which even the "insatiable" public is losing interest. The otherwise hard-boiled voice of *Crime Scene* soon loses its confidence, and often strays into mocking even its professional successes as instances of shocking transgression. In Gelman's world, we learn, anything goes: he "pump[s]" a story with "facts and shock value,"[64] tries to shoehorn himself into a grieving family's wake by posing as a florist,[65] steals erotic photos from a murder scene for good "art" copy.[66]

After witnessing one grisly crime scene involving cannibalism, he reports he went out and had a Blimpie.[67] Running a story about a dead dog's "last bark," Gelman first defends it by saying the dog "made the ultimate sacrifice. He gave his life for a headline." Then he admits "[i]t was definitely time to go."[68] Having absorbed the gallows humor of old-timers and of police, Gelman has clearly had his fill. Having begun his book by encountering a probationary six-month period as a "cub," soon we gather that he views the *entire* experience of crime reporting as probationary. Old-timers now seem inert, in turn, precisely because they want to stay crime reporters: to Gelman himself, by contrast, "cop reporting was no longer . . . a lifetime calling, but rather . . . the low rung on the journalistic ladder . . . Our role had changed from insider to outside observer."[69] In the end, he announces his promotion to the health beat.

Blau's book traces a similar pattern. All the while documenting the futility of the policing he encounters in 1988, Blau realizes that his own routine is subverting his effectiveness and compassion as well. The signs creep in gradually, as when he reflects on the reporter's reflexes on the crime scene:

> Relics caught my eye: A smashed flower vase. A baby shoe. A writer could always use one of these.[70]

> Every week seemed to begin and end with the same kind of trauma.
>
> The big questions about motive (How could anyone *do* such things?) would persist until I arrived at the scene; once I was there, I would feel a letdown as the inexplicability of what I saw sank in. The big answers were buried much deeper than newspapers or television could reach. In Hyde Park, as elsewhere, I was willing to settle for facts. I was beginning to understand the refrain from "Dragnet": "just the facts."[71]

> I had expected to find a broken home with signs of neglect all around . . . And on leaving, I expected to congratulate myself for stomaching it, as though I and not the people living there had endured some inconvenience, some pain.[72]

Albeit still taking pride in this hard-boiled Joe Fridayism, Blau actually tires of the roving eye of naturalistic detail gathering. Now he experiences feedback from what he calls "brittle grief,"[73] a routinized spectatorship that was supposed to provide understanding but produces only a melodrama of futility. Having survived mornings awakening to police scanners, Blau tells us sardonically in the end that he now works a "broader arena" of investigative reporting, and listens to FM. "I don't have to run around with cops on Saturday night," he writes.[74]

In all, then, these decidedly male narratives tell what is, in the annals of the news memoir, a familiar story. It is hard to remember an era when the crime beat was *not* the low rung of the profession. The paradox is that, much as young doctors are exposed to morgues, or cops themselves to difficult traffic intersections, the trade posts cub reporters in crime news to inculcate the restraint on emotions, and the strategic ritual of "objectivity" that the twentieth-century field has long promoted. Consequently, the episodes of boundary blurring these books mention are also thoroughly conventional markers of the genre: a reporter being mistaken for a cop, or an emergency medical technician, or an emergency room doctor. And as Christopher Lasch once observed, the idea that disillusionment is the necessary beginning of wisdom is itself a convention of modern liberal realism generally. At least since Steffens's own hard-boiled tutorial memoir, the idea that life was an unlearning of middle-class beliefs has been the way liberals have customarily seized the high ground of pragmatic realism. Under the cult of the hard-boiled exposure to facts, each generation claims to be more disillusioned, and thus more tough-minded, than the last. Nor is the motif of disillusionment so antithetical to the exposé of the profession. As John Pauly reminds us, demonizing the tabloid tendencies of news is a classic strategy of legitimation by mainstream journalistic practice itself. (Even Lincoln Steffens, one might remember, only moved on from the *New York Post* to a more austere paper of his own.)[75]

Indeed, a crucial point is that these books hardly say that the sickness is confined to the reporter-spectator, the news establishment, or even that fundamental source of mediation, the police themselves. Rather, this pathology is portrayed as inhering *in* events: in the what of news as much as in who writes it. Paradoxically, then, these True Crime stories also begin to describe a journey marked by profound ambivalence for the cohort of the cop shop— the police—left behind to face this disorder. That is, what marks the rookie reporter's initiation into hard-boiled wisdom and fatalism is, first, his entry into the fraternity of the police. Paradoxically, however, this initiation is joined at the hip to a story of professional out-migration. Indeed, it is intriguing that the book that traverses most directly into True Crime territory, Simon's *Homicide*, presents the journalist's rite of passage into cop wisdom as a fait accompli, so absorbed that its genesis need not be described. But in closing, Simon also includes one instance where he helped police subdue a suspect, much to their amusement. Significantly, this is his *only* first-person tale, and he saves it for the very last page of his narrative.[76]

IV

When we turn from the autobiographical dimension of these three narratives to their portraiture of police culture, we discover a symbolic exchange between journalistic and police identities. Moreover, this counterweight to the liberal-realist narrative's story of disillusionment emerges in what becomes a boundary narrative about *class*, about the cop shop alliance of writer and detective on the grounds of their shared labor. In the post-Vietnam years, we might say, the master narrative at work becomes a story of liberalism besieged, and yet effecting a retreat marked by the uneasiness of these journalists about the troops left to defend the cities. Skepticism of policing thus gives way to pity, or to grudging admiration, or to outright awe. Most importantly, it gives way to a *literary* emulation embedded in the aesthetic of the True Crime narrative.

By this boundary blurring, I do not mean to identify the traditional laments of crime news scholarship about "objectivity" and compromised source relationships; it insults these reporters to cast them as blithely unaware of these risks. Although in no sense exposés, these books *do* detail the closed-mindedness, the futility, and the corruption of urban law enforcement in the late 1980s. Bureaucratic inertia, public indifference, and new kinds of violence, mainly gang and drug related, all contribute to an accurate portrait of police impotence in many instances. Blau, for example, is highly critical of the Chicago Police Department's efforts to outmaneuver the drug trade; Gelman documents the futility of the New York force against street violence; Simon describes a Baltimore force inundated with drug-related murders, the hardest cases to solve.[77] Nor does racism go unmentioned: Simon, for one, explicitly discusses the internal racism in the Baltimore force and the class-consciousness that drives detectives' animosity to white *and* black poor alike.[78]

These criticisms of police authority are central to these books' claim to liberal affiliation. And yet despite this *Shame of the Cities* thread, the counter-current in favor of imaginative empathy with cops is quite noticeable. Sometimes this baptism emerges, as in Simon's back cover photo, as explicit mimicry of the police; sometimes this empathetic act fluctuates between self-parody and unintentional confession about fantasies of heroism. At times, the aura of the police serves as protection from the streets. Blau writes: "Sometimes when I drove through a bad neighborhood, I would reach for the handset of the two-way radio and hold it near my mouth in imitation of an undercover cop."[79] In many instances, however, identification serves to connect the *labor* of both professions. Blau, for example, offers this advice to rookie reporters arriving at the scene after a violent crime: "In the beginning [of an interview with relatives of a victim]," he says, "pretend you are a cop. Walk like a cop, hips weighted down as though slinging a gun. Keep your notebook hidden . . . Then stop being a cop. Be curious about everything."[80] At the end of his initiation, Blau admits that, even given that higher police officials had "sold out the rank and file with stupidity and greed," it was "impossible to cover the crime beat without coming to respect" the job cops had to do.[81] (Blau's narrative ends, predictably, with his breaking in a new rookie.) Gelman, meanwhile, writes that he had finally arrived when he was admitted to an undercover cop fraternity,[82] or when, award of awards, a cop gave him a Patrolman's Benevolent Association card to help him negotiate the department's inner channels.[83] Simon, meanwhile, remarks that he felt similar pressures. (Indeed, he might be said to have gone to the heart of the cop shop by actually becoming that police intern.) In *Homicide*'s epilogue, he reports that he altered his appearance so as to not alienate the men he worked with: cut his hair, removed a diamond-stud earring, adopted suits and ties. Like Gelman and Blau, Simon reports that he was often mistaken for a cop and didn't correct the impression.[84] His photo is thus, again, a testament to his initiation.

All three reporters, in fact, *define* the quintessence of professional achievement as empathy with cop consciousness. There is, for instance, absolutely *no* romanticizing of the gangster such as would have been typical in Mark Hellinger's writing. An illustrative episode of changed times comes in *The Cop Shop*, when an officer is shot—as it turns out, by a former policeman driven to madness after years of stress on the job. "As a reporter," Blau writes, "you had to try to understand it thoroughly, as though the tragedy had befallen your partner . . . you feared there was no justice."[85] Even in a moment of cop-to-(ex)cop confrontation, Blau stays decidedly on the police side of the barricade. Simon, meanwhile, departs from his representation of detectives' minds only once, and then only to fictionalize the mind of a criminal on the run who must recognize that cops "own" *him*.[86] Gelman's baptismal moment comes on the heels of covering a cop funeral. In this episode, Gelman's anxiety about tabloid invasiveness (getting a headline quote from a widow grasping a wooden crucifix) is expiated when a police official tells him his story was "some job." Subsequently, he writes a story on police academy classmates of the same officer who had praised his funeral piece, now feeling he has broken through the "thick blue line."[87]

As this line is crossed, the boundary itself seems to blur. In some moments, the imaginative work performed by the empathetic act of crime writing works to rewrite the cop, much as *The Naked City* had, as a professional, white-collar laborer: a hybrid, again, of blue- and white-collar labor value. Here, for example, is Blau's reflection on the collaborative work of firemen and homicide investigators at an arson scene:

> Firemen and police.
>
> You could see them side by side at arson investigations. Firemen hauled water lines and axes. Cops held clipboards, and wore ties knotted at their navels.
>
> Society had messed with the resolve and honesty of police by expecting too much from them. The simple, well-defined role they had played for generations—Stop, thief!—was no longer enough.
>
> Unlike fire, the criminal had become a more complex enemy, one that led them down dark alleyways, into abandoned buildings that were customized fortresses, and around in circles.[88]

The cop is represented here as a fact gatherer, note taker, writer like the reporter himself. Blau's contrast with the firemen casts the physical, collective labor of fire fighting against the white-collar guy holding his clipboard. Indeed, this class inflection, however slight, is important. Despite the artisanal aura of the cop shop, crime news is usually predicated on contact with *detectives*, not beat officers (called by reporters derogatorily, as by detectives, "uniforms"). The episodic, story-to-story, high-wire act of the case narrative reflects the strategy of response-to-call policing so evocative of detectives themselves rushing to the scene. If in True Crime, all *is* 911, both the drudgery and the solving of crime are reserved for an empiricist elite of detectives.

This is the ethos of what Stuart Hall calls the "professional technical neutrality" that crime news so notoriously reinforces when it comes to depicting the police.[89]

Simon's *Homicide* offers easily the fullest merger of police empiricism and journalistic narrative. But the procedural isn't precisely what is being romanced; in this sense the cover photo covers up. For Simon's book turns out to be a *labor-centered* account, focusing on the tension between the underpaid, overworked, but dedicated calling of the detective and a politicized department that values the quantity of cases solved over the quality of work. Unlike *The Naked City*, where the illusion that technocratic labor can keep police work serenely aloof from politics, in these books politics always intrudes. Here, much as in reporters' laments about their own offices, "real police work" becomes so much of a political football that the "last natural police detective in America," who solves cases by sheer instinct and talent, considers early retirement.[90] The Baltimore detective is a quester for truth who nevertheless "endures,"[91] brilliant (again) in his "ownership" of the crime scene,[92] confronting an outside world where "[e]verybody lies,"[93] paramedics are chronic klutzes, and juries are incompetent. The city looms as an ominous, bestial antagonist. Down these mean streets a man must go, down into "an equal and opposing spirit in the streets and alleys," where "something alien and unnatural" is cornering him—just as, in a touch indeed straight out of Capote, an oversize rat corners a cat.[94]

Simon's book likewise offers up a stirring editorial repudiation, again from the cop's perspective, of liberal illusions about crime enforcement. In ways that rehearse long-standing police complaints one can, again, find in Wambaugh, Simon lambastes the standard of utter certainty that television foists upon juries;[95] the illusion that police lying in court about probable cause is anything more than routine; the noble idea that interrogation rooms are free of compulsion ("Police work has always been brutal," Simon writes; "good police work, discreetly so").[96] Regarding the Miranda rules, Simon writes: "Miranda is a symbol and little more, a salve for a collective conscience that cannot reconcile libertarian ideals with what must necessarily occur in a police interrogation room."[97] We should not mistake this for simple uncritical capitulation to the fatalism of his sources; rather, the hard-boiled voice acquires its literary aura via a forceful assimilation of what is cast, importantly, as the detectives' pragmatic realism.

Therefore, the most telling sign of boundary blurring is not in these moments of intrusive editorializing, nor in fraternization and fantasy. Rather, it is how class affiliation embeds itself in the aesthetic of the narrative itself. For example, rhetorically dismissive as they are of TV images of ratiocination and car chases (much as our criticism is), these True Crime narratives actually enfold crime scenes within conventional, mass-cultural images of law enforcement. The policeman is often cast in familiar romantic garb: as the undercover maverick, the master detective, the dedicated loner in trench coat. Take this passage from Simon's text, in which cops satirize a popular icon while the journalist actually recoups it:

> "I always wanted to work a murder in fog," says [Detective] Worden, almost wistful. "Like Sherlock Holmes."
> "Yeah," agrees James. "That guy was always finding bodies in this shit . . . the killer was always named Murray."
> "Moriarty, you mean. Professor Moriarty" . . .
> They do get a murder, a street shooting that stays a whodunit for only as long as it takes Worden to wade into a sea of black faces, a pale wanderer waiting for the crowd's natural hostility to dissipate, a patient, civil cop listening for the anonymous mention of a criminal's name.[98]

I will return momentarily to Simon's contrast of the civil (white) cop and the naturally hostile inner (black) city. For now, it is worth noting how the True Crime aesthetic in these narratives follows the lead of police detectives in, as it were, repossessing the crime scene (or, in cop terms, the scene of the crime) as its domain. Simon's *Homicide* makes detectives' caseloads the dominant organizing principle of its narrative. Cops become more than the protagonists of his story; rather, we view crime through their experience. Street knowledge, reflecting the classic contradiction of crime news, is not precisely "of" the streets; rather it is usually constructed through the policing of those streets. Indeed the very form and modus operandi of a book like *Homicide* perform an act of identification by mimicking, in narrative detail running to nearly six hundred pages, the care, focus, and ownership of the police detective himself. A text like Simon's enshrines the scientific heroism of empirical deduction that the nineteenth century's naturalistic ethos is often said to epitomize.

And yet, if at first glance these books might seem to augur a return to these naturalistic protocols, the fact is that *Homicide* and its more autobiographical counterparts often betray little interest in the social clues that might index anything other than an underclass pathology. We hear too little, for example, linking downtown development and inner-city unemployment; Simon represents his threatening regions as "West Baltimore" or "Billyland," police districts whose cop shop names implicitly signify the kind of people ostensibly typical to them. Valorizing the police's own street experience also seems to breed a discounting of academic knowledge gathering. Very little in these books is said about theories of economic underdevelopment, about debates over the underclass, about different typologies of gang affiliation. In this respect, what a book like Simon's does to the crime scene it does to Baltimore at large: in a substitution crucial to the poetics of True Crime generally, Simon turns the terrain into the property of the homicide investigator, a site of clues not to social conditioning but to individual criminality and predation.[99] When he does fictionalize the vantage point of a criminal mind in that last chapter, rather tellingly it is not a mind driven by any social determinants or compulsions. Rather, it is merely the fear of the hunted quarry. ("Here's the morning line, bunk," Simon writes. "By now, they've marked your blood trail out of the bathroom").[100] Similarly, Simon's entire argument about the interrogation room is predicated on a rather one-sided predicament; that is, how the cop can trap or outwit the "perp" who he, and the reader, already know is guilty.

All too often, the urban community doubles as home both to the perpetrator and a hostile or indifferent citizenry. Here Simon describes the neighborhood around two crime scenes:

The morning newspaper will not print a line about the killing [of a street drug dealer]. The neighborhood, or whatever is left around Gold and Etting that resembles a neighborhood, will move on. West Baltimore, home of the misdemeanor homicide.[101]

***

West Baltimore. You sit on your stoop, you drink Colt 45 from a brown paper bag and you watch the radio car roll slowly around the corner. You see the gunman, you hear the shots, you gather on the far corner to watch the paramedics load what remains of a police officer into the rear of an ambulance. Then you go back to your rowhouse, open another can, and settle in front of the television to watch the replay on the eleven o'clock news. Then you go back to the stoop.[102]

To a degree, this is similar to what Michael Massing has called "ghetto blast-ing," referring to the way journalistic narrative in the 1980s, in the guise of liberal exposé, often implicitly infantilized and delegitimated the communi-ties it portrayed. What might serve as a story of initiation, in this instance, might also work as a story of upward mobility *out* of the streets. And though claiming to go behind the news headline, these narratives actually recapitu-late, as crime news itself often does, the police's tendency to see crime as the by-product of pathology. Contrary to the depiction of Rodriguez's *Always Running*, gangs are seen wholly as criminal associations; criminals (when de-picted at all) are cast as low-life, the very antithesis to the professional cop. And one would never know from these books, any more than one would from the news, that our world-beating figures for prison populations have come largely from jailing the *non*violent offender.[103]

Again, this variant of True Crime thus inherits that fatalism about commu-nity politics and reform so often characteristic of police culture, an "unbelief" in reform even Steffens had noticed in his *Autobiography* (280). Indeed, echo-ing the pall put over police management in these years, all three books charac-terize the crime of the 1980s as predominantly "senseless," "meaningless," or "stupid"—in Gelman's metaphor, crime is epitomized by the "stray bullet."[104] This characterization complements not only crime news' own conventions, but the police's own nostalgia for professional criminals and that supposedly "simple, well-defined role" of crime buster that is, as I've tried to suggest in earlier chapters, as much a phantom in police history as a reality. Even small decisions reflect this dominant view of crime. Blau, for instance, acknowl-edges that he reported official tallies of gang shootings even though everyone knew they were a "joke,"[105] and abided the police censorship that disallowed the appearance of gang members' names in print. Neither concession to the police gestalt was liable to move very deeply past the crime scene, much less broach the individual psychologies of often-adolescent criminals. Similarly, Gelman admits that, whatever "long, involved analyses" psychologists had to offer, he has come around to the cops' view of rapists as "scum bags" who, "unlike killers," have a "sick, addictive desire to feel dominant and invinci-ble."[106] A nickname like Bulldog thus reflects more than the machismo of male cop shop fraternities; rather it captures a dogged defensiveness, a con-ception of policing, and reporting, as standing guard over a territory one owns. One at risk from what is seen, fundamentally, as predation.

V

In not a few of the narratives about police corruption during the 1970s through the 1990s, authors typically resort to flashback or cross-cutting narratives, often looking back at the apprenticeship of cops, good and bad, in the department. In *Serpico* or *Prince of the City*—or, more recently, in books like McAlary's *Good Cop/Bad Cop*—the intended effect is both to provide a portrait of cop acculturation to institutional corruption, and to mark or blur the good cop/bad cop dichotomy in history and in police psychology. In Maas's *Serpico*, there is one such flashback that is particularly striking. In it Detective Frank Serpico, almost exactly Joseph Wambaugh's age, is remembering a Sunday afternoon when, as a child, he had sought solace from his Italian American father, at the moment gardening in the back yard:

> [H]e burst into the greenhouse crying because some kids had taunted him for wearing hand-me-down clothes. His father listened, and then told him a story about a prince who disguised himself in rags to see what the citizens of his kingdom were really like, only to be chased away by them. When the prince returned the next day dressed in full regalia, the townspeople who had hooted at him bowed and scraped, but he sent them packing, telling them they ought to be ashamed of themselves, that he was still the same person. "So you see," his father concluded, "it's not important how a man looks. It's what inside that counts." (28)

In Maas's reading, this rather "banal" tale is clearly meant as an inspirational parable, suggesting son Serpico's own incorruptibility. But in light of books like *Homicide*, we might suggest another slant: rather, it is a tale about the unfairness and ambiguity of undercover (or plainclothes work), where one is exposed to the disorder and corruption of those one is meant to serve. Or, as much, be served *by*. Secretly, one is, to use the familiar phrase, always already the son of territory that (like that Italian American backyard) is one's own: a "prince" of the city. Similar populist motifs are to be found in Robert Daley's book of that title.[107]

Although we have generally failed to notice it, this populist framework is what, in fact, often brings together the various strands of True Crime: the "cop talk" narratives that implicitly or explicitly compare police to the abandoned troops of Vietnam; the Mafia exposés that lounge in the mystique of a fraternity of silence eerily like that of the police; even in the serial-killer phantasms of former policewoman Ann Rule, pitting lonely detectives against pathological, irrational murderers. It is not merely that the hard-boiled, neo-noir conventions described earlier—lonely detective, dark city, senseless crime—work to cast police departments as the underdog defenders of the city. Rather, it is that such a portrait reinvokes the craft-conscious producer ideology, even (as I developed in chapters 2 and 3) a covert ownership or proprietorship of the streets, which have turned against the police.[108] Even the aura of the heroic crime buster is at its core nostalgic. As I have suggested, in police history, the crime-busting ethos is most evocative of America at midcentury, when the prominence of Hoover's G-men, symbol and champions of middle-American normalcy, so dominated the public perception of police power. Yet in these reporter narratives, and indeed in True Crime more generally, crime solving still dominates, cast in a Manichaean battle with a mysterious, senseless entity (fog), Moriarty turned to mayhem. Blau, for instance, likens the new drug wars of the 1980s with Chicago's days of Al Capone, and thus sees today's gangs in rather dated terms; likewise he expresses nostalgia for midcentury police chief O. W. Wilson, the advocate of cop as crime buster. True Crime establishes a connection to this earlier time, even casting policing itself as a lost yet transhistorical knowledge, part of a fatalistic vigilance against recurring social depredation. Simon perhaps best captures this ambiguity, when he describes his Baltimore detective squad as the "land of the forgotten promise,"[109] a world of instinctual duty in a landscape the cop clearly feels has fallen. Crime busting thus bespeaks an ideological faith beneath the cover story about the reporter's initiation into pragmatic, street realism. The journalist is initiated not just into a profession, nor even into policing as such, but into a populist way of seeing the city: into the anxiety that, as many commentators have noted, allowed it to be courted nationwide by the Right in the 1980s.[110]

The cop shop counterpart in the news profession, of course, is the old-timer in trench coat, the Breslin or Mike Barnicle or Mike Royko, hard-drinking, democratic defenders of the urban little guy. Traditionally, this disposition works by venting hostility against "parasitic" classes at the upper reaches of society (bankers, politicians, "boutique" liberals) and at the lower end as well. The ethos is well captured by Breslin's famous "Dies the Victim, Dies the City" (1976), about a man named Allen Burnett murdered on the street, pathetically, for his overcoat. Here is Breslin describing the police lieutenant looking into the file:

> In a city that seems virtually ungoverned, Harold Ruger forms the only municipal presence with any relationship to what is happening on the streets where people live. Politicians attend dinners at hotels with contractors. Bankers discuss interest rates at lunch. Harold Ruger goes into a manila folder on his desk and takes out a picture of Allen Burnett, a young face covered with blood staring from a morgue table. In Allen Burnett's hand there is a piece of the veins of the city of New York.
>
> Dies the victim, dies the city. Nobody flees New York because of accounting malpractice. People run from murder and fire. Those who remain express their fear in words of anger.

In its allegorical collapse of abandoned citizens (and the police) into the city's "naked" body, in its emulation of the dispassion of the morgue, in its controlled anger at parasitic classes, this is boilerplate tabloidism.[111] However, complicating this symbolic journey for the newer generation is their distance from the signs of ethnic and cultural difference that Breslin took as his own. If Gelman's being called Joe College signals tensions born of class or generational differences, Blau's being identified the "short Jewish Guy from New York," or crashing a wake to interview that widow holding a wooden crucifix, speaks to something equally important. That is, being upper middle class, college educated, and in this case a Jewish outsider is linked, by these narratives, to young-professional expectations of journalism. Law enforcement, and its older cop shop news cohort, are cast as Catholic, old working class, and more defensively white. Thus the cop shop comes to represent, at once, a borderland post not only of professional fields, but of ethnicities and divisive racial attitudes. Indeed, this is a crucial subtext to the general cover story of professional disillusionment, which turns out to hinge upon the politics of white resistance: on entertaining the plight, as it were, after white flight.

At first, random observations about cultural differences, or even white-ethnic fraternalism, seem little more than workingman's banter, cop shop humor. When asking about an internal source of rumors, for example, Blau can ask, " 'Does he have an Irish name or a Polish name?' "[112] Simon, likewise, depicts his detective squad room as Catholic territory, in which a rookie is asked, comically, to kiss the ring of his only "true and begotten" lieutenant.[113] The chapter in which Gelman crosses over the thick blue line is called, again in neighborhood terms, "Little Italy," and when he earns his PBA card, it comes from an Irish narcotics cop named (in the original variant) Iron Mike.[114]

Yet if taking up this banter signals acculturation to white-ethnic byways, other subtexts belie it. In *Homicide*, for instance, the detectives' steadfast faith is linked to a "Holy Trinity" of "Evidence," "Witnesses," and "Confessions,"[115] all terms resonant of Catholic faith. Blau, in a contrasting vein, compares interviewing crime victims to talking to his father about the Holocaust,[116] a barely speakable allusion his cop cohorts cannot identify with. And Gelman calls upon *his* Jewish background to contrast struggles with police knowledge that will not go away:

> [Sergeant] Clifford and I came from different backgrounds. He was a Catholic raised on faith in the Lord's word and obedience to anyone of higher rank. I was a Jew told always to question and speak my mind if I did not agree . . . I wanted to be a muckraker; he was a good soldier. In a way, Clifford and I made each other possible. We also made each other miserable. [Someone] once told me that even if I didn't learn anything else, after a year of covering cops, I'd know how to think like an Irish Catholic.[117]

Making "each other possible" and "miserable" perhaps best captures the ethnographic predicament of the cop shop. White and Catholic ethnicity, as it is embodied in the police, seems heroically committed to calling in a way the young crime reporter seemingly cannot be. These young professionals are cast as individualistic participant-observers in a more static, communitarian, fraternal culture. The cop shop is not unlike a guild that bars entrance to a secret, precious, almost mystical knowledge of the streets. Yet white-ethnic culture is also portrayed as a place of static hierarchy, unresponsive to inquisitive (not to say inquiring) minds, pragmatic to a fault. When Gelman's bureau chief tells him, after dealing with a police information officer named Fahey, just to "[d]o what it takes. Just don't get caught," the chief calls this wisdom "Italian Rules."[118]

We might well remind ourselves that these *are* self-consciously liberal-realist narratives, explicitly left-leaning on matters of racial discrimination. Even so, one cannot overlook the ethnocentrism these stereotypes convey. Inescapably, one feels that these are ethnicities seen from the outside, collapsed into a one-dimensional and single urban type.[119] Moreover, this ethnic portraiture provides clues to a demographic subtext that covertly supplements the cover story of liberal disillusionment. Albeit indirectly, each of these narratives also suggests how the phenomenon of *earlier* middle-class white flight—that is, even prior to the post-Vietnam decades—is recouped by the presence of the young, witnessing reporter.

Clearly a surrogate for the suburban reader removed from the crime scenes he depicts, sometimes this narrator is cast explicitly as a prodigal son returned to the city. In his first chapter, Blau describes himself as a young man fresh from suburban reporting, eager to witness the city once again; he points out he had never been mugged and had attended only one funeral in his entire life.[120] In these lights, it is easy to forget he is from New York City. During Gelman's account of his assignment to the Bensonhurst murder of Yusef Hawkins, meanwhile, the reporter discloses that his own father had once attended the same high school as Hawkins's accused killer.[121] Gelman himself looks too Californian, in other words, because his father had taken his own family to LA to escape the infamous New York fiscal crisis of the 1970s.[122] And though we learn virtually nothing about David Simon, it is tempting to interpret his photo, once again, not only as cop or class mimicry, but a cultural makeover. If this is, as the True Crime marketing of these texts suggest, a voyage to an American underside, then it is also a covert reentertainment of the position of whites left to face it every day.[123]

In some instances, this symbolic act of populist reaffiliation with ethnic whites seems quite intentional. A major portion of Simon's text, for example, is devoted to the unselfish quest of one detective named Pellegrini to track down the murderer of an eleven-year-old black girl. His heroic quest for her killer is a sign of his populist commitment to his community regardless of race, public indifference, or political scapegoating: again, the bulldog democratic ethos that *The Naked City*'s Muldoon embodies. And Simon, again most closely attuned to the poetics of police populism, ends with detectives pondering the "fine and beautiful thing"[124] of nailing such a murderer, drinking down the day in a bar, returning home from their shift as their wives and children are just waking up. But at the same time this urban populism also has its not-so-progressive dimensions. Simon also observes that gentrification of the waterfront, a pet project of the African American mayor, is displacing the very bars these working-class heroes frequent.[125] Simon positions the detective squad as the land of the forgotten promise because Baltimore has re-turned, ironically, to boss rule under that mayor, who is politicizing the de-partment, saddling that natural detective with a political red ball, and stocking the department leadership with affirmative-action hires. Gelman, in a similar way, contrasts his move to the health beat with the election of African Ameri-can David Dinkins over Rudolph Giuliani in 1989, a victory the new mayor called a "milestone." But the victory, and politics generally, are cast here as a "meaningless diversion" when seen from the post of the hospital trauma unit and another teenager shot in the streets.[126] "Bulldog" street wisdom here might seem, in retrospect, merely to play to Giuliani's own tune. Blau, albeit perhaps the most critically minded about race of the three authors, closes with a soured friendship between black and white-ethnic police officials, an example of lost racial harmony also symbolic of what has gone bad in the city at large.[127] But even this nostalgia entertains a populism often based in resis-tance to the liberal state for not particularly harmonious racial reasons.[128]

VI

By way of conclusion, I would like to return to Gelman's *Crime Scene*, as he is recounting a vital learning experience at the feet of his idol: as it turns out, Jimmy Breslin himself. It is a story quite evocative of this hybrid genre as a whole: part professional initiation narrative, part an exercise in police affilia-tion, and part populist allegory. And of course it is entirely fitting that Breslin presides in the story. But he presides uneasily.

In a crime story quite like the murder of the fast-food worker to which Simon alludes, a promising eighteen-year-old cheerleader had been killed by a stray bullet while eating with friends at McDonald's. Gelman, still a rookie, is assigned to work the scene with Breslin. The young man marvels at the way his idol is oblivious to pressure, armed with no secret formula except grit and defiance. Breslin even stops at an Irish bar to use the bathroom; he writes his copy on the el. And when a column emerges, it reads, in part:

> Tondelayo Alfred was a freshman at Brooklyn College . . .
>
> Her father is a sergeant in the police department of the City of New York. Somebody said that her mother had been going to college, too. I don't know that. I do know that her city needed Tondelayo Alfred as much as it needs the sunrise.

She was on her way to something, and she was going to take all of us with her, and here comes some degenerate walking in from the street with a gun. She loses her life and we lose her.[129]

This is a progressive voice in part, bulldog in its loyalty to the lost land of the city. True to form, Breslin voices his own hard-boiled identification with police culture and consciousness; he pictures urban crime as predatory, senseless degeneracy; and his sympathetic affiliation with a young African American, Ms. Alfred, is folded into the nostalgic image of the old urban community. To the rookie Gelman, the circuit is complete: by writing this, Breslin proves himself the ultimate working stiff who exhibits shoe leather and determination in filing the tale,[130] thus becoming the true "voice of working-class New York."[131] And Alfred is herself a symbol of that very ethos, since the column implies that "Tondelayo would have stayed and contributed to the city."[132] But the really telling moment comes when Gelman mentions that he had told Breslin that Ms. Alfred had, according to friends, actually hoped to transfer to a college out of state. In other words, Gelman inadvertently discloses that what must be covered over by Breslin's boilerplate allegory about urban violence, a shattered community, and police resilience is Ms. Alfred's own desire to escape that city. Both reporters concluded, however, that this potentially contrary fact was really just a "matter of conjecture."[133] Faced with the prospect that Ms. Alfred might not serve as the symbol of urban populism and community they intended, they nevertheless run the column as is.

In much the same way, these young-professional narratives might be said to be trying to honor the police, to relink urban families, to be Jimmy Breslin again; ultimately, however, this act of populist entertainment encounters its limits. In the end, these reporters seem themselves as eager to leave the post of the cop shop as they once were to join it. It is striking enough, perhaps, that *The Cop Shop* and *Crime Scene* are written not by established reporters at the end of their careers, but by men who are still relatively young. But the pattern they describe may well extend beyond their individual careers. Gelman, for one, tells us that it took one only a few years to acquire seniority on *Newsday*'s crime desk.[134] And Blau tells us that, not long after his departure, his paper just hadn't been staffing the police headquarters beat regularly.[135] Indeed, by the summer of 1995, *New York Newsday*, after suffering devastating cuts in its news staff and its circulation, ceased publication altogether. New

York City, which had thirteen papers at the end of the 1920s, and as many as seven in the early 1960s, was now down to three papers.[136] The *Sun*, meanwhile, finding itself under pressure from Times Mirror, facing various declines in advertising and circulation, enduring staff buyouts, even after a much-heralded computerization, closed up its evening edition in September of 1995. (The *Los Angeles Times*, it might also be added, ended its Washington edition at virtually the same moment.) True Crime surely acquired mass-market legitimacy in the 1980s. But as I've suggested, the more telling possibility may be that the genre provided (hard)cover for what Bourdieu calls a "pathological" (concentrated) news field, indeed an ongoing evacuation of the traditional post of crime reporting.

These three narratives, naturally, cannot recapture the history of crime news in that decade any more than they can stand for the entire phenomenon of True Crime. Like any other genre, True Crime invites a variety of differently articulated cultural readings; as a hybrid form, by definition it makes mass readings of different kinds available to different audiences. Nevertheless, it may be that the various political entertainments I have described, not merely their killer-next-door voyeurism, are what strike chords with some American readers. Moreover, in the effort to out-true True Crime, these books may even shed light on the mainline progenitors of the form. We tend to forget that even Capote's *In Cold Blood* did not center exclusively on its pathological killer, Perry Smith. Rather, a considerable portion of the book—indeed, the dominant focus in its final pages—was devoted to the tedious and yet ultimately successful legwork of a dedicated, coat-and-tie family man, Kansas investigator Alvin Adams Dewey, former sheriff and FBI agent. Capote's True Crime successors might be said not merely to have updated him, but to have enhanced his own police populism. Of course, after the 1980s, we're not in Kansas anymore.

5

Framing the Shooter:
The *Globe,* the Police, and the Streets

I have seen this countless times. The police car pulls up to a corner where teenagers are gathered. The window is rolled down. The officer stares at the youths. They stare back. The officer says to one, "C'mere." He saunters over, conveying to his friends by his elaborately casual style the idea that he is not intimidated by authority. "What's your name"? "Chuck." "Chuck who?" "Chuck Jones." "What'ya doing, Chuck?" "Nothin'." "Got a P.O. [parole officer]?" "Nah." "Sure?" "Yeah." "Stay out of trouble, Chuckie."
> —James Q. Wilson and George L. Kelling Jr., "Broken Windows: The Police and Neighborhood Safety" (1982)

In the United States of the late 1980s and 1990s, in cities large and small, the watchword for urban law enforcement became "community policing." In cities like Houston, Boston, and New York, still reeling from the obvious failures in combating street crime in the previous decade, police departments increasingly turned to decentralized neighborhood management, aiming for greater police visibility and increased public trust. Following a new strand of neoconservative theory, they paid more attention to what began to be called "quality of life" disturbances in those neighborhoods—that is, to the sometimes petty, often gnawing, and sometimes fear-provoking street disorders that so alienated much of the urban citizenry. The police tried strategies like storefront branches, community crime watches, and aggressive street sweeps of prostitutes, drug dealers, and—infamously—street vendors and the homeless.

Rather than being preoccupied with progressive legacies like efficient response to call, it was said, community policing was aimed at improving citizen perceptions of order as much as solving crimes. As one book title had it, the idea was take us *Beyond 911* (1990)—beyond, that is, the ostensibly impersonal, paramilitary, rapid-response policing begun in the 1960s.[1] And above all, the dominant symbol of this back-to-basics approach has become the traditional beat cop—a figure, as it were, once historically repressed but now returning. The symbol emerges, for example, in an article coauthored by Ronald Reagan's former attorney general Edwin Meese in 1990, entitled "Taking Back the Streets: Police Methods that Work"—a title that inverted the sixties rhetoric that had so often pilloried the police officer. Accompanying this article was a Victorian woodcut representing the classic British bobby walking his beat on a snowy night, nightstick sheathed at his side, his boots leaving their marks on his turf (figure 5.1). "The sight of a familiar officer coming down the street on foot," the picture's caption explains, "inspires greater confidence than does an impersonal squad car cruising by."[2]

As a way to turn modern law enforcement back to its roots, community policing soon spread across the nation, receiving the imprimatur of the Clinton Justice Department. All three of the cities in my previous chapter—Baltimore, Chicago, and New York—now have pilot or well-established community policing strategies. The program has also spawned larger, more ambitious experiments like "Business Improvement Districts," in which urban zones have been redesigned with more efficient police oversight in mind—and in which foot patrol plays only a small part. And yet, echoing much of the political script of our day, nostalgia played a central role even in the most technocratic of designs.[3] And that is because community policing has become more than a police strategy. Moreover, it is a cultural narrative, an essentially aphoristic, even folkloric reconstruction of the streets that weaves together the cultural turn against permissiveness, a resurgence of urban populism, and a revived realism that, I have tried to show, so often suffuses urban journalism in our time. In my own regional city of Boston, a return to beat patrol and soon community policing was inaugurated under Police Commissioner Francis "Mickey" Roache, best known for having spearheaded the department's community disorders unit (conceived in 1978), which had investigated

5.1
The sight of a familiar officer, from
Edwin Meese III and Bob Carrico,
"Taking Back the Streets:
Police Methods That Work,"
Policy Review 54 (autumn 1990): 23.
Reprinted with permission of
The Bettmann Archive.

racial incidents in the decades following desegregation. Roache was a South Boston boyhood friend of the then-mayor, Democrat Raymond Flynn, himself elected under the banner of urban populism that sought to restore the power and autonomy, it was said, of "the neighborhoods." In the *Boston Globe*, the newspaper to which I subscribe, Roache had in fact been greeted as an extension of the mayor's "caring" personality.[4] And under Roache's prodding—and later, under that of his colleague William Bratton, who then moved on to become police commissioner in New York City—community policing went on to be called the main reason for a dramatic decline in violent crime in the late 1990s.[5]

To close this book, I would like to try to re-create how, in that decade, I came to know about community policing, and to read its cultural rhetorics in political and criminological theory, in local police policy, and in journalistic representation. To illustrate this broader narrative linkage, this chapter begins by looking at the theory and practice of community policing during

Roache's administration as police commissioner in Boston (1985–93). Along the way, I will also examine the instrumental role played by the theories of James Q. Wilson and George L. Kelling Jr. in solidifying this new approach, in large part by reframing social understandings of the rationality of the young, apprenticing criminal. To succeed, community policing needed not only to rationalize the renewed focus on street disorder, but to do so in ways that addressed the concerns of the Boston constituencies who would, under these new programs, be asked to play along. Simultaneously, community policing also needed to provide a working rationale for quite deeply bureaucratic and still largely white-ethnic police forces, unions, and work traditions. In these lights, the total social narrative provided by community policing—particularly by Wilson and Kelling—was crucial, dovetailing as it did a theory of criminal motivation, recommendations for specific police tactics, and even an implied strategy for achieving local political legitimacy.[6]

And yet, the additionally important if paradoxical fact was that I came to know about community policing not through immediate contact with the policies of Roache, but rather through reading a crime story: the street homicides of two young African American males, Charles Copney and Korey Grant, from gunshots in April of 1991, as they were brought to me by the coverage of a single newspaper, the *Globe* itself. A daily journal founded and (until a few years ago) run under sole family ownership, the *Globe* places itself in roughly a quarter of Boston-area households, including my suburban home in Newton, while achieving circulations well over the half million mark.[7] Although it receives nominal competition from its crosstown tabloid rival, the *Herald*, the *Globe* still dominates local coverage; as one local journalism professor put it, the *Globe* often seems to stand as the city's "dominant civic voice."[8] And as if rising to this role, in the eight months following these homicides, this newspaper devoted, by my rough count, over thirty articles and op-ed pieces to the Copney-Grant case, climaxing in a Sunday magazine essay by staffer and soon Pulitzer Prize–winning author Eileen McNamara, focusing on one defendant, the apparent shooter, a fifteen-year-old boy named Damien Bynoe.[9]

At first glance, this particular case might seem to have little to do with what was changing about urban policing. Rather, from the start, this crime was framed as a test case regarding the criminal adjudication and punishment of juveniles. And yet, what I mean to show is that police knowledge was in fact *constitutive* to this tale, from the most foundational matters of police sources and the *Globe*'s narrative framing, to the mobilization of white-ethnic nostalgia for the lost city, to the enlistment of local columnists in elaborating this tale and feeding *into* the debate over juvenile crime and punishment.[10] Though the police were virtually invisible to the tale as such—invisible because they rendered themselves as part of the victim community itself—they were in fact pivotal knowledge workers in this story. They provided the urban spade work that allowed neoconservative theories, and the journalistic conventions that often unwittingly supplemented them, to initially frame the shooter in this crime story as a rational choice maker of whom those theories were so fond.

Thus, after discussing Roache's implementation of community policing, I will turn to re-creating the *Globe*'s plot as a suburban reader might have encountered it in time. That is, I will trace how a pattern of revelation took place, in part dictated by news conventions, in part by the structure of police and court investigation and prosecution, and in part by local social and political contingencies. Certainly I have chosen this story for specific reasons: because it was a street murder of young African American males; because the shooting was labeled as gang related; because it provoked the familiar refrain about the breakdown of social authority. But most of all, the Copney-Grant story is revealing of the everyday, more mundane reciprocity between the *Globe*'s liberalism and what I have been calling police populism. What I hope to show is that, during the apparent victory of community policing, it has often been the case that the Boston Police Department's own premium on order has found a willing cohort in the *Globe*'s own desire to claim the status of dominant civic voice for its city and—seemingly paradoxically—its increasingly suburban audiences. Where the new theoreticians of community policing put the young street criminal at the center of its cultural storytelling, the *Globe* framed its protagonist, Damien Bynoe, in startlingly similar terms—at least for a time. To use an old newspaper phrase, this framing was perhaps the paper's most distressing "feature."

To an extent, this framing effect is familiar to many in modern media criticism. As my introduction recounts, in recent years contemporary media studies have increasingly emphasized the power of crime news not only in showcasing a law-enforcement view of crime—"showcase" being the word often applied to community policing itself—but by providing an illusory sense of social consensus that itself polices disorder.[11] The news does so, it is often said, by traveling only through "narrowed grooves of institutional meaning," and thus conveying, in Stuart Hall's words, a "professional-technical neutrality" about events. Crime news thus makes expert opinions appear to be "the only forms of intelligibility available."[12] And yet we also need to follow Hall's example and put this high theory on the ground—or, as Bourdieu might have it, in the field. Aside from the need, in particular, to revisit the police knowledge on which crime news inevitably draws, we also need to sharpen our precision about what *kinds* of authority are rendered, by what methods, and unto whom, by both police power and the contemporary kind of storytelling the *Globe* purveys. As with Dora Clark, or Dot King, or the street disorders re-created by Joseph Wambaugh or my True Crime journalists, the Copney-Grant case told interlocking cultural stories that shuffled reader sympathies, suppressed or relocated root causes for the crime, and created new fables of urban decline, neighborhood responsibility, and public civility. Ultimately, however, it was the elusive character of the *Globe*'s framing—in the last analysis, a kind of zero-sum narrative that reordered the community map while affecting liberal dispassion—that raised questions for me, not the least of which was my own placement as a suburban subscriber.

This elusive, double-sided aspect to the *Globe*'s coverage was central to the nostalgic story it told, about the cultural norms about neighborhood and family authority the case threw into question, and the legal repercussions of the Copney-Grant case seemed so naturally (but not at all naturally) to generate. But this nostalgia was not the entire story. For it turns out that community policing in Boston, I hope to show, actually went out under what Stephen Mastrofski has rightly called a "crime attack" strategy, much more suited to modern police approaches than Victorian-style foot patrol ever could be.[13] The contradiction could not have been more striking; indeed, in many ways it was the stimulus for this book. At the moment when Boston police forces were supposedly implementing a caring, personal, neighborhood-oriented community policing strategy—feeling, as it were, our pain—juvenile street crime was being subjected to ever-harsher police and judicial treatment. For those eight months, the ultimate effect may have been mainly that many fixed their attention on the spectacle of lower-class criminality, as the *Globe* itself—in the words of literary critic Frank Lentricchia—made the "fate" of incarceration "known to all."[14]

I

When Mickey Roache succeeded Commissioner Joseph Jordan to a state-mandated five-year term in the winter of 1985, he inherited a department still reeling from budget cuts, public distrust over recent police shootings, and continuing deep racial divides stemming from the desegregation crisis of the 1970s, during which the reputation of the predominantly white police force had been notoriously damaged. At the start of Roache's term, Boston was still a city nearly 60 percent white, with antibusing memories still strong in South Boston; it was also, however, a city racially stratified by *age*, with blacks outnumbering whites by nearly two to one in the public school system. On top of all that, in the late 1970s, the Massachusetts tax-revolt rollback measure, Proposition 2½, had led to the closing of seven neighborhood police stations and (in 1981) six hundred layoffs of uniformed officers. Meanwhile, the department was on the verge of two of the largest corruption scandals in its history, one of which Roache and Flynn had apparently been apprised from the start of their administration. The stagnation of the late 1970s and 1980s described in chapter 4 afflicted the BPD to much the same degree. As but one reflection of political infighting, racial division, and stagnation within the force, not a single civil service exam had been given for sergeant, lieutenant, or captain since 1977. In this context it could seem natural that the *Globe*, among others, would greet Roache as a fresh start.[15]

The theory of community policing did not descend into a vacuum. Rather, it emerged into the particular field of power that was Boston in the late 1980s. Even after the initial parts of Roache's new platform were in place, for instance, the rhetoric of "neighborhood" dominated that of "community," as it had in Ray Flynn's own populist election campaign.[16] In the context of Boston politics, community policing seemed only to legitimate the continuing installation of white-ethnic locals like Roache (in his case, from South Boston) to command positions, because they were, as it was said, from the "neighborhoods." Even five years later, in the postbusing city, to voice support for an "outsider" for the commissioner's post was considered virtually anathema to the debate.[17] Naturally, the neighborhood theme also played to police fraternalism, placating what I have described earlier as the police's sense of street proprietorship; not unimportantly, it also placated police hostility to federal oversight and to affirmative-action policies. Indeed, in a force that finally began to diversify ethnically (at least for African Americans, now about 20 percent of the force), began to add women, and began to get younger, this reaffirmation of "the neighborhood" had a decidedly unprogressive character. Even today, the racial tinges around the terms "neighborhood" and "community" persist. The not-so-subtle consensus was visible even when the commissioner and the Boston Police Patrolmen's Association (BPPA) seemed to be at odds. For instance, BPPA lawyer Frank McGee would belittle community policing as the interfering hand of "federally funded philosophers," as if he meant that local politics should shape police authority. However, the BPPA also complained that Roache's was a "political" appointment and seemed to lament those stagnant civil service exams on the force. In fact, it is likely that neither party wanted the up-and-coming, much less new, "outsiders" to take such exams. Similarly, Roache and his BPPA antagonists could each lampoon federal investigators, liberal "elitists," or even the BPD's own detective division, and thus mutually reinforce the idea of policing as a kind of aldermanic service.[18]

Roache soon undertook several changes that reflected how central policing was to Flynn's populist campaign promise to reinvigorate the neighborhoods. Roache began to reopen those station houses; he claimed to decentralize the police command staff, including adding civilian personnel to positions of authority; he spoke of a pet program in which patrol officers were encouraged to get out of their cars for forty-five minutes each shift, to "walk and talk" (the showcase term for the policy) with community members. Most significantly, Roache reaffirmed the department's commitment to restoring beat patrol, a campaign that had flagged under Jordan's tenure. Recognizing the fading emphasis of crime busting within police management literature like the Rand study of criminal investigation—and, some said, in anticipation of the coming corruption scandal—Roache also attempted to reassign some thirty detectives to beat patrol, chastising not only the division but what he called the "detective's mentality" itself. Backed by Flynn, he maintained experimental "team patrol" units in housing projects, using funds from a federal grant and even sustaining the program when the funds evaporated. And whereas for well over a decade, officers had been assigned to different city sectors on sequential days, Roache lobbied for steady beat patrol, announcing increased foot forces about every year throughout his tenure.[19]

At first, however, Roache's plan did not share in the reformist glow that neoconservative theorists were, at virtually the same time, beginning to fashion around foot patrol. Of course, by the end of his tenure, the *Globe* would cast Roache as a proponent of community policing from the start, albeit an unsuccessful one. In its initial phases of reintroduction, however, beat patrol was described not under this progressive-sounding label, but as a return to "traditional" policing *as such*. The familiar idea of returning to being "just a cop" is, in fact, a time-honored police aphorism: meaning, that is, not just a return to neighborhood beat patrol, but to traditions of informal discretion and, as we'll see, to "busting heads."[20] Moreover, even Roache could be found describing foot patrol itself as an *anti*reform strategy at the time, a rollback of the centralization that earlier managers had sought. Just as importantly, in Boston, Roache's reforms were often described as antiunion, since they tried to assert themselves against the resistance of the BPPA, which at this time held some eighteen hundred of Boston's force of roughly two thousand. For example, as Jordan had before him, Roache tried to institute one-person patrol cars against union objections. It wasn't long, therefore, before rank-and-file resistance to Roache could be felt. Initially, in fact, a local Boston finance commission supported the BPPA's contention that foot patrol was currently too underfunded to be successful. Moreover, innovations like team policing were resisted by police veterans and unions because they conflicted with the ever-growing use of overtime and paid "details" for outside work.[21] And, of course, the mix of nostalgia and therapeutic reassurance embedded in the image of the "caring" cop ran head-on into the crack epidemic and its associated violence in the late 1980s.

It was momentarily fortuitous, then, that the progressive rhetoric of community policing arrived at the moment it did. The principal theorist of the movement was political scientist James Q. Wilson, most notably in the oft-revised *Thinking about Crime* (1975), a book that later added as its center-piece the famous essay "Broken Windows: The Police and Neighborhood Safety," which Wilson coauthored with Northeastern University criminologist George L. Kelling Jr. in 1982. Kelling would himself be a consultant to the Boston Police Department from the mid-1980s onward.[22] Pivoting off the disturbing conjunction of soaring crime rates and the affluence of the 1960s (13–25), Wilson argued that the "root causes" of criminality often cited by liberal and radical criminologists—structural unemployment, racism, family disruption, and more—were in fact either of negligible consequence for understanding street crime or, in any event, beyond the current reach or desires of social policy (46–47). In one bold stroke, this assumption swept

aside not only left-leaning criminology and sociology, but challenged the entire relevance of these disciplines.[23] In turn, police power was subsumed under
the supposedly more pressing field of neighborhood political authority.
"Thinking about crime," Wilson and Kelling argued, could be better concep-
tualized by their hypothesis of the "broken window," the shattered pane of
glass in a building that, in this theory, signaled a community's tacit acceptance
of disorder, thus actually promoting more of it.

Of course, empirical support for this analogy was forthcoming. The "broken window" theory itself claimed to be drawn from a Stanford psychologist,
Philip Zimbardo, who had studied how abandoned cars were treated in disadvantaged and affluent neighborhoods (78). Meanwhile, Wilson and Kelling
cited findings like those of Albert Reiss's *The Police and the Public*, discussed
in chapter 3. Like Reiss, they argued that the "order-maintenance" function
of the beat cop, not crime busting, was a more accurate description of what
police really did (61). Again, the casting of LAPD-style paternalism as "impersonal," and thus ineffective, involved an important redrafting of history.
The broken "window" also covertly made a rhetorical link to the supposedly
separating "window" of the police patrol car (82). Kelling's observations from
the so-called Newark Foot Patrol Experiment of the mid-1970s (published
in 1981) make this rhetorical, quite literary casting apparent:

> The people on the street were primarily black; the officer who walked
> the street was white. The people were made up of "regulars" and
> "strangers." Regulars included both "decent folk" and some drunks and
> derelicts who were always there but who "knew their place." Strangers
> were, well, strangers, and viewed suspiciously, sometimes apprehen-
> sively. The officer (call him Kelly) knew who the regulars were, and
> they knew him . . . Drunks and addicts could sit on the stoops, but
> could not lie down. People could drink on side streets, but not at the
> main intersection. Bottles had to be in paper bags. Talking to, both-
> ering, or begging from people waiting at the bus stop was strictly forbid-
> den. If a dispute erupted between a businessman and a customer, the
> businessman was assumed to be right, especially if the customer was a
> stranger. If a stranger loitered, Kelly would ask him if he had any means
> of support and what his business was . . .
> . . . Sometimes what Kelly did could be described as "enforcing the
> law," but just as often it involved taking informal or extralegal steps to

help protect what the neighborhood had decided was the appropriate level of public order. Some of the things he did probably would not withstand a legal challenge. (77)

Reading semiotically, it is hard not to notice how much the status quo becomes the social good in this passage: in Newark's semantic rewriting, places are "known" and dwellers should return to them.[24] Along with the fundamental differentiation of stranger and "regular," the idea here is to reinstall the recognized hierarchy of a neighborhood, often explicitly identified as stemming from the authority of local businessmen. In this way the mythology of foot patrol presages the private-public partnerships of the 1990s that Kelling would promote (for example, the BID's overseen by private patrol forces).

The broken window also sorted citizens by how well they read its instructions. In stylistic terms, the implied reader of the community policing fable was a citizen who could displace academic (read: liberal) expertise and substitute common sense, a folkloric rationality that allowed Wilson, at various turns, to reduce complex criminological issues to supposedly logical aphorisms. (The parallels to Ronald Reagan, who nominated Wilson time and again to crime commissions, are perhaps obvious.) Yet as in the passage quoted at length above, the aura of folkloric rationality actually addressed different publics. In one sense it directly quoted the script of police populism: it restored "reason" to the cop's understanding of his job. And like earlier police reforms, community policing involved a political re-sorting of the public, a calling upon the cooperative citizen's own deference to informal and discretionary police power in particular. The repaired "broken window" was itself meant to work both as an ordering symbol to the community and a warning to the potential perpetrator. That is, it was a legible symbol, involving certain criteria for public or civil literacy.

Of course the question of how such a window would speak, if it was restored as new, wasn't entirely clear. Rather, the key turn in the argument was that deference to a single meaning (order) was now cast as a litmus test of citizenship itself. That is, the corollary was that criminality was rendered as a rational choice in the Benthamite pleasure-and-pain calculus of Wilson's legible street (143). Here is another folkloric fable that Wilson told, which itself sorted the community on the basis of the already known:

> Most of us are probably not very well informed about the true costs of crime; being law-abiding . . . But persons at risk (young men hanging

around on street corners and thieves who associate with other thieves) have quite different sources of information. These are the accounts of other young men and other thieves who have had a run-in with the police or the courts . . . Judge Bruce McDonald [asterisked as a "fictional name"] is either "Maximum Mac" or "Turn 'Em Loose Bruce" . . . (128)

In other words the law itself now became a sign system to be read, like that broken window.

Or, more precisely, to have *already* been read by the street criminal and his peers. Assuming that aggressive policing and sentencing would have a reverberating effect, of course, meant that this theory risked installing a systemic bias, results that could only be quite self-confirming.[25] But by addressing the police's own ingrained, equally retrospective actuarialism, Wilson's plan cut this corner. Rather, it not only called upon informal mechanisms of community social control, but the criminal's own *prior* "choice" whether or not to consign himself to those mechanisms. The street criminal was, in many ways, rewritten as someone who has already assessed his future, as if imagining lines on a future résumé, and made the wrong reading. Actuarial fatalism also reinforced the rationale for focusing police work on lower-level criminality, because the street criminal, it was now said, was only apprenticing to more serious and violent offenses down the line. (In other words, stop him before he commits a more violent crime.) Contrary to an assumption made by much of our scholarship on the serial killer phenomenon, that is, this type of criminal was *not* specializing in a certain kind of crime. Nor was he really seen as trapped in a repetitive pathology. To be seen that way, after all, was to invite the kinds of psychological expertise being marginalized, a threat we'll see sidelined in the Copney-Grant story. Rather, the young street criminal was seen as on the verge of intentionally expanding his criminal résumé and repertoire. In effect, Wilson simply anticipated the actuarial table and headed back to the perpetrator ready to fill it out (146).[26]

Wilson's new priority category of "predatory crime" thus in effect inverted the hierarchical scheme of August Vollmer, and made each gang member into a future gangster. Robbery, burglary, auto theft, and larceny were themselves often apprenticeship and gang crimes by the young. Of course, one of several glaring contradictions that this emphasis on criminal rationality papered over was that simultaneously rising crime and incarceration rates hardly indicated any real message about consequences was getting through to the street. Nevertheless, street crime was prioritized as not only predatory upon the community but a future threat. Not only, as is commonly pointed out on the left, was street crime prioritized over white-collar crime; it was also emphasized over crimes committed in private areas as well (64). With a characteristic tone of lament, such private-area crimes were sadly acknowledged as beyond the reach of such reforms; hence, for instance, so little attention to rape, so much to property crime and violence between men.

Along with this complex reshuffling of priorities came Wilson and Kelling's further acknowledgment: that some "communities" were so demoralized and crime-ridden so as to make foot patrol useless there (88). (Here, as we'll see in the *Globe*, which often ran Kelling's own op-ed columns, the term "community" had a differential meaning.) In the fatalistic tone that again marked the aura of neoconservatism, with its sad awareness that individual freedoms had exacted too high a price, this point also played to police forces as an audience—where, as we've seen, populism and fatalism were often the warp and weft. Covertly, the corollary even offered an implicit (and even at times self-admittedly racial)[27] presumption about which neighborhoods officer "Kelly" could and couldn't save. Explicitly directed at a localist and yet also differentiated notion of a city, here the term "community" substitutes *for* the boundaries of the municipality itself. Taken as a politics, then, this is essentially a beachhead strategy.[28] The rear flank was left open, meanwhile, for more aggressive and *really* traditional police practices where symbols and softball wouldn't work. As we'll see, Roache and Kelling themselves would move away from the core strategy of foot patrol without sacrificing the comforting aura it had helped to create.

This aura was crucial, nevertheless, to the redrafting of the relationship between citizenship and community authority. Of course, central to the community policing ethos was the idea that citizens' *perception* of lower crime rates actually helped to make the system work. To say the least, community policing advocates have had it more than both ways on the issue of crime measurement. Just as Wilson cited the UCR rates for the 1960s, in order to debunk "root causes," he then cited victimization studies to prove crime was more extensive than these traditional measurements had shown. But then he went on to argue that "perception" of crime was somehow something that could be managed. (Obviously, victim surveys show perception beyond police management.) Moreover, Wilson and Kelling overlooked the basic contradiction that a citizen who *feels* safer (say, a woman who thinks rape rates are down) might actually be putting him- or herself at greater risk by acting as if the streets *are* safer. But in the neoconservative alchemy that betrays the mark of public-relations thinking, the same citizen's presence on the streets would supposedly signal and structure order itself. In the community policing political unconscious, then, a citizen is in some sense him- or herself a beat cop, fully suffused in the notion that nothing succeeds like the appearance of success. The contradiction would repeat itself when, after decades of belittling standard crime measurements, community policing advocates rushed to embrace them when UCR rates fell in the late 1990s.

In the meantime, a new consensus—and a new history to go with it—was securely in place. Indeed, in Department of Justice pamphlets that often quoted Kelling at length, by the 1990s community policing was placed in a progressive history in which the 1960s and 1970s were recast as a period of "Social and Professional Awakening." Now the police were part of a movement for "constructive change."[29] Citing the support of Bill Clinton and Janet Reno, a unique compact was quite directly affirmed: Community policing, it was said, "is democracy in action."[30] Heroically, the "Police Respond[ed] to the Need for Change"[31] with the two-part philosophy theorists had outlined: community partnership and "problem solving" policing. Under this latter rubric, departments were given a list of strategies that, it was said, "exceeds the standard law enforcement emphasis"—though now, contrary to Wilson's realist candor, they seemed tame: helping accident victims, helping resolve neighborhood conflicts, "working with residents and local businesses to improve neighborhood conditions, controlling automobile and pedestrian traffic"—and much, much more.[32]

This is not to say that many of these activities don't have a place; many are valuable. Rather, it was the way such activities often provided cover for what most police officers still thought of as "real" work. Readily acknowledged, for instance, was how better "community partnerships" could actually improve the intelligence gathering that the LAPD or FBI had longed advocated. Meanwhile, "democracy in action," even according to the Bureau of Justice Assistance pamphlet *Understanding Community Policing*, often meant simply that police would respond to "community" (read: local businesses' and authority figures') requests for increased vigilance. Once again, response to call served to supplant any move toward civilian review.

Meanwhile, another clear risk was that criminal activity would be cast not merely as disorderliness or transgression but—since it was ostensibly rational—a refusal of citizenship itself. Straying individuals in the community were now described as making choices " 'based on the opportunities presented by the immediate physical and social characteristics of an area. By [our] manipulating these factors, people will be less inclined to act in an offensive manner.' "[33] Building upon Wilson's assumption that *behavior* was what could be altered,[34] police attention to what were called the "little things" gained legitimacy: once again, burglaries, panhandling, prostitutes, disorderly youths who "regularly assemble," or a disorderly or harassing individual.[35] Yet one such "solution" calls attention to the kinds of tactics that now qualified as addressing an "underlying problem" rather than a root cause:

> Manipulating environmental factors to discourage criminal behavior. This can include collaborative efforts to add better lighting, remove overgrown weeds and trim shrubbery, and seal off vacant apartment buildings.[36]

In a way, the streets themselves were made shallower, dehistoricized. And this emphasis on the disorder-breeding eyesore clearly played into the antithesis of what "Broken Windows" had seemed to propose, a restored community. Rather, now community policing seemed to become a recipe for crime lights, cleared lots, and boarded-up buildings. In this way, disorder was often simply sanitized and secured.[37]

In these crime lights, the eventual direction of Roache's campaign was anything but accidental. What began as aldermanic service, "democracy in action," soon took a harsher turn. Foot patrol was actually returned first to Area C (encompassing parts of Dorchester and South Boston), where a crackdown on public drinking began. Before long, as well, the force under Roache began to pay attention to those "problems," those "little things," that the theorists of community policing had identified. The department stepped up pressure on abandoned cars; they performed sweeps on prostitution, especially on soliciting adjacent to residential neighborhoods; and then came a crackdown on midlevel drug dealing, traditionally a province of federal authority. Almost immediately in March of 1985, Roache announced plans for a special undercover unit based on decoys and disguises to combat street crime. By the first months of 1986, drug arrests had doubled from the same interval of the previous year. In fact, however, *because* of the latitude the theory granted the police in the "order maintenance function"; because it seemed to sanction vocal community "leaders"; because it sanctioned differential policing—because of all this, the more aggressive, order-obsessed side of the community policing philosophy soon took over. The *Globe* reported that the institution of aggressive programs (some of which were first developed in Gates's LAPD) like the "Power Patrol" or "Operation Save" in Area B— Roxbury, Mattapan, and part of Dorchester—aimed at disorderly conduct, drug dealing, and gang violence, supposedly came at the request of community leaders in Roxbury (the Reverend Don Muhammad of the Nation of Islam and local NAACP head Jack E. Robinson). Police graphs boasted of drug-related arrests in Roxbury jumping a stunning 95 percent during the first three months of 1987. From there it was a short step to the department's announcement of a new "stop and frisk" policy in Area B, a policy that Flynn and Roache affirmed even in the face of Supreme Judicial Court declarations of its unconstitutionality. By 1989, arrests overall were reported to be up 20 percent, with a new emphasis on police "visibility" to allay, as theorists had insisted, the fear of crime itself. Police officials now spoke explicitly about arresting criminals for minor infractions *before* they would commit a more violent crime. The "get tough" policy was now the order of the day, and "stop and frisk," of course, ballooned out of control in the aftermath of Carol Stuart's murder.[38]

II

There is little need to rehearse *that* infamous history, which would seem to take us far afield from the Copney-Grant murders.[39] Nor do I mean to suggest that local media, or the *Globe* in particular, simply danced to the department's new tune. Dozens of officers from the Boston-area police, for instance, picketed the *Globe* right in that spring of 1991 over what they deemed unfair coverage of their work.[40] While the Copney-Grant plot was playing out, the *Globe* ran any number of concurrent stories and editorials critical of the department; the paper itself was an advocate of more emphasis on community policing.[41] And yet, it was this particular twist on the *Globe*'s advocacy that meant that the department was held to the bar of the image it was itself intent upon achieving. It followed easily, then, that the *Globe*'s everyday reporting, dutifully covering a press conference like that which inaugurated the Copney-Grant coverage, actually worked in tandem with the BPD's own self-representation as a "community" force from the get-go.

On 20 April 20 1991, eleven-year-old Charles Copney and fifteen-year-old Korey Grant were shot on the doorstep of Copney's home in Roxbury. The next day, the *Globe* opened its metro-section front-page coverage with the story. The stylistic conventions are familiar: under the headline "Boys, 11 and 15, shot dead in Roxbury," the first report opened with the standard recitations of police reports, with names of victims, ages, and addresses, time of shooting, followed up by police descriptions of the crime scene. These are punctuated by an eye-catching, emotional fact about Copney's age:

> Two Boston youths, one of whom had just asked his mother if he could go out and "play," were shot and killed in Roxbury last night, police said.
>
> The youths, Charles Copney of Highland Avenue, who turned 11 on Tuesday, and 15-year-old Korey Grant of 26 South Huntington Ave., died at Boston City Hospital shortly before 9 p.m., Deputy Police Superintendent Willis Saunders said.
>
> Police said the shooting occurred at about 8:10 p.m. on the sidewalk outside 27 Highland Ave. in Roxbury after the two youths, who were friends, were approached by a larger group of youths. An argument broke out, and the assailants opened fire with a high caliber automatic handgun, police said.
>
> Copney and Grant were each struck once, police said.
>
> Police believe that the two youths may have been involved in a fist-fight about two weeks ago, and that the other youths involved in the fight, 14 to 16 years old, are prime suspects in the case, according to two sources close to the investigation.[42]

The report, as usual, is victim centered, with the tradition of last names now applied, uneasily, to children. And yet, as sociologist Gaye Tuchman best reminded us, all facts are qualified by attribution to police authorities. And not unimportantly, the police release, citing with exactitude the time of death and ambulance arrival, announcing suspects in sight, underscores the force's own efficiency. But something different is in the air: for both Commissioner Roache and Mayor Flynn are at the news conference itself. " 'We want the people to know we are hurting also,' " Roache is quoted as saying; " 'We are part of the community and we feel this as much as anyone else.' "[43]

As Bostonians know, Flynn had himself been (affectionately and derogatorily) nicknamed "Mayor 911" for his penchant for showing up at crime scenes and even attending to victims. The sentiments he and Roache expressed above were doubtless heartfelt. Yet my interest here falls on how the framing of the conference differs from the conventional "911" posture police had taken even in the recent past. Roache's rhetorical displacement of the term "public" with "community" was itself indicative of a shift. The conventions within journalistic representation, understood both as a response to sources and as narrative keys, quickly reflected these new conditions in the field. Within the *Globe* itself, even as the emergency medical technician timings reported above reinforced the more traditional image of rapid response, Roache's appearance in fact positioned his department as more than a crime-busting or even a professional force. Rather, he said it was part of the victim community itself.

Of course, the conference served its traditional purpose as a venue for news management. But now even traditional functions took on a different look. In narrative terms, we might say, the press conference now functioned as what James Clifford calls a "spatial practice" for the *Globe* reader, one that bore particularly on what community policing grew to stand for. That is, much as an anthropologist's tent substitutes metonymically for the village s/he reports on—and in turn, for the larger social entity like a nation—here, the news conference functioned partly as a location that "represented" the urban community in the senses of standing for *and* displacing it.[44] The conference venue is, for instance, bridged back, by the *Globe*'s conventional place naming, to the crime itself; those officials present, moreover, are implicitly linked metonymically to "police officers at the scene [of the crime]" who report having seen, for the first time, that emergency medical technician cry.[45] However, the headline's in-situation in Roxbury disguises this neighborhood's actual distance from the news conference (location unidentified), effecting a narrative substitution running through the representation of police authority at this stage. The Boston locality is itself being redrafted. Even the paper's own ritual of objectivity tended to reinforce the police-citizen byplay the theory of community policing called for: echoing police pronouncements, and then typically shuttling to community leaders to get their reaction. And when the new tactics seemed to fail, it was always because there hadn't yet been *enough* community policing.[46] Indeed, as I will show, this very pliability to Wilson and Kelling's mythos allowed even the more liberal *Globe* to have it both ways: reinforcing the claim to community, yet clinging to standard crime-busting measurements, eventually much to Roache's detriment.

Events, meanwhile, were moving. The day after the shooting, three African American males—Bynoe, William Dunn (age sixteen), and Tarahn Harris (age sixteen)—were arrested and subsequently charged with first-degree murder and conspiracy to commit murder. Almost immediately, police authorities, citing community sources and witnesses, leaked the idea that the shooting was the result of gang conflict, specifically revenge on the part of members of one gang, the Trailblazers, for a melee over a girl with another group, the Blackhawks, at the Dudley Square mass-transit (MBTA) station two or three weeks earlier.[47] The following year, the case went through several twists—and, according to many, a shocking outcome. All three defendants were deemed capable of rehabilitation, in the reports of court psychologists at the requisite "transfer" hearings set to determine whether they should be tried as adults. But Dunn and Harris, who apparently did *no* shooting, *were* deemed adults, while *Bynoe*, the shooter, was remanded to the juvenile system, wherein he pleaded guilty, and was committed to the Department of Youth Services. Under existing law at the time, he could be held there only until his twenty-first birthday. To many observers—columnists from the right and left, police and Roxbury leaders, Copney neighbors and Beacon Hill politicians—who had called for adult trials and hard jail time, Bynoe's sentence seemed to illustrate the utter breakdown of juvenile justice. Republican Governor William Weld, formerly of Edwin Meese's criminal justice division, was hardly mavericking when he said the handling of these cases put a "shadow over the state's entire justice system." "A system," Weld added in his remarks to the *Globe*, "that puts a convicted murderer back on the streets just because he turns 21 is a system that has failed."[48] In elections to come, the Copney case would still be a political haymaker for Weld and other law-and-order advocates.

The chain of events I have narrated above might seem a naturally unfolding set of facts that inevitably produced—or, in McNamara's unfortunate pun, "triggered"[49]—the political debate over the punishment of adolescents. But of course what I have rehearsed here is merely a plot, the structure of the story that the *Globe* chose to represent. By contrast, for example, the *Herald*'s tendency, an elaboration of the tabloid tradition discussed in my earlier chapters, was to focus more on crime scene re-creations, witness accounts, forensic detail of the brutality of the crime.[50] Part of the *Globe*'s "civic" posture was, by contrast, to disdain such crime scene details and look for the "big" picture. Indeed, by centering the story on the legal cases of Bynoe and his friends, the *Globe* seemed to begin with the ready-made moral Weld had identified, even if such a conclusion was anything but inevitable.[51] Therefore, rather than triggering its own debate, an already existing debate had framed the story.

Again, at first glance, this debate might seem far afield from community policing or its representation. That is, the frame had already been generated by state legislation previously amended in December of 1990, which (a) mandated that juveniles over the age of fourteen alleged to have committed murder would, at a transfer hearing, have to show that they should *not* be tried as adults; and (2) that all hearings would now be open to the public. (Trial transcripts would still not be.)[52] In fact not only does the *Globe* call up this debate in its very first story—with all the local officials there to signal it—but by its own style of representation as well. The *Globe* signaled this already-there frame, in the first place, by publishing the names of the three juvenile defendants, a departure the law now allowed but not imitated unanimously by area media. In fact this seemingly minor change signaled other, more fundamental ways in which victims, defendants, and the Roxbury community would now be ushered into the *Globe*'s spotlight.[53] And that was because, of course, these legislative reforms had been inspired, in part, by the desire to put the "character" of criminals (as I've been saying, their choices) into public scrutiny. That is, in addition to reversing the presumption of juvenile status for those committing violent crimes, the new law had been intended to enhance the court standing of victims and to reinforce community oversight of the young. (Weld, in fact, had and would continue to lobby for automatic adult trials for *all* juvenile homicide defendants, barring a judge's override.)[54] The *Globe*'s own spotlighting simply followed suit.

The consensus here was as startling as it was contradictory. When Commissioner Roache himself, nominally a Democrat, was quoted by the *Globe* as saying that "everyone who commits" murder "should be treated as an adult," he not only extended Republican Weld's case but exposed its central weakness. The culturally disorderly contradiction here centered both on Bynoe's supposedly rational choice and the utility of exposing him to public view. Having committed a homicide earned the defendants, in Weld's spin on the frame, the status of adults (somewhat like going to a peep show). Meanwhile, the political rhetoric of "man-sized punishments for man-sized crimes," again evocative of Kelling and Wilson's folkloric appeal to "reason," in fact probably worked to reinforce the volatile machismo of the crime itself, a potentially disastrous contradiction for young males some interpreters view as culturally emasculated or caught between ritualized honor and habitual criminality.[55] In the *Globe*, meanwhile, the Copney-Grant case was framed as a "test case," despite the fact that judicial determination would still, by law, include consideration of the defendants' susceptibility to rehabilitation.[56]

Potential cross-purposes and different plots do contest this framing in the early phases of the process. After the *Globe* recites the ambulance arrivals, Mayor Flynn reveals that he is the source of Copney's last request about playing outside. But then he "used the occasion" to call for handgun controls. Complaining that " 'anyone who wants one can obtain a firearm,' " Flynn calls the lack of stricter gun controls a " 'major issue gnawing at the social conscience of America.' "[57] Even this honorable plea situates the loss within a decipherable social allegory, itself later to be contested by columnists and some community members themselves. Despite their evident sincerity, his familiar, even hackneyed phrases identify the story he tells as a cultural master plot that, of course, fit into the broader allegory of Roache's and Flynn's own rise from the "neighborhood." Time intervals now not only contribute to the sense of tragedy, but to social placement:

> Flynn said he spoke to the parents of both children at the hospital. He said Copney's mother had come home from work just before the shooting. According to Flynn, she said the boy had asked her if he could go out to play, and that she replied that he could if he was back indoors by 8:15.
>
> "Five more minutes, and he would have been fine," Flynn said.
>
> "These were two young people from good families who were in the wrong place at the wrong time. Two young people with great potential and a great future were cut down in the prime of life," he said.[58]

In Flynn's peroration about hard-working families threatened by disorder, a populist myth I described in chapter 4, the land of equal opportunity, is put at risk—perhaps making the streets of Roxbury themselves the "wrong" place.[59] Thus, in its opening phase this terrible drama would seem to enact much of what recent theorists suppose: an affirmation of technical efficiency and compassion by police and city authorities—and, more broadly, of Boston's tutelage of Roxbury. Of course, we also need to see that Flynn's speech, attempting to turn the debate to gun control, represents a failed attempt to frame the story against what, henceforth, I will call the "Weld mainframe."

III

This would not, that is, be a story about guns. But beyond highlighting its nearly invisible political sponsor, I refer to the Weld mainframe, in part, to broach a broader analytical problem. And that is that despite the fact that the Boston field lacks the saturnalian diversity of news coverage even twenty years earlier—much less that of the Dora Clark and Dot King cases—the *Globe*'s technical apparatus does allow it to represent, in itself, a variety of story "threads." If a more procedural narrative produces a readerly lockstep through clues, on the *Globe*'s pages we seem to have more options. Thus the simple fact is that determining which frame (or "story," or interpretation) *does* hold sway might seem to depend on what coverage we attend to. The master plot of Copney, Grant, and Bynoe, framed by the Weld-spun debate over adjudication and community oversight, might be seen as something like a central "program" (hence mainframe) from and through which other story-subroutines flow.

I choose these technocratic analogies deliberately. To a degree, the shifting of a story like the Copney-Grant case to front-page status might be seen as "tabloidization," an attempt to rival its crosstown tabloid competitor, the *Herald*.[60] For a Stephen Crane or a Mark Hellinger or a Jimmy Breslin, the physical layout of the daily newspaper (its columns, its back pages) seemed to reembody the city's own byways and alleys itself—a tradition, I will show, some columnists of the *Globe* still draw upon. Yet taken as a whole the *Globe*'s multilayered format suggests, again, something more like an overview, if not an Olympian vantage point, juxtaposing events at will. Thus even the Copney-Grant "story" seems less a text than something more like a hypertext. That is, the *Globe*'s layout repeatedly positioned its relevant columns within a constellation of other stories that one eye or another might read as relevant or peripheral: single stories about homicides with similar facts, family profiles, stories about community marches in Roxbury, cartoons about the NRA. A turn in one of these related plots might well have generated another subroutine of equal depth and duration: for example, the discovery that Willie Dunn had been released by juvenile court judge Paul McGill, despite a Department of Social Services recommendation for incarceration, just three days before the slayings. (A version, that is, of James Q. Wilson's "Turn 'Em Loose Bruce.") That being said, it remains striking how the Weld mainframe held, especially if we consider what subroutines were *not* generated in proximity:

about the latitude or temperament of Judge McGill; about debates around preventive detention or probation; about broader issues like racism or economic opportunities for black youth. (The Dudley Square MBTA trolley station, for instance, was concurrently the site of struggle over contract guarantees for minority and local workers.) The power of the frame was no better indicated in that the "story" stayed on Bynoe; virtually no controversy, for instance, arose over the fact that McGill had *overridden* his court psychologists in regard to the transfers of Dunn and Harris.[61]

Certain long-recognized conventions of news coverage also contributed to the Weld mainframe's durability. For example, following standard news conventions, the victims were consistently cast, as Robert Blau or Mitch Gelman would have seen, as innocents. How else, we might imagine, to account for the unthinkable fact of an eleven-year-old dead on his mother's doorstep?[62] And yet, what was most striking was how the *Globe* not only fixated on the younger bystander, but more to the point allowed his innocence to encompass the apparent target of the shooting, Korey Grant. And if Bynoe would soon gravitate in coverage from an average kid to an ambiguous leader/follower figure, to a learning-disabled, troubled-at-home, machismo-seeking crack dealer, Grant stayed relatively unseen, sometimes portrayed merely as the kid shot while on school vacation visiting his divorced father. Only at the very end, for instance, might we notice that Korey Grant was six feet tall and weighed 235 pounds.[63] As Eileen McNamara would point out, this polarization of coverage disguised the potential similarities of victim and defendant, and thus the cycle of violence itself.[64] Imagine a plot, for example, that begins not at the time of the shooting, but in an earlier scene where Grant terrorizes Bynoe to fear for his life. We cannot imagine it at this point, because except for stray moments (*Harris's* testimony after arrest, which his own lawyer deemed inadmissible, and one neighbor's remarks), police authorities and the prosecution not only narrated all prior events but decided, in effect, when the time of our crime story began. At the transfer hearings, Judge McGill would rely heavily upon the police structure of events about gang initiation and payback.[65]

What this suggests, I think, is that the mainframe also held because of the temporal boundaries it acquired, a fixed time-line convention moving from crime scene to courtroom drama. As I've said, the story began by inscribing a presumption of police efficiency, an already-set job well done. Subsequently, the *Globe*'s plot moved swiftly from being victim centered to a focus on community members' reactions, and then to trial testimony seasoned by relatives' reactions. This is all quite familiar to news theorists, too. Nevertheless, reflecting some of the contradictions of the Weld mainframe, the coverage actually peaked at the transfer hearings, and even then extended only to the sentencing phases. Incarceration, the fate upon which neoconservative thinking so often relies, actually remained in the shadows. (The exception was McNamara's visit to Bynoe, to which I will return).[66] Though it is possible coverage could be renewed if Bynoe commits another crime now that he has been released, the mainframe actually allowed little to clarify the issues that supposedly "governed" it. Or to look beyond it to ever-swelling prisons. From other *Globe* stories, for example, one could also discover that most first-degree murders even under Roache's tenure were actually pleaded out. In fact, of course, *Bynoe* had pleaded out.[67]

Meanwhile, where the *Globe*'s mainframe story legitimated the police's supposed efficiency and their account of the crime itself, it also did so at the expense of the legal system following the arrests. Bureaucratic ineptitude, or so it seemed, was only accentuated as new reports emerged: about Dunn's earlier release, about the court records of Dunn's prior arrest (which his lawyer said were faulty), and more. This seeming litany of inefficiency, albeit part of adversarial justice, nevertheless worked to create a panorama of an inept judicial machine unable to process even "proven" criminals. (There it was again: a criminal's prior choice.)

Meanwhile, *Globe* coverage again followed the reform of court procedures themselves by individuating the defendants, thus reinforcing the neoconservative mainframe's theme of individual moral choice. At moments there is something quite unintentionally horrific about the *Globe*'s rendering of these courtroom determinations of moral character, reminiscent of Dora Clark's spectacle. In complete contradiction to the neoconservatives' idea of the expanding criminal résumé, the *Globe* reports Bynoe as crying, remorseful, and having submitted well to his prior probationary scheme, and thus he is deemed a juvenile subject to the state's care. Dunn and Harris, who cannot or will not submit to this ritual, and having previously used violence in committing crimes, are deemed adults. Bynoe's fellow defendants very nearly ended up invoking, against their will, the image of the superpredator aimed against them. Paired against the still-juvenile Bynoe, that is, it seems almost as if Dunn and Harris are there to illustrate the suitability of incarceration through which the state could actually forgo its rehabilitative responsibilities. A distinction, of course, directly echoing Wilson and Kelling's differentiation of communities.[68]

But however arcane, dismal, and familiar these morality plays seem, the temporal boundaries of the coverage have another consequence, a side effect we often overlook in the cliché news prefix derived from police: the words "gang-related." In the trial phases of its coverage, the *Globe* certainly gives prominence to the voices of those court-appointed psychological experts individuating the assailants. And yet, the *group* dynamic of Bynoe's supposed recruitment to the gang—which was, apparently, central to McGill's differentiation of Dunn and Harris *from* Bynoe—is wholly un-testified-upon in the *Globe* coverage at the time. Indeed, as we shall see, comparing the *Globe* reports to McGill's final reasoning, one might easily conclude he just plain had his facts wrong.

IV

At this point, it is understandable why much media criticism echoes Stuart Hall's sense that journalists lend an aura of "professional-technical neutrality" to their reports. In much of contemporary theory, as I've said, this aura both orchestrates a field of meanings and represents authority itself, in a manner akin to John Fiske's description of the normalizing studio of network news.[69] Or, to put it in narrative terms, the *Globe*, as we shall see, takes on the status of a narrator *and* character in the city. Thus we would seem to have the "channeling" process Hall and others have described. Yet there is an important difference. Subsequently, rival voices actually *do* make an appearance in the *Globe*'s pages, as it were scrimmaging over interpretation much as Weld and Flynn did at the outset of the story. Thus, rather than reading the news as simply exhibiting a monolithic order, much less the familiar surveillance of Foucauldian "policing," we might see that it enacts a very different sorting of community order. A media outlet like the *Globe*, because it operates in a field of print journalism Bourdieu would term "pathological" in its monopolization, must in fact "entertain" local and, in certain ways, rival voices as part of its liberal representational protocols, rather than just simply reproducing those narrow "official" grooves. Otherwise, I would argue, its police stories would not garner the authority that they do.[70] In other words, the *Globe* enacts what Robert K. Manoff has identified as an "only" formal polyphony—that is, the *appearance* of re-creating public debate *in* itself (and thus that "civic voice").[71]

For example, in two articles bracketing the victims' funerals, the *Globe* turned its attention to Roxbury activists and mourners, portraying a community struggling to come up with answers—street counseling, gun buybacks, and more—to combat recurrent violence.[72] Local ministers chastised neighborhoods, churches, and parents for abandoning their disciplinary roles, as did the Reverend Bruce Wall in a Sunday *Globe* op-ed piece. And there were, as well, other culprits momentarily brought out into the light:

> Grant was typical of "the gold in Roxbury that only has to be dug up and refined," Rev. [Michael] Haynes said [at the funeral]. But too frequently it is instead ignored by parents, members of the clergy and elected officials who squander the resource while blaming others, he said.
>
> "Our teen-agers do not make guns. Our teen-agers do not grant liquor licenses and own package stores. Our teen-agers do not grow the narcotics. Our teen-agers do not control television," Rev. Haynes said.
>
> "Older folks do!"
>
> . . . After mourners paid their last respects, Grant's casket was taken . . . His death will have been for naught, Rev. Haynes warned, if it is viewed as just another tragic incident—and not as a turning point.[73]

Haynes's attempts at mobilization are certainly given voice; here, indeed, was a challenge to the neoconservative transformation of children into adults. On the other hand, here also were some of the sentiments that invited the partnership community policing performed. The *Globe's* report, let it be said, seems uncomfortable in the face of this activism, depicting the community, in the first piece, as so "provoked" as to "lay aside its rhetoric"; in the second, the *Globe* observes that Grant "was laid to rest with wails and cries of anger at adults apparently too willing to squander the resources of their young."[74]

That is, if the juvenile court system comes off poorly in *Globe* coverage, the paper exhibits equal guardedness toward what it calls the "Roxbury community" subject to the court's rulings. Along with the racial inflection mentioned earlier, the denomination "community" is now linked with a blurring of the terms "activist" and "resident" as well.[75] Meanwhile, Haynes's heroic call is also partly defused by the bitter aura the *Globe* gives the proceedings.

The conventional sequence from crime scene to funeral actually has a containing effect on Haynes's attempt to dispel the aura of "tragedy" and juvenile responsibility already imposed by the Weld mainframe. Almost inevitably, as the *Globe* depicts it, it is not Rome burning, but quite decidedly Roxbury, a community wallowing in gestures that look rhetorical and futile. And after playing this role, Roxbury is largely reduced to a chorus as coverage returns to the trial scenes.

The similar sidelining of alternative voices appeared in the op-ed pages. Black journalist Derrick Z. Jackson, writing in the *Globe*'s editorial pages, himself pointed to the implicit marginalizing of Roxbury, saying sarcastically that he was grateful "that the *Globe* said 'a phalanx' of friends and relatives" shielded Copney's mother from the glare of the media. At least, Jackson said, this "defied the stereotype." But the two black commentators on this story, Jackson and visiting commentator Wall, were hardly successful in turning coverage in the *Globe* toward, respectively, better educational opportunities or the black church's potential role in supporting families. Rather, it was the aura of hardened "realism" that acquired greater force. This process was nowhere better illuminated than when two reporters, John Ellement and Tom Coakley, commented in passing on the effect of the law now allowing access to the 22 April arraignment in Roxbury juvenile court:

> The small courtroom in Roxbury was filled with relatives of the victims and the teen-agers charged with ending their lives. The number of kin was so large that only a small group of reporters was allowed into the courtroom to represent the public.[76]

This otherwise-incidental aside, perhaps added to refer ironically to the law's intent, also tells much about the *Globe*'s own self-appointed role. At one level, the passage performs a familiar sequence of Fourth Estate substitutions: the reporter stands in for the newspaper, which in turn stands in for the public and its right to know. But in so doing, the aside also performs some of the differentiation of the "community" that community policing itself put in place. For looked at closely, another opposition is generated: that of the reporter/paper/"public" (that "civic voice") versus the kin community of Roxbury. As a chorus, Roxbury is positioned outside the staging area of realistic civil deliberation.

It was only fitting, then, that it was white columnists who arose to voice community rage, in the classic "hard-boiled" populist style. The posture was best represented by *Globe* columnist Mike Barnicle, sometimes called Boston's Jimmy Breslin, who first offered his column "Blood Is Gone, Horror Remains" on 23 April. By this point, Barnicle's reputation was well established as the columnist to whom *Globe* readers looked for police inside dope and for "gritty" urban populism. (All this, despite the fact that Barnicle himself, by now, was a suburbanite.)[77] In earlier columns, for example, Barnicle had complained about the intrusion of yuppie styles on the Boston force ("wearing a Nike jogging outfit" instead of "putting on a blue tunic and doing a hard job, honestly"), about double standards of morality applied to the department, about "sleepless taxpayers" forcing cops to do the work of parents in attending to teenage drinkers on street corners instead of burglaries or robbery. These beat-level attacks, as if copied from the pages of Joseph Wambaugh, were sometimes quite explicitly directed at Roache himself.[78]

Barnicle's first column on these murders, predictably, turns to Copney's death, hammering home its message of sympathy in staccato cadences. In a tradition handed down from Hellinger to Breslin to David Simon, Barnicle begins by casting a natural world indifferent to heart-wrenching details of violence; then he shifts to Gothic terror. Implicitly paralleling the column itself to urban thoroughfares, the effect is pure "Dies the Victim, Dies the City":

> A WILD SPRING RAIN lashed the city Sunday and washed what was left of the baby's blood off the sidewalk where he died Saturday about 8 p.m. on the steps of his own home on Highland Avenue in Roxbury, purportedly killed by the dogs of night who were all quite young and more dangerous than dynamite.

In a case itself marked by machismo (rival gangs, whose names invoked either frontier conflict or pro basketball teams, fighting over a girl), Barnicle's own masculine, hard-boiled voice positions itself "on the street," listening to the heartbeat of the city. This allows the column to pit itself against the assailants, who in Barnicle's account lost an earlier fight and yet returned, gutlessly, with a gun.[79] Like his tabloid predecessors, Barnicle's persona thus supplements the get-tough posture of those seeking "man-sized" punishments; extending and yet also modifying the spatial segmentation Ellement and Coakley had established, Barnicle's "street" wisdom allows the *Globe* to represent bilaterally not only the disinterested public, but the city in its raw materiality. At its core, this double political claim was also central to formulations like James Q. Wilson's: here, claiming both fraternity with Roxbury and yet covertly the ability to supersede it.[80]

And also to deny the *Globe*'s own complicity with the Weld mainframe itself. By molding himself as an urban populist, Barnicle can both appropriate the language of toughness and seem to distance himself from political labels. So he writes that these boys from Roxbury "sit surrounded and ignored by politicians who think of life as a series of abstract notions or quaint theories." Meanwhile, however, these same politicians provide a convenient segue to lapsed authority closer to "home," a home (Boston/Roxbury/the Bynoe family) that has not done its job. The article shifts into testimony by "one of Pat Copney's friends"—the aura of street-level facticity is seasoned by fraternal familiarity with Roxbury—who offers up her solution to the crisis:

> "My son is 16," the woman said. "And I keep my foot in his ass and my fist in his face. That's the down South way. That's how I was raised. Not the Diss way. That's how you teach them respect. This is a Catholic state—and I like Catholics—but we need the electric chair here. We need to fry a couple of these little [expletive]. Then you'll see the rest of them start to pay attention. I truly believe that." [brackets Barnicle's]

Police populism is never far removed from this putative street testimony. Indeed, as if to solidify the urban front, Barnicle juxtaposes this parent's testimony with that of the police, led by a hard-working sergeant in homicide named Herby Spellman, said to be trying to contain his "natural emotion of outrage" too.

Through Spellman's presence, in fact, the initial press conference is alluded to and rewritten. Going that occasion one better, Barnicle now differentiates the police from the politicians, as Mayor Flynn (another male faced down) is implicitly put in his place by Spellman's own words:

> "Copney was in the wrong place at the wrong time," someone said to Spellman [directly echoing Flynn; brackets mine].
>
> "No," Herby Spellman quietly replied. "He was in the right place at the right time. He was a little boy who was going home when his mother told him to, and he got killed. He was in the right place at the right time. It was where he lived."

Of course, this might seem merely populist one-upmanship. In fact Barnicle is only staking a claim the traditional nuclear-family values Flynn himself had invoked, the sacred right to one's home. But drawing upon a narrative syncretism with police ranks themselves, Barnicle also sharpens the social division further, both from Flynn and from Roxbury. Pat Copney has done her job, and Herby Spellman has done his. But implicitly, other parents in Roxbury—the parents of the assailants—had not.

The hard-boiled style thus strikes comradeship with only *part* of Roxbury, the part that expressed nostalgia for discipline and welcomed police and judicial toughness. In conjunction with the example of the policeman, Barnicle shows he too can suppress his rage. Thus the sharp diction of hard-boiled-dom plays off against that supposedly inflated "rhetoric" of community activists. Virtually the same scrimmaging between rage and hard-boiled-dom, internalized in Barnicle's persona, found its way, as well, into the identity and politics of fellow columnist Alan Lupo. In his essay on the case, Lupo found himself in the contradictory position of saying old liberal solutions seemed "obvious" and yet somehow irrelevant. Initially foiling himself to the hard-boiled tradition of the crime beat, saying that he "stopped going to the scenes of most crimes" because he had "lost the hardened shell of a reporter to the more easily penetrated veneer of a father," Lupo tries initially in his column on the affair to defend the social remedies Weld and his cohorts demean as "touchy-feely." But recovering the very voice he claims to have lost, Lupo goes on to write that he could not apply traditional liberal remedies to the "slugs who killed Copney and Grant." It was, he said, "too late to feel sorry for them [the assailants]"; the murderers should be "put away forever." Quite explicitly, that is, "slug" status—a street term echoing Hellinger's *News*, or Mitch Gelman's initiation—now meant adult standing for Bynoe, and that meant jail time.[81]

At this juncture of the plot, particularly when such columns are considered alongside news reports, technical neutrality or disinterest hardly seems to rule the day; nor does an unmediated liberal ideology. Quite the contrary: to achieve its "civic voice," the *Globe* must scrimmage with rival voices of rage, entertain them, to blend police populism with liberal realism. Momentarily, in fact, the need of the hard-boiled columnist to strike fraternity with the streets (and, of course, the police) puts the *Globe*'s more elite liberalism in abeyance even when it came to Damien Bynoe. Or, to put it another way, the populism of the style now seems to extend beyond anger at "politicians" and endanger liberal dominance in the *Globe* itself. Indeed, it might be said that the *Globe* has painted itself into a corner: affirming its own "community" status, working through that metonymic collapse of places (Boston/Roxbury) inaugurated in its first report, invoking (as Flynn had) that time-honored nostalgia for discipline that was part of the "caring" package Roache and Flynn embodied, the *Globe*'s story line necessarily ventriloquized the Weld mainframe even as it claimed, editorially, to dispute it. Yet because both Weld's dominance and the community's rage are figured as threats to the way things ought to be, the coverage must ultimately "cover" itself. In effect, the *Globe* calls up a rewrite.

V

As the legal cases of Tarahn Harris and Willie Dunn lingered on through 1992, 1993, and even 1994, the notes above were struck time and again. Barnicle, for example, returned to the crime in 1994 with a column titled "Getting Away with Murder," complaining about the way the defendants had "court-appointed lawyers and psychiatrists and social workers retained to explain or excuse" their actions, while Copney and Grant had only "undertakers." But as far as the story line in 1991 itself was concerned, staffer Eileen McNamara, in the newspaper's Sunday *Magazine* section, was left with the business of a rewrite. Or perhaps, a "re-left," since it is here, in an extended format, where more conventional liberal accounting is mobilized. Essentially, McNamara's article is a "redress," since it both offsets its hard-boiled predecessors and returns the *Globe* (and hence, its suburban-liberal readers) to the more familiar high ground of civic dispassion. The process of entertainment is thus completed, rage defused, the globe turned on its axis.

The redress is ushered in by a third-person re-creation of Damien Bynoe's consciousness as the lead-in to McNamara's article. We see his thoughts, putatively, at his moment of arrest, a modified internal monologue that then shifts its narrative position around his family:

> He hadn't told his mother, and now there wasn't time. He'd been waiting for hours for the cops to come. Now that they were here, everything was happening too fast. His mother, roused from bed by bare knuckles banging on the door: a detective asking for Damien. Her mouth, dry from sleep, forming the question "what?" over and over, as though she were climbing out of a dream. Enough time to whisper "Hide the bullets" to his kid brother.[82]

At first, by putting the bullets in Bynoe's possession, it is as if McNamara is continuing the hard-boiled realism established by Barnicle and Lupo. She herself deprecates what she calls the "Political messages" and "Legal codes"[83] swirling passionately around Bynoe's case, rhetoric drowned out at the "street level" of reality. But this opening signals a different strategy to come: the re-creation of Bynoe's adolescent mental state as it coped with the familiar dysfunctional contours of his home life—worries about displacement by a new baby his mother takes in;[84] worries about telling his mother, who has been laid off from work, about the crime; thoughts about a father living in Mission Hill.[85] We also learn that Damien Bynoe is learning disabled.[86] And in what follows, we follow something like a five-part circuit of testimony— from Bynoe's mind, to psychological experts, to the victims' families, to Judge McGill, and back to Bynoe again. The sum effect is a surveying sweep, a "taking account" of Bynoe's adolescent confusion, the psychological experts who discount "back end treatments" like incarceration, and—finally—a scene depicting the penitent Bynoe pondering his future while under juvenile lockup. McNamara's account thus seems to undercut the passionate parties who made political sound and fury over the fate of a confused child. Her circuit of testimony is, as well, fundamentally reflective of the liberal journalist's claim to "balance" by seeming to touch all sides of debate.

McNamara's broader retrospective viewpoint, therefore, readjusts the political spin. Her sweep allows her, perhaps most importantly, to recoup (previously feminized) psychological expertise. In effect, after recounting earlier beatings and threats Bynoe experienced at the hands of area gangs, McNamara finally provides that plot that, before, we could not imagine. She offers the fullest recounting of the defense version of the shooting: Bynoe claims he shot out of panic, and didn't know he had hit anyone until he heard it on the late news.[87] Similarly, McNamara sprinkles her scene settings not with crime scene details of blood and pain, as Barnicle had, but with front-end details of social landscape to signal the economic and political deprivation, the "root causes" so typically marginalized by neoconservative theorists of community policing and the *Globe*'s own coverage. For example, we are shown a closed gymnasium, despite a framed portrait of Mayor Flynn (locally known for his basketball prowess) in the Bynoe living room.[88] And two characters' roles are enlarged to fit the rewritten plot. Judge McGill, previously an authoritative, but potentially bungling figure, is now depicted as hard-working, Boston-born and -bred, humanly flawed; perhaps feeling the political heat,

McGill is described as having never bought the defense case, yet having found something to save in Bynoe's character.[89] And finally, if the mother of Charles Copney dominated early coverage (including a sympathetic report of a subsequent, unrelated street robbery), McNamara reintroduces Bynoe's mother, seen delivering a cleaned-up pair of secondhand sneakers to her son in lockup. Indeed, these sneakers emerge as the dominant symbol of McNamara's re-write: for if we hear again that Damien Bynoe indeed sold crack cocaine, we are also told that he did so only in order to buy himself a pair of new "Ewing" Nikes.[90]

Necessarily, McNamara's piece itself still works from within certain givens of the Weld mainframe. After all, she is replying to the debate over juvenile and adult status that put Bynoe in its center. Her novelistic narrative voice not only works to present Bynoe's memories as fact, but to re-present the issue about juvenile rationality implicit in the debate as a whole.[91] But at this point, McNamara is able to eliminate all remaining traces of journalistic identification with street rage or rhetoric. That is, she can contest the *Globe*'s own populism. But it is McNamara's character that itself plays a key role. As a figure mobile to the scene, able to move from Bynoe's mind to judges' chambers with equal facility, McNamara's voice, in fact, might be said only to rechart the trajectory of the *Globe*'s rhetorical positioning as it had evolved during the reporting phrase. That is, she (1) opens with an assertion of fraternity with the street; then (2) re-creates the *Globe*'s own conventional circuit or stopping points of testimony; and then (3) moves from the street (and Roxbury) to the higher ground of liberal-psychological authority, the very expertise Barnicle had ridiculed.[92]

Yet notice: by the time McNamara represents her circuit of Boston opinion, neither Roxbury activists nor the Boston police make any appearance at all. Indeed, politicians, victims' relatives, and ultimately Bynoe himself are fixed into implicitly more limited positions than Harvard psychologists, DYS administrators, or even McNamara's own liberal persona. McNamara's role, in part, is to reassert how the *Globe* itself more customarily represents its own authority: as a mobile dispassionate eye above the fray, that "civic voice" mentioned earlier. The sum effect is that certain voices in the tale are not able to fundamentally challenge the *Globe*'s authority, though they are granted, as it were, "audience." Even Bynoe himself is not, after all, present to us; rather he is ventriloquized by McNamara's representation (and perhaps, even more invisibly, by his lawyer). And there are indications, in fact, that he might actually threaten to disrupt McNamara's repositioning of his case in her new plot. McNamara herself points out that McGill's interpretation of Bynoe's "mom, apple pie, and the American flag" background only six months earlier surprised "even the prosecution."[93] Tarahn Harris, meanwhile, had told detectives that, contrary to one of McGill's main points of differentiation, all *three* defendants had retired to have pizza after the shooting. And if Bynoe says that he only wanted drug money for sneakers, he also says he earned as much as $500 a day as a dealer.[94]

As the street is partly suppressed, Beacon Hill must also be put in its place; this double action is central to the re-creation of liberal "civic" authority. Once having opened up the door to Weld's influence, the *Globe*, under McNamara's guidance, now closes it—in hindsight belittling not only Weld, but "newspapers" (though not itself) for fanning the flames of the debate. McNamara closes with a bitter aside about another street homicide that, lacking the political utility of the Bynoe case, didn't "make the papers."[95] But despite this departure from the original mainframe, one final irony is that McNamara and the *Globe*'s liberal redress can occur only in tandem with reaffirmation of the legitimacy of *juvenile* incarceration. There is no fuller sign of this contradiction than in McNamara's closing portrait of the penitent Bynoe, in the Westborough lockup, awaiting his mother's visit. It is striking, in fact, how McNamara entertains the prospect of systemic dysfunction, but only in the confines of a narrow political, bipartisan frame. In either case, disorder is ultimately set aside again, as both parties at the center would want it to be. Roxbury can still seem like the "wrong place" for Bynoe; juvenile lockup the right one.

VI

The reasoning that Foucault adds to classical Marxist thought is something like the following: if the prison can produce a lower-class criminality upon which we can fix our attention as legally defined criminality, then the criminality of ruling interests . . . may operate outside the lights of justice, "in the shade," as Foucault puts it . . . And this is all to the good of ruling interests. For one thing, so well-defined and enclosed, the class of criminals can be socially contained . . . Crime is the work of the poor. Let that be known to all . . . The way out is the way up: leave the ranks of the exploited; join the ranks of the exploiters.
—Frank Lentricchia, *Ariel and the Police* (1988)

For residents of Boston's disadvantaged neighborhoods, the violent death of the young tears immediately at the very fabric of kin and community. Yet for me, a white middle-aged academic living and working in what is really the not-so-nearby suburb of Newton, such episodes are often—I want to say "merely"—"news." Though the *Globe* seems to put me "in" Boston, the differential application of community policing, after all, does not seem to have me as an object in its path. Even my intentionally intrinsic reading of *Globe* story making inevitably reflects contradictions in my social placement as a reader. My emphasis on the extended process of reading, for example, may reflect a position of privilege, the very ability to read a story longitudinally, at a safe distance, with time for retrospect. Likewise, my description of what I have called the *Globe*'s "entertainment" of street crime reflects a persistent contradiction built into my distance from events. With its "Living" and "Lifestyle" sections, much of the *Globe* is, alas, "for" me.

Nevertheless, I have tried to suggest that, just as my home in the suburbs is very much part of the *Globe*'s recent demographic orbit, so too the story of community policing aims for an audience broader than that of Area B to gain political legitimacy. This consideration seems all the more important given that, the Copney-Grant story tells us, something quite different from professional-technical neutrality now lubricates the political operations of this system. Public criticism directed at traditional liberal remedies—the attack on the so-called "don't blame me" syndrome, for instance—is currently pervasive in American culture. To be sure, though often aimed at televised trials and maligned defense strategies, this anger is often directed not just at remedies for racism and class exploitation, but at their victims. Thus on the one hand, liberal dispassion certainly provides much of the *Globe*'s rationale for its own civic authority, and thus doubtless find a willing ear in a predominantly Democratic suburb like mine. And yet, on the other hand, the paper must also "contain," in both senses, a sense of affiliation or connection with Boston's own streets, an aura that it draws partly from the police, from its populist columnists, and from neoconservatism's own folkloric claims.

Surely the Copney-Grant coverage in the *Globe* demonstrated how strategic the channeling of police populism was to the paper's eventual reclaiming of civic authority. It was not only that a police version of events bounded this coverage's temporal frame, or that Barnicle championed street proprietorship in the ways I have described. Rather, it was that, by these narrative conventions, the *Globe* was able to more covertly represent what community policing had itself brought to redividing an already divided municipality. A columnist like Barnicle may *return*, in his finales, to liberal dispassion himself—for instance, to say we should *not* replace "rehabilitation with rage"—and claim affiliation with an Eileen McNamara. Yet his narrative machismo nevertheless depends on dramatizing his frustration with the task of policing his own anger—thus again, implicitly, containing his anger against part of the "community" with which he supposedly fraternizes. Alan Lupo was even willing to offer up Bynoe as a sacrificial lamb (or "slug") to that anger.[96]

These contradictions also suffused the way the *Globe* itself oversaw Mickey Roache's grim progress and eventual fall from populist grace. In the somewhat self-congratulatory history that the newspaper itself rehearsed, it was the *Globe*'s own "spotlight" teamwork that, right as the murders of Charles Copney and Korey Grant took place, exposed the shoddiness of investigative work on Roache's force and the corruption that still bedeviled it. Two years after the St. Clair Commission recommended his removal, Roache resigned in 1993 to run for mayor.[97] Along the way, the *Globe* would link the use of nonexistent informants—at this writing, an ongoing scandal—to the poor procedures that, the paper argued, had led to too much plea bargaining.[98] In the face of a rising crime and homicide rate, Roache had clearly miscalculated in assuming citizens, or the *Globe* itself, would dispense with the standard measurements of police efficiency, much less abandon 911 as his newfederalist philosophers like Wilson and Kelling told him to. After all, sweeps temporarily raise crime rates, and often only drive criminals to other districts (and even to the suburbs). Even more fundamentally, as reporter Kevin Cullen argued back in 1989, poor or corrupt investigative processes were partly themselves a result *of* the intensity of the sweeps Roache had himself installed.[99]

In these lights it is therefore important to mention, as well, one final denouement of the Copney-Grant case. As I have said, Judge McGill's differentiation of Bynoe from his companions was dependent upon a narrative of gang recruitment that the *Globe*'s mainframe reported. And yet, in January of 1994, Bynoe's companion Willie Dunn was found (not having handled the gun in the murder, supposedly) guilty of gun possession charges, but innocent of "joint venture" in relation to the murder of Copney and Grant. Then, in May of 1994, a Superior Court judge ruled that Sergeant Detective Herbert Spellman—the exact same police representative cited by Barnicle's column—

had given "false or misleading" testimony to the grand jury. All charges against Tarahn Harris were thus dropped.[100]

If we view this outcome only from the vantage point of the Weld mainframe, this might well seem yet another outrage: an affront to the supposed rationality neoconservatism wants to reclaim for our cities. But if anything Harris's fate exposes how fundamental, yet invisible, police officer Herby Spellman had been to the plot that fit into this frame. It is also some measure of how naturalizing the power of this dominant news outlet, the *Globe*, really was—that such an outcome had seemed unthinkable. It is worth repeating, then, that the jury in Dunn's adult trial implicitly repudiated Judge McGill's reasoning about Damien Bynoe's supposed recruitment to a gang—an anomalous postscript that the *Globe*'s 1991 narrative line certainly did not anticipate. (Indeed, if the police botched the background of the shooting, one would never have known it from reading the *Globe* in 1991.) It might be argued that the jury's very presence within these proceedings represents one of the few intrusions of actual public voices into the *Globe*'s otherwise merely "formal" polyphony. Of course, local media only seized upon it, again, as just another sign of the legal system's failure. Partly in response to this case, Massachusetts law amended its provisions to make juveniles convicted of such crimes serve *beyond* the age of twenty-one in an adult lockup. It is often called the "Copney-Grant amendment."[101]

Epilogue

Police Blues

To reconnect cultural analysis to some of the particulars of police history, as I've tried to do here, is surely to engage an often-dismal panorama. Modern policing has been marred by technocratic arrogance, undercut by its own distrust of the public it serves, disabled by self-appointed "minorityism" and its institutional handmaiden, racism. No one can work very long on police culture without coming to respect its profound resistance to change. We might take this observation from Lincoln Steffens's *Autobiography* (1931) as an illustrative postscript:

> [P]olicemen and the rank and file of government officials are either born or brought up in an environment of unbelief. They know facts; they know how things are really done; they don't develop illusions as I did in my protected youth . . . They know that good is rare and short-lived . . .
>
> "Reform, yes," said a cautious reform chief of police . . . "I am willing to lay up with T[heodore] R[oosevelt] but I cannot help keeping one eye on the signs of the failure of reform and the return to Tammany. Tammany is not a wave; it's the sea itself."

Of course, the *Autobiography* is full of such exchanges, illustrating—or so our customary historiography would have it—Steffens's disillusionment with his own earlier liberal naiveté. Yet in the course of writing this book, I came to read such moments differently. It is not only that, as Christopher Lasch pointed out long ago, Steffens's project was not so much to bury liberalism as to resurrect it in a more modern, hard-boiled, realist form.[1] Rather, it is that Steffens chooses to strike perhaps the central theme of his *own* odyssey through the voice of a police captain. At one level proposing itself as a memoir of those "waves" of reform, the *Autobiography* seems, instead, still immersed in the sea of Tammany. Part of my project in this book has been to explain not only the manifest foiling to police power in cultural storytelling, but often the more covert envy or emulation one finds there.

My account, however, is necessarily a partial one. Municipal policing intersects with state and federal law enforcement more extensively than I have been able to explicate; I have also neglected border, corporate, and private policing.[2] On the cultural front, this study has been restricted to metropolitan crime news, a few cases of popular fiction and nonfiction, some strands of liberal exposé, and one film. Yet police power is figured in proletarian novels, union speeches, news photography, comic strips, radio, and more. I obviously have said far too little, perhaps because modern criticism says so much, about various detective genres, or about serial killer narratives, where the veins of contemporary criticism are equally rich. Nor has my emphasis fallen on either high-cultural variations of popular police genres, or recent attempts to subvert those conventions (e.g., in feminist or African American detective fiction). And whereas chapters 2, 3, and 4 discuss important prototypes for prime-time police melodrama and contemporary cop TV, I rarely address television directly. Most of all, I have emphasized the resources, political lessons, and cultural stories writers and other observers have discovered at the police post—and extrapolated, only then, to what some *readers* might have found there.

We also need to acknowledge more candidly the limits of our own role in crafting any portrait of the cultural field and the larger field of power. In this book, I have tried to suggest that even seemingly nonliterary posts, and the narratives emerging from them—institutions that produce academic ethnographies, political theories, even police management literature—are part and parcel of the cultural field itself. The challenge, therefore, is to keep one's eye on changing relations in a given field and moment while recognizing that any account is necessarily partial and contingent. As I've said, it is a snapshot, a constellation of posts and dispositions that inevitably neglects others. At most, one can merely suggest the various forms of interaction that can occur across a given field, indeed between *kinds* of posts. That is, we need to see not only the conversation across the New York news field in the 1890s, or the attempt of Hellinger's *News* to challenge the *Times,* or the *Boston Globe*'s efforts to eclipse community newspapers. In addition, we have to see that Joseph Wambaugh's fiction rehearsed the McCone Commission's findings, or spoke back to the liberal framing of the police as "occupying armies." Or how the science of human relations fused with the midcentury literary reaction against *Black Mask,* superhuman heroes; how James Q. Wilson's theories provided new ground for Mike Barnicle's recycling of the hard-boiled columnist's populism. But no account can capture all such interactions.

Nevertheless, such case studies can also help to loosen the hold of some of the more monolithic and ahistorical notions of policing that inhabit the disciplines and generally resurface in the reflective, instrumental, or propagandistic models used to characterize cultural representation. To use the term "policing" uncritically, as I've suggested throughout, is often to risk reinscribing a historically brittle, one-dimensional, and elite paradigm. We need to remember that Foucault's model, for all its brilliance, was extrapolated from a rather narrow precedent: the eighteenth-century Enlightenment (particularly French) fantasy of political rationality (and with it, surveillance and detection). Foucault's paradigm, to be sure, corresponds in many ways to what I have called the "administrative" and actuarial dimensions of police governance in the twentieth century; surveillance, compulsive record keeping, doubtful presumptions about habitual criminality certainly run from Dora Clark to Damien Bynoe. But what originated as a model promising to particularize the relation of knowledge and cultural representation to power now runs the risk, by its brittle and generalized applications, of just the reverse.[3] In cultural studies, the use of "policing" even threatens to double back upon the understanding of municipal police authority, simultaneously flattening our readings of history, culture, and power. Nor are such "micro"-physical models of power like Foucault's always as attentive to local political authority as they seem.[4]

The panoptical blueprint, for instance, does not offer much help in recapturing historical change, or how and why police authority has been contested over time. Over the last century, American municipal policing has in fact never been unchallenged, nor confined to any single model or practice. Even the revisionist narrative of evolving police professionalism and technocratic impersonality, developed by historians like Joseph Woods and Robert Fogelson, eventually proves too monochromatic. This narrative, though I have relied on it extensively, often ends up mistaking both the symbolic dimensions of police labor and its class contradictions; the different strategies of public relations (e.g., "human relations" or tactical simulations) police managers have used; and the complex relationship to public notions of civility such strategies initiate. Police work, for example, is often contingent not upon mobilizing citizens to their duty—a pattern our paramilitary model often suggests—but in fact simulating and thus often sidelining them. Thus police forces have made a variety of cultural appeals over time: to the humanity of the cop in Weegee's day, to genteel respectability in T. R.'s, to a sense of shared proprietorship of urban neighborhoods (or, rather, some of them) in our own. And yet, as generalized as these appeals seem, they have always left some "publics" out of the picture.

Surveillance, meanwhile, is of course intrinsically part of the police's task. Yet it has not been applied only to the streets, but to cops like Charles Becker and even reporters themselves. Sometimes, it is the collaborative orchestration of zones of shade, between the police and media, that keeps some police tactics out of view. And those blue knights of the beat, as Jerome Skolnick and Joseph Wambaugh both suggest, do not always express simple vassalage to elites; on the contrary, Skolnick showed, the bureaucratic contradictions of their work gives police officers a presumptive, administrative, and often unwarranted feeling of autonomy and entitlement. But no form of police labor is sacrosanct. Even detective work, the mode supposedly at the top of the police echelon, has been given different tactical assignments at different historical moments. In the 1980s and 1990s, many municipalities (like Boston) in fact denigrated it, the pop-culture hype surrounding FBI mind hunting notwithstanding. As we're starting to see, it is everyday police profiling, not the psychopathological profiling of serial killers, that offers a more disturbing consequence of what I have called police actuarialism.

My emphasis on these differential dimensions of police power carries over into my more particularistic portrait of the cultural field. The media does not simply heroicize police professionalism or even implicitly underwrite its technical expertise. In the nineteenth century, the media were just as often liable *not* to fall into lockstep even with local police power, as scholarship on the antebellum penny papers or public prints will tell you; my own portrait of the 1890s suggests a highly differentiated field still in place.[5] Over time, as that news field has succumbed to tabloidization, market concentration, and now suburbanization, the risk of news dependence upon police authority has become more pronounced. But even my final chapter suggests a newspaper like the *Globe*, otherwise monopolizing its local print market, must nevertheless entertain rival voices to garner the authority that it does; the police are marshaled into one phase of coverage, marginalized in the next. As anthropologist Mark Pedelty has observed, as well, the recent tendency to describe a "discursive network which runs through the whole social body" tends to eclipse differentiations in such a body, the hierarchies and specializations it entails.[6] All too often, instead, it is as if the policing function of media would exist regardless of historical changes in police forces themselves; regardless of the rules of access and privacy among news media, police, citizens, and courts; regardless of laws covering the adjudication of street criminals or juveniles; regardless of the stylistic conventions governing media forms—all of which, I've tried to show in this book, have changed over time. Not at all coincidentally, they are in a state of change right now.[7]

Beyond tracking such institutional changes in newspaper making, book markets, academic practice, or law enforcement, I have also tried to reopen the often static genre labels we commonly use—"the" procedural, the documentary "fiction film," True Crime—in order to explore the transfusions that often occur across genres, types of media, and the police post itself. Even the most mainstream of cultural forms are already hybridized in the cultural field, a condition accentuated through the ever-more-prominent phenomenon of media crossover. Stephen Crane's "Eloquence of Grief" is an experimental mixture of fictional and journalistic modes, literally pasting in news clippings and divergent news representations; *The Naked City*'s documentary ethos seems to discount tabloid representation but actually resurrects it. Wambaugh's historical chronicles synthesize Chief Parker's speeches, yet also clearly partake of the new cultural prestige, in the 1960s, of the nonfiction novel of Truman Capote.[8] A book like Simon's *Homicide* is, in some ways, ready-made *as* a crossover book. Born in the cop shop, it synthesizes procedural mystery forms, high naturalist delineation, and police case files. Its episodic case structure was easily redesigned for prime time by adapting, so famously, the clearance board and its red balls to the insistent dramatic pulses of TV.

When it comes to reading texts themselves, I have tried to emphasize Robert Manoff's notion of the "merely formal," yet "mosaic" quality to popular forms that accompany such hybridity. That is, I follow the way texts "paste in" and then orchestrate different meanings and voices (newspaper clippings, speeches from Chief William Parker, voices from Roxbury). To posit this mosaic is also to suggest the drafting or entertainment of ideological possibilities, without succumbing to the simple arguments about escapism or instrumentalism that still dog much of our criticism. Indeed this mosaic quality makes different readings inevitable; helps us explain twists and turns in a given tradition of representation over time; and helps us see how different readers are mobilized or marginalized by a given form. In these ways, by tracing this orchestration, I have tried to suggest how forms exhibit facsimiles of the modern democratic process itself, with its attendant constraints, omissions, and blind spots. A story like the Copney-Grant murders, I have suggested, works from the foundation of the historically contingent form of policing of its day. From that foundation it writes its way, through a mosaic of conventions and voices, into civic ordination itself, actually contributing its flawed conclusions to *legislative* power. If I call some of these texts "entertainments," it is not to suggest their voyeuristic appeal. Rather, it is to show how their "what if" power leverages broader political understandings. And sometimes, what if becomes what is.

In a small way, then, my hope is that some of the more familiar themes in cultural studies concerning the ideological effects of police stories may undergo some historical sharpening. To be sure, our criticism still focuses too much on police "images," too little on the role of cop knowledge. But it is true that audiences have often been fascinated by the police because they embody masculine, authoritarian norms, sometimes even making us reluctant witnesses to the brutality of enforcing the law or going beyond it. In the 1990s, following the television show *Homicide*'s example, interrogation scenes became the order of the day in prime-time TV. As Peter Brooks has recently observed, it is as if the interrogation room "has been created to match the closed and isolated pathological space of the crime scene."[9] Indeed, it is not at all uncommon to see the argument made, in cultural studies of various kinds, that police melodrama is antithetical, say, to constitutional protections holding sway in real-life situations. A television detective's desire to break with official procedure, for instance, or circumvent a legal system that frustrates him—a standard motif in the literary procedural, which I examine in chapter 2—is taken as evidence of a fundamentally reactionary masterplot, usually linked to conservative moralism or ethnic stereotyping. Or, police stories are customarily read as throwbacks to mythical individualist westerns, subvariants of the mystery tradition of Poe or Doyle, or inheritors of the Gothic. But the contortions in such readings are, I think, telling. Stories of metropolitan police officers working collaboratively in multiethnic departments in large urban centers are read as western lawmen; cross-ethnic partnerships as inheritors of the romantic paradigm of noble savagery; procedurals where we know the murderer are called "whodunits"; and so on.[10]

Many of these older conventions do have their place in the modern police stories I have described.[11] Many popular narratives about police authority in the twentieth century reinscribe older notions, for instance, of habitual or amoral criminality. Meanwhile, even figures adversarial to cop culture, like a Stephen Crane or a Mitch Gelman, nevertheless express awe at the masculine (or "man-sized") power and fraternal solidarity of police. Many a police story works to cordon off disadvantaged communities (from the Tenderloin to Roxbury) supposedly beyond the pale of respectability, civility, or a dispassionate public sphere. These are commonly narratives where antipathy to written law is far stronger than allegiance—or, at least, stories where that allegiance is grudging, a matter of a heroic suppression of personal violence or retribution, again a restraint that testifies to a writer's claim to membership in the community of civility.[12] As Todd Gitlin has told us, the Hollywood producers won over by Wambaugh's *Police Story* claimed to identify with the LAPD's self-aggrandizing minorityism in the aftermath of the 1960s.[13]

On the other hand, I have also tried to suggest that these more familiar emphases upon the reactionary, Gothic, or western code of police narratives are partly derivative of the traditional ways we think about the relationship between power and representation to begin with. There is a tendency to approach popular narratives as products of an autonomous culture industry, responding entirely to its own imperatives and formulae, or as a realm of culture separate from police authority itself. In some instances, it means starting with western or *Black Mask* detective conventions, thereby giving prominence to maverick traditions that certainly persist today, but not as pervasively as one might think. (Police dramas on television, for instance, are nearly twice as frequent and long-lasting as private-eye shows.)[14] The critical tracing of a transhistorical archetype or convention can, as well, seem rather self-confirming. Argued to be expressive of its original moment, such a convention nevertheless acquires unusual longevity, making it difficult to mark where any such tradition loses its decisive force.

We need to be aware, therefore, that neglecting the quite modern and material engagements behind our cultural narratives can simply reproduce the assumption that history has no place in their making. Conversely, by that neglect we can unwittingly reinscribe a static and idealized notion of police power or the law itself. But we all know that reporters, for instance, commonly begin their journalistic apprenticeship—as Steffens, Blau, and Gelman did—by working with police departments; that television and Hollywood films not only exploit technical advice from police, but often take pride in their reinforcement of police labor; and that police departments in the real world do a great deal that is *not* constitutional to begin with.

Indeed, we should be cautious about what we think "real" police practice and even criminality supposedly are. Such assumptions often begin with the positing of too sharp a distinction between power and its representation; by unwittingly reinforcing the police's own claim to "human" fellowship; by praising a genre's "realism" simply as a matter of its style. But the interpretive problem goes deeper. In addition, faulty assumptions about "real" crime or policing can arise while unknowingly invoking the knowledge constituted by police themselves. Whether we recognize it or not, police knowledge gathering often informs the static backdrop of the "real" in many current versions of interdisciplinary study. For example, much of our popular culture criticism frequently resorts to federal crime statistics, usually to debunk media images. That is, ostensibly "real" statistics on homicides or burglaries from the Uniform Crime Reports (UCR) are used, for example, to discredit the hysteria of crime news, the sensationalism of True Crime, the unrealistic success rates of cops on TV. Along the way, critics will of course acknowledge the statistical limitations of these records; perhaps they will mention that studies on the *effects* of such distortions on audiences' views are, at best, inconclusive.[15]

For our purposes, however, the more important matter is that, as my second chapter explains, police statistics like the UCR are themselves better understood *as* cultural representations. That is, as texts that reveal how municipal authority was itself reconstructed at midcentury, by enlisting citizens who were willing to align themselves with that power. This is what we are contrasting—not "real" crime as such. A similar caution needs to be applied to an uncritical use of the data generated by ethnographic studies like Albert Reiss's. Reiss's study proposes itself as a sociological exposé of what "real" police work really is; hence its usefulness for back-to-basics polemicists like Wilson and Kelling. However, we have to recognize the political, historical, and ideological assumptions that generated Reiss's data in the first place: an antipathy to civil protest of all kinds; a convenient willingness to overlook the proactive models of policing emerging in cities like Los Angeles; and a deeply flawed ethnographic practice that caused his study to simply, again, ventriloquize the police's own lament about public incivility. And if we use data like Reiss's to discount mass-cultural images of heroic detective work, we also need to recognize that this discounting of professional crime busting has been anticipated, for instance, by Reiss and the Rand Corporation over twenty years ago.[16] When we find ourselves invoking the street-smart aura of liberal realism, we need to recall how this ethos has been so easily assimilated into the grim calculus of neoconservative order management. And, let it be said, to the disadvantage of many communities torn, as Luis Rodriguez suggests, between being subjected to an unbearable police presence and, what can be equally tragic, the absence of any meaningful presence at all.

It may be more useful to turn the common observation about the supposed discontinuity between real policing (or law) and mass culture on its head. Contrary to much of our current understanding of policing in cultural analysis, that is, police power *is* often informal, discretionary, even extralegal.[17] Moreover, if we recognize what I have termed the interstitial position of the police—between law and the *exercise* of power, between the knowledge they gather and distribute, between their anger at social disarray, the order they must impose, and their own sense of lost proprietorship over our cities—we may develop a better sense of why writers, readers, or viewers have been so intrigued by cop knowledge. Within these manifold layers, there are obviously many potential sources of writerly affiliation or reader fraternity. In David Simon's *Homicide*, for instance, the "match" that Peter Brooks describes in the police interrogation is not the by-product of sheer coincidence, any simple public desire for revenge, or an invisible discursive homology. Rather, it is the product of the decidedly Catholic subculture of that Baltimore police squad, and its "Holy Trinity" of "Evidence," "Witnesses," and "Confessions."

Likewise, the literary procedural, inheriting as it often does the internal divisions of the police bureaucracies it represents, actually enables the genre to embody contrary class implications. Institutional police dramas, like *Dragnet* or Quinn Martin's *FBI*, or like the *Naked City* television show that premiered in 1958, may seem to vaunt the managerial imperatives for scientific policing promoted by August Vollmer, William Parker, and their peers. And yet, it is also the procedural's more covert understanding of the working cop's labor situation that also speaks back against those utopian recipes. A refrain like "Just the facts, ma'am" may thus express not only professional routines or authoritarian malaise—but, as well, the vexed labor of policing within Chief Parker's Glass House script. Crossover figures like Joseph Wambaugh or David Simon, who often tried to turn proceduralism upside down, thus opened up television to fables of hard-laboring blue knights who rely more on brute force, blind loyalty to a community they privately believe no longer exists, and thus again those interrogation scenes. To my mind, this underside often drives police melodrama on TV today, and not only for lineal descendants of my texts like *Hill Street Blues* or NBC's *Homicide* itself. Even the drive-by live action shows of cop TV, as sheerly propagandistic and sensationalistic as they are, follow a working cop at the point of his labor, and invite many different readings, as it were, *of* its point.[18]

Despite what some strands of current criticism would insist, then, crime stories are not universal "moral" fables detached from their law enforcement milieu; nor are they, alternatively, simple reflections of technocratic authority. Rather, in the end, it is the gesture signaled by Lincoln Steffens that captures the fullest complexity in the various cop shop encounters I have tried to describe. In a tradition handed down to the likes of Mark Hellinger, Jimmy Breslin, Mike Barnicle, and their True Crime protégés, Steffens portrays the police as a fraternal yet often corrupt culture that initiates the liberal journalist and intellectual into pragmatic and fatalistic realism. The broader symbiosis implied is crucial to my story. Like so many who would follow him, Steffens endows what I have called cop knowledge with an intimate, interstitial, nearly mystical understanding of crime, urban neighborhoods, working-class identity, "fallen" political citizenship, and more. And the gesture persists. When *NYPD Blue* scriptwriter David Milch pens his memoir of the show in 1995, he coauthors the book with the white working-class detective he recruited for the series, splicing in horrific first-person accounts of crime scenes, shocking cases, fatalistic cop humor. When Pulitzer Prize–winning author Tracy Kidder investigates the social fabric of Northampton, Massachusetts, his home town, his guide, source, and principal character is a local community cop. When Spike Lee creates a fiction film of white-ethnic hysteria during New York City's "Summer of Sam," with local vigilantes emulating either the Mafia or the police in their attempts at neighborhood defense, the director's tabloid amanuensis and narrator is Jimmy Breslin, who quotes *The Naked City* with a copycat's obliviousness to attribution.[19]

Nor is this mystique about cop knowledge reserved to literary, journalistic, or mass-cultural representations. On the contrary, an attempt to remythologize the policeman's artisanal code has been visible in social-science formulations, notably in the past half-century, that have attempted to narrate social understanding from the civic authority of the cop on the beat. Capitalizing on the symbolic power of this beat cop, undergirded by the fatalism that some districts can't really be cleaned up, now legitimating the police's "humanity" while reinforcing their long-standing need to separate the worthy citizen from the unworthy, a book like Wilson's *Thinking about Crime* offers itself as more than reform of law enforcement. Rather, as Wilson or his federal sponsors would be the first to insist, it is a new theory of the democratic polity. Of late, that this nostalgia is bound to the vexed class and racial politics of white ethnics makes it all the more complex. Ever so ambiguously, this mystique simultaneously expresses chivalric commitments to, and yet a more problematic covert ownership of, urban streets themselves—a mixed ethos, again, I have called police populism.

It is important to reiterate, one last time, that this populistic thread has emerged in markedly different historical moments, just as the political narratives yoked to police power are anything but uniform across the last one hundred years. Indeed, because it is often cast as a communal, ethnically marked, and even craft knowledge, implemented in informal and discretionary practice, policing remains malleable in its material-symbolic dimension. Yet one effect of the current neoconservative consensus, with its seductive rhetoric of order, community, and the smiling beat cop, is largely meant to make us forget this variability in the past and its potential for change in the future. But in addition, one challenge for me in writing this book, and I hope one contribution of its inevitably eclectic and partial story, has been to keep in mind who the differentiated audiences are for this current appeal—in essence, who is asked to remember or forget what.

A refrain one hears constantly in contemporary cultural criticism, that is, is how modern forms of authority, working in tandem with media power, place citizens in the role of spectators. This strand of thinking has been foundational to my own efforts. But this book is also meant to offer a modest qualification, brought home to me especially as I worked on my last two chapters. And that is: If the organization of the social stage, or the cultural field, necessarily has differentiated positions for its players and its audiences, appeals to protecting "our" freedom, or reaffirming "our" community, are often predicated upon a structure of feeling that makes us, at once, feel we are on the stage as well as onlookers. Asked to look, and to look the other way. Policed; and not.

The new cultural story out there about community policing and that transhistorical beat cop, and indeed this book as a whole, might well be read with this differentiated field of spectatorship, and thus power, in mind. No one, of course, could seem to quarrel with the desire for citizens to take responsibility for their neighborhoods, to have a say in how they are policed. No one, it seems, might quarrel with the current political mantra of "more police officers on the street." Nevertheless, we might begin to think about community policing not merely as a tactical matter in law enforcement that plays to progressive rhetoric and budget-conscious electorates, and the genuine longing of communities and citizens to be free of crime—but as a cultural narrative not merely for the representation of policing, but for the policing of representation. In the hands of its advocates, community policing often becomes not merely order maintenance, but a reordering of political legitimacy that decides, from the post of the beat, which constituencies are in a community and which are not. In its design and in its harsher modifications, furthermore, it often becomes a means to secure a community that it secretly feels unrepresentable, which needs not James Q. Wilson's k/night watchman, but just watching. And certainly it is worth noting that Edwin Meese's "Taking Back the Streets," the article framing the Victorian woodcut I began chapter 5 with, ends by praising the "community policing" of Daryl Gates's LAPD.[20] This is a history and a future that certainly bears rewriting.

Notes

Introduction

1. The high visibility of police officers in television melodrama is matched by unrepresentative effectiveness in dealing with disproportionately high and violent crime rates. On these images, see James M. Carlson, *Prime Time Law Enforcement* (New York: Praeger, 1985); and Joseph
R. Dominick, "Crime and Law Enforcement in the Mass Media," in *Deviance and Mass Media*,
ed. Charles Winick (Beverly Hills: Sage, 1978). These distortions continue in so-called "reality-
based" cop TV: see the studies by Mary Beth Oliver and G. Blake Armstrong, "The Color of
Crime: Perceptions of Caucasians' and African-Americans' Involvement in Crime," and Paul G.
Kooistra, John S. Mahoney, and Saundra D. Westervelt, "The World of Crime According to
'Cops,'" in *Entertaining Crime: Television Reality Programs*, ed. Mark Fishman and Gray Cavender
(New York: Aldine De Grayter, 1998), 19–35 and 147–53 respectively.

2. On political socialization, see Carlson, *Prime Time Law Enforcement*, 3 ff., and George
Berkley, *The Democratic Policeman* (Boston: Beacon Press, 1969), 213.

3. By "interstitial" I mean occupying a space between social parts and everyday relationships—an often invisible negotiating and witnessing role. For a recent chronicle of this mystique,
see the work of Chicago-based analyst Connie Fletcher, in *What Cops Know* (New York: Villard
Books, 1991) and its sequels.

4. Statistics on "gang-related" killings from Michael Bertrand, graphic of "Murder in the
City," from "Boston Police Department of Strategic Planning and Policy Development," *Boston
Herald*, 31 Dec. 1992; the two killings discussed in chapter 5, for instance, were Boston's forty-
fourth and forty-fifth victims of murder generally (L. Kim Tan, "Boy Just an Innocent Bystander," *Boston Herald*, 22 April 1991). As noted in Robert Blau, *The Cop Shop: True Crime on*

the Streets of Chicago (Reading, Mass.: Addison-Wesley Publishing Co., 1993), 22–23, 28, however, police statistics on gang crime and affiliation are notoriously unreliable—not only because of the methods police use to ascertain gang membership, but because police sometimes play down that affiliation because they think gang members are pleased at media recognition. In some cases, "gang-related" means those crimes resulting from organized criminal activity; in others, any connection at all.

5. Of course, recent alarms about superpredators have been based upon suspicious projections at best; U.S. prison populations have been swelled largely by an infusion of *non*violent offenders; and serial killers, I mean to show, are not the key to our crime control strategies that so many recent cultural analyses presume them to be. On current mystifications performed by projections in neoconservative criminology, see esp. William Ayers, *A Kind and Just Parent: The Children of Juvenile Court* (Boston: Beacon Press, 1997), 75–76. On current incarceration rates, see Stephen Donzinger, ed., *The Real War on Crime: The Report of the National Criminal Justice Commission* (New York: Harper Perennial, 1996), 15–17, 101–4.

6. On the national "wound culture," see Mark Seltzer, *Serial Killers* (New York: Routledge, 1998); on community and citizenship, see Marilyn Stasio, "The Killers Next Door: We Can't Get Enough of Them," *New York Times Book Review*, 10 Oct. 1991, 46–47.

7. For one example of this heralding of community policing, see Peter Maas, "Welcome to New York, A Quiet Place," *Parade Magazine*, 10 May 1998, 4–6.

8. I refer here to my "Plotting the Border: John Reed, Pancho Villa, and *Insurgent Mexico*," in *The Cultures of United States Imperialism*, ed. Amy Kaplan and Donald Pease (Durham: Duke University Press, 1993), 340–61, and *The Labor of Words: Literary Professionalism in the Progressive Era* (Athens: University of Georgia Press, 1985), 34–38. Police power is discussed in Eric H. Monkkonen, *Police in Urban America, 1860–1920* (Cambridge: Cambridge University Press, 1981).

9. Despite the enormous influence of Foucault, *Discipline and Punish: The Birth of the Prison*, trans. Alan Sheridan (New York: Pantheon, 1977), Foucault's most explicit redefinition of "policing" is perhaps in "The Political Technologies of Individuals," in *Technologies of the Self*, ed. Luther H. Martin, Huck Gutman, and Patrick H. Hutton (Amherst: University of Massachusetts Press, 1988), 145–62.

Applications of Foucault's model are, of course, legion. D. A. Miller's *The Novel and the Police* (Berkeley and Los Angeles: University of California Press, 1988), most prominently, argues that the European nineteenth-century novel's rhetoric of trivial detail, case-study analysis, and monologic narration was both analogous to Panoptical surveillance and discipline and also a powerful supplement to institutional police power. Victorian writers, Miller acknowledges, rhetorically disavowed the novel's complicity with police institutions and methods, even criticizing systemic abuses around the management of legal power. Yet their fictions, he argues, nevertheless carried out a new premium on surveillance, "imposing on those whom it subjects" Foucault's paradigm of "compulsory visibility." Meanwhile even wider applications of policing are in circulation. In Jacques Donzelot's work, for example, policing is attached to "a much broader meaning that encompassed *all* the methods for developing the quality of the population and the strength of the nation." Jacques Donzelot, *The Policing of Families*, trans. Robert Hurley (New York: Pantheon, 1979), 6–7, emphasis mine. In another recent article, nineteenth-century Britain has been termed witness to the emergence of "the policeman state." The claim, apparently, is that of V. A. C. Gattrell, as cited by Patrick Brantlinger and Donald Ulin, "Policing Nomads: Discourse and Social Control in Early Victorian England," *Cultural Critique* (fall 1993): 34. See also Mark Seltzer's discussion of "lay policing" in *"The Princess Casamassima:* Realism and the Fantasy of Surveillance," in *American Realism: New Essays,* ed. Eric Sundquist (Baltimore: Johns Hopkins University Press, 1982), 96, 101. Compare also Seltzer's *Henry James and the Art of Power* (Ithaca: Cornell University Press, 1984), 180. More characteristically, however, Seltzer follows Foucault in arguing that policing must "bear 'over everything'" (see *Henry James,* 49, or *"The Princess Casamassima,"* 111, both citing Foucault, *Discipline and Punish,* 207, 213).

10. The phrase "narrowed grooves" is from Richard Ericson, Patricia M. Baranek, and Janet B. L. Chan, *Representing Order: Crime, Law, and Justice in the News Media* (Toronto: University of Toronto Press, 1991), 86; realist imperative of "making everything visible" is from Mark Seltzer, *Bodies and Machines* (New York: Routledge, 1992), 95–96; cf. Maren Stange, *Symbols of Ideal Life: Social Documentary Photography in America, 1890–1950* (Cambridge: Cambridge University Press, 1989), esp. 18–26. Quote on news media, emphasis mine, from Ericson, Baranek, and Chan, *Representing Order,* 74. "Police reporter" from Steve Chibnall, "The Crime Reporter: A Study in the Production of Commercial Knowledge," *Sociology* 9 (Jan. 1975): 51.

11. In addition to the work alluded to here, I mean as well to credit studies like those of Samuel Walker and Jerome Skolnick, who have brought such incisive critical energy to police debates; David Papke, who included police memoirs and turn-of-the-century criminology in his analysis and helped shape my understanding of the cultural framing of criminality; and Richard Gid Powers, whose *G-Men: Hoover's FBI in American Popular Culture* (Carbondale: Southern Illinois University Press, 1983) illustrated how cultural representation can loop back into law enforcement policy and practice. I have also obviously benefited enormously from the work of cultural, literary, and journalism critics and historians like Mike Davis, Richard Ericson, Robert Fogelson, Todd Gitlin, Robert Karl Manoff, Amy Kaplan, Stephen Knight, Michael Schudson, Mark Seltzer, Maren Stange, Alan Trachtenberg, and others.

12. Stuart Hall, Chas Critcher, Tony Jefferson, John Clarke, and Brian Roberts, *Policing the Crisis: Mugging, the State, and Law and Order* (New York: Holmes & Meier Publishers, 1978). In this study of a supposed crime wave of mugging in the 1970s, Hall and his collaborators had emphasized how the British media came to represent predatory, violent attacks on "ordinary" citizens as synonymous with crime itself (23). The police and media were said to both "structure" and "amplify" (38) this hysterical conflation and, in so doing, *"reproduce the definitions of the powerful"* (59–60). Worse yet, the British media's "ventriloquism" of "public outrage" actually fed back into the legal system, thereby legitimating tougher sentencing guidelines, stern judicial pronouncements, but relaxed regulations upon police discretion itself.

13. Ian Loader, "Policing and the Social: Questions of Symbolic Power," *British Journal of Sociology* 48 (March 1997): 1–18; quote here from 3. The social scientist quoted is Albert J. Reiss, whose work I critique in chapter 3. Reiss, *The Police and the Public* (New Haven: Yale University Press, 1971), 45. On the information society, see esp. Richard V. Ericson and Kevin D. Haggerty, *Policing the Risk Society* (Toronto: University of Toronto Press, 1997).

14. See, in particular, the recent convergence of interest in legal and narrative authority exemplified by Peter Brooks and Paul Gewirtz, eds., *Law's Stories* (New Haven: Yale University

Press, 1996), or Patricia Williams's commentary on how legal allowances for police "discretion" become precisely the crossroads at which power relations, cultural blind spots, and racism can "strip [the law] clean" of its intent. Williams, *The Alchemy of Race and Rights* (Cambridge: Harvard University Press, 1991), 138–39.

15. For a nevertheless useful analysis of this kind, see James Inciardi and Juliet Dee, "From the Keystone Cops [*sic*] to *Miami Vice:* Images of Policing in American Popular Culture," *Journal of Popular Culture* 21 (autumn 1987): 84–102.

16. McWilliams's account was *Factories in the Field* (Boston: Little, Brown, 1939); Hopkins's was *Our Lawless Police: A Study of the Unlawful Enforcement of the Law* (New York: Viking Press, 1931); Robert M. Fogelson's, *The Los Angeles Riots* (New York: Arno Press, 1969). Following the Watts riots, a commission was appointed by Governor Edmund Brown. This group was headed by John A. McCone, a businessman and former CIA director. Subsequent scholarship has, by and large, found this commission's report to be a whitewash that, in essence, voiced Chief William Parker's views—notably regarding the recommendation that "law enforcement agencies place greater emphasis on their responsibilities for crime prevention." Quote from recommendation 3, Fogelson, *Los Angeles Riots*, 8. *Private* forces have of course experienced phenomenal growth recently—a trend Mike Davis (among others) has described. See Mike Davis, *City of Quartz* (London: Verso, 1990), 240–50.

17. Baldwin's formulation came in "A Report from Occupied Territory," reprinted in *James Baldwin: Collected Essays* (New York: Library of America, 1998), 728–38. Compare "The Police in Protest," a staff report reprinted in Terry R. Armstrong and Kenneth M. Cinnamon, eds., *Power and Authority in Law Enforcement* (Springfield, Ill.: Charles C. Thomas, 1976). Drawing on the Kerner Commission report and the work of Albert Reiss, Jerome Skolnick, and others, the report opined that "James Baldwin's characterization of the police as an army of occupation" required urgent consideration (140). The same idea is struck in W. Eugene Groves and Peter H. Rossi, "Police Perceptions of a Hostile Ghetto: Realism or Projection," in *The Police in Modern Society*, ed. Harlan Hahn (New York: Sage, 1971), 188–89.

18. See Robert M. Fogelson, *Big-City Police* (Cambridge: Harvard University Press, 1977); "no longer eased" from 263; Joe Domanick, *To Protect and to Serve: The LAPD's Century of War in the City of Dreams* (New York: Pocket Books, 1994); and Claire Bond Potter, *War on Crime: Bandits, G-Men, and the Politics of Mass Culture* (New Brunswick: Rutgers University Press, 1998).

19. I refer here to the presentation of Assistant Chief Harv Ferguson of the Seattle Police Department at a roundtable discussion organized by Professor Bill Lyons at the American Studies Association convention, Seattle, Washington, 20 Nov. 1998. Of course, taking racism into account, let alone other inequities of nineteenth-century street justice, renders the current nostalgia for Gilded Age policing more than a little problematic.

20. As Loader puts it: "[I]t is necessary to avoid making a hard and fast distinction between the symbols and practices of police work . . . The routine activities and symbolic forms that comprise the social phenomenon of policing cannot so easily be divided. The craft skills and coercive powers that police officers deploy on a daily basis are not just goal-oriented. They serve too to communicate meaning, not only about the police and their role, but also about power and authority in society." Loader, "Policing and the Social," 9.

21. The theorist most thoroughly focused on the concept of a "field" of cultural representa-

tion is perhaps Bourdieu, though my application is far from rote. I am also thinking here of older formulations, notably those of C. Wright Mills, Raymond Williams, and others. Mills, for example, stressed how citizens live in "second-hand worlds" generated by "the cultural apparatus"—by what, paralleling Bourdieu, he called "the observation posts, the interpretation centers, the presentation depots" that shape meanings and value in a mass society. C. Wright Mills, *Power, Politics, and People*, ed. Irving Louis Horowitz (New York: Oxford University Press, 1963), 405–6. "Field" in Bourdieu's usage refers to the domain of a profession, a realm of knowledge, yet also "a structure of probabilities—of rewards, gains, profits, or sanctions" that is always contested. Quoted in Pierre Bourdieu and Loïc J. D. Wacquant, *An Invitation to Reflexive Sociology* (Chicago: University of Chicago Press, 1992), 18. Posts in such a field, he writes, often defy "any unilinear hierarchization" but are nevertheless internally differentiated and ordered. Pierre Bourdieu, *Field of Cultural Production*, ed. Randal Johnson (Cambridge: Polity, 1993), 43. Posts include all those institutional bodies that produce meaning and value (Bourdieu, *Field*, 37): thus, not only agencies of production (e.g., a newspaper), but of certification, consumption, and collection practices as well (e.g., journalism schools, wire services, library archives). On the materiality of cultural production, and the reciprocally cultural status of material life, see esp. Raymond Williams, "Base and Superstructure in Marxist Cultural Theory," in *Problems in Materialism and Culture* (London: Verso, 1980), 31–49.

22. Renato Rosaldo, *Culture and Truth: The Remaking of Social Analysis* (Boston: Beacon Press, 1993). Pierre Bourdieu's term is *habitus*, a variation on something like Raymond Williams's "structure of feeling" or Gaye Tuchman's "strategic ritual" (Tuchman, "Objectivity as a Strategic Ritual," *American Journal of Sociology* 77 [Jan. 1972]: 660–79), in that it tries to capture the systemic underpinnings and field placements constituting such subjectivity. As Bourdieu explains his term, *habitus* is "the strategy-generating principle enabling agents to cope with unforeseen and ever-changing situations . . . a system of lasting and transposable dispositions which, integrating past experiences, functions at every moment as a matrix of perceptions, appreciations and actions and makes possible the achievement of infinitely diversified tasks" (quoted in Bourdieu and Wacquant, *An Invitation to Reflexive Sociology*, 18). As Randal Johnson elaborates in the introduction to Bourdieu's *Field*, "The habitus is sometimes described as a 'feel for the game,' a 'practical sense' (*sens pratique*) that inclines agents to act and react in specific situations in a manner that is not always calculated and that is not simply a question of conscious obedience to rules. Rather, it is a set of dispositions which generates practices and perceptions. The habitus is the result of a long process of inculcation, beginning in early childhood, which becomes a 'second sense' or a second nature" (5). Relatively autonomous from the larger field of power, the social players in such cultural fields, much as in the sports analogy, are marked by a mixture of "in-difference." That is, they often exhibit obliviousness to anything but their own situation— and yet also a deep investment in it, not unlike Geertz's notion of "deep play." But rather than providing metacultural interpretive power for members of a culture, as in Geertz's model, the games within the field create a kind of inertial weight by their power of investment. Lately, Bourdieu—perhaps to offset those readers and critics who have equated his *habitus* with a more conscious, tactical, or "interest"-based sensibility—has expressed preference for the term *illusio* (Bourdieu and Wacquant, *An Invitation to Reflexive Sociology*, 115–16).

23. Cf. Hall, in "Notes on Deconstructing 'the Popular,'" in *People's History and Socialist*

Theory, ed. Raphael Samuel (London: Routledge and Kegan Paul, 1981): "alongside the false appeals, the foreshortenings, the trivialisation and shortcircuits" of popular culture, "there are also elements of recognition and identification, something approaching a recreation of recognizable experiences and attitudes" (233).

24. Robert K. Manoff, "Modes of War and Modes of Social Address: The Text of SDI," *Journal of Communication* 39 (winter 1989): 68. I use the terms "scrimmaging" and "frame" also to suggest the performative, rule-bound, and yet contested process of meaning-making and ordination enacted in cultural texts. Cf. Todd Gitlin, *The Whole World Is Watching: Mass Media in the Making and Unmaking of the New Left* (Berkeley and Los Angeles: University of California Press, 1980), 6–7; Daniel C. Hallin, *We Keep America on Top of the World* (New York: Routledge, 1994), 81–82.

25. This style of tough-minded "realism" within the liberal intelligentsia is perhaps best described in Christopher Lasch, *The New Radicalism in America* (New York: Knopf, 1963), 255–65, 282, 289. I am relying also upon several more recent studies: Dorothy Ross, "Liberalism," *Encyclopedia of American Political History*, ed. Jack P Greene (New York: Charles Scribner's Sons, 1984), esp. 758–59, quote here from 759; James T. Kloppenberg, *Uncertain Victory: Social Democracy and Progressivism in European and American Thought, 1870–1920* (New York: Oxford University Press, 1986), 267–77; Robert B. Westbrook, "Politics as Consumption: Managing the Modern American Election," in *The Culture of Consumption*, ed. Richard Wightman Fox and T. J. Jackson Lears (New York: Pantheon, 1983), esp. 148–53; Robert B. Westbrook, *John Dewey and American Democracy* (Ithaca: Cornell University Press, 1991), 280 ff.; Eugene Leach, "Mastering the Crowd: Collective Behavior and Mass Society in American Social Thought, 1917–1939," *American Studies* 27 (1986): 99–114; and Michael McGerr, *The Decline of Popular Politics* (New York: Oxford University Press, 1986).

26. Much of our recent scholarship emphasizes the plurality of publics rather than a unified public sphere; see, e.g., the remarks of Nancy Fraser in "Rethinking the Public Sphere: A Contribution to the Critique of Actually Existing Democracy," in *Habermas and the Public Sphere*, ed. Craig Calhoun (Cambridge: MIT Press, 1992), 116; or Mary P. Ryan, "Gender and Public Access: Women's Politics in Nineteenth-Century America," also in Calhoun, esp. 269.

27. The term "populism" has received varied use. As a description of tabloid ideology, see John J. Pauly, "Rupert Murdoch and the Demonology of Professional Journalism," in *Media, Myths, and Narratives: Television and the Press*, ed. James W Carey (Newbury Park, Calif.: Sage Publications, 1988), 246–61. It has also been applied to Britain's Thatcherism, or what Stuart Hall expanded, from "demotic populism" in 1981 (Hall, "Notes," 233) in regard to the tabloids to the reigning "authoritarian populism" in his *The Hard Road to Renewal* (London: Verso, 1988); and even to cultural studies interpreters themselves in Jim McGuigan, *Cultural Populism* (London: Routledge, 1992). I should therefore clarify that my reference here is primarily to the urban legacy of the nineteenth-century American political ethos; for useful descriptions of twentieth-century adaptations, cf. Richard J. Margolis, "The Two Faces of Populism," *New Leader*, April 1983, 8–9; Colin Greer and Barry Goldberg, "Populism, Ethnicity, and Public Policy: An Historical Perspective," in *The New Populism: The Politics of Empowerment*, ed. Harry C. Boyte and Frank Riessman (Philadelphia: Temple University Press, 1986), 174–88; and Christopher Lasch, *The True and Only Heaven* (New York: Norton, 1991). I have nevertheless profited from Hall's

discussion in *Hard Road*, and from Lawrence Grossberg's denomination "popular conservatism" in *We Gotta Get Out of This Place: Popular Conservatism and Postmodern Culture* (New York: Routledge: 1992).

28. Seventy-five percent of those polled from the NYPD's graduating academy class in 1994 said they were Catholic; more white officers had gone to Catholic schools in New York than public schools. Peter T. Kilborn, "Police Profile Stays Much the Same," *New York Times*, 10 Oct. 1994. On New York, see also James Barron, "Survey Places New York Police Last in Hiring of Black Officers," *New York Times*, 8 Oct. 1992; on Los Angeles, see Bettina Boxall and Nicholas Riccardi, "Lack of Diversity in Fire, Police Forces Cited," *Los Angeles Times*, 26 Oct. 1994; on the U.S. Capitol Police, see Kenneth J. Cooper, "Minorities Hold Just 16% of Top Ranks of Capitol Police, Profile Shows," *Washington Post*, 19 May 1993. The Chicago Police Department in the mid-1990s was 66 percent white in a city whose population was 38 percent white. Edward Walsh, "In Chicago, Affirmative Action Looms over Challenge to Police Promotions," *Washington Post*, 30 March 1995.

The term "white ethnic," naturally, brings its own problems. By "white ethnic" I of course mean "male white ethnic," though I mean to underscore a claim to community membership that is somewhat (and problematically so) broader. I also recognize that the label "white ethnic" is often used in the name of interest group pluralism: cf. Eugene J. Cornacchia and Dale C. Nelson, "Historical Differences in the Political Experiences of American Blacks and White Ethnics: Re-visiting an Unresolved Controversy," *Ethnic and Racial Studies* 15 (Jan. 1992): 102–4, esp. 103, and to discount differences among, and discrimination within, these groups themselves (e.g., Irish against Italian). The label often disguises historical change as well: the demise of machine politics, the emergence of white flight, the shifting importance of home ownership, Irish American upward mobility, or the varying degrees of integration and division within urban Catholicism. But my use is not meant to be static: rather, my chapters *track* many of these changes, including the confrontations with Hispanic and black constituencies after the 1960s. For my more qualified use of this term, and its implicit connection to the ethos of urban neighborhoods, I am indebted to John T. McGreevy, *Parish Boundaries: The Catholic Encounter with Race in the Twentieth-Century Urban North* (Chicago: University of Chicago Press, 1996), esp. 13–28; Robert Orsi's discussion of the Italian American *domus* in *The Madonna of 115th Street: Faith and Community in Italian Harlem, 1880–1950* (New Haven: Yale University Press, 1985); and to James T. Fisher's discussion of "street" Catholicism in "Clearing the Streets of the Catholic Lost Generation," *South Atlantic Quarterly* 93 (summer 1994): 603–29 (see esp. 627–28 on *NYPD Blue*).

29. This tendency to conflate police with authority *qua* authority is also evident in more conventional content analyses of television drama: see Carlson, *Prime Time Law Enforcement*; or B. Keith Crew, "Acting like Cops: The Social Reality of Crime and Law on TV Police Dramas," *Marginal Conventions: Popular Culture, Mass Media, and Social Deviance*, ed. Clinton R. Sanders (Bowling Green: Bowling Green State University Popular Press, 1990), 131–43. For this conflation in analyses of source relationships in crime news, see Steven M. Gorelick, " 'Join Our War': The Construction of Ideology in a Newspaper Crimefighting Campaign," *Crime and Delinquency* 35 (July 1989): 421–36; Ericson, Baranek, and Chan, *Representing Order*, esp. 104–5, 86, and 74; and Chibnall, "The Crime Reporter."

30. As Maureen Cain has recently emphasized, one pressing question is how members of the working class came to police themselves *and* others. Maureen Cain, "Some Go Backward, Some Go Forward: Police Work in Comparative Perspective," *Contemporary Sociology* 22 (May 1993): 319–24; point here from 321. I am indebted to Cain's overview.

31. For one account sensitive to this development, see Samuel Walker, *A Critical History of Police Reform* (Lexington, Mass.: Lexington Books, 1977), esp. 162–64.

Chapter One

1. Crane's ambition, declared during the precise week of the Dora Clark episode, was reported in the *Baltimore News*, 14 Sept. 1896; clipping in scrapbooks in the Stephen Crane Collection, Columbia University (hereafter CU). Cf. Ellen Moers, "Theodore Roosevelt, Literary Feller," *Columbia University Forum* 6 (summer 1963): 10–16, esp. 15. See also *The New York City Sketches of Stephen Crane*, ed. R. W. Stallman and E. R. Hagemann (New York: N.Y.U. Press, 1966), a collection cited hereafter and in text as *NYS*. For my account of the Tenderloin's geography, I am indebted to Timothy Gilfoyle's *City of Eros: New York City, Prostitution, and the Commercialization of Sex, 1790–1920* (New York: Norton, 1992). Except where noted, all newspapers cited in this chapter are New York papers; for economy's sake, I have omitted *New York* from the titles.

2. Stallman, *Stephen Crane: A Biography* (New York: G. Braziller, 1968), 220.

3. Roosevelt had actually dined with Jacob Riis and Crane in July; see *The Letters of Theodore Roosevelt*, selected and edited by Elting E. Morison (Cambridge: Harvard University Press, 1951) (hereafter *Roosevelt Letters*), 550. In August, Crane had sent "George's Mother" to Roosevelt for comment; Roosevelt had already written him in July, wanting to talk about *Maggie*. See *The Correspondence of Stephen Crane*, ed. Stanley Wertheim and Paul Sorrentino (New York: Columbia University Press, 1988), letters from Roosevelt of 20 July and 18 Aug. 1896, 1: 241, 249.

4. Crane's own account is "Adventures of a Novelist," reprinted in *NYS* 226–31; "wives and sisters" is from the 17 Sept. 1896 article in the *Journal*, reprinted in *NYS* 223. Scholarly accounts of this episode appear in Stallman, *Stephen Crane*, 218–36, and Olov W. Fryckstedt, "Stephen Crane in the Tenderloin," *Studia Neophilologica* 34 (1962): 135–63. See also Andy Logan, *Against the Evidence: The Becker-Rosenthal Affair* (New York: McCall Publishing, 1970), 107 ff., and Christopher Benfey, *The Double Life of Stephen Crane* (New York, Knopf, 1992), 171–81.

5. Logan's *Against the Evidence* covers this later scandal, often said to be alluded to in the Meyer Wolfsheim sections of F. Scott Fitzgerald's *The Great Gatsby* (1925). For a fine treatment of Gatsby's larger resonance with gangsterism in the 1920s, see Thomas H. Pauly's account in "Gatsby as Gangster," *Studies in American Fiction* 21 (autumn 1993): 225–36.

6. It *is* discussed briefly in Richardson, *The New York Police: Colonial Times to 1901* (New York, Oxford University Press, 1970), 261–62.

7. Here and elsewhere my use of "ordination" derives from Robert C. Allen, *Horrible Prettiness: Burlesque and American Culture* (Chapel Hill: University of North Carolina Press, 1991), 54. For a fine discussion of the relationship of commercial entertainments to machine politics, see (along with Gilfoyle's account) the article by Daniel Czitrom (to whom I must apologize

for an earlier mistake in citing this work): Dan Czitrom, "Underworlds and Underdogs: Big Tim Sullivan and Metropolitan Politics in New York, 1889–1913," *Journal of American History* 78 (Sept. 1991): 536–58.

8. I have tracked the evolution of these readings of Crane in more detail in "Stephen Crane and the Police," *American Quarterly* 48 (June 1996): 275 nn. 4 and 7, 307–8.

9. Crane as a "soldier" going into "battle" from Stallman, *Stephen Crane*, 231, 224. On the original casting of American realism as a liberal "war" on injustice, see esp. Amy Kaplan, *The Social Construction of American Realism* (Chicago: University of Chicago Press, 1988), 15 ff.

10. As Edward Said has suggested, the essence of the Foucauldian paradigm is just such a discursive "dedefinition," in which a given textual operation is "stripped of its esoteric or hermetic elements," thus "making the text assume its affiliation with institutions, offices, agencies." Edward Said, "The Problem of Textuality: Two Exemplary Positions," *Critical Inquiry* 4 (summer 1978): 701. For another account of the role of slum photography in "clearing the streets," see John Tagg, *The Burden of Representation* (Amherst: University of Massachusetts Press, 1988), esp. 150 ff.

11. In Maren Stange's superb work on documentary photography, for example, police reporter Jacob Riis's slide lantern lectures and exhibitions are similarly described as "woven throughout" with "the idea of photography as surveillance, the controlling gaze as a middle-class right and tool" (esp. 18–26; quote from 23). The best and most widely recognized revision of realism's milieu is Kaplan's; on spectatorship, see *Social Construction of American Realism*, esp. 44 ff. See also, from a Jamesonian perspective, the role of spectatorship described in June Howard, *Form and History in American Naturalism* (Chapel Hill: University of North Carolina Press, 1985), esp. 104–41; Crane's *Maggie* is described on 105–6.

12. In fact, there are a few indications that Clark had never been convicted, and that her earlier arraignments also resulted from friction with the police. "Red Badge Man on a Police Rack," *Press*, 17 Oct. 1896, reported that Clark testified that she had been arrested three times before on the same charge and had been found *not* guilty.

13. "[N]aive or duped" from Stallman, *Stephen Crane*, 225; "soldier" from 231; subsequent characterizations from Fryckstedt, "Stephen Crane," 157, and Benfey, *Double Life*, 176. On Roosevelt's actual whereabouts, see *Roosevelt Letters* 559. Katz's article first documented Crane's developing quarrel with Roosevelt, not Tammany, a distinction studies still overlook (see, e.g., Seltzer, *Bodies and Machines*, 203 n. 10). James Colvert's biography of Crane, *Stephen Crane* (New York: Harcourt Brace Jovanovich, 1984), repeats Stallman's account almost verbatim. See instead Joseph Katz, "Stephen Crane: Metropolitan Correspondent," *Kentucky Review* 4 (spring 1983): 39–51. The articles Katz recovered from the *Port Jervis Evening Gazette* are "Poor Police Arrangements at the Bryan Meeting," 20 Aug. 1896; "What an Observant Correspondent Sees Worth Noting," 27 Aug. 1896, which mentions the arrest of an "unoffending and innocent woman on 6th Avenue the other night"; and "An Interesting Letter from Our Correspondent," 8 Sept. 1896. Roosevelt's reply to Crane's protest is well known: see the letter from Roosevelt, 18 Aug. 1896, in *Correspondence of Stephen Crane*, 1:249.

14. On this liberal-realist strain, see note 15 to introduction.

15. As in subsequent chapters, what we're looking at is Bourdieu's "box within a box": that is, keeping our eye on how local partisanship, conventions of crime news, and journalistic depen-

dence upon police power shaped the representational field in which Crane worked, and from which we've made our histories. Bourdieu on the box, *Field*, 172. For similar accounts from the penny press era, see esp. Dan Schiller, *Objectivity and the News* (Philadelphia: University of Pennsylvania Press, 1988), 57–61, 63–65; Alexander Saxton, "Problems of Class and Race in the Origins of the Mass Circulation Press," *American Quarterly* 36 (summer 1984): 211–34; Patricia Cline Cohen, "'Unregulated Youth': Masculinity and Murder in the 1830s City," *Radical History Review* 52 (1992): 33–52; and Amy Gilman Srebnick, "The Death of Mary Rogers, the 'Public Prints,' and the Violence of Representation," *Legal Studies Forum* 2 (1993): 147–69.

16. On Hearst's solicitation, see the letters from H. R. Huxton in Crane's *Correspondence*, 1:255 ff.; for Crane's later view of Hearst, see 2:679.

17. Lincoln Steffens, *The Autobiography of Lincoln Steffens* (New York: Harcourt, 1931), 224.

18. This passage is well discussed by David Ray Papke, *Framing the Criminal* (New York: Archon Books, 1987), 121. On "boodling," see Lincoln Steffens, *The Shame of the Cities* (1904; reprint, New York: Hill and Wang, 1957), 24–25. For a recent synopsis of the balance between Progressivist moralism and "Hamiltonian" means, see Gary Gerstle, "The Protean Character of American Liberalism," *American Historical Review* 99 (Oct. 1994): 1043–73, esp. 1049–52. Mary Ryan gives a good rendering of the substitution of "the public" for the respectable male taxpayer ("Gender and Public Access," 277).

19. In the first grouping I would place standard works including Fogelson, *Big-City Police;* Richardson, *The New York Police;* Jay Stuart Berman, *Police Administration and Progressive Reform* (New York: Greenwood Press, 1987); and, in a much more critical vein, Walker's *A Critical History of Police Reform.* "Clubber" Williams himself, according to Richardson, had hundreds of formal complaints and fines levied against him, but would stay in office until 1895 when Roosevelt removed him (Richardson, *The New York Police*, 59). For more recent revisionist accounts, see Eric H. Monkkonen, *Police in Urban America;* Sidney L. Harring, *Policing a Class Society* (New Brunswick: Rutgers University Press, 1983); David R. Johnson, *Policing the Urban Underworld* (Philadelphia: Temple University Press, 1979); Allen Steinberg, *The Transformation of Criminal Justice* (Chapel Hill: University of North Carolina Press, 1989); Alexander Von Hoffman, "An Officer of the Neighborhood: A Boston Patrolman on the Beat in 1895," *Journal of Social History* 26 (winter 1992): 310–30; and David Montgomery, *Citizen Worker* (Cambridge: Cambridge University Press, 1993). Recent scholarship on the history of the police is helpfully discussed by Maureen Cain's review essay, "Some Go Backward, Some Go Forward."

20. A NYPD manual from 1901 offers prohibitions against sitting, loitering, or lounging on patrol, arguing that the cop "will at all times maintain an erect, soldierly position." New York Police Department, *Manual Containing the Rules and Regulations of the Police Department of the City of New York* (New York: J. W. Pratt, 1901), 100; see also 136. Marching was also required, supposedly, when coming to and from duty (104).

21. Roosevelt discusses these reforms in "Administering the New York Police Force," in *American Ideals / The Strenuous Life / Realizable Ideals*, vol. 13 in *The Works of Theodore Roosevelt* (New York: Charles Scribner's Sons, 1926), 127 ff. For relevant news articles, see "Police Board in Action," *Times*, 7 March 1896; "Bicycle Police to Patrol Whole City," *Journal*, 10 Sept. 1896. Statistics from Richardson, *The New York Police*, 254.

22. This law required any "police officer or constable having notice or knowledge of any

violation" of Sabbath alcohol restrictions to report it to his district attorney; the DA's duty was then to prosecute. As quoted in "Misdirected Zeal," *Times*, 26 Dec. 1896. T. R.'s views in "The Laws Must Be Enforced," in *Campaigns and Controversies*, vol. 14 of *The Works of Theodore Roosevelt*, 181–82—a statement originally given in June 1895; "The Enforcement of Law," same volume, 183–91, also originally published in 1895.

23. See "The Ethnology of the Police," in *Campaigns and Controversies*, 229, and "Administering the New York Police Force," 129. This talk was originally published in 1897. Roosevelt's opinions on racial inheritance were reiterated in *Roosevelt Letters* 555; see also *Roosevelt Letters* 495, where Roosevelt estimated that two-thirds of his appointments had been Catholic.

24. After 1880, for instance, the number of policemen in American cities actually had grown considerably faster than urban population at large. Likewise, turnover in police forces had been diminished considerably, suggesting that political interference (particularly at the rank-and-file level) had been reduced out of the recognized need for greater police efficiency. Although police labor was technically still unprofessional work, wages had actually risen generally in this era, with patrolmen's pay often double that of unskilled or semiskilled labor. On the growth in police numbers, see Montgomery, *Citizen Worker*, 70; on turnover, see Harring, *Policing a Class Society*, 38; on pay see Harring, 42, and Johnson, *Policing the Urban Underworld*, 101. Recent scholarship, however, suggests that this pattern was reversed in the south. See Dennis C. Rousey, *Policing the Southern City: New Orleans, 1805–1889* (Baton Rouge: Louisiana State University Press, 1996).

25. See esp. Papke's discussion of Byrnes and his "crime-stopping" folio, *Framing the Criminal*, 156–58. Czitrom also points out that Inspector Byrnes famously rendered charges *against* a ward boss, "Big Tim" Sullivan (541). On the complexities of police forces' solidarity, see esp. Maureen Cain, "Some Go Forward," 321 ff.

26. On these innovations, see esp. David R. Johnson, *Policing the Urban Underworld*, 110–12.

27. Fragment in the epigraph to the introduction is from *NYS* 259. Steinberg and Montgomery have traced the process whereby locally based, private prosecution of criminal charges in aldermen's courts (one citizen taking another to court), were gradually replaced, in the mid–nineteenth century, by state prosecution in district courts or so-called police courts. In these historians' view, this was a system far less accessible to ordinary people and to the poor. In this sense Foucault's model does indeed help to characterize a new combination of mobility and invisible administration that police power now enacted. Steinberg, however, emphasizes that this new system also made it subject to local partisan corruption.

28. On this earlier vigilance, see esp. Montgomery, *Citizen Worker*, 64–87; Steinberg, *Transformation*, 177. Harring's observation is in *Policing a Class Society*, 40. On the military model in the south, see Rousey, *Policing the Southern City*, 14–24. Rousey's data, moreover, follow Monkonnen's finding that drunk and disorderly vigilance dramatically escalated arrest rates per policeman in the late nineteenth century (*Police in Urban America*, 193).

29. Despite the headlines given to sensational murders since the days of the penny press, Monkonnen's work suggests violent crimes actually remained relatively stable and rare in late nineteenth-century cities, and may have even declined.

30. Von Hoffman, "An Officer of the Neighborhood," 310, 312. I do not mean to suggest these recent revisions are altogether compatible. Against the social-control hypothesis rehearsed by recent police historians, Von Hoffman has argued that, at the street level, urban police

"accommodated and served citizens as much as they disciplined them" (310)—a phenomenon liberal *and* radical historians both concede but tend to minimize. As chapter 5 will show, Von Hoffman's portrait is very much of a piece with the neoconservative recovery of beat patrol in the 1980s.

31. On the police court, see esp. Harring, *Policing a Class Society*, 63–64; Steinberg, *Transformation*, 225; and Monkkonen, *Policing in Urban America*, 103.

32. For admission to the force, Roosevelt's board installed entrance exams covering five subjects: spelling, penmanship, letter writing, simple arithmetic, and the history, government, and geography of the United States. On the exams and Roosevelt's defense, see *Roosevelt Letters* 578–79.

33. "Calling For Policemen," *Post*, 18 Sept. 1896: "President Roosevelt had the new eligible list before him to-day . . . He said he feared many men of the most desirable type . . . from the trades and calling where brains are used and developed . . . were frightened off by the persistent rumors of the necessity for political influence" that the high failure rate on the exams supposedly kept alive. "The majority of those who have either no such belief or no such fear are Irishmen, Irish by birth or of Irish parentage. They are getting on the force, which, it is plain, will have so many of this nationality that its old comic-paper type will not be altered at all."

34. Roosevelt, "Ethnology," 226–35; compare Richardson, *The New York Police*, 259–60. On colonial police forces, see Cain, "Some Go Forward," 320 and Cynthia Enloe, "Ethnicity and Militarization: Factors Shaping the Role of Police in Third World Nations," *Studies in Comparative International Development*, 11 (autumn 1976): 25–38, esp. 33–37.

35. On the centrality of saloons to working-class culture, see Elliot J. Gorn, *The Manly Art: Bare-Knuckle Prize Fighting in America* (Ithaca: Cornell University Press, 1986), 98–99, 133–34; and Czitrom, "Underworlds and Underdogs." Cf. also Roosevelt, "The Law Must Be Enforced," 183–91, with Riis quoted on 190; and in Roosevelt, "Administering," 129. For a typical *Post* lampooning, see "Plenty of Friends Now: Politics in a Police Court," *Post*, 19 Oct. 1896.

36. Paramilitarism is one theme of Berman, *Police Administration and Progressive Reform*, 60–62, and Fogelson, *Big-City Police*, 54 ff. For Roosevelt's own use of the metaphor, see "Ethnology," 232; "Americanism in Municipal Politics," *Campaigns and Controversies*, 198; and his pep talk to district officers, "The Commissioner's Advice . . . ," *Campaigns and Controversies*, 209. On Roosevelt's views during his tenure, see Edmund Morris, *The Rise of Theodore Roosevelt* (New York: Coward, McCann & Geoghegan, 1979), 481–542.

37. Compare D. A. Miller, *Novel and the Police*, 22.

38. Lincoln Steffens, "A Way to Police Reform," typescript on microfilm, Butler Library, Columbia University. Here Steffens explicitly points to the outrage following T. R.'s enforcement of the Raines excise law, saying that policemen who had befriended Roosevelt were later discriminated against within the department. It is unclear whether this is a later version of an unpublished essay Roosevelt had earlier endorsed (see *Roosevelt Letters* 473), but it seems likely. On Roosevelt's own views on police discretion, see "The Law Must Be Enforced," 181–82. Here, in fact, was another possible dimension to the much-ballyhooed restoration of Schmittberger. While Steffens's *Autobiography* paints the restored officer as an innocent good man, valuable for his "sweeping" power, he may well have functioned as the kind of insider that the journalist and police commissioner both theorized about.

39. "Secret Service" identified in "Portraits Do Them Harm," *Times*, 4 Jan. 1896. Riis also applies this title to Byrnes; see *How the Other Half Lives* (1890; reprint, New York: Hill and Wang, 1957), 69.

40. A bill was proposed in the New York State legislature to bar such use in strikes, much to Roosevelt's outrage. For Roosevelt's reasoning on plainclothes "spies," see *Roosevelt Letters* 618, 575–76. Writing in the early 1900s, Steffens refers back, in obvious disgust, to the outcry about using "spies" that had accompanied Roosevelt's reforms.

41. Becker's background is discussed in Logan, *Against the Evidence*, 105–6 and *passim*.

42. As one of the few clues to how Becker might have testified, we have "Not a Grudge, He Says," *Journal*, 19 Sept. 1896. The article notes that Becker "talks like a man who might have had an education in the public schools." In this report, Becker says he will make no statement, but he adds: "but I am ready to make one if Mr. Crane makes a complaint against me. I think I can produce evidence that will surprise him." Following this veiled threat, he says that Crane is mistaken, and that he (Becker) did not take Clark away from a "party of persons with whom she was conversing . . . To do such a thing would be simply suicidal for a man in my position. I am in this business not for glory, but to earn my living honestly. I wish to retain my position, and, if possible, to get ahead."

43. Quotes from Jerome Skolnick, *Justice without Trial: Law Enforcement in Democratic Society* (New York: John Wiley & Sons, 1966), 220–21; "[i]n contrast" from 197, emphasis added. "Police Board in Action," *Times*, 7 March 1896, reports on adoption of Bertillon system; see also Henry F. T. Rhodes, *Alphonse Bertillon: Father of Scientific Detection* (New York: Greenwood Press, 1956), 73–99.

44. Roosevelt, "Administering," 127.

45. On banter, see Skolnick, *Justice without Trial*, 105–6; "Hysteria" from "Adventures," *NYS* 230.

46. The more the administrative ethos is allowed to flourish, Skolnick argues, "the more [patrolmen] demand a *lack of constraint upon initiative*" (*Justice without Trial*, 235; emphasis mine).

47. "Respectable Woman Arrested," *Sun*, 24 Aug. 1896, also gives a clear sense of the assignment Becker is on. Discussing Rosenberg, the *Sun* says he is "assigned by Capt. Chapman to arrest women who are in the streets for immoral purposes." Rosenberg is noted by the *Sun* as repeatedly having charged women "against whom the evidence was very slight." In this instance Rosenberg, while in plainclothes, arrested a woman merely walking ahead of her husband after he had stepped into a cigar store; Rosenberg, however, swore in court that she solicited him. Somewhat typically, the *Times* soft-pedaled the episode: see "Policeman Rosenberg's Mistake," *Times*, 24 Aug. 1896. In one report, Dora Clark said that the initial spark to *her* quarrel with Rosenberg was her misidentification of him as a nonwhite man seeking assignation, a story she told to titters in criminal court. See the *Sun*'s 17 Sept. report, *NYS* 217. The *Sun* also revealed that there was, quite simply, a litany of police disciplinary hearings taking place right as Becker was brought up before Commissioner Grant: "Parker Asks Questions," *Sun*, 1 Oct. 1896.

48. "Officers Moved Around," *Press*, 9 June 1896, speculates that Chief Conlin shook up and reassigned patrolmen upon receiving information from the Parkhurst Society. In his resignation letter of 17 April 1897, Roosevelt underscored that he had made the police not only the enemy of the criminal but the "ally of every movement for good" (*Roosevelt Letters* 594–95).

49. These surrounding controversies are discussed in Berman, *Police Administration*, 103 ff., and Richardson, *The New York Police*, 254 ff. See also "Trouble in Transfers," *Times*, 5 March 1896. Funds were made up by the City Vigilance League, according to Berman, *Police Administration*, 105.

50. On the blurring of boundaries, see also Gilfoyle, *City of Eros*, 243–248.

51. These witnesses are mentioned in "Dora Clark Makes Startling Charges," *Journal*, 8 Oct. 1896, in *NYS* 233.

52. Compare Skolnick, *Justice without Trial*, 210. The papers reported several cases where plainclothes officers had exceeded their authority or not identified themselves: see "Blackmail Charged against the Police," *Journal*, 22 Sept. 1896; "Policemen Reprimanded," *Sun*, 25 Aug. 1896, which discusses policemen Conway and Schroeder of the West 47th Street station and a "third cop, whose name is withheld"; "The 'Other' Woman Was His Prisoner," *Journal*, 8 Sept. 1896, which tells of the failure of Conway to bring the correct prisoner to court. Conway, it is noted in the article, "has been acting as a 'plain clothes man,' his duty being to arrest women at night." The *Sun* also compared Rev. Charles Parkhurst to an entrapping detective, wining and dining his victims to get them to commit crimes; see Candace Stone, *Dana and the Sun* (New York: Dodd, Mead, 1938), 164 ff.

53. This success followed a reorganization of district and precinct lines by Chapman; see "Broadway Squad Change," *Times*, 12 July 1896. The *World* identified Chapman's orchestration of the testimony of James O'Connor in "Crane Had a Gay Night," *NYS* 252. In the *Press* report of the trial on 17 Oct. 1896, Dora Clark singled out Captain Chapman as her persecutor.

54. It is reprinted as "Sixth Avenue" in *NYS* 117.

55. "Portraits Do Them Harm."

56. Becker's partner *is* referred to in "S. Crane and Dora Clark," *Sun*, 17 Sept. 1896, in *NYS* 218.

57. Tramp quoted in "71 Tramps Nabbed," *Sun*, 24 Aug. 1896; cartoon is "The Modern Highwayman," *Press*, 21 Aug. 1896.

58. On the relationship of police precincts to sensationalism, see my *Labor of Words*, 17–39; on this relationship and crime generally in this period, see Papke, *Framing the Criminal*, 59–74.

59. Roosevelt actually called Max Schmittberger "my big stick" (Steffens, *Autobiography*, 279).

60. Necessarily, this means neglecting key newspapers, notably the immigrant press, particularly the German American *Staats-Zeitung*. Roosevelt himself identified the *World* and *Journal* as his main nemeses; see "Administering," 125–26. In *Roosevelt Letters* 470, 488, 502, 508, and passim, he says the *Press* stood by him steadily, the *Tribune* and *Times* more tepidly. Roosevelt claimed the *Sun* was compromised by its involvement with the Tammany machine (*Roosevelt Letters* 508).

61. The editorial page of the *Times* was written by Charles Miller, perhaps Roosevelt's closest ally on an earlier New York committee advocating civil service reform. See F. Fraser Bond, *Mr. Miller of "The Times"* (New York: Charles Scribner's Sons, 1931), 106–8. For typical coverage, see "Wanted—Policemen," *Times*, 17 Sept. 1896; "Work of the Detective Bureau," *Times*, 23 July 1896; "Honesty or False Pretense?" *Times*, 21 Jan. 1896; "Commissioner Parker," *Times*,

21 Aug. 1896; "Mr. Roosevelt's Justice," *Times*, 24 July 1896. Crane coverage in "Stephen Crane as Champion," *Times*, 17 Sept. 1896; "Crane Presses His Charge," *Times*, 17 Oct. 1896.

62. For the *Press*'s anti-Tammany stands on police reform, see "The Police Bill Decision," *Press*, 28 Oct. 1896; "Passion Sways Police Rulers," *Press*, 21 Aug. 1896; "Roosevelt Sets Police Guessing," *Press*, 22 July 1896; "Police Bribery Openly Charged," *Press*, 4 June 1896; "Parker, Pachyderm," *Press*, 4 July 1896; and "Mr. Parker's Little Handsaw," *Press*, 10 June 1896. For some of the *Press*'s experimentation in newer areas, see "Stirring Deeds of Police and Firemen," 21 June 1896; "Night Stick against Knife Saves a Woman from a Brutal Husband," 25 Aug. 1896; "Policeman Kills a Negro Burglar," 31 Aug. 1896; "The Lady Burglar as She Really Is," 7 June 1896; and part of an occasional comic series on the Irish cop, "Casey's Reminiscences of the Ambulance 'Doc,'" 21 June 1896. On Victorian woodcuts and the crime story, see Stange, *Symbols of Ideal Life*, 11–20. Principal *Press* coverage of the Becker episode occurred in "Policeman May Be Tried," 18 Sept. 1896, and "Red Badge Man on a Police Rack," 17 Oct. 1896. This second report says Crane testified that the police had "threatened to blacken his character" to prevent him from testifying. The *Tribune* reports, if anything, trivialized the controversy even further. See "Saved from a Fine by Stephen Crane," *Daily Tribune*, 17 Sept. 1896; "Dora Clark Accuses Two Policemen," *Daily Tribune*, 4 Oct. 1896; "An All-Night Police Trial," *Daily Tribune*, 17 Oct. 1896; "The Letter Reached the Wrong Crane," *Daily Tribune*, 30 Sept. 1896.

63. It is not surprising that Roosevelt thought the *Press* was the most loyal to his cause. Due in part to its local Democratic ties, the *Times* had, in fact, been a bit tepid on the Raines Law— and the *Press* was not. Compare "Misdirected Zeal," *Times*, 26 Dec. 1896, with "Money Piles In from Liquor Men," *Press*, 2 July 1896.

64. See, e.g., "Policeman Was Drunk," *Sun*, 23 Aug. 1896; "Little Rebecca Found," *Sun*, 24 Aug. 1896; "Policeman Arrests Detective," *Sun*, 10 Sept. 1986; "Chief Conlin's Burglar," *Sun*, 13 Sept. 1896; "A Police Court Oration," *Sun*, 14 Sept. 1896.

65. See, e.g., "Police Law Once More," *Sun*, 29 Sept. 1896. On the *Sun*'s antipathy to the Lexow Report and its support of Tammany, see Stone, *Dana and the Sun*, 135–39, 140–42, 164 ff.; on its changing audience in the 1890s, see Janet E. Steele, *"The Sun" Shines for All* (Syracuse: Syracuse University Press, 1993), 79–80, 96–98, 119–20; compare Saxton, "Problems of Class and Race," 234.

66. "Roosevelt Is Right," *Brooklyn Daily Eagle*, 3 Sept. 1896; "Modern Municipal Reform," *Brooklyn Daily Eagle*, 4 Sept. 1896; "The Habitual Criminals Act," *Brooklyn Daily Eagle*, 19 Oct. 1896.

67. "S. Crane and Dora Clark," *Sun*, 17 Sept. 1896, reprinted in *NYS* 217–19; "Novelist Crane Racked," *Sun*, 17 Oct. 1896; ["Stephen Crane said in a New York police court,"] *Brooklyn Daily Eagle*, 17 Sept. 1896; "Mr. Crane's Humiliation," *Brooklyn Daily Eagle*, 16 Oct. 1986; "Mr. Crane and the Police," *Brooklyn Daily Eagle*, 17 Oct. 1896, reprinted in *NYS* 252–54.

68. "The Police Report," *Sun*, 16 Sept. 1896. See also "71 Dock Tramps Nabbed," *Sun*, 24 Aug. 1896, describing a police sweep; and "Policeman Kills a Thief," *Sun*, 21 Sept. 1896; compare "Boy Burglar Shot to Death," *Journal*, 21 Sept. 1896.

69. I discuss the style of *World* Sunday editions more fully in *White Collar Fictions: Class and Social Representation in American Literature, 1885–1925* (Athens: University of Georgia Press,

1992), 40–47. For typical fare, see "M'Laughlin Is Lucky," *World*, 21 Oct. 1896; "Police Force Spoiled Him," *World*, 16 Sept. 1896; " "A Few of the Things that Joining the Force Taught Truly Good Policeman Hughes," *World*, 17 Sept. 1896; "Policemen as Cinderellas," "Reunited in Court," and "Bears Locked in Cells," *World*, 18 Sept. 1896. Compare "A New Trial for McLaughlin," *Brooklyn Daily Eagle*, 20 Oct. 1896.

70. "With Himself as Hero," *World*, 17 Sept. 1896, and "Crane Had a Gay Night," *World*, 16 Oct. 1896, both clippings in CU.

71. For representative fare, see "Conlin Wins the Thief-Taking Match," *Journal*, 10 Oct. 1896; "Torn from His Bride," *Journal*, 24 Oct. 1896; "Boy Burglar Shot to Death," *Journal*, 21 Sept. 1896; "Died Struggling with a Policeman," *Journal*, 21 Sept. 1896; "Brave Policeman's Narrow Escape," *Journal*, 26 Sept. 1896; "Blackmail Charged vs. Police," *Journal*, 22 Sept. 1986.

72. Main coverage in "Crane Risked All," *Journal*, 17 Oct. 1896, reprinted in *NYS* 242–48; "Novelist Crane Was True Blue," *Journal*, 16 Oct. 1896, reprinted in *NYS* 235–38; "A Crime or a Blunder" (*Journal* calling for Becker's trial), *Journal*, 18 Sept. 1896; "Dora Clark Doesn't Appear," *Journal*, 18 Sept. 1896; "Not a Grudge, He Says," *Journal*, 19 Sept. 1896; Crane, "Adventures," *NYS* 229–30.

73. Long quote from *NYS* 223. Cf. my discussion of chivalric "protectionism" in regard to O. Henry in *White Collar Fictions*, 47 ff. On contemporary images of the chorus girl, see Allen, *Horrible Prettiness*, 201 ff.

74. "Adventures," *NYS* 229–30. More typically, according to Kathy Peiss, "while carefully marking the boundary between the fallen and the respectable, a working woman might appropriate part of the prostitute's style as her own." Peiss, *Cheap Amusements: Working Women and Leisure in Turn-of-the-Century New York* (Philadelphia: Temple University Press, 1986), 66; see also 57–59 on street culture.

75. "Crane Risked All," *NYS* 245.

76. The term "affair" obviously carried the aura of contamination by Clark. However, the long-term effect on Crane's reputation may have been overstated. In the collection of obituaries and later reviews housed in CU, for instance, I found virtually no mention of this episode. Crane nevertheless worried about it: in a letter to his brother not unlike a last will and testament, Crane insisted that he had acted "like a man of honor and a gentleman in the case," and that his "Adventures" reported events exactly as they had happened. Letter to William Howe Crane, 29 Nov. 1896, in *The Correspondence of Stephen Crane*, 1:266.

77. Alan Trachtenberg, "Experiments in Another Country: Stephen Crane's City Sketches," in Sundquist, *American Realism*, 148. A similar strategy regarding police mop-ups is at work in the last page of Crane's best war piece, "War Memories," in *Tales of War*, vol. 6 of *The Works of Stephen Crane*, ed. Fredson Bowers (Charlottesville: University Press of Virginia, 1973). Here Crane mocks how "natural-born major-generals" will go on "clucking" about combat where common soldiers remain silent (263).

78. As with the descending social ladder in the *Journal* illustrations, this pattern had itself been prefigured in the finale of Crane's *Maggie*, which not only teases us with several potential misrecognitions—wherein we witness layers of street encounters that may be assignations, solicitations, or pleas for charity—but also makes us wonder whether the "girl of the painted cohorts

of the city" is even the Maggie we've been following in the plot. Trachtenberg, for one, recognizes that the name "Maggie" was "virtually generic" (145). I have written about similar stories of misrecognition, modeled on Crane's example, in "'Broadway Nights': John Reed and the City," *Prospects*, 13 (1988): 273–94. All subsequent citations are from *Stephen Crane: Tales, Sketches, and Reports*, vol. 8 of *The Works of Stephen Crane*.

79. Nearly the exact same sentiments are expressed about the Tenderloin in "In the Broadway Cable Cars" and "A Lovely Jag in a Crowded Car," both *The Works of Stephen Crane*, 8: 361–64. The latter is also an intriguing piece in that the presence of a drunk transforms the space of the cable car into a saloon.

80. On the publicity about Minetta Lane, see the news coverage cited in *The Works of Stephen Crane*, 8:882.

81. Crane, *Active Service* (New York: International Association of Newspapers and Authors, 1901), 199.

82. That summer, as Joseph Katz shows, when Crane had challenged the reformed NYPD for its "blundering" and "mismanagement" of crowds at a rally for Bryan, he singled out a pattern of "brutality" and "unnecessary harshness" that would not, he wrote, "have been possible under the [Tammany] Byrnes regime." See "Poor Police Arrangements at the Bryan Meeting," reprinted in Katz, "Stephen Crane," 44. On the *Sun*'s own standard of "knowing the ropes," see Stone, *Dana and the Sun*, 168.

83. William Dean Howells, "The Police Court," in *Impressions and Experiences* (New York: Harper and Brothers, 1909), 62.

84. "Eloquence" also seems to realign the elliptical centers of Crane's "An Experiment in Misery"—wherein the testimony of the man denominated the "assassin" is "so profound it is unintelligible" (286), and cries of the flophouse are described as "carving" a scar in the "imaginations" of Crane's "youth" (289). Compare Howard's remarks on the "immobility" of the spectator in naturalism, *Form and History in American Naturalism*, 126 and passim.

85. Arrest statistics from Richardson, *The New York Police*, 254.

86. Gilfoyle, *City of Eros*, 243. Intriguingly, "Assaulted a Policeman," *Sun*, 17 Oct. 1896, also discusses the arrest of a *World* reporter named Richard Bell, who claimed he was arrested simply because he was about to expose the revival of vice in the Tenderloin.

87. "[M]achinery that no one owns" from "Eye of Power," 156.

88. Containing these contradictions, he nevertheless thought of himself as a loyal police officer, foiling himself throughout his career to Steffens's and Roosevelt's Max Schmittberger even when a plea-bargaining deal, purportedly to "rat" on his superiors, came to him in prison. "Tell them I'm no Schmittberger," he reportedly growled. See Logan, *Against the Evidence*, esp. 105–17, 139, 260. Quote from prison in 1912, from Logan, *Against the Evidence*, 139.

89. Ross, "Liberalism," 759.

90. In these ways, Crane's experience offers to synthesize the discrepancy often posited between interpretive closure and the violence of judicial rulings. Compare Austin Sarat and Thomas R. Kearns on Robert Cover's thinking in "Making Peace with Violence: Robert Cover on Law and Legal Theory," in their *Law's Violence* (Ann Arbor: University of Michigan Press, 1992), 218–19.

91. I refer here to the (misnamed) Clemencia Arango affair, notorious because *Journal* sketches provided by Frederic Remington re-created a scene that never occurred. See Arthur Lubow, *The Reporter Who Would Be King: A Biography of Richard Harding Davis* (New York: Scribner's, 1982), 143 ff. Roosevelt, "The Law Must Be Enforced," 184. Compare my "Plotting the Border," 340–61.

Chapter Two

1. The film's narrative departs significantly from the screenplay reprinted in *The Naked City*, ed. Matthew Bruccoli (Carbondale: Southern Illinois University Press, 1979). The narrator's comments here, for example, do not appear in Bruccoli. Nevertheless, where possible, page citations of *The Naked City* are from Bruccoli merely for the reader's convenience; in all instances, however, it is the *film* version to which I refer.

2. Bruccoli, *The Naked City*, 70.

3. Filming mirror discussed in Jim Bishop, *The Mark Hellinger Story* (New York: Appleton-Century-Crofts, 1952), 336. Weegee had similarly claimed in his book, *Naked City* (1945; reprint, De Capo Press, 1985) that his photos caught "New Yorkers with their masks off" (11); often unaware of being photographed, these subjects became a "page from life" (12), putatively showing a "real" passage of events. As these book metaphors suggest, Weegee's volume also aimed for documentary simulation.

4. Wald, afterword to Bruccoli, *The Naked City*, 148.

5. Fogelson argues that one can trace the movement in American film and television from police shown as "lower- and lower-middle-class ethnics" to their representation, after the war, as "ordinary middle-class Americans" (*Big-City Police*, 235).

6. Muldoon (called Mulvey in *The Naked City* reprint) was played by Barry Fitzgerald, who was explicitly chosen for his Irish ancestry (Wald, afterword, 124). On Irish American mobility following World War II, see McGreevy, *Parish Boundaries*, 80 ff.

7. The script even suggests that Wald pondered cameo roles for the mayor and his commissioner. Wald had apprenticed during the war under Robert Flaherty, and said he wrote "some thirty" documentary and training films. See Wald, afterword, 136–37. Wald said Hellinger was the source of the connection to O'Dwyer (138).

8. In the years leading up to the Hollywood code of 1934, for instance, the FBI had already been involved in advising movie theaters to hold civic events and lobby displays linked to its sponsored anti-crime films. As Powers points out, the focus on celebrity criminals also allowed the Bureau to disclaim responsibility for the broader crime problem (*G-Men*, 39–47). Cf. Walker, *Critical History*, 151–52. "Lone wolf" from Powers, *G-Men*, 94. On the LAPD's complete script control of the television version of *Dragnet*, see Domanick, *To Protect and to Serve*, 122 ff.

9. Interview with Valentine by S. J. Woolf, "Cops' Cop with a Five-Borough Beat," *New York Times Magazine*, 19 Nov. 1944, 16, 38, 39. Wald and Hellinger remembered being lobbied by this professional civil-servant philosophy. Wald recalled that it was the NYPD detectives themselves who pressed to be represented not like the lazy Irish beat cops of past stereotypes, but as "hard working civil servants" (138). "I have a hunch," Hellinger is similarly quoted as saying, "that most of the real cases are solved by patient hard work." As quoted in Bishop, *The*

Mark Hellinger Story, 329. Jack Webb told a nearly identical story about meeting an LAPD detective on the set of *He Walked by Night*, and then riding with him in a police car. Retold in "Jack Be Nimble!" *Time*, 15 March 1954, reprinted on <http://www.hooked.net/~cbhall/DRAGNET.HTM>.

10. Jack Webb, *The Badge* (Englewood Cliffs, N.J.: Prentice Hall, 1958), v.

11. See Lawrence Treat, *V as in Victim* (New York: Duell, Sloan and Pearce, 1945), 33, 57–58; Hillary Waugh, *Last Seen Wearing* (1956; reprint, Bath, England: Chivers Press, 1985), 51, 66, 133, 189, 204. Or, for more contemporary versions, Laurence Sanders, *The First Deadly Sin* (New York: Berkeley Books, 1973), 269, or Patricia D. Cornwall, *Post-mortem* (New York: Avon Books, 1990), 66.

Relevant criticism on the procedural genre is George N. Dove, *The Police Procedural* (Bowling Green: Bowling Green University Popular Press, 1982); George N. Dove, *The Boys from Grover Avenue: Ed McBain's 87th Precinct Novels* (Bowling Green: Bowling Green University Popular Press, 1985); Peter Messent, ed., *Criminal Proceedings: The Contemporary American Crime Novel* (London: Pluto Press, 1977), esp. 1–21; and Hillary Waugh's own essay, "The Human Rather than the Superhuman Sleuth," in Lucy Freeman, ed., *The Murder Mystique: Crime Writers on Their Art* (New York: Frederick Ungar, 1982). Ed McBain's procedural is usefully discussed in relation to the postwar "structure of feeling"—particularly the new credibility of organized, technological might—in Stephen Knight, *Form and Ideology in Crime Fiction* (Bloomington: Indiana University Press, 1980), 168–93. See also Richard Weisberg, "Law in and as Literature: Self-Generated Meaning in the 'Procedural Novel,' " in *The Comparative Perspective on Literature*, ed. Clayton Koelb and Susan Noakes (Ithaca: Cornell University Press, 1988), 224–32. All page citations in the main text are from Ed McBain, *The Con Man* (1957; reprint, New York: Signet Books, 1974).

12. Wald, afterword, 148.

13. William Stott, *Documentary Expression and Thirties America* (New York: Oxford, 1973), 14. Ellroy quoted in Messent, *Criminal Proceedings*, 11.

14. For an alternative view of the narrator in the film, see Sarah Kozloff, "Humanizing 'The Voice of God': Narration in *The Naked City*," *Cinema Journal* 23 (summer 1994): 41–53. Compare this to Seltzer's reading of Sherlock Holmes's "fantasy of providential supervision" (*"The Princess Casamassima,"* 100), which involves flying over London, removing roofs, and peeping into windows; or D. A. Miller, *Novel and the Police*, 24. Webb called *Dragnet* a "documentary radio and television detective series" (*Badge*, v).

15. I am especially indebted to Saverio Giovacchini on this point. On Weegee's connections with film noir, see Alain Bergala, "Weegee and Film Noir," in *Weegee's World*, ed. Miles Barth (Boston: Little, Brown, 1997), 69–77. Meanwhile, just about everyone involved with *The Naked City* claimed credit for its central procedural emphasis, its narrator, and its shooting strategies. In Cynthia Grenier's interview with director Jules Dassin, in *Sight and Sound* 27 (1957): 141–43, Dassin claimed it was his idea (not Wald's) to film in the streets of New York, "in real interiors, with unknown actors" (142). Producer Hellinger is given credit for the same strategy in Bishop, *The Mark Hellinger Story*, 328–29. Contrary to Wald's overall characterization, Bishop portrays Hellinger as obsessed with this film's production. Dassin disowned the film when he saw it after studio editing; see Grenier, interview with Dassin, 141.

16. A typical version of this rhetorical by-play comes in one of the first procedurals, Hillary Waugh's *Last Seen Wearing* (1952). Here police chief Frank Ford belittles the college-educated, bookish pretensions of his sidekick, while—in parallel fashion—they track down a serial seducer college professor. "'God damn it,'" Ford says at one point, "'spend one afternoon at a college and you start talking like a professor. You're working for a Police department, not a Ph.D.'" (235). In Lawrence Treat's *V as in Victim* (1945), however—though the same by-play is seen (33, 169–70)—it is actually the lab-coated "police science" man who is the secret hero (216).

17. On the 1940 class, see Richardson, *New York Police*, 138. On Vollmer and the MO, see Gene E. Carte and Elaine H. Carte, *Police Reform in the United States: The Era of August Vollmer, 1905–1932* (Berkeley and Los Angeles: University of California Press, 1975), 23. On police watches, see O. W. Wilson, *Police Administration* (New York: McGraw-Hill, 1950), 473 ff. On these developments generally, see Fogelson, *Big-City Police*, 167–268; Carte and Carte, *Police Reform*; Richardson, *New York Police*, 132–57; and Walker, *Critical History*, esp. 139–66. Walker provides the best overview of the developments during the Depression; Carte and Carte a good sense of Vollmer's academic affiliations. Most accounts of the LAPD, meanwhile, still rely on Joseph Gerald Woods, "The Progressives and the Police: Urban Reform and the Professionalization of the Los Angeles Police Department," Ph.D. diss., UCLA, 1973; I have also used his "Police Unions and Police Professionalization: the Los Angeles Model," paper presented to the 1976 annual meeting of the American Society of Criminology, Tucson, Arizona.

18. For insightful accounts of popular conceptions of criminality in these decades, see David E. Ruth, *Inventing the Public Enemy: The Gangster in American Culture, 1918–1934* (Chicago: University of Chicago Press, 1996), 63 ff., and Potter, *War on Crime*, 57 ff. On migratory criminals, see Vollmer, *The Police and Modern Society* (1936; reprint, Montclair, N.J.: Paterson Smith, 1971), 25; for "Bluebeard," see 21. The Wickersham report also affirmed, in the section written by Vollmer, the "crook" as a "migratory worker." National Commission on Law Observance and Enforcement, *Report on Police*, no. 14 (Washington: U.S. Government Printing Office, 1931), 36.

19. Smith, for instance, said that the word "systems" in the title of his work was a lament, since in his view there were "40,000 separate and distinct police agencies in the United States." *Police Systems in the United States*, rev. ed. (New York: Harper & Brothers, 1949), 25. Civil service and civilian oversight, it was argued, were destructive of internal discipline and the need for lifelong tenure for police administrators; see esp. Donald C. Stone, "The Control and Discipline of Police Forces," *Annals of the American Academy of Political and Social Science* 146 (Nov. 1929): 66–71.

20. Vollmer, *Police and Modern Society*, 30, 32. Vollmer, in fact, offered one profile of a serial killer, one James P. ("Bluebeard") Watson, as having an MO just like the criminal in the *Con Man*. Potter persuasively connects "celebrity bandits" to mobility and transience (*War on Crime*, 64, 67).

21. On salaries, see Walker, *Critical History*, 140; Fogelson, *Big-City Police*, 181; on prestige, Fogelson, *Big-City Police*, 234.

22. On delinquency, see O. W. Wilson, *Police Administration*, 3–4; compare the Wickersham report in National Commission, *Report on Police*, 76, 113–16; on symbolic functions of beat cops, see O. W. Wilson, *Police Administration*, 81, and Bruce Smith, *Police Systems*, 19 ff.

As Domanick makes clear, statistical number crunching to prove crime busting vigilance, a lasting legacy for the LAPD into our own day, often provided cover for persisting relationships with local gangsters and vice crime (*To Protect and to Serve*, 55–79). On the importance of record keeping as stressed by the Wickersham Commission, see National Commission, *Report on Police*, 105–10.

23. On Valentine's "muss 'em up," see August Heckscher, *When La Guardia Was Mayor* (New York: Norton, 1978), 109. For these useful accounts, see Fogelson, *Big-City Police*, 219–42; Woods, "Progressives and the Police," 162–219; and Domanick, *To Protect and to Serve*, 99 ff. Domanick gives a full account of the LAPD's intelligence and "red-busting" operations; see, for example, 63 ff. and 76 ff. One typical statement of a Parker admirer: "A close analysis of the efforts of the leadership of the NAACP indicates clearly that they are waging their fight and girding themselves to impose their will upon other races by force, fear, and intimidation." Paul H. Asenhurst, *Police and the People* (Springfield, Ill.: Charles C. Thomas, 1956), 153. For an alternative view of Vollmer's tenure in LA, see Walker, *Critical History*, 130. For information on the NYPD in the 1940s, I have also relied on Frank S. Adams, "Check-up of Police in Gambling Drive Ordered by Mayor," *New York Times*, 28 Aug. 1946; Meyer Berger, "Shake-up in Police Laid to Complaints by Hogan on Laxity," *New York Times*, 12 Dec. 1946; Alexander Feinberg, "Vice Arrest Data Will Be Checked," *New York Times*, 31 Aug. 1946; "O'Dwyer Shakes Up Police in Harlem Election Killing; Inspector De Martino Quits," *New York Times*, 11 Dec. 1946; "Wallander Shifts Police Inspectors," *New York Times*, 11 Oct. 1945.

24. See esp. Potter, *War on Crime*, 4, 108; on public mobilization in the New Deal, see esp. 125 ff. Cf. G. Douglas Gourley, "Police Public Relations," in *New Goals in Police Management*, ed. Bruce Smith, *Annals of the American Academy of Political and Society Science* 291 (1954): 136. Volume hereafter cited as *New Goals*. Parker quoted in O. W. Wilson, ed., *Parker on Police* (Springfield, Ill.: Charles C. Thomas, 1957), 5. Webb's *The Badge*, which reprinted police radio codes for its readers (73), explicitly made its plea for alliance: "either accept Parker and the L.A.P.D. he has fashioned," Webb told readers, "or make a grave and weakening concession to hostile elements" (245).

25. Vollmer, *Police and Modern Society*, 6–7. The "sentimental" attitude of the public was attacked as early as Fosdick's *Crime in America and the Police* (New York: Century, 1920); see esp. 43 ff. Phrases after "sentimental" are from Fosdick (44, 45). For a good summary of this new "democratic realism" that discounted citizen rationality and participation, see Westbrook, *John Dewey*, 280–86. Not surprisingly, Vollmer worked directly with Chicago's Charles Merriam (Carte and Carte, *Police Reform*, 63–64), the chief proponent of this realist philosophy (Westbrook, *John Dewey* 280).

Sources for the following summary of police attitudes include: Donald C. Stone, "The Control and Discipline of Police Forces," *Annals of the American Academy of Political and Social Science* 146 (Nov. 1929): 63–73; Vollmer, *Police and Modern Society*; Smith, *Police Systems*; O. W. Wilson, *Police Administration*; and a series of articles in *New Goals*: William H. Parker, "The Police Challenge in Our Great Cities," 5–13; A. E. Leonard, "Crime Reporting as a Police Management Tool," 127–34; Gourley, "Police Public Relations," 135–42; Stanley R. Schrotel, "Changing Patrol Methods," 46–53; Paul L. Kirk, "Progress in Criminal Investigation," 54–62.

26. Gourley, "Police Public Relations," 136.

27. Logan's *Against the Evidence* details how Becker's graft—and, indeed, the homicide it-self—were taken as symbolic of the older police system and its invulnerability to reform (260). For Fosdick's comments, see "Detective Becker and the Courts," *Harper's Weekly*, 4 April 1914, 10–11.

28. *Police Systems*, 5.

29. On fool and knave, see Smith, *Police Systems*, 19. On Fosdick's connection to Woodrow Wilson on this point, compare Raymond B. Fosdick, *Chronicle of a Generation: An Autobiography* (New York: Harper and Bros., 1958), 129 and 46–47.

30. Vollmer, *Police and Modern Society*, 236–37.

31. For the widespread perception of a crime wave in the twenties, see John R. Brazil, "Murder Trials, Murder, and Twenties America," *American Quarterly* 33 (summer 1981): 163–84, esp. 179–80. Steffens published his views *in* the twenties: e.g., in "How I Made a Crime Wave," *Bookman* 68 (Dec. 1928): 416–19, later incorporated into his *Autobiography*. Fosdick also cites a speech by muckraker Brand Whitlock from 1916 ridiculing the impact of moral crusading on police morale (*Chronicle*, 54–55). Meanwhile, Lippmann wrote during Prohibition: "We find ourselves revolving in a circle of impotence in which we outlaw intolerantly the satisfaction of certain persistent human desires and then tolerate what we have prohibited." "The Underworld, A Stultified Conscience," *Forum* 75 (Feb. 1931): 65. Lippmann in fact argued that what distinguished an "underworld" from mere criminality was that it performed "services for which there is some kind of public demand." "The Underworld, Our Secret Servant," *Forum* 75 (Jan. 1931): 1–4; "services" from 1. On the broader shift in reform liberalism, see Gerstle, "The Protean Character," 1047 ff.; Ross, "Liberalism," 759–60.

32. Fosdick, *Chronicle*, 44. Leonard, "Crime Reporting." 127, credits the International Association of the Chiefs of Police with starting the drive toward the UCR, as does Walker, *Critical History*, 155–56. Bruce Smith was the technical staff director for the project. Adopted by IACP in 1929 after Smith's study a year earlier, the project was soon taken over by the FBI. Walker claims as well that the "seven felonies" emphasis distracted the focus of policing from lesser street crimes and disorderly conduct. See the terribly important essay, Walker, " 'Broken Windows' and Fractured History: The Use and Misuse of History in Recent Police Patrol Analysis," *Justice Quarterly* 1 (1984): 75–90, esp. 77–78.

33. The public must be told, Parker said in his usual sociological abstraction, that *"the police function is a basic component of man's government by man which has determined the character and permanence of every social structure since human beings first sought collective security"* ("The Police Challenge," 6, emphasis his). But, as Parker put it, the "police function" wasn't "considered by the members of the electorate to be a vital element of their life together" (5).

34. Asenhurst, *Police and the People*, 21; Valentine quoted in Woolf, "Cops' Cop," 39. There were, to be sure, shortages of police officers during the war—a situation that may have increased the necessity of citizen employees. Complaints about shortages were common; see "Valentine Retires; La Guardia Delays Naming Successor," *New York Times*, 15 Sept. 1945.

35. Wilson, *Police Administration*, 3, 412, 413.

36. In the 1970s, James Q. Wilson would be citing Vollmer on precisely this matter: the 18+ offender. James Q. Wilson, *Thinking about Crime*, rev. 3d ed. (New York: Vintage Books,

1985), 141–42 and *passim*. Woods also mentions the "efficiency" of permanent booking information on repeat offenders, a LAPD innovation ("Progressives and the Police," 427).

37. Wilson on "important groups" in *Police Administration*, 7; Gourley on publics in "Police Public Relations," 137; on the poll rankings, see Gourley, "Police Public Relations," 140.

38. On unreliable witnesses, see Kirk, "Progress in Criminal Investigation," 57. Domanick points out that Davis wanted *every* LA citizen fingerprinted (*To Protect and to Serve*, 53). On Valentine and the lineups, see *New York Times*, 13 Oct. 1945. Weegee was himself fascinated with what he called the "pie van"; see notes 58 and 59 below.

39. Elijah Adlow, *Policemen and People* (Boston: William Rochfort, 1947), 4, 9, 10, 15–21.

40. On making people and the bellhop, see Asenhurst, *Police and the People*, 134. Statistics on the LAPD's own minority recruitment in this period are provided by Woods, "Progressives and the Police," 459, 463.

41. The UCR might also be understood in relation to time-honored resistance to civilian review boards. On this campaign in LA, see Woods, "Progressives and the Police," 472 ff. Fact on Winchell and Hellinger from Wald, afterword, 140.

42. Ruth, *Inventing the Public Enemy*, 106.

43. Again, Wald also remembered cops' disdain for the "glamour boys" of Hammett and Chandler (afterword, 138). On censorship, see Geoffrey O'Brien, *Hardboiled America: The Lurid Years of Paperbacks* (New York: Van Nostrand Reinhold, 1981), 119.

44. The case received front page coverage nearly every day for two weeks of March 1923. "Half hundred" from "Mitchell and Wife Meet in Private Car and Separate Later," *New York Times*, 28 March 1923. See also "Fight for Letters Killed Girl Model," *New York Times*, 21 March 1923. There is one allusion in the film to the 1920s: the family members in the photograph on the chief detective's desk are described in the script as from that period. But Muldoon is also a widower. The district attorney's office was attacked again for its handling of the case in 1933: see *New York Times*, 2 June 1933.

45. I am indebted here to Brazil especially and to Michael Schudson, *Discovering the News* (New York: Basic Books, 1978). See esp. Brazil, "Murder Trials," 165; on police heroes in the *News*, see John D. Stevens, *Sensationalism and the New York Press* (New York: Freedom Forum Media Studies Center, Columbia University, 1991), 130; on Pulitzer and Hearst's displacement, see Stevens, *Sensationalism and the New York Press*, 112. In the late twenties, Lippmann predicted that tabloidism would run its course; the older, more "conservative" style, he sometimes said, was reviving. Lippmann hopefully paralleled the exhaustion of the penny press and "yellow journalism" not only—as his mentor Steffens had—to romantic fiction, but to older notions of democratic consent that were themselves being reformed. Since "the commodity" that the new journalism dealt with was no longer "human interest," Lippmann argued, but "the approximation of objective fact, it is free also of subserviency to the whims of the public." The new journalism thus opened the door to "the use of trained intelligence in newspaper work." "Two Revolutions in the American Press," *Yale Review* 20 (March 1931): 438, 440. This was a case Lippmann had been arguing since *Public Opinion* (1922).

46. The best account of this is the chapter called "Discovering Sweeney" in John Chapman, *Tell It to Sweeney: An Informal History of the New York Daily News* (1961; reprint, Westport, Conn.:

Greenwood Press, 1997), 133–45; fondly recalled in Pete Hamill, *News Is a Verb: Journalism at the End of the Twentieth Century* (New York: Ballantine Publishing Group, 1998), 54–78.

47. This point is made explicitly in the script reprinted in Bruccoli, *The Naked City*, 25.

48. My generalizations here stem from extensive comparisons of *News* and *Times* coverage. Julia Harpman was continuously the main author of *News* coverage; her byline is given for all but a few articles. Quotes here from her "Model Slain, Her Gems Gone," *News*, 16 March 1923; "Model's Death Showers Fiery Light on Broadway Jackals," 18 March 1923; "'Angel' Planned to Wed Model," 21 March 1923; "King 'Angel' Defies Accuser," 19 March 1923; and "King 'Angel' Rich Bostonian," 20 March 1923. King's "Angel," however, turned out to be a Philadelphian. *New York Times* coverage customarily had no bylines. In addition to those cited earlier and subsequently, articles consulted include: "$1,000 Bond, Last Gift by Mitchell to Girl, Missing," *New York Times*, 27 March 1923; "'Angel' Planned to Wed Model," *New York Daily News*, 12 March 1923; "'Angel' Ready to Drop Mask," *New York Daily News*, 22 March 1923; "Comb Is Chief Clue to Man Who Killed and Robbed Model," *New York Times*, 17 March 1923; "Daugherty Bares King Threat," *New York Daily News*, 29 March 1923; "Daugherty's Caller Was Frank Keenan," *New York Times*, 1 April 1923; "Daugherty's Son in King Case," *New York Daily News*, 27 March 1923; "Friend of Model Killed Her," *New York Daily News*, 30 March 1923; "J. K. Mitchell, Kin of E. T. Stotesbury, Slain Girl's Friend," *New York Times*, 25 March 1923; "Marshall's Secret Guarded in Murder," *New York Times*, 22 March 1923; "Murder of Model Not Part of Plot," *New York Times*, 20 March 1923; "Police Trail King Plotters," *New York Daily News*, 26 March 1923; "Prosecutor Calls Reticent 'Marshall,'" *New York Times*, 24 March 1923; "Prosecutor Seeks Daugherty's Help," *New York Times*, 28 March 1923; "Say Model's Slayer Wanted His Letters," *New York Times*, 18 March 1923; "Shorn Mask Bares Stotesbury's Son-in-Law as Model's 'Angel,'" *New York Daily News*, 25 March 1923; "Slain Model's Brother Faces Mitchell," *New York Daily News*, 1 April 1923; "Slain Model's Suitor Held," *New York Daily News*, 17 March 1923; "Son of Daugherty Sought," *New York Daily News*, 28 March 1923; "Spotlight on Mitchell's Past," *New York Daily News*, 31 March 1923; "Umbrella Provides New Clue in Murder," *New York Times*, 23 March 1923; "Witnesses at Odds in Model's Murder," *New York Times*, 19 March 1923.

49. In 1923, the editors of the *New Republic* had in fact singled out the King case for the way it showed "tabloidization" was hardly a phenomenon limited to the *News* or *Mirror*. If Hearst's *American* devoted 30,000 words to it over two weeks, by their count the *Times* had devoted 28,000. "Dorothy Keenan and 'Mr. Marshall,'" *New Republic*, 11 April 1923, 175–76.

50. "Say Model's Slayer."

51. Particularly when contrasted with the saturnalia of chapter 1, or compared with the two-newspaper cities of today, what Schudson casts as a polarized field (between tabloid and what he calls "objective" camps) can seem, in a longer view, equally a trend toward what Bourdieu calls a "pathological" cultural field. For typical *Times* casting, see also "Find Model Dead, Her Jewels Gone," *New York Times*, 16 March 1923.

52. Brazil, "Murder Trials," 167.

53. Hall, "Notes," 233.

54. On underworld fraternity, see Mark Hellinger, *Moon over Broadway* (New York: William

Faro, 1931), 225; on cons see Hellinger, *The Ten Million* (New York: Farrar & Rinehart, 1934), 59–67.

55. Compare, for instance, the panoramic effect of "Characters of Broadway," in Hellinger, *Moon over Broadway*, 243–72, to the O. Henry mannerisms I discuss in *White Collar Fictions*, 26–55. O. Henry is explicitly referred to in *The Ten Million*, 3, 363, as well. Hellinger later tried, of course, to distance himself from this tabloid role (*Moon over Broadway*, 100–103); many of his stories, in fact, present themselves as decades old.

56. Hellinger, *Moon over Broadway*, 160–61.

57. Ibid., 224.

58. [Fellig,] *Weegee by Weegee* (1961; reprint, New York: De Capo Press, 1975), esp. 36–98. Notably, Weegee also said that Walter Winchell had a police radio, and, like himself, "liked to play cops and robbers" (54).

59. Quotes from [Fellig,] *Weegee by Weegee*, 36, 42, 59. On helping the police, see 56, 61, 74. In his *Naked City*, on photographing fires, he writes:

> At fires I also make shots of the crowds watching the fires . . . for the detectives and fire marshals who are always on the scene . . . on the look out for pyromaniacs . . . jealous lovers . . . thrill seekers . . . disappointed would-be firemen . . . who having failed their examinations will start fires . . . Also at fires where there are rescues . . . different firemen will take credit for such rescues . . . my photos decide who did make the rescue and end all disputes (52).

60. Weegee cited in comparison to O. Henry in Miles Orvell, "Weegee's Voyeurism and the Mastery of Urban Disorder," *American Art* 6 (winter 1992): 23.

61. In one of his rare interviews, McBain claimed that "[t]he police procedure was learned from cops, and it is as unvaried and as disciplined as the pattern of a bull fight." Where invention and imagination entered into his books at all, McBain claimed, was "in the guise of the various people the cops meet along the way." Quoted in interview in *The Writer*, April 1969, 111.

62. That this plot was prototypical in an ideological sense is suggested not only by its direct parallel in Vollmer's writings (see note 63 below), but in Webb's *The Badge*, which uses a serial burglar who preys on lonely women as its boilerplate crime (3–20). Waugh's *Last Seen Wearing* also focuses on a compulsive seducer.

63. This particular plot focused on a con Vollmer himself had said was archetypal for criminality in the new age: a man who starts with an ad in a love letters column, victimizing an innocent woman (Vollmer, *Police and Modern Society*, 43). Both these texts connect a "con" to violent crime, in part to demonstrate the organized character of crime and also the seriousness of even the most petty of rackets. Potter also shows how FBI literature connected social pathology to consumerism (*War on Crime*, 59 ff.).

64. Bruccoli, *The Naked City*, 132.

65. Ibid., 125.

66. My point is that this is more than the traditional voice of the Manhattan savant, derived from examples like Eugene Sue, George Foster, or even Stephen Crane. Wald claimed that he created the idea of the narrator as a combination of Walt Whitman and Thomas Wolfe; see

Kozloff, "Humanizing 'The Voice of God,'" 43. Not unimportantly, however, Wald also himself was a tabloid reader and fan and established his credibility with Hellinger that way (Wald, afterword, 135–36).

67. Neal Gabler, *Winchell: Gossip, Power, and the Culture of Celebrity* (New York: Knopf, 1994), 81. Gabler's view of the tabloid is quite consistent with Miles Orvell's, who has argued persuasively that Weegee's art was grounded in tabloid "newsworthiness," a vision of "urban chaos" ("Weegee's Voyeurism," 23). Orvell also sees Weegee's art as a "retort" to the more sympathetic documentary idiom of the New Deal (27). My only qualifications here are that Weegee's mass-cultural voyeurism included some O. Henryesque patronizing of "little people," and his voyeurism extended to a fascination with police power.

68. I discuss this affiliation more extensively in chapter 4, and in my discussion of Mike Barnicle in chapter 5. But even Joseph Wambaugh took issue with the "robotic" image of *Dragnet* and *Adam-12* as contrary to the best interests of police as workers. See Cecil Smith, "Humanizing the Television Cop," *Los Angeles Times*, 19 March 1973.

69. See "Wallander Shifts Police Inspectors," *New York Times*, 11 Oct. 1945. The line-up provided another occasion for Weegee's envy of police authority. In the pie wagon photo ([Fellig] 160), his caption says of the line-up: "[W]here they are questioned by police officials on a platform with a strong light on their faces . . . as detectives in the darkened room study them . . . and make mental notes for future reference" ([Fellig] 160). Weegee also refers to criminals as "scum" and says he feels no pity when they ask not to be photographed (160 ff.)

70. Ruth, *Inventing the Public Enemy*, 28.

71. As Larry Landrum observes, the public is cast as "childlike in its unreasoned impulsiveness and emotionalism while corruption from within is treated as an aberration." Larry Landrum, "Instrumental Texts and Stereotyping in *Hill Street Blues:* The Police Procedural on Television," *MELUS* 11 (autumn 1994): 93. My argument is meant to demur slightly, however, from Landrum's sense that the public is seen as an "anti-structural crowd" and is thus "assaulted" by the procedural form.

72. Bruccoli, *The Naked City*, 34.

73. *The Naked City*, it might be added, also worked partly to sanitize its victim, suppressing the drafted lines in which, in Wald's screenplay, Dr. Stoneman spoke of Jean Dexter's "unnatural hungers" (Bruccoli, *The Naked City*, 119). Precisely as *The Con Man* does, Hellinger's film must turn its feminine victim into more conventional normalcy, a rural migrant with loving parents left behind, an icon of eight million lives of loneliness each with their own (crime) story. Dorothy Keenan's mother, however, lived at 309 West 101st Street; see "Find Model Dead, Her Jewels Gone," *New York Times*, 16 March 1923. In the film, Jean Dexter is a migrant from New Jersey. In *The Con Man*, the floater is a daughter of Scranton coal miners. I am especially grateful to Alex Chasin for her insights about the film's antipathy to Jean Dexter's rogue sexuality.

74. Compare the photo sequence of Sinatra and a fan in Weegee's *Naked City*, 33. His captions are similarly full of laments about public gawking that doesn't actually see (or admit to watching), the way the camera or detective eyes work. Of one such sidewalk killing (79) in Little Italy, Weegee writes: "Detectives tried to question the people in the neighborhood . . . but they were all deaf . . . dumb . . . and blind . . . not having seen or heard anything" (79). What the photo shows, however, is over a dozen citizens leaning out of buildings looking at that scene.

75. Webb also shows a deluge of amateurs who distract pros from the case (*Badge*, 32). It is intriguing, as well, how whitewashed *The Naked City* is: an elevator man identified as a "Negro" was central to the actual case, and the original script's call for a "Negro" maid—also the case in Dot King's murder—never made it to the film. See "Witnesses at Odds in Model's Murder," *New York Times*, 19 March 1923; "$100,000 Blackmail Plot on Mitchell Led to King Murder," *New York Times*, 26 March 1923.

76. In the Dot King murder, the maid's assistance actually proved central. She provided the tip to the police that a blackmail scheme was afoot; see "$100,000 Blackmail Plot." And acting district attorney Pecora was charged repeatedly with protecting the well-to-do; in the film, the police can pillory the rich with impunity, in order to establish their own class authority.

77. The procedural, that is, would seem to reverse Miller's thesis about the Victorian novel, wherein literal policemen are rhetorically discounted or marginalized so as to foreground the novel's supplementary "amateur" economy of social control (*Novel and the Police*, 13–16, 41 ff.). Meanwhile, a name like "Jimmy" marks Halloran's juvenility and sidekick status.

78. Hellinger, *Moon over Broadway*, 67.

79. There is, of course, a modest renaissance of interest in Weegee's work now, as prototypical of postmodern pop: in this vein the Barth volume, *Weegee's World*, is one sign.

80. Landrum, "Instrumental Texts," 93.

81. References here especially to Armstrong and Cinnamon, "The Police in Protest," 131–90. See also my introduction, note 17.

82. In the end, the New York police commissioner went so far as to say King/Keenan's killer was "known" to the police, but that the "final shred" of evidence needed to indict was lacking; see "Elwell's Slayer Known to Police," *New York Times*, 21 Oct. 1923. One suspect in the case, Albert Guimares, *was* indicted on previous charges of stock swindling, in Boston; see "Lays Ruin to Slain Model," *New York Times*, 19 Dec. 1923.

83. A police shake-up on Manhattan's East Side followed shortly upon the election of William O'Dwyer and the murder of Joseph Scottoriggio, a Republican district captain, apparently by underworld figures: "O'Dwyer Shakes Up Police in Harlem Election Killing; Inspector De Martino Quits," *New York Times*, 11 Dec. 1946; Meyer Berger, "Shake-up in Police Laid to Complaints by Hogan on Laxity," *New York Times*, 12 Dec. 1946. The full story of New York's scandal is told in George Walsh, *Public Enemies: The Mayor, the Mob, and the Crime That Was* (New York: Norton, 1980). On Valentine's departure, see Irving Spiegel, "Valentine Ends 42 Years on Force to Begin Career in Radio, Movies," *New York Times*, 7 Sept. 1945.

Chapter Three

1. The police union lawyer is Frank McGee, profiled by Eileen McNamara, "Calling for Backup," *Boston Globe Sunday Magazine*, 12 April 1992, 16 ff. On the lessons of Vietnam, see the profile of new Boston police commissioner Paul Evans by Kevin Cullen, "The Neighborhood Cop," *Boston Globe Magazine*, 7 Jan. 1996, 29. On comparisons of street gangs to the Vietcong, see Davis, *City of Quartz*, 258, 293.

2. Jack Webb reports in 1958 that the International City Managers Association, long a locus

of police politics, called the LAPD "probably the most soundly organized large police department in the country" (*The Badge*, 86). In one survey in 1960, LA also led the nation in base salaries for police. Ralph Katz, "Police Pay Here Topped in 3 Cities," *New York Times*, 22 March 1960.

3. It has always been telling that the famous "Black Dahlia" case—which confounded all attempts to solve it—is mythologically bound to the LAPD's own repudiation of the crimebusting ethos. See, e.g., Webb, *The Badge*, 22 ff. On the LAPD invention of the *real* "dragnet," see Domanick, *To Protect and to Serve*, 53–54; on its Red Squads, 63 ff.; on "bum blockades," 60–63. Jerome Hopkins also singled out the LA forces as the worst perpetrators in his survey of the "third degree" and dragnet policing (*Our Lawless Police*, 152 ff.); Webb played up the "western" individualism of Parker (*The Badge*, 245). Domanick argues, however, that the new paramilitary style did not actually adopt its extreme cast until the late 1960s, and that proactive policing—internally known as "the grip"—was obsolete as soon as it was implemented (*To Protect and to Serve*, 108 ff.).

4. In New York City and Philadelphia, cops were actually prohibited from living in their precincts; see Jonathan Rubenstein, *City Police* (New York: Farrar, Strauss, and Giroux: 1973), 27; and Peter Maas, *Serpico: The Cop Who Defied the System* (New York: Viking Press, 1973), 104. As Woods also points out, under charter section 202, the LAPD maintained complete control over its disciplinary procedures ("Progressives and the Police," 9). On beat assignments and rotation, see Fogelson, *Big-City Police*, 219–42, and Albert J. Reiss, *The Police and the Public* (New Haven: Yale University Press, 1971), 5. On boot camp–style academy training, see also Woods, "Progressives and the Police," 429.

5. As in many cities, the very reforms hailed as producing professionalism—the abolishing of residency requirements for officers, character checks, even minority recruitment—were only managed in a notoriously discriminatory way. Joseph Woods's portrait in "Progressives and the Police" in particular showed how successive generations of Los Angeles police leadership, seeming to reject the more aggressive strategy of trade unionism defeated in the Boston police strike of 1919, had nevertheless used the leverage of their Police Protective League to secure collective benefits, steer ballot initiatives, and arrive at nearly complete departmental autonomy from civilian control. On the white-ethnic insulation provided in part by civil service rules, see Fogelson, *Big-City Police*, 248–63. As Fogelson also points out (260–62), these racial and ethnic patterns were overlooked in neoconservative arguments, rehearsed by James Q. Wilson and others, that police practices were still decentralized and institutionally heterogeneous. For the persistence of these problems recently, see Geeta Anand and Matthew Brelis, "Police Cadet System Failing Minorities," *Boston Globe*, 25 July 1996.

6. On this territorial and moral imperative, see esp. Steve Herbert, *Policing Space: Territoriality and the Los Angeles Police Department* (Minneapolis: University of Minnesota Press, 1997), 141–60. Herbert also describes how this "siege mentality" affects beat patrol, as the Christopher Commission maintained (118–21).

7. This fact on Watts participation cited in the entry on Wambaugh in *Current Biography* (New York: H. W. Wilson Co., 1980), 419. *New Centurions* was on the *New York Times* hardcover best-seller list for thirty-two weeks, and another twelve in paperback; *The Blue Knight*, in hardcover and paperback, spent nearly thirty-eight weeks on the *Publisher's Weekly* best-seller list.

Keith L. Justice, *Bestseller Index: All Books, by Author, on the Lists of Publishers Weekly and the New York Times through 1990* (Jefferson, N.C.: McFarland, 1998).

8. The title *New Centurions* itself alluded to Parker's mythos, which explicitly connected whiteness to the mythology of pioneering. In one speech, for example, Parker referred proudly to the "Caucasians" who had settled America, a nation that "was created by people with iron in their spines, with belief in their souls." But now, he said, the "holy designation" of the "City of Angeles" was being threatened by a "handful of parasites" who would turn it into "the city of the devils" (reprinted in O. W. Wilson, ed. *Parker on Police*, 29, 32). See also the television interview in which Parker explicitly pitted support for the department as protection against Negroes, quoted in Steve Herbert, *Policing Space*, 81. Robert Fogelson first noted Wambaugh's rookies seem to represent the new demographic police profile of the postwar period—or, at least, its supposedly ideal types: college-educated, ethnically diverse cops with middle-class values (*Big-City Police*, 235).

Parker's fanaticism doubtless seems exceptional. Yet just as the McCone Commission would, even early twentieth-century police reformers characteristically attributed poor police authority to having to work with foreign-born and Negro migrant populations; this was in fact point 5 in the Wickersham report of 1931 (National Commission, *Report on Police*, 6).

9. Walker, " 'Broken Windows' and Fractured History." Here Walker provides a useful critique, as well, of the "watchman" myth deployed by Edwin Meese, James Q. Wilson, and others. Again, this is the rotten-apple moralism described in Armstrong and Cinnamon, *Power and Authority in Law Enforcement*, 148.

10. The familiar differentiation of the LAPD as a "western-style," and hence "apolitical," department can be very misleading. As in the east, the department remained rife with political infighting and nepotism; nor was the pattern of Police Protective League activism in Los Angeles so different from that in Detroit, Boston, or even New York. On Detroit, see William Serrin, "God Help Our City," *Atlantic*, July 1969, 115–21; on New York, see Ed Cray, "The Politics of Blue Power," *Nation*, 21 April 1969, 493–96; on Boston, see McNamara, "Calling for Backup."

11. Reiss's work was actually begun in 1962, establishing the basis for his more elaborate survey at the behest of the National Crime Commission of 1965, which publicized his findings. Thus, though his *book* postdates Skolnick's and critiques it, it is more accurate to say the two are in conversation throughout this decade. Skolnick's work, for instance, is referred to in Reiss, *Police and the Public*, 88 n. 11.

12. Again, on the LAPD's complete script control of *Dragnet*, for instance, see Domanick, *To Protect and to Serve*, 122 ff. See also Fogelson, *Big-City Police*, 237.

13. In one *Police Story* episode called "The Execution," the radio dispatcher is called "Operations," indicating her central role in the paramilitary style. On the commendation, see Jerry Cohen, "Wealth Boring, Wambaugh's Back on Beat," *Los Angeles Times*, 14 Feb. 1973.

14. On this "minorityism" see, e.g., Woods, "Progressives and the Police," 481. As I will show, Wambaugh lays claim to a supposedly pluralist cop fraternity by working through the consciousness of a Mexican American character.

15. Wambaugh's father is discussed in Steven V. Roberts, "Cop of the Year," *Esquire*, Dec. 1973, 151. The G-man also refers to "G2," which was Parker's code name for his intelligence division (Woods, "Progressives and the Police," 445).

16. Here I would like to acknowledge George Lipsitz's many brilliant commentaries upon how this period has been rewritten by neoconservative histories. See also David Glover and Cora Kaplan, "Guns in the House of Culture? Crime Fiction and the Politics of the Popular," in *Cultural Studies*, ed. Lawrence Grossberg, Cary Nelson, and Paula A. Treichler (New York: Routledge, 1992), esp. 216, on the rewriting of radicalism.

17. The additional measures, of course, were clearance rates, an invention of the IACP's own committee on the UCR (Fogelson, *Big-City Police*, 264–65). As Fogelson points out, this measure also reflects police insularity, since it measures not crimes solved but "the percentage of crimes known to the police that the police believe they have solved" (265). See also my discussion in chapter 4 of David Simon's use of these rates to characterize police labor.

18. See, e.g., George Berkley, "How the Police Work," *New Republic*, 2 Aug. 1969, 15–18, a preview of his *The Democratic Policeman*. Berkley's analysis particularly exposed myths regarding the supposedly "civil service" character to U.S. departments. As Terris shows, training and education requirements still lagged; only 7 percent of polled officers in leading police departments in the mid-1960s had a college degree; Bruce J. Terris, "The Role of the Police," *Annals of the American Academy of Political Science* 347 (Nov. 1967): 62. Polling police morale before and after five years of reforms by O. W. Wilson in Chicago, James Q. Wilson's claim was that increased professionalization could not eliminate feelings of police alienation and citizen hostility. Yet this only begged the question as to whether "professionalization" was what had actually taken place. See James Q. Wilson, "Police Morale, Reform, and Citizen Respect: The Chicago Case," in David J. Bordua, ed., *The Police: Six Sociological Essays* (New York: John Wiley & Sons, 1967), 137–62.

19. As I've said, current studies like Herbert's *Policing Space* (1997) suggest this philosophy still drives the LAPD. The reality of this increased danger, however, was and is hotly debated. As Berkley pointed out in the 1960s ("How the Police Work," 15), the President's Crime Commission reported that the number of U.S. citizens killed by policemen far outstripped the number of policemen killed, actually the *reverse* of the situation in many European countries. See also Andrew Hacker, "Safety Last," *New York Review of Books*, 15 Sept. 1977, 5–6, and Terris, "The Role of the Police," 61 n. 6, which argues that the rate of police fatalities was, in 1955, about one third of what they were in mining, half in the construction trade, and so forth.

20. Herbert, *Policing Space*, 141–60. The staff report is "The Police in Protest," reprinted in Armstrong and Cinnamon, *Power and Authority in Law Enforcement*, 131–90. Under the rotten-apple doctrine held by most policeman, the report said, "crime and disorder are attributable mainly to the intentions of evil individuals; human behavior transcends past experience, culture, society, and other external forces and should be understood in terms of wrong choices deliberately made" (148). John Gregory Dunne also gives an especially good account of this philosophy in Daryl Gates's thinking in "Law and Disorder in LA," *New York Review of Books*, 10 Oct. 1991, 23–29, and 24 Oct 1991; see esp. 65.

21. On the riot's start, see Domanick, *To Protect and to Serve*, 179–80.

22. Seymour Martin Lipset, "Why Cops Hate Liberals—and Vice Versa," *Atlantic*, July 1969, 76–83. Lipset's characterizations were echoed by the National Commission on the Causes and Prevention of Violence; again, compare Armstrong and Cinnamon, *Power and Authority in Law Enforcement*, 147–49. During these years, The *Nation* also ran a special issue on the police,

which it called "America's only fully armed minority"; see *Nation*, 21 April 1969 (quote here from the cover). The Supreme Court's incursions into police work are discussed in Herbert L. Packer, "Policing the Police: Nine Men Are Not Enough," *New Republic*, 4 Sept. 1965, 17–21; see also "Cop Watching," editorial in the *New Republic*, 3 Dec. 1966, 9.

23. The National Commission on the Causes and Prevention of Violence report itself typifies this change in emphasis: "What happened during the Chicago Convention," it says, ". . . is not something totally different from police work *in practice* . . . The problem is definitely not one unfortunate outburst of misbehavior on the part of a few officers" (reprinted in Armstrong and Cinnamon, *Power and Authority in Law Enforcement*, 137).

24. Post-riot surveys have always shown a long history of police intimidation and mutual hostility in what we now call South Central LA. This history was discussed, for example, in Terris, "The Role of the Police," 60. Carl Werthman and Irving Piliavin's study also discusses the fact that many local patrolmen in Oakland and San Francisco in these years "tend[ed] to consider *all residents* of 'bad' neighborhoods rather weakly committed to whatever moral order they make it their business to enforce, and this transforms most of the people who use the streets in these neighborhoods into good candidates for suspicion." Werthman and Piliavin, "Gang Members and the Police," in Bordua, *The Police*, 56–98; quote from 76. See also Harlan Hahn, "Cops and Rioters: Ghetto Perceptions of Social Conflict and Control," in Hahn, *The Police in Modern Society*, 135–51; and Groves and Rossi, in Hahn, 175–91.

25. This interplay between emphasizing managerial order and deemphasizing civilian oversight was evident in a profile of Parker's successor, Tom Reddin; see Linda McVeigh Mathews, "Chief Reddin: New Style at the Top," *Atlantic*, July 1969, 84–93. Puffing Reddin's new emphasis on community relations, Mathews wrote: "What most poor black and Latin people . . . were waiting for was a sign that the attitudes and actions of the lowly patrolman had been reformed. The chief, to his credit, was well aware of the need for reforms at the street level; but the patrolman's behavior was the one thing Reddin could not control. He struggled manfully to sell his ideas to the line officers." (91–92). Reddin's declaration of 1968 as "The Year of the Policeman" was given positive backing in "Responsibility in 'the Year of the Police.'" *Life*, 22 March 1968, 4. The turn on the "order maintenance function of the police" and civilian oversight, compared to neighborhood "balkanization," was also made in James Q. Wilson, "What Makes a Better Policeman," *Atlantic*, July 1969, 134.

26. On recent thinking on the "public" sphere, please see note 26, introduction.

27. Walker, " 'Broken Windows' and Fractured History," esp. 80–81. See also Peter K. Manning, "Community Policing," *American Journal of Police* 3 (1984): 205–27. For one use of the argument about "impersonalization" from the 1960s themselves, see Wilson, "Police Morale," 159–61.

28. On the limits of ethnographic realism, see George Marcus, *Anthropology as Cultural Critique* (Chicago: University of Chicago Press, 1986). As but one example of the limits to Reiss's approach, see Terris, who cites studies of Cincinnati, Washington, D.C., and Los Angeles to show a high degree of hostility to the police: in South Central Los Angeles following the Watts riot, over 90 percent of black males under thirty-five believed subjection to insulting language, improper search, unnecessary force, or being beaten in custody occurred in their district ("The Role of the Police," 60). Terris also claims that in San Diego alone, "aggressive patrol" meant

some four hundred thousand citizens in a single year were stopped "on the basis of little or no evidence" (63).

29. In other words, even information that might have broadened Reiss's own sense of when a crime occurs is turned to reinforce his model. For instance, he turns his speculation about insurance on its head, and says with little evidence the following: "Thus, when citizens call the police, they are often seeking personal gain" (68). In some instances, even revisionist historians seem only to play into these neoconservative assaults on the norm of crime-busting. Fogelson, for instance, cites Reiss's study to debunk the crime-busting ethos (*Big-City Police*, 266). Like Reiss, Fogelson uses efficiency as a criterion and then acknowledges that crime is notoriously difficult to measure (see 274–75). Compare Wilson, "Police Morale," 143, 158.

30. George T. Payton, *Patrol Procedure* (Los Angeles: Legal Book Corp., 1967), 143, 144. On Panoptical power in the LAPD, cf. Davis, *City of Quartz*, and Herbert, *Policing Space*, 17–23.

31. Focusing only on actual, logged-in encounters also leads one to believe that when officers are simply patrolling in their cars, they're not "policing"—when obviously the entire system is predicated on a visible, proactive police presence. Yet Reiss actually advocates against preventative patrol, saying it will work only when crime is routine and organized (101–2)—that is, built upon vice and gang patrol models that the LAPD had been emphasizing for decades. And not surprisingly, Reiss's reservations about civilian review were also pronounced (209 ff.).

32. On Parker's crusades in this regard, see Davis, *City of Quartz*, 294–96. John Hersey found a similar attitude in Detroit: see *The Algiers Motel Incident* (New York: Bantam, 1968), 85–86.

33. Payton's POST textbook refers to homosexuality as a "perversion" (309), adding that the "active" (out of the closet) homosexual "is almost like an alcoholic, he must abstain or he has the tendency to go wild" (309). Woods points out that one of the more infamous smear tactics of the Protective League's "special" unit was its attempt to defeat a liberal Republican U.S. senator by fabricating an arrest for a homosexual offense ("Progressives and the Police," 10).

34. Similar attitudes among police officers in Detroit were found by Hersey; see *The Algiers Motel Incident*, 58, 62, 96–97. Compare my introduction, note 17, and the report in Fogelson, *Los Angeles Riots*, 5–6, 8–9. As Fogelson points out, police not only underestimated the number of participants in the riot; subsequent analyses showed that young adults (not minors) made up the large majority of arrestees; that riot participants were, if anything, slightly better educated than their peers; and that the great majority were employed and had lived in LA for at least five years (121–22).

35. *The New Centurions* (1970; reprint, New York: Dell, 1984), 171. Further citations in text. In the TV *Blue Knight* and *Police Story*, this claim became a cliché: guilty defendants, black and white, can recite their constitutional rights verbatim, and are protected by white liberals and shady lawyers.

36. Mike Davis makes clear how Hollywood was a political force in Los Angeles history (*City of Quartz*, 141, 143).

37. For one recent rendering of this mystique, see Fletcher, *What Cops Know*. Cf. Reiss, *Police and the Public*, 5–6. I take up this matter of street proprietorship more directly in chapter 4.

38. In the *Police Story* episode "Year of the Dragon," the vexation of this paternalism arises

when a cop decides to use an Asian American witness against "her own people." "Are you a friend of hers?" one character asks the detective. "I'm not sure," the cop responds. Later, he tries to go easy on a young Asian intimidated into gang participation. As in *The Blue Knight*, however, this paternalism is literally short-lived: the cops drop the kid at his "crib," and the gang arrives to shoot him.

39. Wambaugh hoped to inject this fraternal knowledge back into mass fiction and TV. He spoke literally about assigning "good, tough cops" to keep Hollywood producers in line. Interview with Joyce Haber, "For Joseph Wambaugh, The Beat Goes On," *Los Angeles Times Calendar*, 4 Nov. 1973, 19. As mentioned in chapter 2, Wambaugh also spoke in the press about working against a kind of feedback loop that kidded cops into thinking they were the "dehumanized robots" procedural TV told them they were. On this point, see Cecil Smith, "Humanizing."

40. Several episodes of *Police Story*—e.g., "The Empty Weapon" and "Officer Needs Help"—dramatize this, notably around firing weapons. In the former episode, street training by a veteran bluecoat is explicitly played off against the advice of detectives.

41. "If you want to be loved," I remember Wambaugh growling on *The MacNeil-Lehrer Hour* after the riots following the Rodney King verdict, "become a fireman" (probably not an exact quote on my part). On unmanning: in one particularly vivid instance, the rookie who loses his intestines in a shooting says he now has a "pussy" (*New Centurions*, 251)—in a chapter entitled, again playing off sacred knowledge gathering, "Conception."

For Wambaugh's views of the King riots and their aftermath, particularly the work of the Christopher Commission, see Robert Scheer's interview, *Los Angeles Times*, 14 July 1991. In this interview, Wambaugh called police work "emotionally . . . the most dangerous work on earth," its main killer a "premature cynicism." Although he praises the achievements of Chief Parker, Wambaugh also felt the "paramilitary" emphasis of the LAPD had gone too far; that cops were "individuals" who needed to be leaders; and that more women officers were needed.

42. On patrol officers' feeling of abandonment by their commanders see Herbert, *Policing Space*, 75 ff.

43. For echoes of these medieval notions of community in Catholic social thought, see McGreevy, *Parish Boundaries*, 43; for Parker's Catholicism in a traditionally Protestant subculture, see Woods, "Progressives and the Police," 421. See also the description of one beat cop's rousting in Michael Norman, "One Cop, Eight Square Blocks," *New York Times Magazine*, 12 Dec. 1993, 62 ff. Mathews also points out that reemphasizing the beat cop was part of Reddin's reforms in the post-Parker era (87). But as Chief Reddin's publicist fed *Harper's* stories about a renewed commitment to community involvement, SWAT was also installed on Reddin's watch (Domanick, *To Protect and to Serve*, 207).

44. Once again Wambaugh's counter-ethnography is there to tell us, for example, that it is morally bankrupt college professors and "professional" subversives who are, in fact, fueling the protest movement.

45. In the TV pilot for *The Blue Knight*, likewise, Bumper Morgan outwits an African American urban arms merchant (and former transvestite) who speaks of "the movement" and "by any means necessary," but who drives a silver Thunderbird and dresses like Superfly.

46. Nearing retirement himself (resigning officially on 8 March 1974), Wambaugh claimed he preferred to stay a "working cop" rather than be promoted. See Cohen, "Wealth Boring."

This is the kind of ironic reversal Bourdieu relishes: see, for instance, *Field*, 164. Wambaugh typically portrayed his encounter with Hollywood in terms of friction and disenchantment, which led him to form his own production company. On *Police Story*, he said: " 'I'm trying to tell them what a police show should be about, what police life is all about. And so far they're giving me cops-and-robbers stories . . .they say [their audience] likes sirens and they like chases and they like the caper.' " Roberts, "Cop of the Year," 153. Meanwhile, his relations with the LAPD were actually strained on occasion: there was initial friction with Ed Davis over the fact that the *New Centurions* was released without department permission; a publisher spokesperson also claimed Davis wanted changes. Wambaugh, of course, initially decided to return to the force after becoming a novelist, but reversed himself when his status as "celebrity cop" made police work impossible. See Cohen, "Wealth Boring," 3. Wambaugh was also embroiled in a small controversy in which officers were asked to contribute to a bust for Mayor Sam Yorty; Wambaugh refused. See Lee Dye, "Collection for Bronze Bust Stirs Police Row," *Los Angeles Times*, 28 Jan. 1972.

47. The ambiguity of Wambaugh's covert departure from the official line is indicated, for instance, in his frequent depictions of what is now known as "testilying." Whether when talking to reporters, testifying in court, or filling out arrest reports, Wambaugh shows, cops learn to create police stories, palliative renderings that honor the very rules of law (e.g., search and seizure) and demeanor that, in practice, make their work impossible (e.g., *New Centurions*, 23, 102; *Blue Knight*, 194). In other words, we learn in reading Wambaugh's novels that cops are forced to manufacture their own cover stories to appease the public. The potentially self-defeating irony here is clear.

48. See, for instance, Lawrence's assessments of Arab motives, tactics, and organization in the *Seven Pillars of Wisdom* (New York: Penguin Books, 1982), 343 ff. We know, of course, that Lawrence also counseled future spies; see the selections from his 1917 manual for political officers, "Handling Hejaz Arabs," in *Lawrence of Arabia: The Literary Impulse*, ed. Stanley Weintraub and Rodelle Weintraub (Baton Rouge: Louisiana State University Press, 1975), 11–12.

49. On Mexican Americans on the LAPD, see Woods, "Progressives and the Police," 462 ff. For another historian's view on the adjacent position of such groups within the black-white axis, see McGreevy, *Parish Boundaries*, 105.

50. Luis Rodriguez, *Always Running* (New York: Touchstone, 1993).

51. Not coincidentally, Daryl Gates argued that this is one way to differentiate Chicano gangs from other kinds: they argue, he said, over "turf." See Daryl F. Gates and Robert K. Jackson, "Gang Violence in L.A.," *Police Chief* 57 (Nov. 1990): 20.

52. Rodriguez's memoir actually discusses a Chicano youth leader, Miguel Robles, who aspires to be a police officer, but is shot by sheriff's deputies. Rodriguez, *Always Running*, 201.

53. Gitlin, *Inside Prime Time* (New York: Pantheon, 1983), 279–80. Wambaugh himself discusses his preference for a chronicle (nonserialized) format, with relative unknowns standing in for LAPD officers—and thus, unknown actors—in Haber, "For Joseph Wambaugh," 19.

In popular culture studies, *Police Story* still receives praise for the authenticity of its re-creation of police routine, as well as its avoidance of melodramatic violence; see, e.g., Robert S. Alley, "Television Drama," in *Television: The Critical View*, 2d ed., ed. Horace Newcomb (New York: Oxford University Press, 1979), 97. The most frequently cited element of praise, however, has been that Wambaugh's pop cops were "human beings"; see, e.g., Roberts, "Cop of the Year," 150; Smith, "Humanizing," 17.

Nearly every *Police Story* episode would have at least one domestic scene, often emphasizing the stress police work placed on it: a missed dance recital, a wife who wants a divorce, and so forth.

54. These remarks reflect my analysis of about a dozen *Police Story* episodes. In "The Empty Weapon," the Gothic re-creation of the invasion of civil space seems quite intentional: a street gang invades a helpless witness's living room (after she has been watching TV). The camera, as in countless slasher films, stalks her up the stairs; when she returns, her living room walls are covered with street graffiti.

55. Daryl Gates, Domanick reminds us in *To Protect and to Serve*, was a reluctant field commander during the riots, and was shamed by the arrival of the national guard, as well as embarrassed by the tactical strategy of withdrawing from the streets and letting the disorder rage (184).

Chapter Four

1. For information on the typical cover cue, see Rosemary Herbert, "Publishers Agree: True Crime Does Pay," *Publisher's Weekly*, 1 June 1990, 35–36.

2. That film's original title, one recalls, had itself *been* "Homicide" (Wald, afterword, 144).

3. *Homicide* won two mystery genre prizes (specifically the Hugo and Anthony awards).

4. See, e.g., Alex M. Durham III, H. Preston Elrod, and Patrick T. Kinkade, "Images of Crime and Justice: Murder and the 'True Crime' Genre," *Journal of Criminal Justice* 23 (1995): 143–52. Durham, Elrod, and Kinkade argue that homicide is the subject in almost 80 percent of their fifty-volume sample of True Crime, while in the Uniform Crime Reports, murder accounts for less than 1 percent of total crimes annually. For scholarship taking a similar line regarding crime news, see my introduction, note 10. Some of these studies might well bear comparison, however, to victimization studies rather than the UCR.

5. On the effect of being "on the case"—an obvious parallel to the police procedural, to which *Homicide* has been compared—see Deborah Cameron and Elizabeth Frazer, *The Lust to Kill: A Feminist Investigation of Serial Murder* (New York: New York University Press, 1987), 49, and the discussion of Jeffrey Dahmer and the FBI in Richard Tithecott, *Of Men and Monsters: Jeffrey Dahmer and the Construction of the Serial Killer* (Madison: University of Wisconsin Press, 1997), 17–33. Robin Anderson argues that cop TV was part of an attempt to define street-level narcotics users in the inner city as the *cause* of crime, thereby ratifying excessive force and questionable search-and-seizure tactics by the police—offering, she rightly adds, "an untenable script and equally untenable public policy." Robin Anderson, "'Reality' TV and Criminal Justice," *The Humanist*, Sept./Oct. 1994, 8–13; quote from 13.

6. Simon's detectives track a possible serial criminal, the unidentified "Fish Man" suspected of killing a young black girl.

7. For representative scholarship on these traditions and their contemporary extrapolations, see Cameron and Frazer, *The Lust to Kill*; Philip Jenkins, *Using Murder: The Social Construction*

of Serial Homicide (New York: A. de Gruyter, 1994); Tithecott, *Of Men and Monsters;* and Seltzer, *Serial Killers.* The best account of nineteenth-century sensational antecedents and their "ritual of noncomprehension" is Karen Halttunnen, *Murder Most Foul: The Killer and the American Gothic Imagination* (Cambridge: Harvard University Press, 1998). Public commentary on True Crime has often been quite moralistic. *Los Angeles Times Book Review* editor Jack Miles, for instance, has said he sees no social utility whatsoever in the genre. Jack Miles, "Imagining Mayhem: Fictional Violence versus 'True Crime,'" *North American Review* 276 (Dec. 1991): 57–68. Others, like *New York Times Book Review* crime columnist Marilyn Stasio, said True Crime spoke to "the collapse of community fellowship and citizen responsibility" in the culture at large ("The Killers Next Door," 46–47).

8. And, perhaps, set aside female writers and readers, as I have discussed briefly in relation to the police procedural. Here again, "real" crime is displayed as an affair between men, much like policing and journalism themselves, esp. in Mitch Gelman, *Crime Scene: On the Streets with a Rookie Police Reporter* (New York: Times Books, 1992). Yet Ann Rule is herself an ex-policewoman and typically casts her stories of pathological crimes as police "files" with dedicated white-collar heroes with technical lingo, their experience always recorded as veteran status: "Hank Gruber, nineteen years a cop . . ." Edna Buchanan's memoir, meanwhile, devotes entire sections to police portraits, men described (in a review of *Homicide*) as "tough guys" who "daily face a job like no other . . . Without the black humor that makes them laugh, they would surely cry." "Tales from the Crypt: *Homicide*," *Los Angeles Times Book Review*, 30 June 1991, 2. See also Buchanan's *The Corpse Had a Familiar Face* (New York: Charter Books, 1987).

9. Here by "entertainment," I mean to describe an ideological foray, an "as if" imagining more covert than what is commonly deemed "cultural work." I mean to forecast, as well, my argument about political hegemony, civic authority, and news reading in chapter 5.

10. Blau's jacket copy described the book as showing the "evolution from rookie to seasoned police reporter, in tandem with Chicago's own loss of innocence"; Gelman's as a "shocking true crime with a story about coming of age in the vortex of an American city under siege"; Simon's as a voyage into the "dark side of the American experience."

11. For my overall account of these changes, I have relied particularly on Anthony Smith, *Goodbye Gutenberg: The Newspaper Revolution of the 1980's* (New York: Oxford University Press, 1980); Joan Didion, *After Henry* (New York: Simon and Schuster, 1992); William Glaberson, "Legacy of a Dead Newspaper: A Bottom-Line Legacy," *New York Times*, 24 July 1995; Glaberson, "*Newsday* Tests Just How Deep Cuts Can Go," *New York Times*, 2 Oct. 1995; John W. Anderson, "Tab War in NYC," *Washington Journalism Review*, July/August 1988, 25–29; Karen Rothmyer, "*Newsday* Goes for the Big Apple," *Columbia Journalism Review*, Sept./Oct. 1986, 42–46; James Boylan, "Alicia's Little Tabloid," *Columbia Journalism Review*, Jan./Feb. 1991, 53–55; James Sterngold, "Times Mirror Chief Stresses Primacy of Newspapers," *New York Times*, 28 July 1995; "A Worthy Competitor" (editorial), *New York Times*, 17 July 1995; Bob Herbert, "Tabloid Troubles," *New York Times*, 17 July 1995; Geneva Overholser, "The Death of a Paper," *Washington Post*, 23 July 1995; and Malcolm Gladwell, "New York Newsday to Close," *Washington Post*, 15 July 1995.

12. Smith, *Goodbye Gutenberg*, 146.

13. Hamill's *News Is a Verb* is one newsman's attempt to come to terms with these changes.

14. On the *Los Angeles Times*'s strategy in particular, see Glaberson, "Legacy." Hamill makes this point extensively in *News Is a Verb*, 54 ff.; see also my discussion of the tabloid in chapter 2.

15. Hamill, *News Is a Verb*, 27.

16. Gelman, *Crime Scene*, 25, 78.

17. Herbert, "Tabloid Troubles." Hamill makes a similar point, but about editors (*News Is a Verb*, 37).

18. For one account of this transformation, see Didion, *After Henry*, 220–50.

19. Smith, *Goodbye Gutenberg*, 151.

20. Though there are indications that alternative weeklies now began to thrive—often reproduced, as in my home Boston region, by chains—Anthony Smith reports that the zoning of the *Los Angeles Times* led to "no fewer than nine community papers" closing up (*Goodbye Gutenberg*, 150). On the nine *Chicago Tribune* editions, see Smith, 144. And as Sterngold reports, when the *Los Angeles Times* was faced with its own cost-cutting drives, it could then cut back on some of its zoned editions, as well as its Spanish-language publication ("Times Mirror Chief").

21. This phenomenon illustrates well Bourdieu's frequent comparisons of "field" to magnetic field (*Field*, 148), in that any shift in one post alters the entire field; in this sense, rather than a monolithic "trend," seemingly divergent conventions make each other possible.

22. For my overall account of these developments in policing, I have relied especially on Stephen D. Mastrofski, "The Prospects of Change in Police Patrol: A Decade in Review," *American Journal of Police* 9 (1990): 1–79; Samuel Walker, "Does Anyone Remember Team Policing? Lessons of the Team Policing Experience for Community Policing," *American Journal of Police* 12 (1993): 33–57; Andrew H. Malcolm, "Civilian Boards on Wane As Watchdogs of Police," *New York Times*, 10 Feb. 1975; Jack Greene, "Foot Patrol and Community Policing: Past Practices and Future Prospects," *American Journal of Police* 6 (1987): 1–16; Herbert Beigel and Allen Beigel, *Beneath the Badge: A Story of Police Corruption* (New York: Harper and Row, 1977); and Jerome Skolnick, *The New Blue Line: Police Innovation in Six American Cities* (New York: Free Press, 1986). See also "Spending on Police Levels Off," *New York Times*, 3 Feb. 1986; Michael Oreskes, "Fiscal Crisis Still Haunts the Police," *New York Times*, 6 July 1985; Ken Peak, Robert Bradshaw, and Ronald W. Glensor, "Improving Citizen Perceptions of the Police: 'Back to Basics' with a Community Policing Strategy," *Journal of Criminal Justice* 20 (1992): 25–40; McNamara, "Calling for Backup"; I also discuss George L. Kelling and Catherine M. Coles, *Fixing Broken Windows* (New York: Simon and Schuster, 1996), in my next chapter.

23. Blau, *The Cop Shop*, 65.

24. On deadly-force reforms, see Skolnick, *New Blue Line*, 85–87; on civilian incorporation, Mastrofski, "The Prospects of Change," 21, and Skolnick, 25. On the lack of growth and spending, see "Spending on Police Levels Off" and Mastrofski, 11, 14, 21. On New York hiring, see Oreskes, "Fiscal Crisis." Statistics on ethnic composition from Fogelson, *Big-City Police*, 287, and Barron, "Survey Places New York Police." In southern California, meanwhile, police command structures were more segregated than rank and file, and one ACLU study ranked Compton forces among the most segregated (Bettina Boxall and Nicholas Riccardi, "Lack of Diversity in Fire, Police Forces Cited," *Los Angeles Times*, 26 Oct. 1994). In a 1994 *New York Times* poll, 55 percent of the white members of the NYPD's graduating class said they now lived outside New York City, and 25 percent said they had gone to a Catholic high school in New York City,

slightly more than had gone to a city public school. Meanwhile, 76 percent of black graduates had attended public school, and 88 percent said they lived in the city, roughly the same rates as for Hispanic graduates (Kilborn, "Police Profile").

25. In New York, for instance, there were month-to-month scandals about the hog tying or beating of suspects, the Tompkins Square riot, and finally extensive drug dealing in the 77th precinct house; in Chicago, over eighty indictments of police officers in the early 1970s. For news items dealing with these incidents see, e.g., Sam Roberts, "Police at Crossroads: A Chance to Turn Rising Adversity into Advantage," *New York Times*, 9 May 1985; Joseph P. Fried, "Two Queens Officers Convicted in Stun-Gun Trial," *New York Times*, 3 May 1986; Todd S. Purdum, "86 on New York Police Force Faced Arrest in '85," *New York Times*, 9 Feb. 1986; Purdum, "City Police Strengthened by '72 Panel," *New York Times*, 31 March 1986; and Purdum, "Ward, Citing Suspect's Death, Issues Ban Against Hogtying," *New York Times*, 18 Feb. 1987. Luis Rodriguez's memoir itself, of course, means to address the ongoing standoff in the 1990s that had, he shows, roots in his own childhood (see chapter 3).

26. For my understanding of Ward's tenure, I have relied on Martin Gottlieb, "13 Police Suspensions: Lessons of '68," *New York Times*, 25 Sept. 1986; David E. Pitt, "Roots of Tompkins Sq. Clash Seen in Young and Inexperienced Officer Corps," *New York Times*, 25 Aug. 1988; Oreskes, "Fiscal Crisis"; Roberts, "Police at Crossroads"; and the articles by Todd Purdum already cited, as well as "Suspensions Stir Accountability Issue," *New York Times*, 24 Sept. 1986, and "Ward's 5 Years at the Helm: Higher Goals Remain Elusive," *New York Times*, 27 Oct. 1988.

27. On corruption by skilled crime busters, see Maas, *Serpico*, 167; Robert Daley, *Prince of the City* (Boston: Houghton Mifflin, 1978), 5–6, 64, 279, 292. Beigel and Beigel point out that this idea of an independent career vice squad was one of O. W. Wilson's ideas (*Beneath the Badge*, 30–31); lacking real administrative oversight, they argue, the system may have actually reinforced the cultivation of payoff schemes.

28. On "bending granite," see Walker, "Does Anyone Remember," 41–43. On generalist conceptions, see Peak, Bradshaw, and Glensor, "Improving Citizen Perceptions," 27, and Skolnick, *New Blue Line*, 46.

29. As Pritchard points out, homicide has long been the *only* crime more likely to be reported upon than not. David Pritchard, "Race, Homicide, and Newspapers," *Journalism Quarterly* 63 (autumn 1985): 500–507.

30. See esp. Mastrofski, "The Prospects of Change," 32, 41. Mastrofski also cites FBI statistics to note that, between 1977 and 1986, total *arrests* in cities of over 250,000 increased from sixty-seven to seventy-five per thousand, with a related shift toward violent offenses and the harsher forms of street disorder and away from property offenses and lesser forms of disorder. Arrests for aggravated assault were up 42 percent, burglary down 28 percent; arrests for drug abuse up 68 percent, yet vagrancy down 26 percent (55–56). Some of this shift, as Mastrofski points out, is of course affected by the incidence of homelessness itself and the availability—or lack of it—of suitable treatment centers for "follow ups" on such arrests.

31. I will argue in chapter 5 that it was not until later that a *synthesis* was fashioned within neoconservative and federal circles that was more appetizing to police managerialism. Then the particular 1990s cast to community policing could successfully emerge: that is, as various "crime

attack" models emerged, more in tune with departments' prior self-image as crime busters. On these models, see Mastrofski, "The Prospects of Change," 34–36. On the measurement of clearance rates, see Peter W. Greenwood, *The Rand Criminal Investigation Study: Its Findings and Impacts to Date* (Santa Monica: Rand Corporation, 1979), 3. For additional discussion of clearance rates, see chapter 3, note 17.

32. Skolnick, *New Blue Line*, 4–5. Walker, "Does Anyone Remember," similarly refers to the "systematic demolition" of the ideas advanced by the likes of O. W. Wilson in these years (79); more recently, Kelling and Coles review these "failures" (*Fixing Broken Windows*, 71–102). On the failures of civilian review, see Malcolm, "Civilian Boards"; Beigel and Beigel, *Beneath the Badge*, 153. On criminal investigation procedures, see esp. Greenwood, *Rand Criminal Investigation Study*, 3–4. Here I quote the *Study*'s definition of index crimes.

33. On fear reduction measurements, see esp. Lee P. Brown, "Neighborhood-Oriented Policing," *American Journal of Police* 9 (1990): 197–207. On the resistance to efficiency measures, see Walker, "Does Anyone Remember," 42, and McNamara, " Calling for Backup."

34. On the Baltimore program, see Andrew Malcolm, "Fear Is Target in This War on Crime," *New York Times*, 24 March 1989.

35. I discuss these earlier conventions in *The Labor of Words*, 33–38; see also Vance Thompson, "The Police Reporter," *Lippincott's*, Aug. 1898, 283.

36. Gelman, *Crime Scene*, 11.

37. Ibid., 71, 158.

38. Ibid., 40, 43.

39. Blau, *Cop Shop*, 2, 13, 42.

40. David Simon, *Homicide: A Year on the Killing Streets* (Boston: Houghton Mifflin, 1991), 6, 99, 299.

41. Blau, *Cop Shop*, 20.

42. See, e.g., Pritchard, "Race, Homicide, and Newspapers," 502.

43. Gelman, *Crime Scene*, 9.

44. Blau, *Cop Shop*, 159.

45. Gelman, *Crime Scene*, 60.

46. Blau, *Cop Shop*, 162.

47. Ibid., 165.

48. Simon, *Homicide*, 188, 418.

49. Blau, *Cop Shop*, 172.

50. Simon, *Homicide*, 418.

51. Blau, *Cop Shop*, 1, 7, 13–14.

52. Ibid., 3.

53. Ibid., 4.

54. Ibid., 56.

55. Gelman, *Crime Scene*, 20–21.

56. Ibid., 103.

57. Ibid., 172.

58. Blau, *Cop Shop*, 175.

59. Gelman, *Crime Scene*, 43.

60. Ibid., 144.

61. Ibid., 41.

62. Ibid., 159.

63. For their discussion of these unconventional stories see Gelman, *Crime Scene*, 57–59; Blau, *Cop Shop*, 170–71; on conventions around rape see Helen Benedict, *Virgin or Vamp: How the Press Covers Sex Crimes* (New York: Oxford University Press, 1992).

64. Gelman, *Crime Scene*, 235.

65. Ibid., 101.

66. Ibid., 240.

67. Ibid., 242.

68. Ibid., 271.

69. Ibid., 73.

70. Blau, *Cop Shop*, 58.

71. Ibid., 182.

72. Ibid., 185.

73. Ibid., 188.

74. Ibid., 251.

75. On objectivity as the restraint of emotions, see Tuchman, "Objectivity"; compare Russell Baker, *The Good Times* (New York: William Morrow, 1989), 77, 88, or Harrison Salisbury, *A Journey for Our Times* (New York: Harper & Row, 1983). On being mistaken for other professions, see Baker, 53–54; Riis, *How the Other Half Lives*, 154; Wilson, *Labor of Words*, 37. On demonizing the tabloid, see John Pauly, "Rupert Murdoch," 252.

76. Simon, *Homicide*, 599.

77. Ibid., 53.

78. Ibid., 104, 231, 398–99.

79. Blau, *Cop Shop*, 25.

80. Ibid.

81. Ibid., 247.

82. Gelman, *Crime Scene*, 116–17.

83. Ibid., 122.

84. Simon, *Homicide*, 596.

85. Blau, *Cop Shop*, 54.

86. Simon, *Homicide*, 578–85.

87. Gelman, *Crime Scene*, 116, 119.

88. Blau, *Cop Shop*, 61.

89. Stuart Hall, "Culture, Media, and the Ideological Effect," in *Mass Communication and Society*, ed. James Curran, Michael Gurevitch, and Janet Woollacott (Beverly Hills: Sage, 1977), 343. My argument, however, is that this technical ethos is mediated by the Breslinesque populism I describe subsequently in this chapter. See also my revision of Hall's idea in chapter 5.

90. Simon, *Homicide*, 312, 317, 323.

91. Ibid,. 22.

92. Ibid,. 76–77.

93. Ibid., 32.

94. Ibid., 67–68.

95. Ibid., 456.

96. Ibid., 548.

97. Ibid., 200.

98. Ibid., 533–34.

99. Compare Gorelick, "Join Our War," 425. The most striking instance of this is the pivotal crime scene of the tenement house at 702 Newington, described as a place so degraded that "the rubicons of human existence have all been crossed" (Simon, *Homicide*, 134).

100. Simon, *Homicide*, 580.

101. Ibid., 6.

102. Ibid., 147.

103. On gangs' departures from traditional criminal subcultures, see Ruth Horowitz and Gary Schwartz, "Honor, Normative Ambiguity, and Gang Violence," *American Sociological Review* 39 (1974): 238–51; and Howard S. Erlanger, "Estrangement, Machismo, and Gang Violence," *Social Science Quarterly* 60 (1979): 235–48. On prison populations, see Donzinger, *The Real War on Crime*, 15–17, 101–4. See also Michael Massing, "Ghetto Blasting," *New Yorker*, 16 Jan. 1995, 32–37.

104. Gelman, *Crime Scene*, 49.

105. Blau, *Cop Shop*, 28.

106. Ibid., 152. In this way these books recall the antipathy to psychological expertise or explanation found in True Crime monthlies; compare Cameron and Frazer, *The Lust to Kill*, 46.

107. Robert Orsi usefully discusses the ambivalence, as well, with which Italian American neighborhoods viewed the Mafia, another important reference point for cop fraternalism; see Orsi, *The Madonna of 115th Street*, 103–4. On the centrality of the *domus* see Orsi, 75–106.

108. Ironically, even corruption was fueled by this ethos and its ethnic dimensions. Daley (deputy police commissioner in New York, from 1971 to 1972, and now a True Crime author) points out that many cops in New York felt scapegoated by the Knapp Commission investigation of 1972. Once again, fraternalism made its presence felt. As Daley writes, "Cops had their own ten commandments, and the first of them was this: If you are walking along a street and find a dime, your partner gets a nickel" (*Prince of the City*, 278).

109. Simon, *Homicide*, 316.

110. On these dimensions to urban populism, see Lasch, *True and Only Heaven*, 504 ff.; on the political swing, see Walter Dean Burnham, "The 1980 Earthquake: Realignment, Reaction, or What?" in *The Hidden Election: Politics and Economics in the 1980 Presidential Campaign*, ed. Thomas Ferguson and Joel Rogers (New York: Pantheon, 1981), 98–140. On the possible route taken by agrarian populism, see Lasch, *True and Only Heaven*, 223–35.

111. As Michael O'Neill writes, Breslin's "greatest invention is his own public persona . . . a cigar-chomping, hard-drinking . . . ordinary guy . . . stumbling through life like a plumber from Queens, living in bars . . . companion of the poor and near-poor." From *The World According to Breslin*, ed. Michael J. O'Neill (New York: McGraw-Hill, 1985), ix; quote in text from "Dies the Victim, Dies the City," O'Neill, 9. I discuss nearly identical columns by Barnicle in my next chapter.

112. Blau, *Cop Shop*, 249.

113. Simon, *Homicide*, 41.

114. The additional variant refers, of course, to Mike Tyson. A perceptive account of the roots of the white-ethnic commitment to urban neighborhoods is McGreevy, *Parish Boundaries*, esp. 18–20, 24, 29–53.

115. Simon, *Homicide*, 73.

116. Blau, *Cop Shop*, 24.

117. Gelman, *Crime Scene*, 89.

118. Ibid., 38. McGreevy points out that the percentage of the non–African American population in the urban North that was Catholic actually grew markedly between the early 1950s and the 1970s (*Parish Boundaries*, 132, table 5.1). Moreover, as racial segregation moved to the national stage, cross-Catholic integration became increasingly sanctioned at the parish level by the church (83). Daley, meanwhile, attributes the New York police's notorious "code of silence" to Italian roots—specifically, Sicilian notions of honor (*Prince of the City*, 133).

119. In Gelman's narrative, this broaches explicit bias, as in, "Unlike Lori, who was Jewish, and could consider such a decision intellectually, if not emotionally, Billy's mother was a devout Catholic" (*Crime Scene*, 155).

120. Blau, *Cop Shop*, 2, 4.

121. Gelman, *Crime Scene*, 228.

122. Ibid., 12–13.

123. On white flight and the new challenges therefore faced by urban white-ethnic machines, see McGreevy, *Parish Boundaries*, 84 ff., and Steven P. Erie, *Rainbow's End: Irish-Americans and the Dilemmas of Urban Machine Politics, 1840–1985* (Berkeley and Los Angeles: University of California Press, 1988), 140–90.

124. Simon, *Homicide*, 584.

125. Ibid., 240.

126. Gelman, *Crime Scene*, 254.

127. Blau, *Cop Shop*, 248.

128. The relationship between white ethnicity and populism's potentially progressive and/ or reactionary character is usefully discussed by Greer and Goldberg, "Populism, Ethnicity, and Public Policy," 174–88. See also Pete Hamill, "The Revolt of the White Lower Middle Class," in *Irrational Ravings* (New York: G. P. Putnam's Sons, 1971), 384–95. On Catholic lay resistance to housing desegregation, see McGreevy, *Parish Boundaries*, 180 ff. And perhaps because of the high percentage of relatives on the force, studies sometimes suggest, Catholics often resist civilian review (McGreevy, *Parish Boundaries*, 182).

129. Gelman, *Crime Scene*, 70.

130. Ibid., 71.

131. Ibid., 65.

132. Ibid., 70.

133. Ibid.

134. Ibid., 271.

135. Blau, *Cop Shop*, 271.

136. On these changes, see the *New York Times* editorial, "A Worthy Competitor."

Chapter Five

1. Michael K. Sparrow, Mark H. Moore, and David M. Kennedy, *Beyond 911* (New York: Basic Books, 1990). For a good summary of community policing scholarship, see Lisa M. Reichers and Roy R. Roberg, "Community Policing: A Critical Review of Underlying Assumptions," *Journal of Police Science and Administration* 17 (1990): 105–14.

Community policing has begun to develop its own chronicle, although much of it—as I shall show—is suffused with a self-congratulatory flattening of history. In *Fixing Broken Windows* (1996), for instance, George L. Kelling Jr. and Joanna Coles are forced to refer to "Kelling" in the third person while recounting his own advocacy, while nevertheless seeming to offer an impartial history. See, for example, *Fixing Broken Windows*, 130, 138. For a sample of current debate on the effectiveness of New York's experiments, see James Lardner, "Can You Believe the New York Miracle?" *New York Review of Books*, 14 Aug. 1977, 54–58.

2. Edwin Meese III and Bob Carrico, "Taking Back the Streets: Police Methods that Work," *Policy Review* 54 (autumn 1990): 29.

3. Business improvement districts (BIDs) described in Kelling and Coles, *Fixing Broken Windows*, 113 ff. Kelling and Coles also describe an early movement to restore New York's Bryant Park, following up on a police operation called "Operation Crossroads" aimed at reducing drug dealing in the park. The effort was led by the head of the adjacent New York Public Library, with support and funding from the Rockefeller Foundation. This movement came up with ten essential characteristics for maintaining the park, and Kelling and Coles summarize them:

> minimal sanitation levels maintained—parks had to be clean and litter-free; a sense of security—with full-time policing of facilities; adequate lighting—the park could not be turned over to predators at night; physical facilities maintained—vandalism and graffiti had to be attended to immediately; excellent concessions—with high quality food and service provisions; beautiful flowers and trees; clean, well-run restrooms—with no need for public urination or defecation; interesting entertainment programs—which would bring visitors to the park; key elements of design—the park would be visually transparent, with wide, unobstructed entrances, at least one fountain, so as to be pleasant while facilitating the operation of normal social control; and clearly posted rules—notifying everyone of expected behavior in the park. (112)

4. This profile cut across both *Globe* and *Herald* coverage, including editorials. See Steve Marantz, "Lots of Praise from Community on Appointment," *Boston Globe*, 1 Feb. 1985; Kevin Cullen, "Roache: 'Quiet and Modest Man' for Sensitive Job," *Boston Herald*, 1 Feb. 1985, which points to the fact that Roache carried "rosary beads" in his pocket and married his "high school sweetheart," literally "the girl next door"; Joan Vennochi, "Flynn Is Binding Police Department Closely to City Hall," *Boston Globe*, 15 March 1985; Andrea Estes, "Police Boss Aims to Boost Morale," *Boston Herald*, 2 Feb. 1985; and "Police Need More than Interim Chief" (editorial), *Boston Herald*, 2 Feb. 1985.

5. See National Institute of Justice, *Community Policing in Chicago: Year Two* (Washington, D.C.: U.S. Department of Justice, 1995); on Baltimore, see Paul W. Valentine, "Reno Sees and Praises 'Old Fashioned Policing' Program in Baltimore," *Washington Post*, 17 Feb. 1994. New

York's program is well known; for an early statement, see Brown, "Neighborhood-Oriented Policing."

6. James Q. Wilson and George L. Kelling Jr., "Broken Windows: The Police and Neighborhood Safety" (1982), reprinted in Wilson, *Thinking about Crime.* To address possible confusion here—as I mention below, sometimes generated by Wilson's own slippery use of the first person—I will refer to these *joint* authors only when citing their essay, again as reprinted in the third (1985) edition of *Thinking about Crime*, from which all other citations henceforth come.

7. On circulation, see Steve Lohr, "Times' Co.'s Strategy: Dominate Northeast," *New York Times*, 12 June 1993.

8. Journalism professor is Ralph Whitehead on "civic voice" as quoted in Sarah Rimer, "No Babe Ruth Reprise, but Still a Sense of Loss," *New York Times*, 12 June 1993. During the "Boston Hoax" seminar on the Charles Stuart case, it was estimated by *Globe*'s editors that only about 15 percent of the paper's sales were from newsstands—as opposed to some 80 percent of the tabloid *Herald*'s sales. *The Boston Hoax: The Police, the Press, and the Public*, dir. David Deutsch (Alexandria, Va.: PBS Video, 1990). Charles Stuart was the man who claimed that he and his pregnant wife had been shot by a black assailant as they sat in their Toyota outside a Boston hospital in the fall of 1989; his wife's death resulted in a local media frenzy—some broadcasts calling the Stuarts a "Cinderella" couple—while the police department ran aggressive raids into the city's Mission Hill district. Following Stuart's apparent suicide in January of 1990, it became clear Stuart had engineered his wife's murder, and probably shot her himself.

Subsequently, the *Globe* was bought by the *New York Times*, once again exhibiting the trends toward concentration discussed in this chapter. When I tried to track down a Boston-based community newspaper to provide a neighborhood alternative to the *Globe*, I could discover only one such paper, the Dorchester-based *Bay State Banner* (see subsequent citations). One well-known paper, the East Boston *Community News*, closed up shop in 1989; see Gloria Negri, "Money Woes Silence East Boston Paper's Roar," *Boston Globe*, 21 May 1989. The *Herald* coverage of the Copney-Grant case was also considerable, and yet very different, as I discuss below.

9. I also have tried to include not merely daily news coverage, but the *Globe* in a fuller scope: its magazine articles, editorials, even the featured columnists who often steer coverage and re-write it. I am indebted to Lee Bernstein for this insight. Originally, I relied on the *Globe*'s own print index as a starting place, though its listings on the crime per se often seemed incomplete. Consequently, I have also consulted 1991 and 1992 listings under the following headings: those of the defendants and the victims; "homicide"; "gangs"; and "murders and murder attempts," in Boston.

10. Of course, the *Globe* itself has been the object of any number of critical studies citing its news mismanagement, religious intolerance, and bias. The results have not been flattering, especially with regard to race. See, e.g., Kirk Johnson, "Black and White in Boston," *Columbia Journalism Review*, May/June 1987, 50–52; Carolyn Martindale, "Selected Newspaper Coverage of Causes of Black Protest," *Journalism Quarterly* 66 (winter 1989): 920–23, 964; and the most direct attack, William Alberts, "What's Black, White, and Racist All Over?" in *From Access to Power: Black Politics in Boston*, ed. James Jennings and Mel King (Cambridge, Mass.: Schenkman Books, 1986), 137–74. For an interesting survey of in-house assessments, see David Shaw, "Negative News and Little Else," *Los Angeles Times*, 11 Oct. 1990.

11. Much of our criticism reinforces the notion that crime news inscribes a "set of procedures not to know," its "coverage" covering over, in the case of street gangs, the underlying conditions of deindustrialization and unemployment, differences between ethnic gangs, the role of the dominant society's own penchant for violence. On "not to know," see Mark Fishman, "Crime Waves as Ideology," *Social Problems* 25 (June 1978): 531. Or, as Gorelick summarizes the familiar position, "crime news ideology" often works by "abstracting" crime "from its historical foundations and structural circumstances and by conveying the resulting fragments of information as universal or natural features of the social world" ("Join Our War," 425). For the complaint that the news usually casts adolescent violence as pathological behavior, see Horowitz and Schwartz, "Honor"; Erlanger, "Estrangement"; and Joan Moore, *Going Down to the Barrio* (Philadelphia: Temple University Press, 1991).

12. Cf. Hall et al., *Policing the Crisis*, 76, 343. "[N]arrowed grooves" from Ericson, Baranek, and Chan, *Representing Order*, 86; "intelligibility" from Hall et al., *Policing the Crisis*, 343.

13. Subsequent accounts of community policing have been unusually frank about this difference; Kelling and Coles, for instance, differentiate a "soft" community policing approach from their preference for a hard one, such as William Bratton's in New York (*Fixing Broken Windows*, 145). The emphasis is unmistakable: "Bratton's message about the business of the NYPD in a community policing strategy focuses on crime. The logic is this: first, *even though policing involves broad and numerous functions*, the *core function* of police is crime control" (145, emphasis mine). Or, later: "The themes that continually shape the discussion are Bratton's four guiding methods of crime control: accurate and timely intelligence; rapid deployment; effective tactics, and relentless follow up and assessment" (147).

14. Frank Lentricchia, *Ariel and the Police: Michel Foucault, William James, Wallace Stevens* (Madison: University of Wisconsin Press, 1988), 85–86.

15. Statistics on Boston's racial composition, attitudes toward busing, and age stratification from Thomas C. O'Connor, *The Boston Irish: A Political History* (Boston: Northeastern University Press, 1995), 270, 273, 274. Of course, nonwhites as a whole outnumber whites in school-age populations.

16. This campaign is described, albeit briefly, in O'Connor, *Boston Irish*, 270–73. See also Erie's different slant, emphasizing Mel King's registration drives (187). "Neighborhood" autonomy, of course, has been directed not only along racial lines, but at downtown development urged by liberal mayors of the past. Cf. O'Connor, 246. and Erie, 177–79.

17. See, e.g., Toni Locy and Indira A. R. Lakshmanan, "Look Outside for Top Cop, Some Officers Say," *Boston Globe*, 4 Feb. 1991. For a somewhat upbeat rendering of Flynn's racial politics, see O'Connor, *Boston Irish*, 276 ff.

18. McGee quoted in Daniel Golden, "A Failure to Communicate," *Boston Globe Sunday Magazine*, 17 Feb. 1991, 44. Thomas O'Connor states that African Americans were about 25 percent of Boston's population by this time (*Boston Irish*, 270). Black officers also made up a disproportionate number of authors of disciplinary complaints sustained within departmental review (Golden, 58). Roache's position became clearer, I think, when as a mayoral candidate in 1993, he proposed the halting of affirmative action in the department; see Brian McGrory, "Roache Defends His Record on Race," *Boston Globe*, 3 Sept. 1993.

19. Steve Marantz, "Roache to Put 30 Detectives on Street Patrol," *Boston Globe*, 22 Aug.

1985; Steve Marantz, "Roache Says New Plan for Patrol by Autumn," *Boston Globe*, 3 July 1985; Steve Marantz, "Comr. Roache: 'I've Taken On a Marathon,'" *Boston Globe*, 4 Nov. 1985; Steve Marantz, "Police Plan Patrol Shift to Areas of High Crime," *Boston Globe*, 20 Jan. 1991. See also Maria Alvarez, "Police Call Beefed-Up Patrols in Roxbury Effective," *Boston Globe*, 11 Jan. 1991; Brian Mooney, "Flynn's Running Mate Gets Top Police Job," *Boston Herald*, 1 Feb. 1985; Brian Mooney and Kevin Cullen, "Flynn Gives Old Pal Police Reins," *Boston Herald*, 1 Feb. 1985; "'Mickey' Roache Faces the Future" (editorial), *Boston Herald*, 15 March 1985.

20. See, e.g., the profiles of the outgoing Jordan: Steve Marantz, "The Traffic Cop Who Got to the Top," *Boston Globe*, 16 Jan. 1985, and Kevin Cullen, "'Cop's Cop' Bows Out," *Boston Herald*, 16 Jan. 1985. Compare the use of this formulation in regard to New York's commissioner Valentine in the 1940s, in S. J. Woolf's title. Even an academic review of this early experiment refers to it as "foot patrol"; see William J. Bowers and John H. Hirsch, "The Impact of Foot Patrol Staffing on Crime and Disorder in Boston: An Unmet Promise," *American Journal of Police* 6 (spring 1987): 17–44, which concludes that the experiment afforded "little, if any, crime control or order maintenance effects" (18).

21. For retrospective accounts, see Golden, "Failure to Communicate," 43–44; Toni Locy, "Arrest Numbers That Don't Add Up," *Boston Globe*, 7 April 1991; Toni Locy, "Poor Police Work Hampers Investigations," *Boston Globe*, 7 April 1991; Tony Locy, "Progress Seen in Combatting Gangs, Say Police, Flynn Aide," *Boston Globe*, 23 April 1991; Doreen E. Iudica, "City to Add Police on Streets in Effort to Reduce Violence," *Boston Globe*, 11 Jan. 1991; on restoration of beat patrol, Marantz, "The Traffic Cop"; Alexander Reid, "Patrol Plan Gets Initial Support in Neighborhoods," *Boston Globe*, 30 Jan. 1991; and an earlier piece, Gary McMillan, "Roache Moving Early on his 5 Priorities," *Boston Globe*, 15 March 1985. On union resistance, Steve Marantz, "Police Patrol Plan Falls Short, FinCom Study Says," *Boston Globe*, 2 Oct. 1985. According to Golden, the Boston Police Patrolmen's Association contract dictated that such assignments be "last in line for paid details [overtime]" (44). By the end of Roache's term, team policing had been cut from eighty to forty-three officers, in half the housing projects initially covered. Joan Hechlinger, "Police Head Pledges to Keep Project Patrols if U.S. Funds Run Out," *Boston Globe*, 5 June 1986; Michael K. Frisby, "City to Continue Patrolling Housing Projects," *Boston Globe*, 10 March 1987.

22. On Kelling's role in Boston, see Golden, "Failure to Communicate." Compare also George F. Kelling, "Searching for More Than a Quick Fix to Boston Police Corruption," *Boston Globe*, 15 Nov. 1987.

23. Disparaging remarks about rival disciplines are frequently made in Wilson's *Thinking about Crime*. For example, "In short, criminology could not form the basis for much police advice . . . but that did not prevent criminologists from advising" (54). Or "Sociology, for all its claims to understand structure, is at heart a profoundly subjectivist discipline" (56). Instead, we need to "find out what works in the real world" (57).

24. To underscore how fictive this kind of storytelling was, see the epigraph to this chapter, which is Wilson and Kelling's depiction of a street encounter (82)—shifted into the authority of the first-person singular even though we are told, initially, the article on which it was based was coauthored. It cultivates the characters of the police plot quite adroitly, encoding a presumed lie in the street person who is seen, quite literally, as a potential "perp."

25. See, again, the parable-like description in the passage asking the reader to fantasize. The imperative voice is quite adroit, really, as is the melodrama of victimization: "Imagine a young man walking down the street at night with nothing on his mind but a desire for good times and high living. Suddenly he sees a little old lady standing alone on a dark corner stuffing the proceeds of her recently cashed social security check into her purse" (118).

26. For this idea in practice, see Kelling and Coles, *Fixing Broken Windows*, 146. This subtle difference marks the importance of incarceration to the neoconservative plan: jailing for small crimes supposedly prevents more serious ones from ever happening; criminals dealt with in the aggregate are punished for crimes they have yet to commit. Wilson asks: "But how do we know who these high-rate, repeat criminals are? Knowing the nature of the present offense is not a good clue. The reason for this is quite simple—most street criminals do not specialize. Today's robber can be tomorrow's burglar and the next day's car thief" (*Thinking about Crime*, 155). Once again, this allowed Wilson to suggest substituting, in determining sentence length, a demographic profile of a career criminal virtually independent of the crimes any *one* perpetrator had actually committed. Again in important ways, the serial killer isn't as much a cultural signature of our times as is often suggested. On the street-level criminalization of gang members *as a class*, see Davis, *City of Quartz*, 278 ff.

27. On this score, Wilson's manipulation of the fatalism of neoconservative engineering was simply incredible:

> [H]ow do we ensure that age or skin color or national origin or harmless mannerisms will not also become the basis for distinguishing the undesirable from the desirable? How do we ensure, in short, that the police do not become the agents of neighborhood bigotry?
>
> I can offer no wholly satisfactory answer to this important question. I am not confident that there *is* a satisfactory answer, except to hope that by their selection, training, and supervision, the police will be inculcated with a clear sense of the outer limit of their discretionary authority. (*Thinking about Crime*, 84–85)

Having so discounted professional training, Wilson now fell back on it; having set his entire platform on transgressing legal authority through "discretion," he now hoped departments would somehow know where to draw the line.

28. Compare Mike Davis on the courting of middle-class "blacklash"; *City of Quartz*, 289 ff.

29. Pamphlet prepared by the Bureau of Justice Assistance, *Understanding Community Policing: A Framework for Action* (Washington, D.C.: U.S. Department of Justice, 1994), 7.

30. Ibid., 4.

31. Ibid., 11.

32. Ibid., sample problems and solutions on 19–20. See also National Institute of Justice, *Community Policing Strategies* (Washington, D.C.: U.S. Department of Justice, 1995).

33. Eck and Spellman, quoted in *Understanding Community Policing*, 17–18.

34. Wilson, *Thinking about Crime*, 50.

35. *Understanding Community Policing*, 19–20.

36. Ibid., 20.

37. Again, Kelling and Coles list "intelligence" gathering as William Bratton's first principle (*Fixing Broken Windows*, 147). I am also indebted here to Mike Davis's analysis of the subtle

interplay between the reorganization of urban space and social control—and, moreover, how even "beautifying" can have such effects. See Davis's discussion of Frank Gehry, *City of Quartz*, 236–40.

38. On these crime attack programs, see Eduardo Paz-Martinez, " 'Power Patrol' Unit with 20 Police Officers Moves into Area B," *Boston Globe*, 19 April 1987; Kevin Cullen, "Stemming the Cocaine Fountain," *Boston Globe*, 21 July 1986; Patricia Wen, "Crushing Blow for Some Car Owners," *Boston Globe*, 26 June 1986; Kevin Cullen, "Police Move to Increase Visibility," *Boston Globe*, 22 Feb. 1990; Kevin Cullen, "90 Suspected 'Johns' Nabbed in Boston," *Boston Globe*, 21 July 1986. For other related stories, see Joan Maddock, "Community Participation Needed to Eliminate Crime, Speakers Say," *Boston Globe*, 10 Aug. 1986; Diego Ribadeneira, "Mean Streets: The Beat of the Power Patrol," *Boston Globe*, 5 Feb. 1988; Jerry Thomas, "Police Sweep of Gangs Deemed a Success," *Boston Globe*, 21 May 1989; Kevin Cullen, "Doubts Raised On Police Sweep," *Boston Globe*, 22 March 1990; Kevin Cullen, "Hub Police Going Under Cover," *Boston Herald*, 15 March 1985. Fortunately, the *Globe* reported, the BPD also learned about prevention programs from the LA example; see Larry Tye, "Bostonians Look to Los Angeles on Gang Control," *Boston Globe*, 30 March 1990.

39. See, however, note 8 above.

40. The protest was joined by the Boston Police Patrolman's Association, as well as union leaders from the state and metropolitan District Commission forces; see "Police Protest Globe Coverage of Department," *Boston Globe*, 23 May 1991.

41. For the continuing endorsement of this approach, see Kevin Cullen, "The Neighborhood Cop," *Boston Globe Magazine*, 7 Jan. 1996, 14, 24–30: a profile of new commissioner Paul Evans that itself begins at a community meeting where Evans refers back to "Gene Dumas and John Kelly," the cops in his own South Boston neighborhood in his childhood. Cullen also claims that Evans, as a Vietnam veteran, was embraced by Southie, which lost as many sons "as almost any other community in America" (29). Cullen's summary of community policing is provided on 27.

42. Adrian Walker and Richard Higgins, "Boys, 11 and 15, Shot Dead in Roxbury," *Boston Globe*, 21 April 1991.

43. Ibid., 29.

44. James Clifford, "Traveling Cultures," in Grossberg et al., *Cultural Studies*, 96–116, esp. 98.

45. EMT reported as crying in Walker and Higgins, "Boys, 11 and 15," 29.

46. Exemplary here were Michael Jonas, "Wanted: Cops Walking the Beat," *Boston Globe*, 16 Sept. 1990, and Sean Mooney, "Theorists Offer Blueprints for a Refocused Boston Force," *Boston Globe*, 3 Dec. 1990.

47. Background to the crime first reported by John Ellement and Tom Coakley, "Three Youths Named, Charged in Slayings," *Boston Globe*, 23 April 1991; Renée Graham, "Suspect in Killings Called Follower, Peer Leader," *Boston Globe*, 8 May 1991.

48. Weld quoted in Eileen McNamara, "When Children Kill: Crime, Punishment, and the Debate over Juvenile Justice," *Boston Globe Sunday Magazine*, 24 Nov. 1991, 48.

49. Ibid, 17.

50. See, e.g., Alice McQuillan, "2 Hub Youths Shot Dead," *Boston Herald*, 21 April 1991;

Tan, "Boy Just an Innocent Bystander," *Boston Herald*, 22 April 1991; Sarah Koch, "Victim's Mom in a State of Shock," *Boston Herald*, 22 April 1991; Ralph Ranalli and Sarah Koch, "Juvenile Slay Suspects Held on High Cash Bail," *Boston Herald*, 23 April 1991; Ralph Ranalli and Sarah Koch, "Surviving Dance with Death," *Boston Herald*, 24 April 1991.

51. At the time Weld commented, the system might even be said to have worked, given that the killers were quickly found, trials held, and potential punishment allotted to two defendants deemed beyond juvenile rehabilitation (Dunn and Harris) and one (Bynoe) who was not. In retrospect, therefore, we should acknowledge that the *Globe* might have, for example, made a defendant other than Bynoe its protagonist, or asked how (with no prior record of violence) he could have committed such an act, or moved on—as the *Bay State Banner* did—to subsequent episodes of violent crime. After its first report, "Two Roxbury Youths Killed," by next week the *Banner* moved on to the murder of an elderly citizen; subsequently, aside from editorials and coverage of gang truces, the *Banner* devoted only passing attention to the case, reporting Bynoe's plea in a single, factual "News Note," 22 Aug. 1991.

52. Some simplification may have already occurred in *Globe* coverage, since the law actually mandated such a hearing "whenever the commonwealth so requests" and for other crimes, including manslaughter. The 1990 amendment established a "rebuttable presumption" that the child endangered the public and was "not amenable to rehabilitation within the juvenile justice system." *Annotated Laws of Massachusetts, Cumulative Supplement to Chapters 113–121* (Rochester, N.Y.: Lawyers Cooperative Publishing, 1994), chapter 119, section 61, 437. Under section 60a, transcripts of the trial were not open to the public, except with written consent by the judge (434). But compare Brian McGrory, "Roxbury Shooting Suspects Face New, Tougher Juvenile Law," *Boston Globe*, 24 April 1991.

53. On other news treatments, see Chris Black and Doris Sue Wong, "Naming of Youths Draws Much Debate," *Boston Globe*, 23 April 1991; see also the comments of "More Change is Needed" (editorial), *Bay State Banner*, 2 May 1991. The *Herald* did name all three; see Charles Craig, "Teen-Slay Law Used for 1st Time," *Boston Herald*, 23 April 1991, which mentions three networks that refrained.

54. On Weld's position, see Doris Sue Wong, "Youth to Face Trial as Adult, Murder Suspect, 16, Said to Lack Remorse," *Boston Globe*, 9 Oct. 1991.

55. Roache quoted in Ellement and Coakley, "Three Youths." Phrase "man-sized punishments for man-sized crimes" quoted in McNamara, "When Children Kill," 17. However, a significant strain of scholarship on violent behavior among so-called "traditional" gangs, often Chicano gangs, disputes their pathological character or their roots in a "criminalized" subculture. Instead, adolescents or delinquents are seen as torn between quite conventional, even chivalric codes, and criminal necessity. Often such adolescent estrangement is linked to the marginal position or political strength of the broader ethnic community. Thus, seemingly petty disputes escalate precipitously. Cf. Horowitz and Schwartz, "Honor"; Erlanger, "Estrangement"; and of course Rodriguez, *Always Running*.

56. Section 61 actually provided for court determinations on factors including "the family, school and social history of the child" (*Annotated Laws*, 215). Again, the shift was in the "rebuttable presumption" (216) now put to the defendant. On the debate, see Elizabeth Levitan Spaid, "Bay State Debates Youth Trial Policy," *Christian Science Monitor*, 20 Nov. 1991; and David

Treadwell, "Law May Portend Tougher Punishment for Juveniles," *Los Angeles Times*, 12 Dec. 1990.

57. Flynn as quoted in Walker and Higgins, "Boys, 11 and 15."

58. Ibid.

59. Again I am indebted to Lentricchia's formulation, quoted earlier in this chapter. Content analyses often point out that an implicit discrediting of staying in the community, such as I discuss in chapter 4, is often structured into news coverage that features prominent black professionals who do not in fact live in inner-city districts; see Kirk Johnson, "Black and White." McNamara actually makes the point that none of Bynoe's well-known relatives remain in his neighborhood ("When Children Kill," 39).

60. And so it was charged—for one, in the Columbia University seminar hosted by Fred Friendly, "The Boston Hoax."

61. On Dunn's release, see Brian McGrory, "Suspect Reportedly Freed 3 Days before Slayings," *Boston Globe*, 1 May 1991. On the MBTA, see "Dudley Station Fix-up to Use Local Workers," *Bay State Banner*, 2 May 1991; see also "Time for Preventive Detention" (editorial), *Bay State Banner*, 9 May 1991. On the court psychologists, see McGrory, "Suspect"; Doris Sue Wong, "Second Juvenile to Be Tried as Adult in Roxbury Slayings," *Boston Globe*, 12 Oct 1991.

62. Again, this is a horrific tragedy. Nevertheless, it is worth noting that the media's focus on younger victims and defendants overlooks the recent findings that suggest many gangs are aging due to fewer employment opportunities for young men who would have grown "out" of the gang's daily routine. See the summary in Scott Cummings and Daniel J. Monti, eds. *Gangs: The Origins and Impact of Contemporary Youth Gangs in the United States* (Albany: State University of New York Press, 1993), 310 ff.

63. A good indication of Bynoe's evolution is provided by Doris Sue Wong, "Witnesses Profile Murder Suspect, 16," *Boston Globe*, 15 Aug. 1991; on Grant's size, see McNamara, "When Children Kill," 45. Of course, perhaps a journalistic taboo on interrogating the victim's character was at work here; at least one columnist, Mike Barnicle, remarked upon the uneasy adjacency of this story to the William Kennedy Smith rape trial ("Blood Is Gone, Horror Remains," *Boston Globe*, 23 April 1991). But if anything *Herald* coverage more clearly highlighted Grant as the target, as well as emphasizing witness accounts; see Tan, "Boy Just an Innocent Bystander," and Ralph Ranalli and Sarah Koch, "Roxbury Residents Confront Wave of Violence," *Boston Herald*, 24 April 1991, which quotes Grant's mother: "I feel like they came looking for my son."

64. Attention to this cycle does appear in other *Globe* coverage; see Charles A. Radin, "Adrift in a 'Culture of Impulse,' Children Turn on One Another," *Boston Globe*, 28 April 1991, and Adrian Walker, "Of Violence and the Young," and "Search for Safe Haven in Gang Turns Tragic in Fatal Gunfire," both in *Boston Globe*, 28 April 1991. But what is striking is that these fine articles do not seem to affect coverage of the Bynoe plot per se.

65. On the relevance of the neighbor's remarks, see the two articles by Alexander Reid, "Testimony Puts Slaying Suspects at Scene," *Boston Globe*, 18 May 1991, and "Lawyer Wants Statements Thrown Out in Murder Case," *Boston Globe*, 23 May 1991. The *Globe's* Adrian Walker reported ("Search for Safe Haven") police opinion that Grant participated in the Dudley station fight but was not a Blackhawk, a contention of his parents as well (Tom Coakley and David Arnold, "Victims Relied on Family, Kin Say," *Boston Globe*, 23 April 1991). This obscured the

fact that the gang was just in-formation (Walker, "Search for Safe Haven") and that, on this basis, Bynoe was equally no Trailblazer, as some gang members told the court-appointed psychologist (Wong, "Witnesses Profile").

66. This shortening of the story is in fact more common than not; see Pritchard, "Race, Homicide, and Newspapers," 502–5.

67. In part due to poor investigative work, Locy writes, prosecutors plea-bargained first-degree murder arrests over 60 percent of the time (Toni Locy, "Poor Police Work Hampers Investigations," *Boston Globe*, 7 April 1991). Compare David Friend's series on the Los Angeles Criminal Justice System in the *Los Angeles Times*, 16 Dec. 1990 to 22 Dec. 1990. Of course, pleading *itself* spoke, potentially, to an administrative justice in which even public defenders comply.

68. For these determinations, see Wong, "Witnesses Profile," and Wong, "Youth to Face."

69. Cf. John Z. Fiske, *Reading the Popular* (Boston: Unwin Hyman, 1989), 149–84.

70. See my earlier use of "entertaining," in chapter 4, note 9.

71. Manoff, "Modes of War," 68.

72. The two articles are Renée Graham, "In Roxbury, a Call to Remove the Guns, Save the Children," *Boston Globe*, 24 April 1991, and David Arnold, "Boys Eulogized with Bitter Regrets," *Boston Globe*, 27 April 1991. See also Jordanna Hart, "At Roxbury Boys and Girls Club, It was a Time to Grieve: 200 Children Remember 2 Slain Peers," *Boston Globe*, 26 April 1991.

73. Arnold, "Boys Eulogized." The *Herald*'s coverage quoted, among many speakers, Haynes's appeal to local youth to stay in school and make Roxbury "a better place to live." Joe Heany and Harvey Dickson, "Two Young Murder Victims Are Mourned," *Boston Herald*, 27 April 1991.

74. Not surprisingly, the *Bay State Banner* depicted this activism—including an extended truce between the implicated gangs negotiated by Shaker Abdulla Ali—in a much more positive light; see "Gang Truce Extended in Bid to Keep Peace," 9 June 1991; Judy Castillo, "Drug-Fighters Mount Vigil against Dorchester Dealers," 27 June 1991; Dorothy A. Clark, "Activist Minister Steps Up Efforts to Stop Gang Fights," 22 Aug. 1991.

75. It is a cliché to say that "community" is a homogenizing term that in practice means focusing largely on male, religious figures in such districts. The implications of this label go beyond this study; nevertheless, it is both important and tragic that it is the high incidence of funerals that provides the venue for such news prominence. Females are rarely given anything but "neighbor" or kin status in these reports. And ironically, in its initial reports, the *Bay State Banner* quoted Copney's neighbors as blaming outsiders from other neighborhoods ("Two Roxbury Youths Killed in Highland Park Shooting," 25 April 1991).

76. Ellement and Coakley, "Three Youths." Compare Derrick Z. Jackson, "A Show of Strength," *Boston Globe*, 24 April 1991.

77. Thus, while many may mock the now-suburban "inauthenticity" of a Mike Barnicle—following his recent firing—his position in fact may be quite symbolic—a surrogate position, as I've suggested in chapter 4, for the ambivalence of white flight itself. See the recent profile in defense of Barnicle prior to his dismissal: David Warsh, "The Lawyer and the Columnist," *Boston Globe*, 28 June 1998.

78. As Christopher Lydon put it in his dismissal of Barnicle's failures during the Stuart case,

it often seemed as if Barnicle's columns came from the back of a police cruiser. Christopher Lydon, "The Boston Hoax: She Fought It, He Bought It," *Washington Journalism Review*, March 1990, 56–61. Apparently, Barnicle has a brother who is a homicide detective (Warsh). Quotes from Barnicle's "Of Double Standards," *Boston Globe*, 6 March 1985, and "No Arrest for the Weary," *Boston Globe*, 14 June 1987; for a direct attack on Roache, see, e.g., "Police Beat: Tale of Woe," *Boston Globe*, 8 Oct. 1987.

79. All further passages from Barnicle, "Blood Is Gone." The claim of gutlessness is, for instance, identical to the testimony of one unnamed Blackhawk quoted in the *Globe* (Walker, "Search for Safe Haven"): "The rules were no guns, no knives, no sticks, no chains . . . But they got jealous when we won the fight [at Dudley Square]. And they didn't come back with their hands, they came back with guns."

80. Certainly relevant here is the *Banner*'s report that Barnicle would subsequently receive a "Thumbs Down" award from the National Association of Black Journalists for allegedly saying in a television interview that he "knew more about being black in Boston than any black reporter in the city"; by contrast, Jackson and McNamara won prizes. "Newsnotes," *Bay State Banner*, 8 Aug. 1991.

81. Of course, the way that Barnicle and Lupo both struck the paternal posture and underlined the importance of parental discipline worked in tandem with an array of Roxbury activists who were, in fact, preaching much the same thing (except that some included the police in those authorities to be distrusted). Alan Lupo, "The Obvious Solutions to Violent Crime," *Boston Globe*, 23 April 1991; compare his earlier "Getting Tough: Does It Work?" *Boston Globe*, 4 June 1989. Some of those in Roxbury, in fact, voiced solutions quite compatible with those of Governor Weld. Consider the *Bay State Banner* editorials, "More Change Is Needed"; "Times Have changed!" 14 Nov. 1991, which explicitly supports Weld's desire to make adult trials mandatory; and "A Bold Initiative," 16 May 1991, which praises Councilor Bruce Bolling's proposed ordinance to make parents responsible for the criminal conduct of minor children. Community leaders, of course, were in fact split over the power patrols and stop and frisk; see Peter S. Cannellos, "Anticrime Activist Reports Death Threat," *Boston Globe*, 20 Nov. 1989. To believe such communities express ideological unanimity is similar to accepting the familiar neoconservative claim that disadvantaged communities as a *whole* are the ones who have invited aggressive, even paramilitary policing. On this issue, see esp. Davis, *City of Quartz*, 289 ff.

82. McNamara, "When Children Kill," 14.

83. Ibid., 15.

84. Ibid., 14.

85. Ibid., 38.

86. Ibid.

87. Ibid., 46.

88. Ibid., 38.

89. Ibid., 46–48.

90. Ibid., 38. For the report on the robbery, see Vanee Staunton, "Mother of Slain Boy Is Robbed of Memento," *Boston Globe*, 20 June 1991. Patrick Ewing, of course, played high school basketball in nearby Cambridge. For a terribly important exploration of the complicity of con-

sumer desire with the drug culture, see William Finnegan, *Cold New World: Growing Up in a Harder Country* (New York: Random House, 1998).

91. I call this "novelistic" because of its omniscient re-creations of a central figure's (Bynoe's) consciousness; specific rendering of set scenes in given time (the courtroom, Bynoe's cell); "jurid-ical" sweep of multiple viewpoints both to represent social differences and construct a narrative consensus. See Elizabeth Deeds Ermarth, *Realism and Consensus in the English Novel* (Princeton: Princeton University Press, 1983); cf. Fiske, *Reading the Popular*, 155.

92. As to what generated its more hidden, internecine debate, we may never know: as with Bynoe's trial, the transcript of the *Globe*'s city room is not public. There were, however, leaked reports of a city room battle over affirmative action, salaries, career advancement, and "ghetto beats" at the *Globe*, notably swirling around Renée Graham, who contributed to the Bynoe cover-age; see the *Bay State Banner:* "Racial Tensions at *Globe*," 5 Dec. 1991, and Brian Wright O'Con-nor, "*Globe* Flap Underscores Tensions of Tight Economy," 19 Dec. 1991.

93. McNamara, "When Children Kill," 48.

94. Ibid., 38. For the discrepancy over pizza, compare McNamara, "When Children Kill," 48, with Reid, "Testimony Puts Slaying Suspects at Scene."

95. McNamara, "When Children Kill," 48. As Pritchard notes, studies actually show that homicide is in fact *the* only crime more likely to make the papers than not ("Race, Homicide, and Newspapers," 502), but cases with a white suspect are much more likely to appear than with a black (507).

96. "Rehabilitation" and rage balanced in Mike Barnicle, "Getting Away with Murder," *Boston Globe*, 6 Jan. 1994.

97. In the *Globe*'s own rendering: "after a four-part series in the Globe questioned the depart-ment's supervision, management, and ability to solve crimes," an independent commission (the St. Clair Commission) was established to investigate the department. The commission found mismanagement in the police department and called for Roache's dismissal, advice Mayor Flynn ignored. John Ellement, "Some Say Top Cop Should Be Outsider," *Boston Globe*, 4 Feb. 1994; "Reviving the St. Clair Commission" (editorial), *Boston Globe*, 1 Oct. 1993. In the Locy series, the *Globe* revealed that Boston ranked twenty-eighth out of thirty major cities in homicides solved. See also Geeta Anand, "Superior Officers' Union Blasts Roache," *Boston Globe*, 3 Nov. 1995.

98. Rather incredibly, the new pressure to arrest had apparently led, in 1988, to a practice whereby nearly *all* drug-related warrants used "unnamed" informants (Sean Murphy, "Boston Police Curbing Use of Informants," *Boston Globe*, 6 May 1990). The murder of Officer Sherman Griffiths in 1988, during a botched drug raid—and following a detective's admissions of fals-ified informants to gain those warrants—had spurred the formation of the Schwartz Commis-sion in 1988. See Locy, "Arrest Numbers That Don't Add Up." In the Kahn documentary, the profiled detective, Stanley Philbin, comments: "Drugs Are Here to Stay. Let me tell you. We'll never stop it. Not at this level. You know, on the street. No way . . . I think it should be as legal as booze is. We could direct our police efforts in other directions." *FRONTLINE: Street Cop*, dir. Richard Kahn, aired originally on PBS on 31 March 1987; from transcript, 26. Courtesy WGBH Education Foundation. Nonetheless, as an interviewed expert in a closing

roundtable, George Kelling is alone in giving a modest approval to aggressive street arrests if they are "skillfully used, properly supervised, with all respect for, uh, civil rights" (29; pause in transcript).

99. See Kevin Cullen, "Arrest Numbers May Add Up to Trouble," *Boston Globe*, 1 March 1989, and David Armstrong, "Cities' Crime Moves to the Suburbs," *Boston Globe*, 19 May 1997. See also Shelby Siems, "Police Force Felt the Mayor's Hand," *Christian Science Daily Monitor*, 25 June 1993.

100. On these outcomes, see Paul Langner, "Roxbury Teen-ager Acquitted of Murders but Gets Prison on Gun Conviction," *Boston Globe*, 4 Jan. 1994; Maggie Mulvihill, "Judge: Cop, Prosecutor Misled Jury in Double Slay Case," *Boston Herald*, 30 June 1994; and John Ellement, "Murder Charges Dropped in '91 Case," *Boston Globe*, 20 May 1994.

101. On this new amendment, which partly resulted from lobbying efforts by the victims' parents, see David Weber, "Law Lets Teen-age Shooter Get Five Years for Murder," *Boston Herald*, 14 Jan. 1994, and Jocelyn Meek, "Killer in Law-Changing Case Gets Freedom as He Turns 21," *Boston Globe*, 6 June 1996.

Epilogue

1. Steffens, *Autobiography*, 280. Steffens may have adopted this memory from his one-time mentor, Jacob Riis; compare Riis's observation about "the policeman on the corner, who is addicted to a professional unbelief in reform of any kind" in *How the Other Half Lives*, 30.

2. Again, Mike Davis (among others) has described this recent trend. See *City of Quartz*, 240–50.

3. Toward the end of his career, Foucault seemed aware of this risk. Reminding American audiences of the broader, European cast to his intended usage of the term "policing," he referred to the wider political technology of the nascent state and its designing of a field of human sciences, within which what Americans call policing—law enforcement—only had a narrower and more negative role. See esp. Foucault, "The Political Technologies of Individuals."

4. Foucauldian and Marxian models, for example, have important differences that have tended to be suppressed in our accounts of "scopic" power. As Edward Said has observed, for example, even if we agree with Foucault's notion of a relatively autonomous "micro-physics" of power "exercised rather than possessed," this hardly means that other forms of class or state power need to be relegated "to the status of superannuated nineteenth-century conceptions of political economy" ("The Problem of Textuality," 710). For another discussion of this tension between Marxian (specifically Gramscian) and Foucauldian models of news analysis, see Fiske, *Reading the Popular*, 149–84.

5. Foucault himself actually warned that the private ownership of journalism compromised the Panoptical paradigm. His observations come in an interview in "The Eye of Power":

FOUCAULT: . . . almost all of the eighteenth century reformers . . . overlooked the real conditions of possibility of opinion, the "media" of opinion, a materiality caught up in the mechanisms of the economy and power in its forms of the press, publishing, and later the cinema and television.

PERROT: When you say they overlooked the media, you mean that they failed to see the necessity of working through the media?

FOUCAULT: And failed to see that these media would necessarily be under the command of economico-political interests . . . Basically it was journalism, that capital invention of the nineteenth century, which made evident all the utopian character of this politics of the gaze.

In *Power/Knowledge: Selected Interviews and Writings, 1972–1977*, ed. and trans. Colin Gordon (New York: Pantheon Press, 1980), 161–62. Examples of the news carnival within the nineteenth-century press are provided by Saxton and Patricia Cline Cohen, among many others.

6. Like all complex organisms, Pedelty adds, "the 'social body' contains nodal centers, hierarchies of control and specialization. Press power, for example, is coalesced into hierarchical regimes . . . to ignore these is to fall prey to a sort of vulgar idealism." Pedelty, *War Stories* (New York: Routledge, 1995), 6. "[W]hole social body" is Pedelty quoting Foucault.

7. Hall et al., *Policing the Crisis* played considerable attention, by contrast, to the style of police forces (see 46 ff.) and to the judicial system, as well as to the social production of news. Moore actually mentions the reeducation of *Los Angeles Times* reporter Bob Baker; see *Going Down to the Barrio*, 249 n. 1.

8. Wambaugh has recently been rediscovered as an experimental writer of nonfiction, his conscious model being Truman Capote. See, e.g., R. Thomas Berner, *The Literature of Journalism: Text and Context* (State College, Pa.: Strata Publishing, 1999), 155–74.

9. Peter Brooks, "Storytelling without Fear? Confession in Law and Literature," in Gewirtz and Brooks, *Law's Stories*, 118.

10. On the discontinuities between romance traditions of crime busting and actual law enforcement, see, e.g., the analysis of Crew, "Acting like Cops"; Todd Gitlin, "We Build Excitement: Car Commercials and *Miami Vice*," *Watching Television*, ed. Todd Gitlin (New York: Pantheon, 1986), 136–61; Henry Nash Smith, *Virgin Land* (Cambridge: Harvard University Press, 1950), on Deadwood Dick, 90–111; Carlson, *Prime Time Law Enforcement*, 137–51.

11. Of course, few analysts today would argue that such cultural narratives express a single ideological, cultural, or political valence; much less do they agree on what it might be. For every critic who rehashes the claim about the literary procedural's "ring of authenticity," there is another who argues that reading crime news or watching *Miami Vice* is a "moral" exercise that has little to do with learning about law or crime. "[R]ing of authenticity" from Waugh, "The Human Rather than the Superhuman," 39; on the essentially moral "workout" of crime reading or viewing, see Jack Katz, "What Makes Crime 'News'?" *Media, Culture, and Society* 9 (1987): 48 and passim, and Crew, "Acting like Cops." The contradiction about escapism appears, for instance, in Inciardi and Dee, "From the Keystone Cops [*sic*]."

12. Manoff, "Modes of War," 68.

13. Gitlin recounts, for example, the words of Stan Gerber, a producer of *Police Story*, in the 1970s:

"We were close to chaos, close to suspicion of institutions in the early seventies. The blue line was there to preserve what was left, what was the semblance of what used to be one helluva government when it served the people . . . I thought we were on the way to success when, about the second or third year I was at UCLA . . . a woman came up to me and said, 'You're just as bad as they are.' . . . I said, 'What do you mean?' She said, 'You're making them like human beings.' And I said, 'You gave me a compliment.' I showed the warts and the pimples, I showed them being brutal because they were frustrated . . . People don't realize the kind of life they live. See, they thought they were the minority. They felt they had to cluster together in a group, nobody understood them. And I showed where they could be damned and vilified, but soon as you're in trouble you yell for the police, not the firemen, not anybody else, *the police*."

As quoted in Gitlin, *Inside Prime Time*, 243. For more traditional accounts of such dependence in crime reporting, see esp. Mark Fishman, *Manufacturing the News* (Austin: University of Texas Press, 1980); or Chibnall, "The Crime Reporter," 50.

14. Inciardi and Dee, "From the Keystone Cops [*sic*]," 100.

15. As I discuss in chapter 4, this is a standard tactic in news criticism. For its use in television criticism, see, e.g., Carlson, *Prime Time Law Enforcement*, 48 ff.; and, in the reading of True Crime, see Durham, Elrod, and Kinkade, "Images of Crime." But contrast Jack Katz, 59 and passim.

16. The complaint of Inciardi and Dee is by no means atypical, but it demonstrates how our criticism can simply prove a pale echo of the realist and now neoconservative line. "In addition to creating exaggerated public expectations," they write about cop shows, "such programs promote the idea that fighting crime is the chief function of police, as opposed to preventing crime, directing traffic, and keeping the peace" ("From the Keystone Cops [*sic*]," 100).

17. For instance, D. A. Miller argues in *The Novel and the Police* that "[w]hat most sharply differentiates the legal economy of police power from the 'amateur' economy of its supplement is precisely the latter's policy of *discretion*" (15, emphasis his). Here Miller demonstrates precisely the risk of equating "policing" with detectivism and with law, and indeed accepting the novel's own elitism (that is, discretion as an upper-class capability). As I have argued, discretion (in its positive and negative aspects) is a capacity inscribed even in the most bureaucratic of imperatives behind policing.

18. Contrast the arguments of Robin Anderson, cited on 134 above.

19. David Milch and Bill Clark, *True Blue: The Real Stories behind NYPD Blue* (New York: William Morrow, 1995); Tracy Kidder, *Home Town* (New York: Random House, 1999); and *Summer of Sam* (motion picture), written and directed by Spike Lee, 1999. See my earlier discussion of Steffens, 25–26 above.

20. Meese and Carrico, "Taking Back the Streets," 29.

Index

Index